MEDJUGORJE: THE '90's

— The Triumph of the Heart —

MEDJUGORJE: THE '90's

— *The Triumph of the Heart* —

Sister Emmanuel

OUR LADY'S CENTER FOR PEACE
820 E. GRAY STREET
LOUISVILLE, KY 40202
(502) 568-MARY

Queenship
PUBLISHING COMPANY
Santa Barbara, CA

©1997 Children of Medjugorje

Library of Congress Number #98-068710

Published by:
Queenship Publishing
P.O. Box 42028
Santa Barbara, CA 93140-2028
(800) 647-9882 • (805) 957-4893 • Fax: (805) 957-1631

Printed in the United States of America

ISBN: 1-57918-104-8

I know that this book of our own Sister Emmanuel will do a great deal of good. Her untiring work —both writings and talks—to hasten the triumph of the Immaculate Heart of Mary is peppered with many reports of personal conversion. It goes without saying that we do not know now what will be the final judgment of the Church concerning the events at Medjugorje; but we *can* say that in this little village the world has been graced with a new Marian awakening without precedent, carrying forward the work of renewal in the Spirit. The most humble folk are touched by the evangelical message and return to the sacraments. Hundreds of thousands of both men and women give themselves over to fasting and the rosary. And all these good fruits have induced the Community of the Beatitudes to consecrate itself to the service of the pilgrims, so that these fruits may remain among us and serve the greater good of the Church.

Ephraim, Deacon and Founder of
the Community of the Beatitudes

CONTENTS

I - YEAR 1990

II - YEAR 1991

III - YEAR 1992

IV - YEAR 1993

V - YEAR 1994

VI - YEAR 1995

VII - YEAR 1996

VIII - YEAR 1997

Appendix 1

Appendix 2

A BISHOP SPEAKS OUT ON MEDJUGORJE

Medjugorje! The apparitions have been taking place for over fifteen years, and they have not stopped today. The "visionaries" continue to... see, and to receive "messages." Things are happening. The Church has not yet spoken definitively, waiting for the outcome of careful examination in a spirit of openness to events.

And what if it is all the work of the Devil? He would be a pretty pathetic Devil indeed, and one who has shot himself in the foot! He would have been getting in his own way on a grand scale and destroying his own evil wiles! For everything about Medjugorje works to bring back souls to God, to restore to the world the only true peace—the peace given by God.

So she talks too much, this "Virgin of the Balkans"? That's the sardonic opinion of some unabashed skeptics. Have they eyes but do not see, and ears but do not hear? Clearly the voice in the messages of Medjugorje is that of a motherly and strong woman who does not pamper her children, but teaches them, exhorts and pushes them to assume greater responsibility for the future of our planet: *"A large part of what will happen depends on your prayers."*

But what sort of prayers? Not rote pious murmurings, but prayers full of life, of joy! Prayer that expresses the desire for sacrifice and renunciation, the longing for the resurrection of the world, following in the steps of the Savior! The Gospa calls for a radical conversion, a change of heart, inspired by the breath of the Spirit: we must learn to truly live our faith, *"not in words or thought alone, but through example."* This is no new message, but the urgency is new, compelling us to put into practice the new commandment of love of God and one's neighbor. They cannot be separated. Conversion is needed in all aspects of life.

This is what remains with me above all else, from the message of Medjugorje, from *The Triumph of the Heart*. Sister Emmanuel has given us a powerful book that stirs in us memories of our profession of faith during the

Easter vigil: we are called upon to renounce Satan and all his works, to take seriously the Word of God and the words of the Credo, to *live* fully the reality of the sacraments—in a word, to truly live! With the help of fasting and the rosary.

We must allow God all the time he wills to take for the transfiguration of all time and space before the Holy Face of the One who is, was, and will come again. God is mankind's future. And God himself confirms once more in our day, with signs and wonders, the work of the Spirit, in the heart-to-heart intimacy of Jesus and Mary. Some of the testimony in this book moved me to tears. May it be a source of grace for the reader too. My message to you, the reader, is to pray, to work for reconciliation in your own life, to love, to act.

I have already seen some remarkable about-faces among the faithful in my own diocese after contact with the loving concern of the Gospa! And listening to my inner urging, I too wanted to go to the Source itself...

So in the middle of winter I went secretly to Medjugorje with, in my heart, the full weight of twenty years as a bishop. I went to ask forgiveness for my failings and to give thanks. I climbed up Mt. Krizevac, sometimes on my knees, tears running down my face. In my chest there beat a heart of such gentleness and humility that it didn't feel like me... My Lord and my God, it isn't me anymore! I left Medjugorje, at fifty-three years of age, with all the strength of a new heart and a new spirit, ready for the mission that both fills me with burning passion and carries me as well: all is joy and hope, thirst for justice and peace, with Mary. Today I bear witness.

This book, then, is an important document in the "Medjugorje dossier." It is a loud and clear call to all of us, a call to the conversion of our hearts. Deo gratias! Magnificat!

> Monsignor Gilbert Aubry
> Bishop of St. Denis (Reunion Island)
>
> August 15, 1996
> Feast of the Assumption of Mary

(In May 1998, the Vatican sent Mngr. Aubry a letter on Medjugorje. See Appendix 2)

A Brief Overview of the Events at Medjugorje

In the heart of Herzegovina, in the former Yugoslavia, there is a Croatian village of a thousand souls nestled between two hills, Krizevac and Podbrdo (the name "Medjugorje" means "between the mountains").The people, all hard-working country folk making their living from the soil, barely managed to survive by growing tobacco and grapes. Until recently they lived in a state of political repression under the eagle eye of the omnipresent Communist militia. The parish church was in the hands of the fiery Franciscan priest, Fr. Jozo Zovko.

On June 24, 1981, the Feast of St. John the Precursor, the village was thrown into turmoil by an extraordinary happening. A few teenagers were walking along the path by Podbrdo hill when they saw a shining silhouette of a lady holding a baby in her arms. The next day she returned and revealed her identity: *"I am the Blessed Virgin Mary."* The group of 6 visionaries was then formed definitively and consisted of Marija Pavlovic, Vicka Ivankovic, Mirjana Dragicevic, Ivanka Ivankovic, Ivan Dragicevic, and Jakov Colo.

Every day the Gospa (the Croatian word for Our Lady) reappeared, giving the children "messages" for themselves, for the parish, and for the world: messages of peace and the need for conversion and love in order to bring back to the Heart of God our poor humanity lost in darkness so far from the Lord! Since 1987 these messages have been given once a month. The Gospa also gives each visionary certain secrets which will be revealed through the intermediary of a priest chosen by the visionary, at a time the Gospa decides.

Father Jozo quickly came to believe in the apparitions for he saw Our

Lady himself one day in the church. The Bishop of Mostar, Monsignor Zanic, at first believed too, but later was convinced that the whole thing had been cooked up by the Franciscans. A rift then developed which exists today.

In 1986 Monsignor Zanic provided Cardinal Ratzinger with a negative report on the apparitions, but the Cardinal removed Zanic from the case and gave the investigation over to a new Commission formed of Yugoslavian bishops with Monsignor Komarica (from Banja Luka) at its head. This Commission is open to further developments and has not concluded its investigations.

In April 1991 this Commission officially accepted Medjugorje as a place of prayer, and authorized it as a place of worship. Private pilgrimages are authorized there. On August 21, 1996, Doctor Navarro Valls, the spokesman for the Holy See, made explicit the position of Rome: "You cannot say people cannot go there until it has been proven false. This has not been said, so anyone can go if they want" (CNS Publication, August 21, 1996). "When Catholic faithful go anywhere, they are entitled to spiritual care, so the Church does not forbid priests to accompany lay-organized trips to Medjugorje in Bosnia-Herzegovina," he added.

Since June 25, 1981, more than 20 million pilgrims have come to this little village to pray and experience conversion, making Medjugorje one of the most frequented sanctuaries in the entire world.

FOREWORD

It is almost midnight, and the stony path down the hill is a river of twinkling lights under the quiet summer night sky. The Gospa has just appeared on Podbrdo hill, and now the thousands of pilgrims are pouring down into the valley of Medjugorje where they are staying.

The cry of a young child pierces the night despite the din of a bumper-to-bumper traffic jam of taxis, buses and vehicles of every description. The little boy is only 3, and he is screaming to the astonishment of his parents. Everything was fine until he realized it was now over and that he had to go home to bed. He refuses to get in the taxi, and big fat tears run down his plump cheeks.

"But it's so late, honey! Come on, sweetie, it's time to go home," pleads his mother.

"I don't wanna!" he cries, bucking and thrashing with all his puny strength.

"But why don't you want to? We can't leave you here all alone!"

But nothing doing; the child gets more and more upset and inarticulate. His parents are stumped and try the gentle approach:

"Look, if you won't come home to bed, what are we going to do with you, huh?"

"I wanna go back!"

"Go back where, sweetie?"

"Back up!"

"Up there on the hill? But why? It's all over!"

"I wanna see her again, I wanna see her again!"

"See who?"

"The lady!"

That night was long indeed for this tiny little French boy who experienced the first "night of the soul" of his life. To have seen and not to see any longer...! He was truly inconsolable. And these cries of grief said more about Medjugorje than any book could ever do.

Medjugorje is above all a place where hearts are set on fire. Every day heaven's gates are opened and out pours the great gift from above, the fire of blazing Love. Mary is the chalice that overflows with his Love! There are no words that can adequately express the reality of what is going on here.

Was another book on Medjugorje really needed? The visionaries, Vicka, Jakov and Mirjana, don't have much truck with books, so why should I think they're important? Jesus never wrote anything except for a few words scratched in the sand with his finger to make sure that they would be swept away...

I don't really believe in books on Medjugorje; I believe in the action of the Holy Spirit. Nor do I really believe in television programs on the visionaries; I believe in the Heart of Mary and her plan to bring all her children back to the Father, always with her own, often surprising, methods!

I don't have much faith in highbrow interviews, even when they hit the headlines of excellent newspapers; I believe more in the silent ones who, without a soul knowing, love God so much that they come to resemble him...

I believe in the children too young to talk, but who uphold the world through their innocence and their silent suffering.

"Prayer with the heart is not something which can be learned from books, and cannot be learned from studying," the Blessed Mother tells us in Medjugorje. *"It is learned through living it!"* The realism of the Incarnation is one the most appealing aspects of the personality of Our Lady. A real Jewish mother!

Despite this beautiful reality, I hope I won't shock anyone if I say in all simplicity that the Blessed Mother called upon me to write this book, with an insistence that I could not resist. I did resist, for months, trying to appeal to her good heart: "Look at all those hours that I could spend praying for your intentions rather than scribbling away..." But to no avail—her request that I write the book kept beating away at my heart in wave after wave, gently but firmly, until I gave in... And that is why you have this book in your hands today!

For, in fact, we must spread Mary's messages at Medjugorje by all means at our disposal. It is her will that *all* her children throughout the entire world hear her appeal, and we are still far from this goal! But she surely did not want another published collection of her messages, which tend to become a somewhat cold "listing" of her words; and there are already plenty of excellent commentaries[1] on the messages that have appeared in periodicals. We don't really need any more!

What the Gospa wanted, then, from me was to write something that would express in a new way the "marriage" of 2 realities that God has united and man must not rend asunder: namely, the Word from on high and the transforming action of this Word in the stuff of everyday human living. Every month the Gospa speaks to us, but her words only illumine and accompany her action, her prodigious work in our hearts and lives. She speaks and she acts, indissolubly.

My job, then, was one of a humble scribe who doesn't just transmit her messages,[2] but captures as well the most moving, the most overwhelming episodes in human lives that show the fruit of her work here in the world. In the Gospel we do not find a mere listing of Jesus' words, but the whole living context in which he spoke them! Through eyewitness accounts we see Jesus in his daily life, walking in the mountains, climbing into Zebedee's boat. We see him surrounded by all kinds of different people — we get to enjoy the personality of Peter as well as the intense love of Mary Magdalen, we are somehow reassured when one of the apostles makes a blooper...

In Medjugorje the Blessed Mother, too, chose a specific human context to receive her messages; real people who could let them grow in their hearts, who would live them. It is necessary to enter into this incarnation in order to understand the messages with the heart and to encounter the One who comes each day, corporeally, with her smile and her tears to touch and see real children and true Croatians peasants-perfectly normal people. She touches us also through them in our very human reality with all the joys and sorrows of life today.

You will find, then, a chapter after each monthly message that tells a particular story. The most beautiful testimonies naturally are the most humble ones from those hundreds of pilgrims who write us: "I didn't see or feel anything extraordinary when I was there, but when I got home I began to pray. I began to love, to put God first. I now feel such a deep joy! My life will never be the same..."

But I mostly write of more spectacular experiences because they are examples for all of us and illustrate the manifold ways of our Mother who uses electronics as easily as the stars of heaven or the tears of a child to tell us of her love. (First names have occasionally been changed, for the sake of anonymity.) These stories have not necessarily been told in chronological order. Rather, they are a sort of impressionistic picture which will instill in the reader deep love and wondering admiration for that extraordinary woman called Mary of Nazareth, Mary of Medjugorje.

This book covers the 1990's and will go up to the year 2000, God willing. I begin in 1990, because I only arrived in the village in December of 1989.

Referring to the title of the present book: *The Triumph of the Heart*, people ask me, "yes, but whose heart?"

Of course, I mean the Immaculate Heart of Mary which here more than anywhere else goes from victory to victory... Because out of all the villages of the world, Medjugorje is like Mary's heel with which she crushes the head of the Serpent in today's world. But I also mean the Heart of Jesus, the unique source as well as the end goal of all Mary's victories.

Lastly, let us not forget the hearts of all of us wretched sinners and your heart too, dear reader. For there is no darkness or misery or secret despair that the Queen of Peace does not want to reach out and heal with her touch today in order that just like François or Karen or Colette in this book, you may know deep down inside that the power of Love conquers all, no matter what the situation may be, if only you will open up your heart!

> Sister Emmanuel
> Community of the Beatitudes
> Bijakovici, August 22, 1997
> (Feast of Mary, Queen of Heaven)

---

[1] You can get Fr. Slavko's commentaries on the Internet; see "How to Get the Monthly Messages" in the Appendix.

[2] For the Gospa's messages of the 25th we have used for the sake of consistency the official translations produced by the parish of Medjugorje. The parish wished to stick very faithfully to the literal translation of the message received in Croatian. There are some expressions and turns of phrase that appear awkward to the English-speaking reader, but, on the other hand, they add a little "local color" and charm to the translation!

1990

— MESSAGE OF JANUARY 25, 1990 —

"Dear children! Today I invite you to decide for God once again and to choose him before everything and above everything, so that he may work miracles in your life and that day by day your life may become joy with him. Therefore, little children, pray and do not permit Satan to work in your life through mis-understandings, not understanding and not accepting one another. Pray that you may be able to comprehend the greatness and the beauty of the gift of life. Thank you for having responded to my call."

TRIPLE DOSE FOR RAPHAEL!

It was almost dusk and there were no signposts to indicate the village with the unpronounceable name in the middle of nowhere. Did it really exist? What on earth was I doing here? Me, a hooligan converted at the thunderclap of the Holy Spirit and re-baptized by total immersion in a Free Protestant church. Me, Raphael, scourge of Catholics, in the land of the rosary beads! If my pastor could only see me now... But I wanted to know what was really going on here...

"So," I said to the Lord, "OK, the Catholics have the Holy Spirit even when they are on their knees in front of a plaster saint, but I want you to explain to me this story about the apparitions of Mary!"

After our stay in Ars (France), we headed straight to Rome and then Medjugorje, without schedule or program. All of us were dyed-in-the-wool Protestants, except for Peter, an unbeliever. He was a businessman, and in a deep depression after 2 suicide attempts. I was taking him along with his 2 children just in case he attempted to stab himself in the belly again in our absence. I glanced into the rearview mirror. He was happily conversing with Alex, a Mennonite professor (the Mennonites are a strict Protestant evangelical sect). Catherine, a "daughter of Luther," was talking shop with my wife.

The road turned. Then suddenly, out of the blue, the 2 towers of the brightly lit church emerged. We were in *the* village.

"There's nothing here; no hotel, no restaurant, not even a shop. Two thousand kilometers just to see this church in the middle of a field!"

Peter cursed his luck. A peasant offered a few square feet of shade for us to pitch our tents. Still, we had to be discreet because of the Communists. Up overhead loomed the immense monolithic cross. It was visible for miles around. We got organized.

The peasants shared their water with us even though there was only a feeble trickle stagnating at the bottom of the well, as it hadn't rained for a month.

The entire valley was bathed in a silken light. Time seemed suspended in the pastel dome vaulting the surrounding mountains. The following afternoon I was reading the Bible in the church. Suddenly I sensed an air of agitation from behind. Someone shouted something in Croatian. I saw people blessing themselves frantically and making a mad rush for the door. Commies coming? I went out. Some 50 people were looking in the direction of the cross on Mount Krizevac. My raised eyes widened at the sight of the immense lights surging for almost a mile around the cross. The sky danced around the cross as if endless suns of an unknown pastel blue color were rising and vanishing from one instant to the next. There were no clouds in the area, and the sun wasn't even in that part of the sky to dazzle us, either. "That's it, I've flipped! Look somewhere else," I thought. "Don't allow yourself to be influenced!" Everything else seemed normal around me. A dog sniffed at the base of a tree. Another glance upward, and still the dance of the lights continued for some time. Perplexed, I went back to the tent.

On the third day, we were picnicking in the shade of some trees; conversation was animated, and Peter's children were playing alongside a vineyard. "Hey! Raphael! Come and look! It's turning, it's turning!"

Little Michael was jumping up and down next to me. No one paid any attention to him. He tugged at the hem of my T-shirt until I gave up and asked, "What's the matter?"

"Look, it's turning!" he said, gesturing. He pointed his tiny index finger towards the hill. I came out from under the trees and lifted my eyes towards the cross. My first thought was: "It's an hallucination!"

The immense cross was rotating. I rubbed my eyes, looked down at my sandals, thought about my business, and scooped up a ball of hard dirt. But the cross was still turning, faster and faster. So fast, it became transparent and even disappeared.

I felt for my pulse. The ole' neurons seemed to be functioning within normal range. I called over to Alex, the *professor*. Discreetly and without saying anything else, I pointed vaguely in the direction of the mountain. "Do you see anything, Alex?"

He made a Jerry Lewis grimace and his glasses jumped to the tip of his nose. "I can't believe it! The cross is turning.

"Keep quiet about it! Shut up!"

I called to the others, without saying what it was all about. Soon all seven of us, watch in hand, were observing the phenomenon which lasted for almost a quarter of an hour.

The avalanche of signs continued.

Peter had a long scar from the time he had plunged a knife in his abdomen after his wife left him. We were often shirtless at the camp site. He approached me, his mouth gaping. "Look!"

The scar had almost disappeared.

I couldn't take any more of these signs. So I said to God, "No, Lord, I still cannot pray to Mary or repeat the same prayers over and over again 100 times. Allow me to attend an apparition in the chapel. I know it is reserved for the priests and religious, but you could make it happen."

That evening, I waited beside the chapel door. A Franciscan was mounting guard, and I said an interior prayer. Someone pulled me by the sleeve. It was the friar. He said something I didn't understand, and pushed me into the chapel. I found myself in the front row just as the visionaries arrived. They began to recite the Hail Mary, and I prayed to God to protect me from the Evil One. I discreetly observed the people immersed in that prayer. Suddenly there was a big "Boom!" In perfect synchronization the 6 visionaries slammed down on their knees. I felt the pain in my kneecaps, out of sympathy.

The people in the front row put their hands on the visionaries' shoulders. I put mine on Vicka's arm.

I had read in a book that, once in ecstasy, the visionaries became completely insensitive to pain and as heavy as blocks of stone. As no one was watching, I pinched Vicka harder and harder. No reaction. Well, so what! Fakirs also stick needles into their bodies! Then I pushed her, gently at first. What a riot if both of us had fallen flat on our stomachs! But no, nothing. So I got in a good position, my bottom braced on my heels... Vicka was praying bolt upright, with nothing to balance on. I pushed her with all the force of my 175 pounds. It was then, at that moment, that I encountered the supernatural. I felt as if I were pushing a block of granite, when all I had in front of me was a teenage girl. My spine tingled; something was going on here...

Up periscope. I looked around. The peace of this place was so palpable that I could almost touch it. I asked God again to protect me. I thought that maybe I was missing some essential point. For the first time in my life, I prayed to Our Lady, "If you are there, if you are part of God's plan, show me. I want to be sure of it."

I raised my eyes towards the place above the table, the place where the visionaries' eyes were fixed.

A light appeared. It was like a ray of sunlight coming through a windowpane, but thick as a young tree. The ray shyly descended and penetrated my heart. From the moment the ray touched my chest, I felt my fears melt away and vanish. I had never felt such a deep plenitude before in my life. All my being dissolved in a flood of gentleness, sweetness, and love. Nothing else existed except an enfolding tenderness. I could have died there of pure love.

My experience took hold of me again as I made my way back to the tent. Alex looked at me and, frowning, asked, "What's happened to you? Your face seems to be radiant with light."

Three months! It took 3 months for me to come back down to earth. Three months when everything was so easy—praying, loving, dying.

I was reconciled with the Church, with Mary, and with myself. Peter converted and now leads a group of young Christians. Glory be to God!

— MESSAGE OF FEBRUARY 25, 1990 —

"Dear children! I invite you to surrender to God. In this season I especially want you to renounce all the things to which you are attached but which are hurting your spiritual life. Therefore, little children, decide completely for God, and do not allow Satan to come into your life through those things that hurt both you and your spiritual life.

"Little children, God is offering himself to you in fullness, and you can discover and recognize him only in prayer. Therefore make a decision for prayer. Thank you for having responded to my call."

I'M THE SECOND Curé OF ARS

On this particular morning in Medjugorje I was giving a talk to French pilgrims in the little video room next to the Adoration chapel. After an extensive explanation on the call to holiness launched by Mary to the world,[1] I told myself, "What they need now is a striking example, something they will remember..." An anecdote from the life of the holy Curé of Ars (the French priest, patron saint of all clergy) came to mind.

"You have all heard of the holy Curé of Ars. You know how he brought the most hardened sinners back to God. He radiated such a depth of holiness! His numerous victories over souls angered Satan greatly. So Satan would often come and torment him in order to hinder his good work. Even during the night Satan's barbs prevented the holy priest from sleeping. The Evil One tried to burn his bed, among other things... One

---

[1] *"Dear children, today I am calling you to holiness. Without holiness, you cannot live"* (7.10.86); *"I am your Mother and therefore I want to lead you all to complete holiness"* (5.25.87).

day, after the Curé of Ars had snatched many souls from his power, Satan lost his temper and, furious, confided this secret to him: 'If there were even 3 people like you in France, I could not set foot in this country anymore!'"

Three great saints like the Curé of Ars would have been enough to prevent Satan from getting his grip on France? Can you imagine that? How powerful the holiness of a single man is! A saint can do much more for his country than a president!

However, there still lacked the 2 other saints who could have helped the Curé of Ars in his work protecting France from the Evil One.

Looking at the group in front of me I asked, "Who among you is willing to be one of those 2 missing saints?"

Total dismay registered on all faces! No one was expecting such a challenge! While I waited for a response, making it perfectly clear that I wasn't going on until some volunteers stepped forward, I saw 2 tiny little hands go up in the front row.

"I am, Sister, I am!"

"Me too!"

Two little girls, ages 7 and 8, were taking up the challenge! They would become the 2 saints vital for France. I took a deep swallow and tried hard to keep back the tears. It had to be children who would answer with all their hearts, their pure little hearts!

After the talk, I explained to both of them how to become a saint and how happy the Gospa would be with their decision. I told them how much she would help them day by day, without ever letting go of them, and how precious their yes was to her. Together, the 2 young children decided to live out the messages and to help each other in this task.. And off they went!

Three years later, I was giving a talk in the south of France near Nice. A large crowd had gathered, and I had just checked the microphone before beginning when I felt a little hand pulling at my scapular. I turned around and saw the sweet little face of a 10-year-old. She smiled broadly as she said, "Sister, do you recognize me? I am the second Curé of Ars!"

How could I ever have forgotten? Once again tears came to my eyes. I had a hard time holding them back.[2]

---

[2] This story and others are found in the cassette *Holiness Means Happiness* by Sr. Emmanuel. Available at "Children of Medjugorje Tapes," PO Box 899, Notre Dame, IN, USA 46556; Fax: (219) 287-7875. ENGLAND: (44) 1-342-893-230. NEW ZEALAND: (64) 9-41-83-428. SINGAPORE: (65) 337-32-77. E-mail orders to: dnolan@childrenofmedjugorje.com

"Oh, wonderful!" I whispered.

Then she pointed to her friend. "What about her, Sister? Do you recognize her too? She's the third Curé of Ars!"

These two little munchkins had kept their promise to Our Lady against all odds. Three years later, they had come with pride and joy to let me know!

"It's hard, sometimes," one of them told me after the talk, "especially at school. Some people make fun of us, but we don't let them push us around. We feel that Our Lady truly helps us and it's great!

"By the way, I wanted to ask you something. The other day one kid insulted me on purpose in front of everybody, after class. What he said was really nasty. Do you think I'll get the crown of martyrdom?"

The Kingdom of God belongs to children and to those who resemble them. Little Sophie still writes to me. She is now thinking of the religious life. Let's pray for her!

— MESSAGE OF MARCH 25, 1990 —

"Dear children! I am with you even if you are not conscious of it. I want to protect you from everything that Satan offers you and through which he wants to destroy you. As I bore Jesus in my womb, so also, dear children, do I wish to bear you into holiness.

"God wants to save you and sends you messages through men, nature, and so many things which can only help you to understand that you must change the direction of your life. Therefore, little children, understand also the greatness of the gift which God is giving you through me, so that I may protect you with my mantle and lead you to the joy of life. Thank you for having responded to my call."

RENDEZVOUS AT THE BLUE CROSS

That evening, when we were gathered around the huge dish of spaghetti that Marija had cooked, she told us "It's absolutely incredible what some guides have invented about the events of the first days! Listen! Just the other day, a pilgrim asked me if the Gospa had really chosen the color blue to paint the cross. Imagine!"

I thought to myself, "Sounds like a good introduction. Looks like we're going to hear something new and different!"

"The Blue Cross business really started," Marija continued, "when the militia actually forbade the people to go up the hill. We (the visionaries) were passing by and suddenly the Gospa appeared to us. It was totally unexpected! We prayed and we sang. At that time, the militiamen were looking for us and they were angrily searching over the whole area. They passed very near us, but it was as though they were blind. They didn't see us! They didn't hear us singing, either. It was unreal! They simply walked by and went on talking as if we weren't there, even though we had been singing only a few yards away from them!

"From that day on, the Gospa appeared very often at the site. However, the militia never found us. It was like our refuge. Then, one day, someone erected a cross there and painted it blue. We then would say, 'We're going to the Blue Cross.' But it was definitely not the Gospa who chose the color!"

Little Michael started to cry and Marija got up to nurse him. For Marija, it's all one seamless reality: seeing the Gospa, and breast-feeding her baby. She goes from one to the other with the ease typical of pure hearts.

"Only a few pilgrims know of the Blue Cross, but they should be encouraged to go and pray there. It's a place chosen by the Gospa."

Yes, Marija is right. The Blue Cross is typical of the places chosen by Mary. There is nothing there! I mean, nothing extraordinary. This place of apparitions (there have been hundreds of them) is located a few yards off the road at the foot of the hill of Podbrdo, and symbolizes the humility of the local landscape. Stones protrude from the red soil. There are small shrubs here and there, too puny to protect from the sun, and thorny bushes that ensure that you can't move without getting scratched. Moreover, there is hardly enough flat space on the ground to enable you to kneel without quickly losing your balance!

Mary has never stopped visiting the Blue Cross. Ivan's prayer group still gathers there frequently on Tuesday and Friday nights. I have seen great graces granted there both to myself and to pilgrims. (When my heart is burdened, I go there and always leave with a great peace.)

One summer evening in 1994, a crowd gathered around Ivan at the Blue Cross and fervent prayers ascended to heaven. Suddenly, the voices stopped. It was the silence of the moment of the apparition. The Mother of God was standing there in front of us. Three minutes passed. Suddenly, the silence was broken by the noise of some stones rolling. There were whispers and a small commotion. Something was happening over on the left. What was up?

A young girl told me the whole story the next day. She was an unbeliever and, of course, never went to church. She was typical of other French teenagers; God was the least of her worries. He was the distant One about whom nobody ever talked to her. And the catechism? Forgotten long ago! Only her grandmother went to church on Sundays. Well, that's okay for her, she's old and anyway that was her thing. Who could blame her for it?

One day her grandmother decided to go by bus to Medjugorje. In spite of her poor health she insisted on going! So she asked her granddaughter to go with her. They made the following arrangement:

"I'll pay for your trip," said the grandmother, "and you'll see what a beautiful country Yugoslavia is. In exchange, you can help me out when I need it." The magic word "Yugoslavia" worked well. The deal was done!

That night Valérie accompanied her grandmother to the Blue Cross. Valérie herself knew that all these people were praying and waiting for Our Lady to come, but not her! She wasn't expecting anything. As far as she was concerned, it was a lot of nonsense!

Her grandmother was standing, since she couldn't kneel, while the young girl was surrounded by so many people that she couldn't see a thing. However, the gathering had hardly entered into the moments of silence when Valérie saw Our Lady. She looked, and looked again... Yes, it was truly Our Lady! She was there! She had actually come! She smiled with a smile unknown on earth. Two minutes passed before Valérie decided to try to get a better view of her. She stepped up on a stone next to the low wall. She couldn't help making small sounds of exclamation. Her grandmother understood that she was *seeing something* and tried to join her on the stone. Bad decision! That's when we heard the sound of stones rolling. Both fell together!

"When I managed to stand up," the girl said to me, "Our Lady wasn't there anymore, it was all over."

She added, with a guilty look, "But, Sister, tell me: Why did she appear to me and not to someone else, when you had all come to pray to her?"

"Maybe that's exactly why she chose you! You were the only one who wasn't praying to her and who wasn't even expecting her at all. She had been looking for you for a long time. But last night she wanted you to find her! She is *your mother*, you know, and from now on she won't let you down."

"Oh, but I won't let her down either! If you had only seen her, Sister, how beautiful she is, so beautiful..."

— MESSAGE OF APRIL 25, 1990 —

"Dear children! Today I invite you to accept with seriousness and to live the messages which I am giving you. I am with you and I desire, dear children, that each one of you be ever closer to my heart. Therefore, little children, pray and seek the will of God in your everyday life. I desire that each one of you discover the way of holiness and grow in it until eternity. I will pray for you and intercede for you before God that you understand the greatness of this gift which God is giving me that I can be with you. Thank you for having responded to my call."

FRANCE, WHERE ARE YOU?

When she was 14, she had only one thought: "Save France." This was a girl with the spirit of Joan of Arc. Her name is Florence de Gardelle. However, this youthful enthusiasm turned out to be only a passing fancy for Florence soon put God in the place reserved for him by the overwhelming majority of the French...on the back burner. More precisely, she didn't put him anywhere! She picked up the way of thinking of her family. God? Never met the guy!

She married Bernard, who went to Mass on Sundays and who insisted on her presence by his side at church "for the sake of the children." Florence didn't pray, but saw her duty through to the end, waiting for the *Ite Missa Est* when she could make a bolt for the door. The important things in her life were dancing, bridge, theater- nothing really bad, but worldly things. The children didn't enjoy life at all.

Florence was shy and reserved, but she had a good job at IBM and she handled it well. In November of 1987, she met her friend Rosemonde who had just come back from Yugoslavia and told her all about her trip. That was the day when the Gospa got a toehold in the Gardelle family! Florence picked up the book which Rosemonde had lent her: *Medjugorje, récits et messages* ["Medjugorje, Stories and Messages"] by Father Laurentin. She devoured it, reading throughout the night. Before the sun came up, Florence said, "I have to go there immediately! I don't care how, I've got to go!" The call was irresistible.

For the next few days, she searched and searched...but none of the priests she asked could give her any information. There was nothing in the newspapers, and the travel agents had never heard of it.

"Medjugorje? No, that's not in our books!"

But Florence wouldn't be beaten and, in the beginning of December, she set off for Medjugorje in a small group.

There was no heat in the Croatian accommodation; it was freezing inside, outside, and in the church, too. The rain didn't stop for 5 days. Florence and her group wandered around with no guide. Time dragged on interminably. They killed it by going for walks in the mud... In short, they were all wondering what they were doing in such a hole! In her naive way, Florence had thought that she was going to see the Blessed Mother. She had been watching out for her for 4 days, but...nothing!

On the last day she decided to go to Marija's home, and she and her friends tagged along with some Americans who, luckily, had made an appointment with the visionary. The rain was pouring down and everyone was squeezed into Marija's tiny courtyard where the translator sheltered her under an immense umbrella. Florence was fascinated by what Marija had to say. When the group broke up, she couldn't move-she was glued to the spot.

Daylight was fading fast; it was twilight. As usual, Marija started to climb her little staircase to go back into the house when she stopped dead. She turned to Florence, whom she didn't know from a hole in the wall, and looking straight at her, said to her, "The Gospa says that few French people come to Medjugorje, but that those of you who are here will receive much grace, and that when you return to your families there will be many graces because she is calling you!"

With that, she left. (Today, Florence can remember clearly every single word uttered by Marija as if it had only just happened.)

Florence and her friends were astounded. Lost in a tide of Americans, Germans and Italians, our poor little French pilgrims had already been deeply moved by the messages that Marija had been relating. Now they had been rewarded with a message specially for them! Florence started to cry in silence. She was still crying when she stepped on the plane. Bernard was waiting for her in Nice.

"Well?" he asked, once they were in the car.

Florence, the taciturn, launched into a flabbergasting speech about Our Lady, about Marija, about the messages and about the extraordinary moment the previous evening... Bernard wondered if his wife was the same woman. Here she was, talking non-stop—he couldn't get a word in edgewise! While she was talking, Florence relived all the graces she had felt at Marija's, the indescribable flow of peace which invades the heart until you think it's going to burst with happiness. She cried throughout the entire story of what had happened. The car stopped in front of the house, but neither Bernard nor Florence could move. Bernard, too, was weeping, a thing unheard of with this rather reserved couple. Side by side they sobbed on and on—the Gospa had found a second toehold in the Gardelle family!

Florence's life had been turned upside-down. She couldn't stop talking about it. She had changed beyond all recognition. Medjugorje came into every conversation and everyone had to hear about it. The most surprising part is that no one thought her a crank. Believers and atheists alike hung on her every word...grace was flowing into everyone's hearts. Her usual social life was swept aside in order to make room for meetings about Medjugorje, and the Gospa began to wreak havoc in Nice. The most unlikely people started to say, "We want to go there!" In the end, Gaetan, the most recalcitrant of tough cookies who shouted his wife down each time she suggested going to Medjugorje, Gaetan of the unrelenting "Niet!," said to Florence, "What about organizing a coach trip?"

He was the one who started the pilgrimages in the southeast of France, because Florence needed help to get the project going. The "little flowers" (of grace) spread through all the families affected by Medjugorje. The Gospa comes close to working miracles: cures for drug addiction or alcoholism, reconciliation of divorcing couples, family reconciliations, even the most minor material favors!

One youngster who gave his parents a lot of heartache left home one night through the window. Two weeks of anxiety then followed for the parents, who didn't know that he'd ended up at Medjugorje! After 2 weeks there, he was broke. He found a car that was returning to France, but the occupants were just as destitute as he was. They had just enough money to fill the tank with gas. They prayed and set off. That one full tank, which shouldn't have gotten them any farther than Zadar, took them to the banks of the Loire where they lived! The young man is now on the way to becoming a priest.

Bertrand, Florence's son, was more used to discotheques than churches and had experimented with drugs. One day, his mother told him she was off to Medjugorje.

"I'll come with you!"

"Bertrand, you know there aren't any night clubs in Medjugorje..."

But at the appointed hour, Bertrand was there, ready to go. Once in Medjugorje, he behaved like a lost soul up to the moment when he listened to Father Jozo and felt the presence of the Blessed Mother. The last night there, he decided to climb Krizevac with a buddy.

Arriving at the cross, he saw 3 flashes of light.[1] "I'll never be anxious anymore!" he told his mother the next day.

Florence's sister-in-law was transformed. All she wanted to do was to spread the word about Our Lady. She organized a charter flight for Medjugorje. Her fashionable dinner parties were transformed into video-dinners where her guests learned all about Medjugorje in 60 minutes before taking their places at the table!

One of the sweetest fruits is the blossoming of vocations. Medjugorje coaches have become the most astonishing hotbeds of budding religious vocations! Florence knew how to work on the Lord's feelings. From the beginning, she would say to him "In each coach, the devil tries to throw a monkey wrench in the works. You know how hard it is sometimes to beat him. You can rely on me not to get discouraged, but in return I want 4 vocations from this coach!"

And she got them! When there were several buses, she raised the stakes. She's lost count of the number of seminarians (and other vocations) who heard the call at Medjugorje. What's more, this holy blackmail, the kind of thing women did in biblical days, has taught everyone that the Lord is a good business partner...

I think people like Florence have struck gold!

Now, there are more French pilgrims at Medjugorje than any other nationality. I can't think about this without tears coming to my eyes because I see a glimmer of hope for the resurrection of my country, foretold by Marthe Robin (see photos) in 1936 to Father Finet: [2]

"France is going to sink very low, lower than any other country because of her arrogance... There will be nothing left. In her misery, she will remember God and cry out to him, and it will be the Blessed Mother who will come to save her.

"France will find her vocation again as eldest daughter of the Church. She will be the place with the greatest outpouring of the Holy Spirit, and she will send missionaries all over the world again." [3]

Couldn't we recognize the Gospa of Medjugorje in this "Blessed Mother who will come to save France" from her tragic spiritual desert? How can we fail to notice the magnificent work of the Queen of Peace who is rebuilding the fabric of French (and every other) Christianity from within, weakened as it is by the Prince of Lies and by those secret societies which, perfectly legally, shoot down God's commandments?

---

[1] The visionaries always see 3 flashes of light just before the apparition takes place.

[2] Marthe also foretold in 1936 that among the satanic falsehoods which were going to disappear would be Communism and Freemasonry, thanks to the Blessed Mother Mary. Marthe often talked about France's sublime calling and how dear to Mary's heart that country is. *"France will get back on her feet when her young people find the courage to declare their faith again."* They will be close to Mary's heart, as St. Louis-Marie Grignion de Montfort has clearly indicated.

There's a story worth telling here: on March 25, 1966, Our Lady herself had left a little book of St. Louis-Marie de Montfort, "True Devotion to Mary" (A. E. Tan Books and Publishers, Rockford, IL, USA 61105) on Marthe's bed, telling her, *"This is the book that I'd like to see spread throughout the world."* Father Finet was puzzled to see it, because no one had been in Marthe's bedroom.

"What's that, my child?" he asked.

"That's Mommy, Father," replied Marthe.

(See *Martha Robin, The Cross and The Joy,* by Rev. Raymond Peyret, Alba House, NY: Society of Saint Paul, 2187 Victory Blvd., Staten Island, NY 10314.)

[3] In October 1993, after her honeymoon with Paolo in France, Marija said to me, "Seeing France was for us a tragedy. Your churches are full of dust; there's no faith left! The churches which are well preserved have been turned into museums; prayer has disappeared. Still, I see that the Gospa is calling many French people here. She'll convert France here at Medjugorje."

— Message of May 25, 1990 —

"Dear children! I invite you to decide with seriousness to live this novena. Consecrate the time to prayer and to sacrifice. I am with you and I desire to help you to grow in renunciation and mortification, that you may be able to understand the beauty of the life of people who go on giving themselves to me in a special way.

"Dear children, God blesses you day after day and desires a change of your life. Therefore, pray that you may have the strength to change your life. Thank you for having responded to my call."

PODBRDO BY NIGHT

This evening once again, Marija tells us about the days of the first apparitions.

"The Gospa often asked us to pray for her intentions and for the plans she was bringing to pass.[1] One day, she asked us to pray a novena for something very important. She invited all the villagers to go to the Apparition Hill between 2:00 and 3:00 a.m. for 9 nights consecutively. Many villagers answered her call. Our Lady appeared to us (visionaries) and, on the ninth night, something incredible happened. During the apparition, the villagers saw stars falling from the sky. They were shooting towards the place where the Gospa was standing, attracted by her presence as if by a magnet. The stars slipped over the Gospa, covered her in a mantle of light, and then fell to the earth. After touching the ground, they flew up again to the sky, their numbers increasing to infinity.

"At the sight of these stars falling from the sky, the villagers grew very frightened and some of them started to scream.[2] They cried out, 'It's the end of the world! It's doomsday!'"

"They were so afraid that they stayed all night on the hill to pray.

"We, the visionaries, didn't see any of this, because during the apparition, the Gospa looked as she normally looked and we couldn't see the sky, nor the stars, nor anything happening around us. After our ecstasy, the villagers told us what had happened. We were overjoyed because, at the time, we were under the constant threat of being sent to jail. Therefore, we said to ourselves, 'Great! Because if we go to jail, the whole village will be able to testify in our place to what the Gospa does here. Now, she has new witnesses!'"

---

[1] Vicka told me that the Gospa usually kept her plans secret, but sometimes she would say what they were.

[2] Just as in Fatima on Oct. 13, 1917!

— MESSAGE OF JUNE 25, 1990 —

"Dear children! Today I desire to thank you for all your sacrifices and for all your prayers. I am blessing you with my special motherly blessing. I invite you all to decide for God, so that from day to day you will discover his will in prayer. I desire, dear children, to call all of you to a full conversion so that joy will be in your hearts. I am happy that you are here today in such great numbers.

"Thank you for having responded to my call."

TETKA'S CREATURES

Tetka started to work as a shepherdess at the age of 7 and since then she hasn't stopped. She belongs to the noble and strong race chosen by the Gospa in Medjugorje, a people whose faith is simple and complete: "God is God."

Tetka's heart constantly beats in unison with nature and with the Creator. She knows each of her 40 ewes by name, just as she knows every nook and cranny of the Medjugorje valley. Even today, you will find her sitting on a rock in the Sivric area of the village, spinning wool to the rhythm of the rosary while keeping a vigilant eye over her flock. Every evening, just before Mass, she puts on her best dress and makes her way towards the church. Off she goes! She winds her way down the little red stony paths which run along the fields. Nothing ever stops her, come hail or come "burra" (the freezing cold wind which howls through the valley in winter). The July heat waves haven't stopped her either. Her roof is the sky and her security is walking with God.

Her company is a delight for me. The very sight of her face, so full of light, is enough to make anyone understand why Our Lady has chosen this village. There is no theology and no subtleties in the language of these people, neither any bookish knowledge! What they have is simply centuries of humble and attentive listening to the whisperings of God in their hearts. Because these people have poured out their tears and blood in the valleys of Herzegovina, God is their only great friend, the only one they can truly rely on. He is the

Almighty, the Lord of their Creed which has resisted Islam and Communism.

When I am in Tetka's company, I learn more about God than in a convent. With her, everything is clear and simple. Like all Croatians in the area, she speaks of the most tender things in a commanding voice, like a general haranguing his troops before a battle... It's part of her charm! The invasion of the thousands of pilgrims into her territory hasn't changed her habits at all.

Naturally, some of the things these foreigners do surprise her greatly, but I suspect that she praises the Lord for her good fortune. He made her the happiest woman of all by letting her watch over her flock, far from the crazy world where most people can't tell their right from their left.

Tetka lives with her nephews, Petar, Anka and Mladen, who are good friends of mine. One day Petar said to me, "Sister, several ewes are sick. They are going to die and we are afraid the whole flock might be contaminated."

I felt sorry for him and uttered a few banal words to express my sympathy when, all of a sudden, a bright idea struck my tiny little brain. I remembered how in her message of December 25, 1988, the Gospa asked us to carry her *"Special Motherly Blessing to every creature."* I had often wondered, "What does she mean by *every creature*? Can animals receive her blessing too?"

For this family, the loss of an entire flock would be a real catastrophe. It was definitely not the right time to plunge into an analytical exegesis! This was a time for quick action!

"Petar," I said in a challenging tone, "the solution to your problem lies once again in what the Gospa has said. To be more precise, in her message concerning the *Special Motherly Blessing* ... "

Petar gave me a bewildered look: Come again?!!!?

I knew it! He had never heard of this message! The temptation to tease him a little was too strong to resist. So I gave him one of my outraged looks and said, "What? Am I hearing right? You, a *Croatian citizen,* a man *born* in Medjugorje and *you* don't know this message? And that it takes a *foreigner* to let you know what *your* Gospa has told you, in *your* mother tongue, in *your* own village?"

He smiled. I had hit the nail on the head! He would never forget the message I was about to tell him...

"She said: *'Today, I am giving you my special blessing. Carry it to every creature so that each one may have peace. Thank you for answering my call.'* When she said 'creature,' she definitely meant animals too.[1] (I promised myself I would check this with Marija). This means that you must go among your flock and pray for it to receive the Gospa's blessing..."

Petar gave me another of his bewildered looks: Come again?!!!?

I knew it! He had his little ways and this was certainly not one of them! In Herzegovina, you cannot break a farmer's ways just like that.

"Sister," he said, 'I would rather have *you* do this. You're a nun, it would surely be more effective if you did it!"

Done deal! I promised him that I would come back later in the afternoon with some brothers and sisters of my community. When the time came, Tetka took her flock outside and all of us, *6 foreigners*, started to pray. For the very first time I was praying for little woolly critters instead of human beings, and I could feel the joy of the Creator among us. Everything was done in a very simple way. I explained to Petar that the Gospa had not indicated any formula or specific way to confer this blessing, which meant that we could pray as we wished, with the heart.

I must say that all the sick ewes recovered quickly and that no other disease ever affected the flock over the last few years. Secretly because they are very modest about these things — Petar and Tetka have probably kept on giving their flock the blessing of the Queen of the Universe!

------

[1] There was a time in France when Jesus Christ had a much bigger place in hearts, and peasants used to bless their flocks as well as their fields. During the periods of the Rogations, there were processions throughout the countryside. A priest would lead, followed by the villagers, and all would sing to their Creator, blessing the cultivated areas. The Gospa is quite obviously inviting us to resume this beautiful tradition. This would also be a good opportunity to cleanse our villages of the more or less shabby practices which have taken over; I am referring to the so-called healers and people with gifts and powers.

It should be emphasized that many of these powers are rooted in witchcraft (even if the woman in question has a statue of Our Lady of Lourdes in her living room), and that some "healing gifts" acquired by such and such a healer have often been given by Satan himself, in some previous generation of that family. It should also be known that Satan never really gives anything. The supposed gift only consists in shifting the pain from one part of the body to another part of the person's being. People believe in these wonders, and thus, the health of their hearts and souls can easily be destroyed. For instance, your swollen knee seems to be healed, when suddenly, you start spending your nights having anxiety attacks, or you can't stand your spouse anymore. Little by little, your soul is imprisoned, even if, for a while, your body seems to be recovering its health.

The age-old prayers of the Church as well as the blessings she offers are among our many treasures which we can use to meet our needs.

In Medjugorje, Our Lady invites us to use them. For example, she recommends the use of holy water or the carrying of blessed articles with us. If we use pagan means to protect ourselves or to kill pain, we take an enormous risk of opening the doors to the Enemy.

— MESSAGE OF JULY 25, 1990 —

"Dear children! Today I invite you to peace. I have come here as the Queen of Peace and I desire to enrich you with my motherly peace. Dear children, I love you and I desire to bring all of you to the peace which only God gives and which enriches every heart. I invite you to become carriers and witnesses of my peace to this unpeaceful world. Let peace reign in the whole world which is without peace and longs for peace. I bless you with my motherly blessing.

"Thank you for having responded to my call."

UNCLE VIC IS CONCEALING SOMETHING...?!

Springtime 1995! Uncle Victor *really* didn't want to go to Medjugorje with his wife. He preferred his garden. I should add that his wife, Shirley-*holier-than-thou* since her first pilgrimage the previous year had never ceased to plague him with the idea. She had wanted him to go in order to be converted at the feet of the Gospa. While he was grumbling, "Me, convert? It'll be a cold day in hell...!" Shirley, a very enterprising woman, managed to find a little house for sale, smaller than their own and more appropriate for them in their retirement. She suggested that it would be a good idea to move.

But give up his beloved garden? Oh no! That would be the last straw for Uncle Victor! So Shirley decided to resort to blackmail. "If you come with me on a pilgrimage, I promise we won't move!" After all, his garden was worth a sacrifice! So he agreed grudgingly to go on a pilgrimage with her. But what a pilgrimage! To Bosnia-Herzegovina!

"We have Lourdes, Paray-le-Monial and Lisieux right here, in our own country! Why must we go to *Bosnia-Herzegovina*? While you're at it, we could just as well go to eastern Kazakhstan or South Kamchatka?!"

Bravely, he boarded the coach with a group of pilgrims from the west of France. Fortunately, they had an understanding guide who also had a good sense of humor and didn't bore them to tears with endless pieties. He'd had many Uncle Victors before and knew that the Gospa had her own ways of speaking to their hearts. So on the way to Medjugorje there were not too many prayers or too much fasting.

Once there Victor stood aside and watched things progress, although, I might add, not without making a few remarks from time to time, just to dissociate himself from the group and get a rise out of other people. Nevertheless he followed them everywhere and went, without excessive grumbling, to daily Mass, the rosary, the Stations of the Cross, visits to the visionaries, and even a climb to Apparition Hill on the last day.

Shirley was rather surprised. She had expected the worst! Well, so much the better; Our Lady seemed to have answered her prayers. Still, before leaving, she had serious worries. Uncle Vic looked rather strange. He wasn't the same anymore. Against all odds, he had told his bewildered wife, "If you want me to come back with you next year, it's okay with me, dear!"

No doubt, something weird had happened! Shirley watched, scrutinized, waited and kept an attentive eye on Vic. During the journey back home, she didn't dare ask him anything, although she was dying to. Back home, the minute Uncle Vic got in the door he took the phone in hand and summoned all his children to gather at the house the following Sunday. He had, he said, something important to tell them.

Shirley had obviously no chance of finding out the secret before the hour when all the children would be there with their father. All sorts of possibilities started to run through her mind, and she grew more and more puzzled. All the more so because her husband had changed—he didn't send her packing all the time anymore, he was thoughtful and silent. Even his garden wasn't as important to him now. There was definitely something up with him.

She was completely mystified. She had always been the chatterbox in the family. Now all she could do was bite her lip and ask herself, "What on earth could he have to say to the kids that is so important?!"

Everything was different now. She even confided in one of her friends, "What have we done for God to merit this?" She spent her day crying. "So the pilgrimage didn't go well?" her friend asked her.

"Yes, of course it did, on the contrary!"

She explained that she was crying from joy and gratitude!

The neighbors even asked, "What has happened to your husband? He's not the man we used to know."

Even their mischievous 7-year-old granddaughter deliberately cornered her grandfather someplace apart and asked him, "Grandpa, why don't you tell me what happened to you? I promise that I won't tell anyone! Did you fall on your head? You're not like before..."

Meals also were very different. Uncle Vic never really had any appetite before. He wouldn't swallow anything solid and threw up the smallest mouthful. Liquids were all he would take. Now, his appetite was back. With gusto he ate everything his delighted spouse cooked for him!

But most of all, he who used to lead the life of a recluse, isolated in his garden, began to be of great help to his wife. Whenever the opportunity arose, he offered to take her places, go shopping, carry bags, etc.

One day when Shirley woke up, she couldn't help asking him, "Victor, what's up with you? We used to spend our days shouting at one another. Nowadays we don't say very much to one another anymore... And what is it that you want to tell the kids anyway?"

What Uncle Victor had to tell the children was the key to this unbelievable change in him.

At this point in our story I should point out that, 2 years earlier, the family had been shaken and weakened, torn apart even, by a terrible sorrow. The pain penetrated each member of the family so deeply that they were heartbroken. One of Victor's and Shirley's sons, Tanguy, had been killed in an accident. He was 31 and the father of a little girl.

Uncle Vic began his explanation :

"Do you remember that last day in Medjugorje when we were on Apparition Hill? I was behind you as usual when suddenly I saw, coming from the village in the valley below, a little cloud with sparkling edges. It was so bright that I couldn't take my eyes off it. There was nothing else in the sky. Remember? The weather was beautiful. And that cloud came slowly up to me, on the hill. To my great surprise, it stopped right in front of me, about 3 feet above the ground! There were 2 people inside the cloud, or rather, a person and a silhouette of someone else. I couldn't see the face of the silhouette, so don't even ask me who it was because I have no idea. The other person wore something that looked like a white veil.

And that person was...it was..."

Uncle Vic broke down. His tears prevented him from continuing. But the motherly heart of his wife already understood, and Uncle Victor confirmed it by whispering, "It was Tanguy, our son! Alive! And he talked to me! He said, *'Daddy, this is Tanguy, your son who does not forget you. I am happy. Tell them all to pray for peace...especially tell my brother and my sisters this. Tell my daughter, too."*

"I saw that his feet were not touching the ground. After Tanguy spoke, the cloud lifted and went back up into the sky."

At last! Uncle Victor had revealed his secret.

"Why didn't you tell me right away?" asked his wife, deeply moved.

"You would have thought that I was crazy!" he replied.

The following Sunday the children came and listened to the same message from heaven. They were deeply affected. The impact was all the more effective that the message was related to them by Grandpa, the former skeptic and grouch!

Now that Grandma Shirley's prayers have been answered, beyond her wildest expectations, she daily wonders, "Lord, what have we done to deserve such a grace?!"

— MESSAGE OF AUGUST 25, 1990 —

"Dear children! Today I desire to invite you to take with seriousness and put into practice the messages which I am giving you. You know, little children, that I am with you and I desire to lead you along the same path to heaven, which is beautiful for those who discover it in prayer. Therefore, little children, do not forget that these messages which I am giving you have to be put into your everyday life in order that you might be able to say: 'There, I have taken the messages and tried to live them.' Dear children, I am protecting you before the heavenly Father by my own prayers. Thank you for having responded to my call."

IVANKA'S MOM

Ivanka was the first of the 6 visionaries to see the Lady. On June 24, 1981, she was out walking with Mirjana in the hamlet of Bijakovici, along the path which runs at the foot of the hill of Podbrdo.

The following day, she was also the first to ask the Lady a question. Ivanka's mother had died 2 months earlier. *"She is happy, she is with me,"* the Lady answered.

Some time later, on Ivanka's birthday, Our Lady surprised her by appearing with Ivanka's mother.[1] The young girl was struck by her mother's beauty. She was much more beautiful than ever before! And this

---

[1]Father Svetozar Kraljevic transcribed a large part of the early interviews of the visionaries conducted by Fr. Jozo and recorded on tape in *The Apparitions of Our Lady at Medjugorje*, ed. Michael Scanlon T.O.R., Franciscan Herald Press, 1424 W. 51 St., Chicago, IL, USA 60609. Price: $ 9.50. In this author's opinion this is the best book ever written on Medjugorje. Since the audio tapes were stolen by the Communists, this book is all the more precious as documentation.

would not be a one-time surprise, for it happened 5 times! On June 25, 1991, the Gospa returned again with Ivanka's mother. Ivanka could hardly believe her eyes. When she saw her mother, she was even more beautiful than before. Amazingly beautiful!

Why had her mother changed? Marija Pavlovic gives us the answer.

When the Gospa showed her heaven[2] and the intense happiness of the elect, she explained that in heaven, saints grow in happiness. This crescendo in their happiness is linked to God's infinite greatness. God is so great that we will never cease discovering him. Each time we discover a new aspect of his greatness, our love grows. As our love grows, our beauty increases. That was the reason why Ivanka's mother appeared even more beautiful when she came the second time.

"*I am beautiful because I love,*" the Gospa once told Jelena Vasilj, who was absolutely amazed by her beauty. "*If you want to be beautiful, love!*" It must be that in heaven nothing could possibly be static. Love implies the ever-changing movement of exchange, as within the Holy Trinity. So, heaven is full of activity!

Another experience related by Marija also illustrates this movement quite well. While the visionaries were praying before the Gospa, Marija noticed that the face of Our Lady was changing, becoming more and more joyful. It was as though the least prayer from Marija filled her with a new joy. The beauty and splendor of her face grew with each new joy. It became more and more radiant. Then Marija asked, "Why are you more beautiful and joyful when I pray?"

"*It is because with each Ave you say my joy increases.*"

Little by little, Marija was also flooded with the joy of Mary.

Even on this earth, we can start to live this crescendo of happiness within our hearts. Each prayer from the heart opens the heavens above and lets us in. Do you want to look beautiful? The Gospa gives you the recipe. And no cosmetics compete with hers!

---

[2]Marija saw images of heaven; she was not taken there like Jakov and Vicka.

— Message of September 25, 1990 —

"Dear children! I invite you to pray with the heart in order that your prayer may be a conversation with God. I desire each one of you to dedicate more time to God. Satan is strong and wants to destroy and deceive you in many ways. Therefore, dear children, pray every day that your life will be good for yourselves and for all those you meet.

"I am with you and I am protecting you even though Satan wishes to destroy my plans and to hinder the desires which the Heavenly Father wants to realize here. Thank you for having responded to my call."

THE GOSPA COLLECTS PENDULUMS

"Sister, Sister!"

Bridget was about to leave. The bus was waiting for her. What on earth could she need to tell me so urgently that she's running over to me like this?

"Just a minute, there's good news!" she puffed, gasping for breath. "Tomorrow, when you go to Apparition Hill, get as close as possible to the pile of stones under the cross. Then, pick up the big black stone on the left side. Under it, you will find my pendulum... I left it there. I'm done with it!"

"And what am I supposed to do with it?" I asked, laughing.

The bus driver blew the horn. She ran to it and shouted, "Leave it there, it's for her!"

One more pendulum, I said to myself as I watched her leave. The Gospa owns the world's biggest collection of pendulums. (New Age crystals) Who would have thought!

This reminds me of an amusing story. A group of 60 pilgrims from Paris had spent 5 days in Medjugorje, and grace had truly moved their hearts very powerfully. They all went to confession, even those who were the hardest nuts to crack. Such an outcome could only have pleased the Gospa. But then, Father Luciano, an Italian Franciscan, unintentionally opened a can of worms.

"Come and speak to us about the Bible, Father," Geneviève, the leader of a group, innocently asked him.

On their final evening the whole group hung on Father Luciano's every word, for they had been receiving unexpected insights from his teaching. While commenting on the first of the "ten words,"[1] ("Thou shalt have no other gods before me"), he gave a startling description of all the false idols worshiped today in our pagan society, which people unconsciously and so naively accept. He left nothing out! Some pilgrims started to squirm in their seats, for no one escaped the cutting edge of the gospel of the Lord. Their idols, whether big or small, were brought into broad daylight and now required a closer look...

Father Luciano had really opened up a hornet's' nest. But the climax of the evening came when he asked the group, "Does anyone here carry a pendulum?" The pilgrims stared at one another. They hesitated, fidgeted, and looked uneasy. Suddenly a perfectly straight-looking nun took a pendulum out of her pocket, saying, "Yes, I do!"

Fifty-nine pairs of eyes looked at her, and the group burst out laughing. Her courage emboldened even the most hesitant among them. One by one, they took pendulums from their pocketbooks or pockets. Sixty pilgrims and 50 pendulums!

The night was a very long night indeed, the longest of the pilgrimage, because 50 confessions were heard before the pilgrims caught the morning plane. Once again, guess who pocketed the pendulums? The Gospa!

Moved by a sudden inspiration, Father Luciano had put his finger on one of the most sensitive spots of today's society. Like a good shepherd, he saved his sheep from the polluted water that was poisoning them and led them to the amazing life-giving spring which is the Word of God.

"It's simple," he explained before the long sleepless night with the 50 absolutions. "Man is often hungry for 'knowledge.' Yet, only God gives us true knowledge, knowledge which leads to life and unity in love with him.

---

[1] The Bible does not mention the "Ten Commandments," but the "Ten Words." They are words that give life and stave off death.

Satan is shrewd and clever. He will try to take advantage of this hunger which man experiences (not to mention woman!). He proposes something which looks like knowledge, but in fact only gives information. As early as Genesis his strategies are visible: 'What! God forbade you to eat this fruit! But on the contrary! Your eyes will be opened. You will have knowledge! You will be like gods!'"

When lured by this bait (this "con job," I would say), Eve is ready to swap her union with God for a song, in order to obtain "knowledge." She bites into the fruit and at that very moment death enters into the world! Today, things haven't changed a bit. Satan's age-old tricks turn out to be as efficient as ever, if not more so. In the Bible, the Word of God concerning all divination methods and the acquisition of "information" by spiritualistic means is crystal-clear (see Deuteronomy 18:9-12). It is an "abomination." Many are the verses in which God warns his people against such pagan ways which lead to death.[2]

Regarding pendulums and other such devices which are supposed to "give information," the most significant excerpt can be found in the Book of Hosea 4:12 and the following lines. God reproaches the priests and the people who desert him, the Living God, to give themselves up to whoring: **"My people consult a piece of wood, and their divining rod gives them oracles. For a spirit of whoredom has led them astray and they have played the whore, forsaking their God."**

Father Luciano added, "They make you believe that a little ball made of paper-mâché, a ring on a thread, or a piece of wood is able to give you information which will benefit you! But what makes your pendulum move? Magnetism makes my compass move and helps me locate the north. But I don't use the compass to look for my soul-mate, for happiness, or for my keys!

"What makes the pendulum swing in a particular direction? How could a ball of paper-mâché be used as a road sign to walk in the ways of God? Saint John gives us 4 conditions for walking in the light; turning away from sin, observing God's commandments (and the commandment of Love), being wary of the world and being wary of the antichrists (1 John 3 and 4).

"If we search for information on how to be happy (through money,

---

[2] Hence the traps still current today, such as theosophy, scientology, extrasensory perception, spiritualism, and various "New Age" beliefs and practices. They offer knowledge disconnected from the Bible for the most part.

love, success...), we have to admit that objectively, where love is concerned, experience has proven that pendulums have really messed up our lives. As to our health... Well if it worked, it would be covered by our HMO's!

"What about money problems? Maybe it works, maybe not. But who is behind it? Are terrible anxieties and temptations to commit suicide the price one has to pay? Only God is free of penalty. Being a child of the heavenly Father, it's enough for me to know that the swinging pendulum offends him. I don't need any further explanations or demonstrations to refrain from using it because I don't want to offend the Father. I love him and I love his Providence. Pendulum or Providence... make your choice!"

Today, the information race rules us. We want information, at all costs. Satan has been whispering the same sweet nothings in our ear ever since Adam and Eve: "You must know everything. Come to me because your God is concealing things from you.[3]" No! Do not swap your soul, your eternal life, for these false lights! In Jesus, we have everything. He is the Way, the Truth and the Life.

"And this is eternal life, that they may know you, the only true God, and Jesus Christ whom you have sent." (John 17:3)

If the Gospa has cried bitterly, *"You have forgotten the Bible,"* it is because she sees her beloved children dying. It is the cry of a mother who sees the Destroyer approaching her little one. She sees him seducing her child who is defenseless because he has not taken up the sword that is the Word of God, and made it his own in order to defeat Satan.

That night, what the pilgrims had once considered a precious treasure was thrown in the waste paper basket. In the following years some of them returned to Medjugorje and they testified as to how this "renunciation" had freed them. Their pendulum was once their idol. Before they realized, it had reduced them to slavery. Fortunately, the Gospa broke their chains!

In other words, if you have a pendulum you are invited to come and add to the Gospa's collection here in Medjugorje. She already has them in all sizes and shapes!

---

[3] Satan always wants to make us believe that God is concealing something, and he tries to attract us through false information. Look up relevant passages concerning divination: Ez 21:29; Mic 3:11; 2 Kings 23:5; I Sam 15:23.

— MESSAGE OF OCTOBER 25, 1990 —

"Dear children! Today I call you to pray in a special way and to offer up sacrifices and good deeds for peace in the world. Satan is strong and with all his strength, desires to destroy the peace which comes from God. Therefore, dear children, pray in a special way with me for peace.

"I am with you and I desire to help you with my prayers and I desire to guide you on the path of peace. I bless you with my motherly blessing. Do not forget to live the messages of peace. "Thank you for having responded to my call."

VICKA AND JAKOV DISAPPEARED!

In 1981, the visionaries all lived in the same area in the Bijakovici district at the foot of Podbrdo. At that time, the militia continuously harassed them, always keeping a close eye on them. Their families lived in constant anxiety. They lived under a permanent threat because seeing the Gospa was considered a major crime against the Communist regime, and the authorities took it very seriously.

---

[1] Today this tumble-downed cottage is a mere ruin: the roof has fallen in, and the walls are in a dilapidated state. Some people have come to retrieve a few stones or tiles here and there. In a word, the ruin could soon disappear. Such a shame! This piece of land belongs to 8 joint owners, and each one of them has his own idea about it. Marija has told me it should be fixed up and made into a museum. We just cannot let this house disappear! So many beautiful things have happened there! After all, in Lourdes, people do visit the Soubirous house. You should tell the pilgrims to come and see this house and explain what happened there, and ask them to pray... If no one does anything, in a year it will be too late, nothing will be left of it.

[2] She died a year later, leaving Jakov at the age of 12. His uncle, Filip Dragicevic, took care of him, and Jakov lived in his house until he married Anna Lisa in April 1993.

One particular afternoon Jakov and Vicka, his cousin, managed—God alone knows how—to evade the general surveillance. They were on their way back from Citluk. They decided to go to Jakov's and ask his mother for something to eat because they were hungry. Pilgrims who have met with Mirjana and Ivan at their homes have passed in front of this miserable tumbled-down cottage, or rather, what was left of it.[1] Jakov's mother, Jaka,[2] was very poor.

Both Jaka and her son Jakov lived in 2 tiny rooms, without running water or any modern facilities, as was common in the days before the Gospa came to Medjugorje. At that time, people slept on the floor. They had no heat and were often hungry. They worked in the tobacco fields to the point of exhaustion. If a person fell ill, he just had to cope with it, because no one but God could help him out...

Breathless, Vicka and Jakov entered the house. They told Jaka how hungry they were. While Jaka was fixing a small snack for them, they went off together. Ten minutes later, she called them. No answer! It was exactly 3:20 p.m. She went into the other room. No one! Her heart skipped a beat. They couldn't have left the house without her seeing them! She kept turning over in her mind every minute that had passed since their arrival. They had to be there! It was impossible for them not to be because she had heard them chatting just a few minutes before. She felt dizzy from anxiety. "What if the militia... No! How could they have taken them without coming through the kitchen?"

She rushed out, totally distraught, and met Ivan's mother coming down the path.

"Have you seen Jakov and Vicka?"

"No, I haven't!"

She went up the road and questioned her neighbors. She entered the blue house.

"Well, no..." answered Vicka's mother, Zlata, shaking her head.

As fast as lightning the rumor spread that Jakov and Vicka had disappeared. People's hearts were torn! All the inhabitants of Bijakovici considered the visionaries like their own children, their own treasures.

At this point we can't help thinking of Joseph and Mary in Jerusalem, searching anxiously for their little 12-year-old *Yeshua*...

The minutes ticked by, but the children had vanished into thin air. Vicka's mother was absolutely positive that she hadn't seen them around either. In fact, no one had seen them. Broken-hearted, Jaka went home. She paced up and down in the kitchen. She took another look in the empty room where she had last seen them, hoping against all hope that she would find them there, and there would be an end to this nightmare. But no one was there! She removed the 2 plates of food she had prepared. They were cold now. She put the old saucepan back in its place, but her mind was haunted by the most terrible scenes a mother could imagine.

In the Balkans, ancestral memory is heavily laden. There, people don't need horror movies to be reminded of atrocities. Jaka went outside and sat under the small tree next to the house. From this vantage point she would be able to watch out for them. Suddenly, at 3:50 p.m., she thought she heard a noise. She couldn't believe her ears. It came from the house!

"Jakov, is that you?"

"Yes," answered Vicka always a step ahead of the others! With Jakov she was just finishing praying the Magnificat, the prayer they always said after apparitions.

Jakov ran out of the house, looking overjoyed, and shouted to his mother, "Mommy, Mommy! We went to heaven! We saw heaven!"

"Heaven!?! No... That's not possible! I can't believe you went to heaven!"

So what had really happened?.

— MESSAGE OF NOVEMBER 25, 1990 —

"Dear children! Today I invite you to do works of mercy with love and out of love for me and for your and my brothers and sisters. Dear children, all that you do for others, do it with great joy and humility towards God.

"I am with you and day after day I offer your sacrifices and prayers to God for the salvation of the world. Thank you for having responded to my call."

SUDDENLY THE ROOF OPENED

"Jakov, please tell us...," the pilgrims always ask.

"The Gospa came and she took us with her. But Vicka was with me. Go and ask her, she'll tell you..."

(Jakov, even today, is a very reserved young man, and even Anna Lisa his wife only gets measured doses of the treasures given to him by Our Lady).

Vicka, on the contrary, doesn't need to be asked twice to tell about her "journey to the beyond"!

"We weren't expecting it," she says. "The Gospa came into the room while Jakov's mother was in the kitchen fixing something for our lunch. Then, she offered to take us both with her to visit heaven, purgatory and hell. We were so astounded that, at that time, neither Jakov nor I could answer yes. Jakov said to her, 'Take Vicka with you. She has a lot of brothers and sisters, but I am all alone with my mother.' (To tell the truth, he doubted we would ever get back alive from such an adventure!)

"As for me," Vicka adds, "all that was going through my mind was, 'Where will we end up going and how long will it take?' In the end, since we saw how much the Gospa wanted to take us along with her, we accepted, and we got there!"

"There?" I asked Vicka. "But how did you get there?"

"As soon as we said yes, the roof opened and there we were!"

"Did you leave with your body?"

"Yes, just as we are now! The Gospa took Jakov by her left hand and me by the right and we left with her. First, she showed us heaven."

"So you went into heaven just like that? You just walked straight in?"

"Of course not!" Vicka said. "We went in the door!"

"What kind of door was it?"

"A normal door! We saw Saint Peter standing by the door and the Gospa opened it..."

"Saint Peter? What did he look like?"

"Well, just the way he looked on earth!"

"Which means...?"

"Between 60 and 70 years old, not very tall but not short either, slightly curly gray hair, rather stocky..."

"Didn't he open the door for you?"

"No, the Gospa opened it herself without a key. She told me he was Saint Peter. He didn't say anything; we simply nodded from a distance."

"Did he look surprised to see you?"

"No, why would he? You know, we were with the Gospa, so..."

Vicka described the scene just as she would tell about a recent stroll in the company of her relatives in the nearby countryside. To her, there was no barrier between heavenly and earthly matters. She felt fully at home in both worlds. She even looked somewhat surprised at some of my questions. Strangely enough, though, she was not aware that her experience was a treasure for mankind. The language of heaven, so familiar to her, opens a window on a completely different world for today's society, for the sightless people that we are...

"Heaven is a big wide space, limitless. There is a glowing light that doesn't exist on earth. I saw many people, and they are all very, very happy. They sing, they dance... They communicate in a way unknown on earth. They know each other from the inside. They wear long robes. I noticed 3 different colors, but these colors are not like the ones on earth. They look like yellow, gray and red. There are also some angels with them. The Gospa explained everything to us. *'See how happy these people are,'* she said. *'They lack for nothing!'*"

"Vicka, can you describe the happiness that the saints experience in heaven?"

"No, I can't describe it to you because no words on earth can express it. The happiness of the elect—I could experience it myself, but I can't talk to you about it. I can only live it in my heart."

"Didn't you feel like staying there and not coming back to earth?"

She answered, smiling, "Yes! But one can't think only about oneself! You know, our greatest joy is to make the Gospa happy, and we know that she wishes to keep us here a little while more in order to bring her messages to the world. It's a great joy to share her messages! As long as she needs us for that, I'm ready! When she wishes to take me with her, I'm also ready! That's her plan, not mine!"

"And the chosen people in heaven, could they see you too?"

"Of course they could! We were there with them!"

"Can you describe them to me?"

"They were about 30 years old. They were very, very beautiful. No one was too short or too tall. There was no one skinny, fat, or crippled. They were all very good-looking."

"Then, I wonder why Saint Peter was older and dressed like on earth?"

At that she paused for a moment in silence… It had never occurred to her to wonder about that.

"That's how it is! I told you what I saw."

"So, if your bodies were totally in heaven with the Gospa, they were not on earth in Jakov's house any longer?"

"Of course, not! Our bodies disappeared from Jakov's house. Everyone looked for us. It lasted 20 minutes in all."

For now, that's all the details available from Vicka. For her, the most important thing is to have begun to taste the inexpressible happiness of heaven, that pure peace, that promise beyond any shadow of doubt. The intellectual will surely try and pick apart this account given "off the cuff" by Vicka. Besides having a second witness in Jakov, the most convincing proof that they really visited heaven is Vicka's heavenly joy that she radiates to all who meet her. How many thousands of people have found hope again after just seeing her beautiful smile?

— MESSAGE OF DECEMBER 25, 1990 —

"Dear children! Today I invite you in a special way to pray for peace. Dear children, without peace you cannot experience the birth of little Jesus, neither today nor in your daily lives. Therefore pray to the Lord of Peace that he may protect you with his mantle and that he may help you to comprehend the greatness and the importance of peace in your hearts. In this way you shall be able to spread peace from your heart throughout the whole world. I am with you and I intercede for you before God.

"Pray because Satan wants to destroy my plans of peace. Be reconciled with one another and by means of your lives help peace reign in the whole earth. Thank you for having responded to my call."

I WON'T GO TO PURGATORY!

When I talk to pilgrim groups about the messages and the graces given by Mary in Medjugorje, I like to trap them with the question: "Who among you thinks that he will go to purgatory?"

The result is always a catastrophe... Almost everyone raises his hand! If this takes place towards the end of their pilgrimage, I do not hesitate to let them know—with a smile, naturally—what I really think about their reaction: "This is terrible! But just terrible! You haven't understood a word of the Gospa's messages. You have to stay here for at least 3 more days!"

Next, I use Vicka's testimony. Little by little, they begin to relax and are willing to give up their old ideas, tinged with fatality. A final test at the end of the talk shows that no one intends to go to purgatory any more. Phew!...

But let's get back to Vicka's story:

"After showing us heaven, Our Lady took us to purgatory," she told us. "It's a very dark place and we could hardly see anything because of a very thick kind of smoke, gray like ash. We could sense that there were many people there, but we couldn't see their faces because of the smoke. Nevertheless, we could hear them move and scream. There were many of them and they were suffering a lot. We could also hear some thumps, as if people were banging themselves. The Gospa told us, '*See how much these people suffer! They are waiting for your prayers to be able to go to heaven.*'"

"Later on, Our Lady told us more about purgatory. I was amazed to hear that persons consecrated to God, nuns and even priests, were there. I asked the Gospa how consecrated people could possibly go to purgatory. She answered, '*Yes, these persons were consecrated to God, but there was no love in their lives. This is why they are in purgatory.*'"

"Before we left purgatory, the Gospa strongly recommended that we pray daily for the poor souls in purgatory."

I asked, "Vicka, did you feel in yourself the sufferings of these people just as you felt the happiness of the elect?"

"When we were in purgatory," she said, "the Gospa gave us a special grace so that we could bear being there. Without this strength, we wouldn't have been able to tolerate it. It's one thing to think about purgatory and another to see it! Today I feel a deep sorrow when I think about these souls who suffer so much, and I pray for them. Of course, I wish that each one could go to heaven! Still, right at that moment, we felt a strength which does not belong to earth. It was unique, just for the occasion."

So that's how Vicka summed up in a few words her visit to purgatory, but she gave us the main aspects. Later on, Our Lady spoke about this reality in 4 messages[1] which corroborate the teaching of the Church. They also confirm the testimonies of some canonized mystics who lived experiences similar to those of Vicka and Jakov.[2]

---

[1] In a message of January 1983, Our Lady explained the different levels in purgatory. Some are close to hell and some are close to heaven. By praying for souls, we gain intercessors who help us in our lives.

[2] St. Catherine of Genoa (Italy), Blessed Marie of Bethlehem (Israel), the Holy Curé of Ars (France), Blessed Faustina (Poland), etc....

Between 1981 and 1984, when asked by the visionaries about the lot of such and such a deceased person, the Gospa would sometimes answer, "*He is with me*," or sometimes, "*You must pray for him.*" This is how Jakov was granted the great joy on September 5, 1983, of learning that his mother was already in heaven. She had died that same day. I asked Vicka some questions about this.

"In your opinion," I said to her, "what in Jaka's life made her go to heaven so quickly?"

"It's very simple!" Vicka answered. "She did all her little daily tasks with love, with her whole heart! God entrusts a job to each one of us. You write books, and I speak to pilgrims. We must do it with the heart. That's what makes it great! God doesn't ask us to move mountains and put them somewhere else! It's the little daily things that matter to him. Many people are too complicated. No, Jaka never did anything extraordinary, but God saw how big her heart was!"[3]

In 1984, the Gospa put an end to "personal questions." Nevertheless, during the recent war, I understood from roundabout conversations with Vicka that the Gospa had given information on such and such a Croatian soldier from the region who was reported missing or killed in action. At that time, only a few pilgrims were coming to the village, and Vicka spent most of her time comforting the local families affected by the war.

One evening she told me, "Many of our men have disappeared. During the apparition we talked a lot about this, and now I must go and visit their families... You know, they are waiting in great anxiety." I chose not to ask Vicka any more questions, but these simple words had already told me much.

For us who are still on earth, the main thing is not to know whether such and such a relative of ours is still in purgatory or already in heaven. What is *really* important is to discover the treasure brought to us on a silver platter by the Gospa, the treasure she offers to us through her school of love in Medjugorje. Whoever joins her school will not go to purgatory![4] No way!

---

[3] When asked the same question, Jakov answered, "She was a good Christian! She took the Ten Commandments seriously. What God invites us to live, she lived every day, and faithfully." She also lived the Gospa's messages.

Our decision to become saints totally fits in with the plans God has designed for us. Pride has nothing to do with this decision—although I often hear this argument. (Such reasoning would imply that Therese the Little Flower, the Blessed Sr. Faustina, and the Curé of Ars were guilty of the sin of pride!)

In her messages, Our Lady has given us many powerful means of going straight to heaven. Whoever lives these messages already feels the joy of heaven in his heart. It is not the kind of joy which comes from the human satisfaction we feel when everything is going our way. It is the divine joy that never leaves you, even in the midst of hardships. I like to quote these words that the Blessed Mother said to Jelena Vasilj in 1986:

"If you would abandon yourselves to me, you will not even feel the passage from this life to the next life. You will begin to live the life of heaven on earth."

But our journey with Vicka is not yet finished...

---

[4] Nowadays, only a few parishes teach the faithful the basic truth of what happens after death. This terrible lack leads some of the faithful to neglect their deceased ones. Some even become attracted by false doctrines, such as nothingness after death, or reincarnation. This ignorance often generates anxiety. To try and fill this gap, I wrote the booklet *The Amazing Secret of the Souls in Purgatory*, available from Queenship Publishing Co., PO Box 42028, Santa Barbara, CA, USA 93140-2028. Tel: (800) 647-9882; Fax: (805) 957-1631.

— FLASHBACK ON 1990 —

February 2: While in the USA, Mirjana received this message as she was praying for unbelievers with Our Lady:

> "I have been with you nine years. For nine years I wanted to tell you that God, your Father, is the only way, truth, and life. I wish to show you the way to eternal life. I wish to be your tie, your connection to the profound faith. Listen to me!
>
> "Take your rosary and get your children, your families with you. This is the way to come to salvation. Give your good example to your children; give a good example to those who do not believe. You will not have happiness on this earth, neither will you come to heaven if you do not have pure and humble hearts, and do not fulfill the law of God. I am asking for your help to join me to pray for those who do not believe. You are helping me very little. You have little charity or love for your neighbor, and God gave you the love and showed you how you should forgive and love others. For that reason, reconcile and purify your soul. Take your rosary and pray it. All your sufferings take patiently. You should remember that Jesus was patiently suffering for you.
>
> "Let me be your Mother and your tie to God, to the eternal life. Do not impose your faith on the unbelievers. Show it to them by your example and pray for them. My children, pray!"

March 25: Sr. Emmanuel founded the association "Enfants de Medjugorje" (Children of Medjugorje) in France. Its aim is to spread the messages through every possible means. In December 1995, the association "Children of Medjugorje" was established in the USA: PO Box 1110, Notre Dame, IN 46556. On the Internet: http://www.nd.edu/~mary/Emmanuel.html. Its head is Denis Nolan.

June 25: The second "Youth Festival," led by Father Tomislav Vlasic, was organized on the initiative of Ernest William from England.

October 21: The President of the Commission, Msgr. Komarica, celebrated evening Mass in Medjugorje. According to the custom of the Church, it was a recognition of Medjugorje as a place of prayer and worship. It also meant that private pilgrimages are permitted. "I am coming in the name of the Yugoslavian Episcopal Commission and of all bishops," he stated in his homily. "Other bishops of the Commission will also come to celebrate Mass here in the future." (And so it happened). "The Commission recognizes the good fruits of prayer and conversion in Medjugorje."

October 23-24: Marija Pavlovic visited Moscow with Msgr. Hnilica and Fr. Orec (Medjugorje's parish priest at the time). Our Lady appeared to her in a church. A huge crowd gathered for the occasion and many people were in tears. "It reminds me of the first days of the apparitions," Marija shared.

1991

— Message of January 25, 1991 —

"Dear children! Today like never before, I invite you to prayer. Let your prayer be a prayer for peace. Satan is strong and desires to destroy not only human life, but also nature and the planet on which you live. Therefore, dear children, pray that through prayer you can protect yourselves with God's blessing of peace. God has sent me among you so that I may help you. If you so wish, grasp the rosary. Even one rosary alone can work miracles in the world and in your lives. I bless you and I remain with you for as long as it is God's will. Thank you for not betraying my presence here and I thank you because your response is serving the good and peace. Thank you for having responded to my call."

DOES HELL EXIST?

Vicka never studied theology. I doubt she ever will! Nevertheless, theologians enjoy meeting her and I often have the opportunity of accompanying some of them to her house. They are deeply moved, and when they leave they say they feel somehow "readjusted" because all the knowledge they had acquired through years of studying had just been summed up in a few simple words by a mere country girl without any cultural background. Yet she spoke with the assurance of someone who has touched the realities of the Faith. She has sometimes even corrected them, bringing them back to the heart of the matter. Whenever a theologian requested me as a translator and started to ask questions which were not connected with the essentials of the Faith, I knew in advance what Vicka's answer (as well as those of the other visionaries) would be: "The Gospa didn't tell us anything about that."

It can be said that the 6 children Our Lady chose to become "visionaries" have no theological curiosity. Is this deliberate?

At the beginning of my stay in Medjugorje, I couldn't help asking some of the visionaries: "Hasn't it ever occurred to you to ask the Gospa why this or why that?" (things I thought would be very interesting to know, about Jesus and Our Lady herself).

"No, why?" Vicka looked surprised. "You know, when the Gospa has something important to tell us, she brings it up herself. We don't ask questions, because if she doesn't say anything on a subject, it means that it's not that important..."

This way of thinking is more readily accepted in the village of Medjugorje than it would be in the halls of our universities! But that's probably the way Our Lady wants it, in order to help us focus anew on the basic truths of the Faith on which our Christian lives rest, and without which they would collapse. We are living at a time when everything is indeed collapsing!

Nowadays, who believes that hell exists? Who will explain to the faithful why, during Holy Mass, we ask God: "Save us from final damnation and count us among those you have chosen...,"[1] or, "Save us from the fires of hell"?[2]

In Medjugorje the Gospa has not hesitated to clarify this point from the very beginning, for she knows that words are often not enough; she "showed" us what exists, so that we might believe. She wants to save us from ignorance, from today's cloudy thinking, because ignorance in the spiritual battle is the weapon of the defeated.[3]

---

[1] Eucharistic prayer No. 1.

[2] Angel's prayer in Fatima (to be said at the end of each decade of the rosary).

"After visiting purgatory," Vicka added, "the Gospa showed us hell. It's a terrible place. There is a huge fire in the middle of it. This fire is not like the fires we have on earth. We even saw perfectly average people, those you would meet on the street, who threw themselves into this fire. No one was pushing them. They dove into the fire down to different depths. When they came out from it they looked like wild beasts. They were screaming their hatred and rebellion and blaspheming. We could hardly believe they once had been human beings, considering how much they were changed and how deformed they had become.[4]

"In front of this, we were terrified. We didn't understand how such a horrible thing could happen to these people. We saw a beautiful young lady throw herself into the fire. When she came out, she looked like a monster. However, Our Lady's presence reassured us.

"The Gospa explained to us what we were seeing and said:
'These people go to hell of their own will. It is their choice, their decision. Do not be afraid! God has given freedom to everyone. On earth, everyone can decide for God, or against God. Some people, while on earth, always do everything against God, against his will, consciously. These people introduce hell into their own hearts. And when they die, if they do not repent, this same hell goes on.'

"'Gospa,' we asked, 'can these people get out of hell?'

"'Hell will never end. Those who are in hell do not want to receive anything from God anymore; they freely decided to be far from God, forever! God cannot force anyone to love him!'"

I then played the devil's advocate, to back Vicka into a corner.

"What about God?" I said. "His heart is full of love. Doesn't he care about his children? How can he let them be lost forever? Isn't he almighty? Why doesn't he place a barrier before hell, for instance, or why doesn't he

---

[3] Even within the Church, some people deny the existence of hell. Some pilgrims related to me, "My parish priest said that hell does not exist, that there is no point in believing in such things anymore..." When confronted with such situations, which are more and more frequent, we must answer kindly but firmly: "Father, is this your personal opinion, or the Faith given by the Bible and the tradition of the Church?" The Old and the New Testaments, as well as the Magisterium of the Church, teach us that hell does exist. [See *Catechism of the Catholic Church*, published by Doubleday: "The teaching of the Church affirms the existence of hell and its eternity" (§ 1037).

[4] These words are so serious that I checked them carefully again with Vicka before printing them.

take in his arms all those who are about to jump into the fire in order to convince them to join him rather than Satan? They would understand their mistake!"

"But God does everything he can to save us! Everything! Jesus died for each one of us and his great love is for all of us. He always invites us to come closer to his heart, but what can he possibly do when confronted with someone who rejects his love? Nothing! You can't force love!"

At this point the visit ended. According to our earthly clocks, it had lasted 20 minutes. However, for Vicka and Jakov, time had been suspended. They had escaped from our limits of time and space. At the end of the apparition, the Gospa entrusted them with a mission.

"I showed you this," she said, *"so that you would know that it exists and so that you can tell others."*[5]

"And how did you get back to Jaka's?" I asked.

"Just the way we left! We went down through the roof and found ourselves once again in the room!"

---

[5] The most famous "visit to hell" is that of Teresa of Avila. In 1917, Our Lady also showed hell to the three little children of Fatima, who consequently wouldn't stop sacrificing themselves for sinners (see the book *Fatima in Lucia's Own Words*, ed. Fra Louis Kondor, SVD, Vice-Postulation Centre, Apartado, 6, P-2496 FATIMA Codex, Portugal). The French mystic Marthe Robin also related her impressive visit to hell with Our Lady (not yet published).

In 1936, Blessed Sr. Faustina from Poland also told of her own experience: "Today, in the company of an angel, I visited hell. It is a place of great agony and it covers a large area! Of all the torments I have seen, the greatest is the loss of God... I would have died as I watched the tortures, if the Power of the Almighty had not supported me! Let sinners know that the nature of their sufferings shall be that of their sins, for all eternity. I am writing this on an order from God so that no one will seek an excuse, saying that 'nobody ever went there,' and that 'nobody knows what really happens there'! I, Sister Faustina, by an order of God, went into the depths of hell to testify that hell does exist! [...] I noticed one thing: that most of the souls there are those who disbelieved that there is a hell." (See *Divine Mercy in My Soul*, 741, October 20, 1936, published by Marian Helpers Press, Eden Hill, Stockbridge, MA 01262.)

In January 1983, Father Tomislav Vlasic asked Mirjana if many people went to hell. "I recently asked the Gospa just that question," answered Mirjana. "She says that nowadays the majority of people go to purgatory, the second largest category of people go to hell, and only a small number of people go directly to heaven. She told me that those who are in hell have ceased to think about God positively; they blaspheme more and more and are already a part of hell. They choose not to be delivered from hell."

— Message of February 25, 1991 —

"Dear children! Today, I invite you to decide for God, because distance from God is the fruit of lack of peace in your hearts. God is only peace. Therefore, approach him through your personal prayer and then live peace in your hearts. In this way peace will flow from your hearts like a river into the whole world. Do not talk about peace, but make peace. I am blessing each of you and each good decision of yours. Thank you for having responded to my call."

A SILENT BLESSING

For 10 years, Sonia had suffered from deep depression. Neither the kindness of her family nor medical care had succeeded in pulling her out of the dark hole she was in, and everyone feared the worst. Concerns of suicide were haunting the household. The solution of a chemical straitjacket was far too inhuman to face, so the family tried everything else they could think of.

One day, a group of friends dropped over at Sonia's for a drink. Among them was Eric, a Medjugorje pilgrim. He had never met Sonia before, and was torn at the sight of her deep suffering. Without telling anyone, he gave her the special motherly blessing of Our Lady, silently. Then the group left, promising to keep in touch.

A few months later, Eric met with a friend who belonged to the group, and he asked how Sonia was doing.

"Do you mean you don't know?" he replied. "Well, she couldn't be better! Would you believe it? Her recovery was spectacular and totally unexpected! And guess what she said? 'It's funny, but since that day you visited me, I felt life coming back. Something clicked inside me and less than a month later I was on my feet again!'"

Eric's testimony reminds me of Bertrand's. He was a male nurse living in Paris who just hated his job. Every day he saw young people die of AIDS without any spiritual help, and he was torn because he couldn't assist them either—this big hospital was understaffed for financial reasons, and the nurses had hardly enough time to give the minimum care to patients before hurrying into the next room. "It's worse than inhuman," he said, "it's criminal! The dying should never be treated like this!"

One day, while in Medjugorje, Bertrand heard about the special blessing of the Gospa. When he came back a year later, he was a totally changed person.

"It's fantastic! The Gospa has found the solution for me. When I have to sprint to give an AIDS victim his treatment, I silently give him the special motherly blessing, and know that Mary herself will take him under her mantle when he dies. Once, a dying AIDS victim was even cured!"

What is this special motherly blessing all about? We must refer to the words Marija received on the mountain as well as in the monthly messages.[1] I remember how, in December 1989, one of my first conversations with Marija dealt with what she called the "special motherly blessing." At that time, being completely naive as far as Croatian culture and the Gospa's "ways" were concerned, I asked questions which were completely out of place.

"Marija, what's the difference between all the blessings given here by Our Lady? Once she gave her 'solemn blessing' (August 15, 1985), then her 'motherly blessing' (December 19, 1985), and she has also said, 'I bless you with the blessing of God' (June 25, 1987). She also gave the 'blessing of joy' (July 25, 1988), and lastly the famous 'special motherly blessing' that she wanted us to transmit to every living creature. Can you explain the differences?"

The reply I got was certainly scanty! "I don't know, the Gospa

---

[1] The visionaries are very strict when it comes to their testimony. They will only speak about the messages they personally received. Marija is the one to whom the Gospa has spoken of this special motherly blessing, and it is useless to ask the other visionaries about it: they will only answer, "The Gospa didn't tell me anything about that." Similarly, on the subject of sickness, it is Vicka who has received the messages, and the others will not talk about them. When one of the visionaries says, "The Gospa hasn't said anything about this," he is speaking only for himself. This attitude is the guarantee of the truthfulness of their testimony.

never said anything about this." You can imagine how disappointed I was!

People say that you learn by doing; seeing the visionaries prompts us to live instead of asking questions! Let's keep our feet on the ground.

If someone offers me a piece of fruit, I take it, I thank the person and then eat it—the apple, orange or banana. Each fruit fulfills its task in my body without my understanding exactly how. I am nourished, and that's what matters!

It's the same with the gifts of God (although of a different order). He gives me what he knows is good for me, and I either take it or don't. If I accept it, the Creator knows in what ways this gift will bear fruit in me, according to his divine law. This is all we need to know. I can rest peacefully, trusting him entirely. At the Last Supper Jesus did not say, "Understand this and eat it"; he said **"Take this and eat it."**

Did Our Lady give a "special motherly blessing" at Medjugorje? Then it is for me to receive it gratefully. Did she ask me to transmit it to every creature? I transmit it. OK, she didn't provide a "user's manual," so I manage without it, and transmit the blessing with all my heart.

One day, Marija told me that she herself gave this "special motherly blessing" in a very simple way. For example, she would say:

"Here, I have received the 'special motherly blessing' of the Gospa and I pass it on to you."

"Is this what the Gospa instructed you to say?"

"No, we are free to say the prayers we like, from the heart."

"Do you lay on hands?"

"No, the Gospa didn't say so."

"Can you pass this blessing on to a group?"

"No, only to one person at a time."

I've noticed that , if our hearts are attentive, Our Lady herself shows us whom to bless. When we are confronted by unbelievers or people who totally reject prayer, we can transmit this blessing silently. Different kinds of graces are then poured out upon these people, such as peace, joy, conversion, etc.

In the late 1980's, with the great enthusiasm generated by the rediscovery of the gifts of God through Mary, all went well. But even the best things can turn sour if man adds his sin to them and tries to appropriate the divine in order to serve his ego. You can't package the divine. You can't sell it. You can't deal with it according to our miserable human standards. Some deviances have taken place, especially in the United States. The point is not to launch "an apostolate of the special motherly blessing" by means of brochures, talks, and even answering machines, which could eventually lead one day to ridiculous lengths such as giving the blessing by answering machine or fax!! Inspired by the Gospa, Marija said clearly not to do this. I myself saw several "diviners" or "faith healers" who were causing real trouble in their groups of pilgrims. One of them asked me: "Sister, I want to receive the special blessing from you alone." I knew his intention was not pure. I refused, and explained that this gift was absolutely not a magnetic force or fluid, that it has nothing to do with something magic that people could pass on to one another.

This is so typical of Satan, sneaking in his dirty tricks precisely where Our Lady wants to give us her treasures! (Therefore, to avoid confusion, I gave the blessing silently.)

Today the situation is still a delicate one. On the one hand, Marija declares positively that the Gospa did ask us to bestow her blessing, but, on the other hand, the Enemy has sown weeds in Medjugorje's good earth. For my part, I think that, once again, illumination comes from the Bible. *"Read the Sacred Scriptures,"* Mary tells us, *"in order to fully understand the message of my appearance here."*

❊ ❊ ❊ ❊

In Hebrew, the root of the word *berakhah* (blessing) is "knee." You kneel before God, you prostrate yourself before him. The derivative *berakhot* means gift, grace, and peace. The Greek and Latin words have lost most of the wonderful meaning of the word blessing. Once a child leaves its mother's womb, it spends most of its time on its mother's lap, sitting on her knee almost day and night. That is where the child receives its first gifts.

"Benedire," which literally means "to say good," is the Latin word for "blessing." So far, so good, but what happened to the knees? What happened to the lap where the child is tenderly caressed and comforted and receives the overflowing love of its mother's heart?

When we praise the name of the Lord, when we worship him, we call down his gifts and graces into the world. The relationship between man and God is vertical, whereas Satan wants to reduce everything to the horizontal plane. The Gospa draws the blessings and all the gifts she gives us from God. On August 15, 1985, she said: *"I am blessing you with the solemn blessing that God grants me."* In the Bible, men who, like Abraham, have received a special blessing, are the carriers of that blessing to others: "In you all the families of the earth shall be blessed," and, "I will bless those who bless you" (Genesis 12:3).

In the beginning, God blessed man and gave him the power to bless the whole of creation, animals and plants, in order to bestow upon them the benefits received from God (Genesis 1:28).

Noah, in his turn, passed the special blessings of God on to his sons so that they could found a new humanity, renewed in the Spirit (Genesis 9:1).

The patriarchs transmitted irrevocable blessings to their sons, blessings which fulfilled what they prophesied and in turn applied to their descendants in a real manner (Genesis 48:18 and 49:28).

Aaron, Moses, David and Solomon, shepherds of the people, transmitted God's blessing in a very real way. Ceremonies, holy assemblies, words, gestures and liturgies existed for this purpose.

Mary of Nazareth was herself blessed by Elizabeth and by Simeon in the Temple. During the celebration of Shabbat, Joseph the Righteous blessed his Son, Jesus. He used a formula which harkens back to the blessings granted in earlier times to Benjamin and Manasseh. (Mary's father blessed her according to the blessing formula used for Rachel and Leah, which was reserved for girls.)

All these blessings were part of the Holy Family's life, as they were part of the life of the entire Jewish people, and then later the Judeo-Christian people. Fathers were commanded by Jewish law to pass on to their children the divine blessing received by Abraham, Isaac and Jacob, from generation to generation.

The Bible teaches us that a blessing is also an eschatological grace, because those who bless are looking to the coming of the Messiah. Isn't Mary coming to Medjugorje precisely to prepare her children for the Second Coming of her Son, just as John the Baptist had prepared his first coming? The fact that she chose June 24 (the Feast of St. John the Baptist) as the date of her first apparition is highly significant. We need her special motherly blessing to prepare ourselves.

In the spirit of the Bible, a blessing is also enriched in the very act of bestowal. It is increased and expanded.

I give and I receive a hundredfold; that is the dynamic of the Kingdom! He who doesn't bless runs the risk of impoverishing and dissipating the gift of God within himself. The Gospa has asked us to live her messages and spread them, and to bear witness to them. Why did she add the passing on of this blessing? Because witnessing will not replace the blessing; it is another reality altogether. The Gospa asks parents to give the example, to be carriers of peace, but she also asks them to bless their children. Children need this in order to grow. Witnessing does not transmit **protection** as blessing does. Witnessing also does not transmit the **covenant** concluded by God with Abraham and Moses on Mount Sinai.

Witnessing generates a good influence; it draws people. But blessing is **an invisible action.** Mary, for instance, takes what is God's and gives it to us. This gift changes our souls directly, much beyond our understanding.

Each time she comes, the Queen of Peace blesses the visionaries and all those who are gathered there to pray. The dose given to the "non-visionaries" that we are is not any less! I have no diploma in Marian theology, and I sometimes have to cope with the little I know, so I say to myself: "She comes and she sees the wretched poverty of my soul. She loves me and she bears all the most beautiful gifts of God. She is my mother and she has several blessings to give me. Which one is she going to choose? I think she is going to give me the best of her blessings today, out of pure love! And I take it without asking any useless questions, because, as far as I know, it's the best way to take hold of the Kingdom of heaven."

— MESSAGE OF MARCH 25, 1991 —

"Dear children! Again today I invite you to live the Passion of Jesus in prayer, and in union with him. Decide to give more time to God who gave you these days of grace. Therefore, dear children, pray, and renew in a special way the love for Jesus in your hearts. I am with you and I accompany you with my blessing and my prayers. Thank you for having responded to my call."

JESUS CRUCIFIED

Our Lady seems to choose unbelievers and children to manifest herself. Nevertheless, last month, an Irish priest had an overwhelming experience! He had decided to do the Stations of the Cross and to climb Mount Krizevac on his own.

Upon reaching the twelfth station he prayed before Christ crucified. Suddenly Jesus' face began to come to life. Swollen from the blows he had received, bleeding, Jesus slowly shook his head from side to side, like a wounded man whose pain has become unbearable. His eyes expressed an unfathomable love and sadness, as they looked straight into those of the priest. His silent look of anguish was an appeal that struck the priest like a thunderbolt.

It was too great a shock for the Irish father; he turned his head away to avert this sight. His heart beat wildly as he wondered whether he had lost his mind. He looked once again at the cross, but Jesus kept on moving and watching him. A look of profound contemplation took place between the High Priest crucified and this priest living in our crucified world.

Trembling from head to toe, the priest went down the mountain and joined his party. The sweetness of the look which flowed from his eyes was so great that they hardly recognized him. They all prayed together and the blessing streamed from him like a deep, peacefully flowing river.

"Today's world is special," the priest said. "The wounds of Jesus are intolerable." Only then did he relate his experience to his friends. He would never be the same man again.

"The face of Jesus has been printed in my heart, like a seal on wax," he declared.

— MESSAGE OF APRIL 25, 1991 —

"Dear children! Today I invite you all so that your prayer be prayer with the heart. Let each of you find time for prayer so that in prayer you discover God. I do not desire you to talk about prayer, but to pray. Let each of your days be filled with prayer of gratitude to God for life and for all that you have. I do not desire your life to pass by in words but that you glorify God with deeds. I am with you and I am grateful to God for every moment spent with you. Thank you for having responded to my call."

IT'S ME, PAUL!

Pilgrims, even today, often ask how to "pray with the heart."[1] They are very relieved to learn, after their experience of Medjugorje's great simplicity, that they had already known it but were not aware of it. They arrive with intellectual concerns but go back home with the solid good sense of children, of little ones, those to whom the mysteries of the Kingdom are revealed.

A French priest gave us a marvelous illustration of "prayer with the heart" one day in church by relating a trivial event which took place in Paris:

Paul spent most of his time in the open. So he really appreciated St. Jacques Church porch, where he used to beg. To be honest, we must add that a bottle of wine was keeping him company. Among his many illnesses, he suffered from cirrhosis of the liver—another faithful companion of his. You could tell by the color of his face. People in the neighborhood expected him to disappear sooner or later. However, nobody was really that interested in him.

Still, a good-hearted lady of the parish, Mrs. N., had initiated some kind of dialogue with him. The terrible loneliness of this man saddened her.

She had also noticed that, in the morning, he would temporarily leave his spot in the porch, go into the church—as empty as ever—sit on a pew in the front row, and face the tabernacle. He would sit there and do nothing...

One day she said to him, "Paul, I've seen you walk into the church many times. But what do you do while sitting there? You have no rosary, no prayer book, you even at times doze a little... What do you do over there? Do you pray?"

"How could I possibly pray?!! I can't even remember a word of the prayers I was taught at Sunday school when I was a kid! I have forgotten everything! What do I do? It's simple! I go to the tabernacle where Jesus is all alone in his little box, and I tell him: 'Jesus! It's me, Paul! I've come to see you!' and I sit there for a while just to show I'm around!"

Mrs. N. was speechless. She never forgot what he said. Days came and went as usual. Then one day, what was bound to happen, happened. Paul disappeared from the porch. Was he sick? Dead, maybe? Mrs. N. decided to find out and finally spotted him in a hospital. She visited him. Poor Paul. He was a dreadful sight! He was covered with tubing and his complexion was gray and pasty. He looked like someone who was about to die. In addition, the medical prognosis was less than optimistic.

She returned the next day, expecting to hear bad news... But no, Paul was sitting bolt upright in his bed, clean-shaven, looking fresh and completely changed. An expression of immeasurable joy emanated from his face. He looked radiant.

Mrs. N. rubbed her eyes. Without a doubt, it was he!

"Paul! This is unbelievable. You're resurrected! You are not the same person anymore. What on earth happened to you?"

"Well, it all happened this morning. I wasn't too well, you know, and suddenly I saw someone coming in and standing at the foot of my bed. He was handsome, so handsome...you can't even imagine! He smiled at me and said: *'Paul! It is I, Jesus! I've come to see you!'*"

---

[1] "Praying with the heart" is to go to God, just as we are, and with all that we've got. If we have nothing to give, then we should go with nothing. Like the destitute widow in the Gospel, Paul had probably consoled Jesus more than tons of others. Don't miss Fr. Slavko's book, *Praying With the Heart*, available from the Florida Center for Peace, PO Box 431305, Miami, FL, USA 33143. Tel: (305) 666-5000; Fax: (305) 668-9804.

— MESSAGE OF MAY 25, 1991 —

"Dear children! Today I invite all of you who have heard my message of peace to realize it with seriousness and with love in your life. There are many who think that they are doing a lot by talking about the messages, but do not live them. Dear children, I invite you to life and to change all the negative in you, so that it all turns into the positive and life. Dear children, I am with you and I desire to help each of you to live and by living, to witness the good news. I am here, dear children, to help you and lead you to heaven, and in heaven is the joy through which you can already live heaven now. Thank you for having responded to my call!"

I HAD ONE FOOT IN HELL
AND I DIDN'T KNOW IT!

All the residents of Medjugorje know Patrick, the English-speaking Canadian who attends the 3-hour evening service every day in the church, along with his wife, Nancy. You'll find him praying the Divine Mercy rosary or the prayers of St. Bridget during the long homilies in Croatian. (See photo)

I thought I knew him too, until the day when he told me his story. Here are his own words:

I'm 56 years old; I have been married 3 times and divorced twice (both times because of my adulteries). Before I read the messages of Medjugorje, I never even owned a Bible. I was in the car business in Canada for 30 years and my only god was money. I used to roll high. I knew each and every way to make big money. When my eldest son asked me, "Dad, what is God?," I gave him a 20-dollar bill and said, "This is your god. The more of this you have, the closer to God you're going to be."

I had no relationship with the Church whatsoever. Although I was born a Catholic, I never lived my faith. Nancy and I stayed together for years without being married and it didn't really matter, because everybody was doing it. However, after 7 years, we finally decided to get married. I organized a super wedding party up on a mountain, rented a helicopter, and had a civil ceremony with an orchestra playing New Age music.

But 6 weeks later, Nancy came out with: "I don't think we're married. I don't feel married!"

I replied, "Here is your wedding certificate!"

She said, "No, my mom didn't come and we didn't go to church."

"Okay," I said, "if that's what you want, go find a church!"

It was only then that I discovered that my ex-wife had applied for and obtained the annulment of our marriage, 20 years earlier. So there was no obstacle to my marrying Nancy in the Church.

Slowly but surely, Our Lady began her moves. The ceremony took place a few weeks later in a church called "The Immaculate Heart of Mary," probably the only church of this name in Canada!

I had to go to confession before the wedding, and I did. It was a matter-of-fact approach to confession, certainly not done "with the heart." After our wedding in the church, however, we still didn't pray, go to Mass, or do anything like that. We weren't involved in anything religious; the only difference now was that we had a Catholic wedding certificate.

My 4 kids (3 sons and a daughter) were having a tough time. In fact, they led terrible lives with alcohol, drugs, and divorce. I wasn't overly preoccupied, though, because all parents have problems with their kids.

One day, we were moving and I found a package from Croatia. It had been sent ages before by Nancy's brother who is Croatian. Nobody had ever really opened the package, but Nancy handed it to me and said, "Here you are, my dear pagan husband. If someone has to throw this away, that will be you. It'll be on your conscience!"

It was a Saturday night. I remember very clearly opening the package. It contained the first messages of Medjugorje, carefully gathered and translated for us by Nancy's brother. I took out the first sheet of paper and read one of the messages of Medjugorje. The first message I ever read was: *"I have come to call the world to conversion for the last time."*

At that moment, something happened within my heart. It didn't take an hour, it didn't take 10 minutes—it happened instantly. My heart melted, and I began to cry. I couldn't help it. The tears kept flowing down my face. I had never read anything like this before, and I didn't even know what Medjugorje was.

I didn't know anything about the messages. All I read was, *"I have come to call the world to conversion for the last time,"* and I knew that was meant for me. I knew Our Lady was talking to me. The second message I read was, *"I have come to tell you that God exists."* I don't think I ever really believed in God until I read this message. It put everything into perspective; it made everything look real. All of the Catholic teaching I had received since I was little was real! It wasn't a bedtime story. It wasn't a fairy tale. It wasn't something that somebody had made up. The Bible was real!

Getting rid of these messages was now out of the question. I wouldn't let go of them! I read them all, the whole book! I held onto them and, for a week, just walked around with the messages in my hand. We were moving out and there was a great confusion, but I wouldn't let go of *the* messages. I read them and reread them, until they penetrated deep into my heart and into my soul. I had found the pot of gold at the end of the rainbow!

While we were moving out, I heard that there was going to be a Marian conference in Eugene, Oregon. Although we were in Canada and it was a 2-day drive, I said to Nancy: "We're going to Eugene, Oregon! We're going to this conference!"

"What about the house?" she asked.

"It doesn't matter, we're going."

There, I met thousands of people who felt just like I did about Our Lady, about the way she speaks to the world today. People had handbooks on Medjugorje, on Fatima, books by Father Gobbi. I had never seen anything like it! During Mass, there was a healing prayer. Father Ken Roberts said to us: "Consecrate your children to the Immaculate Heart of Mary!"

I stood up, still in tears—I hadn't stopped crying from my first message of Medjugorje—and I said to Mary: "Blessed Mother, take my children! I beg you, because I've been such a poor parent! I know you'll do better than me."

So, I consecrated my 4 kids. It was tremendously moving for me, because I didn't know what to do with the children. I had no idea. They were living decadent lives beyond anything imaginable. But, slowly, after the conference, everything began to change in our family. Father Ken Roberts had also said, "Give up something you love the most."

I really loved Nancy and I really loved coffee...so, I gave up coffee!

The messages of Medjugorje have been the grace of my life. They transformed my ways completely. I was in such a pattern that if it had not been for the messages, I know I could have divorced again and again. I was on a treadmill, and I had big money... Now, there is no way I could possibly think of committing adultery again. The love that Our Lady has placed between Nancy and me is unbelievable. It is a grace from God.

My son, who was taking drugs and got kicked out of school at the age of 16, has converted and has been baptized. He is now contemplating the priesthood. If someone in the family takes the first step, Our Lady does the rest. If these messages of Medjugorje touch just one person in a family, slowly the whole family changes!

The second miracle in our lives is my other son. He was a notorious unbeliever until he came to Medjugorje last Christmas and found the faith (confession, First Communion, etc.). My other kids and my parents are now also on the right road although it is not always easy.[1] One of them joined the "Oasis of Peace" city and is thinking about the priesthood.

Another thing, within a week of reading the messages of Our Lady, I said to Nancy, "We're going to Medjugorje!"

We have lived there now since 1993. We arrived with nothing. But on the third day of our arrival, Nancy was already translating for Father Jozo. We had work and a roof over our heads. As for me, my whole life is now devoted to helping the pilgrims who come here and to spreading the messages in every way I can.

I love Our Lady immensely. She saved my life, because... I had a foot in hell and I didn't even know it!

---

[1] (Jesus to St. Mechtilde): *"So long as a sinner remains in his sin I am linked to him as by a chain, stretched out on the Cross. But as soon as he experiences conversion, he undoes my chains, and as if I had been let down from my Cross I go to him as I did to Joseph of Arimathea, with my grace and my mercy, and I put myself in his power so that he can do with me what he wills."*

— Message of June 25, 1991 —

"Dear children! Today on this great day which you have given to me, I wish to bless all of you and to say: These days while I am with you are days of grace. I desire to teach you and help you to walk the way of holiness. There are many people who do not desire to understand my messages and to accept with seriousness what I am saying. But you I therefore call and ask that by your lives and by your daily living you witness my presence. If you pray, God will help you to discover the true reason for my coming.

"Therefore, little children, pray and read the Sacred Scriptures so as to discover through the Sacred Scriptures the message contained for you in my comings. Thank you for having responded to my call."

THE 24 HOURS OF THE GOSPA

One day, as it is often the case, I was on the hill of Podbrdo. I love to pray there for a long time before Our Lady's apparition time and welcome her in my heart, away from the crowd. The apparition in Medjugorje is at 5:40 p.m. (6:40 p.m. in the summer).

That day, I said to Our Lady, "As you are coming back in 24 hours, I will prepare a present for you and I'll offer it tomorrow."

What gift? I had no clue! The thought crossed my mind that I should examine some of my little ways. There it was! Since the age of 14, I had had a bad habit of scratching my lips with my nails, sometimes until they bled. I couldn't help it. A dermatologist told me that I ran a risk of developing cancer of the lip which could quickly spread to other parts of my body. Despite the warning, I kept on doing it. It was beyond my control even though my life was in danger. So, I made a promise to Our

Lady: "For the next 24 hours, I'll try my very best not to scratch my lips. But I beg you, please, help me!"

When our rendezvous came the next day, it had worked! All the repeated attacks (very numerous) had been overcome—Our Lady had helped me a great deal, and I offered my present to her with a glad heart. Then I decided to prepare another present for her, a new victory over something in particular within the next 24 hours. "What about the same thing?" I asked myself. That's what I did, and she received the same gift again. For a whole week, I did the same thing each time I met Our Lady. And guess what? After 7 days my dreadful habit had completely disappeared! It was over and done with—gone! I never gave it another thought. Mary had touched my body and my nervous system and cured it. She had uprooted the evil from me. I was overjoyed and felt so grateful!

The story does not end here…

As I thanked Mary with all my heart in prayer, she helped me understand that she wanted to work in the same manner with each and every one of her children. Then, some of the words she had said in the past came to my mind in a splendid new light:

"I am your Mother, this is why I come."

"Whenever you need me, call me."

"If you have difficulties or if you need anything, come to me!"

"God has allowed me to help you every day by graces, to protect you from evil."

"Dear children, allow God to perform miracles in your lives."

I understood that we were missing the boat regarding an immense capital of graces, and that we were millions of miles away from realizing how helpful Mary's daily "visitations" could be for us. We had been snoring on the watch! *"No, dear children, you do not understand the importance of my comings,"* Mary says to us. And Vicka adds, "What the Gospa does in Medjugorje has never been done anywhere else before and will not be done again. It is unique in history."

However, it is not too late. I am amazed to discover how happy God's people are to learn about the good news of the daily "visitations" of the Gospa. For any parish priest who welcomes a witness of Medjugorje, it is both a shock and a joy to see his church suddenly full to the brim with a crowd who wouldn't consider leaving even after 3 or 4 hours of testimonies and prayer! Isn't this an amazing sign of the immense thirst people have to actually touch their Mother's heart—a heart that gives life, a heart that is real, healing, compassionate and inexpressibly tender?

Yes, the people of God are happy to find their Mother and to enter into a new kindred spirit with her. In Medjugorje, heaven has opened up and we can touch it as never before.

When Our Lady appears, the visionaries see her in 3 dimensions, as one would see a normal person on earth. They can shake her hand, hug her, pull her veil and at the same time ask her a favor. They can laugh and cry with her too: she is completely real, incarnate, alive and infinitely beautiful.

"We have been seeing her for 16 years now," says Marija, "but we don't get used to it. Each day, we experience a greater joy."

But for us who do not *see*, who do not *hear*, who do not experience ecstasy while speaking to the Queen of Heaven, is our lot consequently inferior and sadly negligible?

Absolutely not! This is the keystone of God's gift in Medjugorje. I, a poor sinner with no charisms, I can receive wherever I am, the same graces from heaven as I would if my name were Vicka, Marija, Ivan, Mirjana, Jakov or Ivanka. On this point, I did my own checking with the visionaries who often hear: "How lucky you are to see Our Lady! What a delight it must be! If only it could happen to me…"

I asked Vicka, "Vicka, when you see Our Lady, do you receive very special graces?"

"Oh, yes! The Gospa said that she gives us graces she has never given anyone before in the world's history."

"What about me? Since I don't see anything, am I going to receive fewer graces than you, even if I open my heart?"

"Of course not! If you open your heart, you will receive the same graces as I do. She herself said so! We are not better than others. The Gospa is very pleased when people come to Medjugorje, as she has made an oasis of peace of this place, and she calls us all here. But if you really can't get here, but open your heart widely at the time when she appears, then, wherever you are, you will receive the same graces we, the visionaries, do."

The answer was crystal-clear: Mary's visitations and the fantastic capital of graces they bring are not reserved for some rare chosen people. They are intended for each and every one of us—for you who are reading this book, for your family, and for all those who open the innermost doors of their hearts at the time of the apparitions.

At 6:40 p.m.—when Mary descends from heaven to talk and pray with her beloved children—all those who wish can stop for a few minutes, wherever they are, in order to welcome her in a very special way. In so doing, they are in communion with Medjugorje and with thousands of people all around the world who already live this appointment... (Some people set an alarm on their watches!) Day after day, 24 hours after 24 hours, such remarkable things happen that the testimonies wouldn't fit in several books. I experience such a great joy every day when I plunge my heart into my Mother's heart! I know that, come what may, she will be back in 24 hours, and there is no real loneliness anymore. Every day, I am another cousin Elizabeth who cries out, "Why am I so favored that the Mother of my Lord should come to me?"

What a joy to offer every day a little present to Our Lady and to decide with her upon a practical thing to overcome, or the fault within me that needs conversion. Whatever I am addicted to—tobacco, alcohol, pornographic videos, or cookies—I can renounce them for 24 hours. If I beat my wife (or husband), I can stop for 24 hours!

I know that I may be too weak to keep such a promise for 8 months, or even a single month, but a 24-hour time period definitely fits into my poor range of capabilities.

Mary is well aware of this. That is why she often answers, *"Day after day, love will grow within you. I am by your side in order to help you have this love reach its fullness."*

"One day at a time" is her motif. Twenty-four hours is her time unit. Mother Teresa also draws our attention to the importance of today, as being the time of grace: "Yesterday has gone, tomorrow is not yet here, I only have today to love."

At each visitation of hers, Mary takes hold of our hearts, imprinting within them her indescribable beauty... She said, *"Dear children, give me your heart so that I can transform it and that it can resemble my heart."*

She grasps the little present we give her with loving alacrity. Then she achieves her incredible work within us: *"I want to purify you of the consequences of your past sins;" "I want to enrich you with my motherly peace."*

The Woman who comes to me is the **Woman who crushes the Serpent's head.** All the infernal powers and demons tremble before her, because she is the Immaculate One and she has received the grace to defeat Satan.

Each time I meet her, I receive the One who is stronger than the evil that inhabits me. She tears up the evil within me by the roots.

Throughout the world we are suffering from the lack of good exorcists. With the proliferation of either conscious or unconscious satanic practices, a growing number of people are deeply tortured by the powers of darkness. Who is there to take them in, to listen to them and to help them? Where and how can they be helped? Their voices echo in the desert.

Here comes our Mother to the rescue! She will not abandon her children to the sad fate that the atheism so dominant in the world today reserves for them. The greatest exorcisms are performed during these meetings with the Queen of Peace as if by miracle! What a psychiatrist can't do in 10 years, Mary does in no time at all. She is Queen!

"Your sufferings are also mine." (April 1992)

"Dear children, don't forget that I ask you for sacrifices in order to help and to expel Satan from you." (September 1986)

Besides, Mary's comings are also a very effective antidote against New Age confusions in which God's incarnation is denied. Medjugorje helps us rediscover the realism of the spiritual life. Mary is not someone with an airy-fairy mentality. She has us plunge into the concrete realities of life in the sight of the Living God and not of some impersonal energy. She liberates us from the New Age esotericism which produces new false gods and bamboozles believers everyday.[1]

The day Ralph Martin filmed the interview on Medjugorje with me for the programs of Mother Angelica[2], we had gone for a quick lunch to a restaurant with him and our friend Denis Nolan. While we were eating, the hour of the apparition came... A few months later, I received a letter from Ralph:

Dear Sister Emmanuel,   10/18/95

Praise be to God!

It was a great joy to hear from you. It's amazing how faxes are changing the world.

Anne and I both enjoyed very much being with you and as in June have received graces through your visit. We hope our paths cross often!

I'd be happy to write a few lines about what I said in the restaurant after the taping and what's happened since.

When the alarm of your watch went off at 12:40 p.m. at the restaurant and we all paused to welcome Our Lady to the earth and to our hearts, I had a very strong sense of Mary's presence with me and a wordless communication which was nevertheless very clear that Mary was there to teach me. I found myself saying to her over and over from my heart, "Mary, you have a lot to teach me, I really need you to teach me about humility, purity and love, and so much more." And I know she is and will. I'm very grateful to God for sending Mary to us, and even to me! After you left I went out to K-Mart and bought a watch (it only cost $5.99[3]) with an alarm which my daughters were able to figure out how to set to ring at the right time. It's been ringing faithfully since and even when I'm with other people, I'm able if only for a few brief moments to join you all in welcoming Mary to the earth and our hearts and praying for the success of her mission."

> United with you in Jesus
> Your brother,
> Ralph

---

[1] The audio tape *Holiness Means Happiness* in which Sr. Emmanuel gives her own testimony is available from Children of Medjugorje (see the appendix at the end of the book for information on obtaining audio tapes).

[2] A one hour TV special hosted by Ralph Martin: *Sister Emmanuel of Medjugorje: Mary's Messenger*, is now available on video from Renewal Ministries, P.O. Box 8229, Ann Arbor, MI 48107. Tel: (313) 662-1730. Price $15.00.

[3] We hesitated to publish this detail, but we found it quite "American" (and funny), and as the saying goes, *When in America, do as the Americans do!*

— MESSAGE OF JULY 25, 1991 —

"Dear Children! Today I invite you to pray for peace. At this time peace is being threatened in a special way, and I am seeking from you to renew fasting and prayer in your families. Dear children, I desire you to grasp the seriousness of the situation and that much of what will happen depends on your prayers, yet you are praying a little bit. Dear children, I am with you and I am inviting you to begin to pray and fast seriously as in the first days of my coming. Thank you for having responded to my call.

I WAS AN ALCOHOLIC

Shortly after my healing, I was invited to the States to talk about Medjugorje. I couldn't possibly hold back the discovery of the "24 hours of the Gospa"! After having explained everything carefully, I asked the 5000 Americans who were listening to me, "Send me your testimonies!" The very first letter I received touched me tremendously:[1]

"Last September, I attended your talk in Pittsburgh. I'm 30. I had been a widow for a few months before I went to hear you. My life had become a living hell. I couldn't cope with the absence of my husband. I missed his voice, his footsteps in the house. My not being able to see him, to talk to him, had become such torture that I wanted to die. I was so distraught with the pain of loneliness and despair that only my death would put an end to it. Therefore I had decided to commit suicide. The reason why I went to your talk is still a mystery to me.

"One thing in particular had struck me from that evening, for I had never considered the apparitions from this angle before: 'Our Lady comes to visit me, personally, at my home, in my situation today...!' On the very next day, I decided to give the *24 hours of the Gospa* a try. When the time of Mary's visitation came, I literally collapsed into her arms (even though I couldn't see her) and I sobbed there for a while against her heart. I had no other present to give her but my total distress, and I told her over and over again, 'Take my despair, take my miserable, screwed-up life! I've had it!'

"Sister, you might not believe me, but I'm telling you the truth! I don't know how it happened, but now I am the happiest woman in the world! I am content with my lot! Our Lady poured her own joy into my heart, she took my despair away. I'm so madly in love with her! She truly is a mother, it's amazing! Her own heart is in me, and I can't find the words to tell you how much I love my life now..."[1] (Patricia).

When in France, I would never let pass an opportunity to speak about this either. One day, a lady who had attended a talk I had given in Toulouse 3 months earlier came to see me in Medjugorje. All the pilgrims who were traveling with her already knew about the miracle she was eager to tell me:

"I am 60. I had been an alcoholic for 10 years. As a result of this, I had severe health problems. As regards my family, they were falling apart, above all, my children for I had made their lives a misery. But it was beyond my control. I had tried one treatment after the other. I had even been prayed over several times by a prayer group, but nothing would do, white wine was still white wine to me, you know!

"When I heard how you had been healed by the Gospa, it gave me an idea. Remember? We prayed for a few minutes during your talk! We kept silent for the apparition at 6:40 p.m. Then I told myself,… 'It's now or never! For once, I should try and offer Mary a present!' So I promised her that I wouldn't drink a drop of alcohol for the next 24 hours. I knew it was far beyond my capabilities, but you had told us that she would help us keep our promise. And it worked! It has been really hard: glasses of white wine kept flashing by my eyes and I had to hold on really hard, because a promise is a promise. However, the next day, I was really happy to offer my gift to her. Immediately after the time of the apparition, I had to go to a party at some friends' and, naturally, I was offered a drink. A glass of white wine! I took the glass but at the first swallow I almost spat out the first sip—wine made me feel disgusted! Sister, since that day, I no longer drink, and it's not even an effort![2]

"But the most beautiful part of it is that, right after this, Our Lady started a chain conversion in my family." (Jeanine)

What detoxification treatments and psychologists were not able to achieve in 10 years, the Gospa did within 24 hours! And whom did she choose in this family to be her Son's apostle? The person who had caused the most damage!

---

[1] Psychiatrists and their ever numerous customers might find this testimony interesting.

[2] Jeanine had a relapse 6 months later, but thanks to prayer she recovered again in just a few days.

— Message of August 25, 1991 —

"Dear children! Today also I invite you to prayer, now as never before when my plan has begun to be realized. Satan is strong and wants to sweep away my plans of peace and joy and make you think that my Son is not strong in his decision.

Therefore, I call all of you, dear children to pray and fast still most firmly. I invite you to renunciation for nine days so that with your help everything I wanted to realize through the secrets I began in Fatima may be fulfilled. I call you, dear children, to grasp the importance of my coming and the seriousness of the situation. I want to save all souls and present them to God. Therefore, let us pray that everything I have begun be fully realized. Thank you for having responded to my call."

THE PRAVDA CONTAINED THE TRUTH!

Fatima! For the first time (and the only time) at Medjugorje the Gospa mentioned another place of apparitions in a message. She mentioned Fatima exactly 7 years after Pope John Paul II, her "most beloved son," had done so. But let's take a look at what happened 7 years before.

On March 20, 1984, Bishop Pavol Hnilica, SJ, a close friend of Karol Wojtyla's for many years, was in India with Mother Teresa, and discussed with her the Holy Father's plan to solemnly consecrate Russia and the whole world to the Immaculate Heart of Mary, and fulfill Our Lady's request in Fatima. This consecration was to take place on March 25, or 5 days from then!

"What a pity I can't be in Moscow for March 25!" he said to Mother Teresa. "There will be no one there in Russia for this consecration!"

"You go," she replied firmly. "Here, take my rosary. I will pray for you!"

"But they'll never let me across the border!"

"Go ahead! Our Lady will open the doors of Russia for you!"

The bishop gripped both Mother Teresa's faith[1] and her rosary, and off he went. The Russian Customs officer, as expected, was an iron curtain. "No way you pass the border!" he said to the 2 travelers (Father Leo accompanied the bishop). Then he poured out the juiciest words in the dictionary of Communist blasphemies. Our travelers insisted and set themselves to wait. The temperature hovered around 0° Fahrenheit. Rosary beads clicked non-stop. Meanwhile, the Customs officer tried every 15 minutes to call his boss, but the contraption wouldn't work. At dawn, frantic, he yelled, "Buzz off! Get lost! I don't want to see you anymore!"

The Gospa had opened the doors of Russia, in her own way...

On March 25, the bishop reached the Kremlin. He walked into the deconsecrated church, ironically named by the regime "Museum of Atheism,"[2] though many people went there secretly to venerate the icons, under the guise of admiring the works of art.

The bishop's heart pounded wildly. This former prisoner of Communist jails regarded this event as a sheer miracle. He bought the Pravda and stood behind what was formerly an altar. In the newspaper, he placed the text written by Pope John Paul II for the consecration of the world. The Pope had entrusted him with the entire "Communist world," a territory that stretched from Berlin through Moscow to the furthermost bounds of China. After 50 years, this was the first time he had ever set foot in Russia! His shepherd's heart was bursting with emotion, but he had to play it cool; he was being watched. To avoid attracting attention while he was offering up the sublime prayer of the consecration to the Mother of God, he pretended to be carefully reading the *Pravda*.[3]

"What a good Communist!" the tourists probably thought. "Look how attentively he's reading the *Pravda*!"

As a matter of fact, on that day, the *Pravda* did contain the truth! (Once in a while does no harm!)

The bishop celebrated the Eucharist in his pocket, the way he used to do in jail, and off he went without further ado. He was overjoyed! He had been able to live this consecration in communion with the bishops of the world as the "Lady" of Fatima had asked! A dramatic page had been turned in the history of Communism!

Back in Rome, he was invited by the Pope for breakfast, a breakfast that lasted 3 hours! Bishop Hnilica related everything to the Pope, how he had been able to be in the Kremlin on the very day the Holy Father himself was consecrating the world to the Immaculate Heart of Mary. The Pope was deeply moved and exclaimed, "The Blessed Mother led you by the hand!"

"No, Holiness," responded the bishop, "she carried me in her arms!"

The Pope then asked, "On your way back from Moscow, did you stop at Medjugorje?"

"No, Holy Father. The Vatican advised me not to."

With a wave of the hand John Paul II swept the objection away. "Go there incognito and tell me what you have seen."

The Pope then showed his visitor into his library. He picked up a book by Father Laurentin, read some messages of the Gospa, and said, "You see, Pavol, Medjugorje is the continuation and fulfillment of Fatima!" (A few years later he would tell him, "Today the world has lost its sense of the supernatural. It finds it again in Medjugorje, through prayer, fasting, and the sacrament of confession.")

Since then, Bishop Hnilica has become a great supporter of Medjugorje. Even today the Pope regularly asks him, "So, Pavol, what's the news of Medjugorje!"

On March 25, 1994, Bishop Hnilica came to Medjugorje to celebrate the tenth anniversary of the consecration.

It seems that Pope John Paul II has supernatural insights into Medjugorje. He confided to Bishop Hnilica that, on May 13, 1981, when he was the victim of an assassination attempt, it was Our Lady of Fatima who protected him from death. (Forty days later, the Gospa began to appear in Medjugorje.) The Pope shared these wonderful words with his friend: "And why did she save my life? After having spent 3 months between life and death, only then did I understand that the only means of solving the problems of the world and those of the Church was the conversion of Russia, according to the message of Fatima."[4]

If Medjugorje fulfills Fatima...then how great is our hope! We know that the Pope places all his hopes in Marian groups, and Medjugorje groups in particular, because he acknowledges their unfailing faithfulness to the Church through prayer, fasting, and recourse to the sacraments.

And how could I fail to mention here the happiness of Sr. Lucy herself, whose visions of Our Lady have continued since 1917, and to whom Mary now speaks of her work in Medjugorje![5]

[1] On April 8, 1992, Mother Teresa wrote to Denis Nolan in her own hand: "I am afraid I will not be able to come for the National Conference [on Medjugorje] due to my health—though I will be with you with my prayers. We are all praying one Hail Mary before Holy Mass to Our Lady of Medjugorje..."

[2] In this same former "Museum of Atheism," the Gospa appeared to a crowd that was in tears; they had gathered to pray with Marija Pavlovic in October 1990.

[3] "Pravda" means "truth" in Russian.

[4] Bishop Hnilica shares these conversations on the tape *Fatima*, which can be ordered by writing to: Resurrection Tapes, 3927 E. Lake St., Minneapolis, MN 55406, reference 94ND04. Price: $5.00.

[5] This was reported by Sr. Lucy's nephew, Father Salinho, a Salesian priest who lives in Portugal. Needless to say, these apparitions pertain to Sr. Lucy's private mystical life and, therefore, will not be the object of an official statement during her lifetime. Happily, Pope John Paul II maintains a close relationship with Sr. Lucy.

— MESSAGE OF SEPTEMBER 25, 1991 —

"Dear children! Today in a special way I invite you all to prayer and renunciation. For now as never before Satan wants to show the world his shameful face by which he wants to seduce as many people as possible onto the way of death and sin. Therefore, dear children, help my Immaculate Heart to triumph in this sinful world. I beseech all of you to offer prayers and sacrifices for my intentions so I can present them to God for what is most necessary. Forget your desires, dear children, and pray for what God desires, and not for what you desire. Thank you for having responded to my call."

PLEASE, LORD, STOP HIM!

Helping the Immaculate Heart to triumph in this sinful world is one of the motif that Medjugorje and Fatima have in common. A *sinful world* is the gentle expression Mary uses in Medjugorje to name the evil we must vanquish. She didn't spare the children of Fatima or the children of Medjugorje, she didn't hide from their eyes the appalling horrors which await unrepentant sinners. She showed them hell. What remedy did she offer? Living in her Immaculate Heart through our consecration to her, and thus becoming co-redeemers along with her Son—sacrificing ourselves for sinners, so that they no longer reject God's mercy, but convert while they still have time.[1]

The Lord once gave me a remarkable lesson on the spirit of sacrifice. It had more impact than 50 books on the subject. One morning, I decided to go to the 10 o'clock Mass, in English. It was being celebrated by an American priest on pilgrimage in Medjugorje. Everything went well until the homily when things started to go sour! The priest began on a speech totally disconnected from the Gospel and, as far as I could hear, also disconnected from God. He launched into a series of lyrical-philosophical reflections, and God did not seem to be anywhere on the horizon. In addition, it went on and on!

As I had hardly slept the previous night, I began fidgeting and looking at my watch. I should have looked at things in a more positive manner…

"Please Jesus, do something!," I cried to the Lord. "Stop him! But before you do so, please let him say at least one sentence to nurture my soul."

To my amazement, the priest suddenly cut short his homily and proceeded quietly back to his seat. Before he had the chance to sit down, he looked as if he had received an electrical shock. He quickly made his way back to the microphone and said out of the blue, "Excuse me, I forgot to tell you something important: The only activity worth anything in life, *the only one*, is to sacrifice oneself for the salvation of souls!"[2]

Then he returned to his seat.

"O Lord!" I said, still trembling with astonishment, "I got your message, loud and clear!"

---

[1] Our Lady said to the children of Fatima, *"Many souls go to hell because there is no one to pray and sacrifice themselves for them."*

[2] This is eminently the activity of Christ and can only be granted by him through a grace of participation. One of the most beautiful examples that I know of is Marthe Robin.

In the 30's, as Jesus was preparing her to found the "Foyers of Charity", he asked her (among other things), to offer herself in atonement for all the profanations and sacrileges that so many priests commit. He led her to understand that for a long time he had searched a soul who would accept to represent all mankind before God, a soul who would be granted the immeasurable grace to live and let herself be continually crucified for his Father and for himself. Jesus confided to her that souls he could unite to his complete mystery and who were ready to accept his will in order to reach perfect union with the Father and with him, were very rare. Jesus even told her the following which gives us food for thought. *"They all step back when I insist…"*

Marthe offered him her complete *"yes"* and did so daily.

(These words were reported to me by Fr. Bondallaz, a close friend of Marthe's, who has gone to the Father.)

— Message of October 25, 1991 —

"Dear children! Pray! Pray! Pray!"

STORY OF ANOTHER SOUL

"Good-bye, Georgette. If I see you in Medjugorje, don't be upset if I ask you to show me your passport. I'll have to make sure that it's really you!"

That's how I took my leave from Georgette last year in Montreal. The quip about the passport is a private joke between us. It's her fault, actually—she sometimes bilocates to Medjugorje! I wonder if her "second body" also carries a passport...

Georgette doesn't like people to talk about her. I hope she will forgive me for doing so!

Georgette Faniel was born in 1915 in Montreal. She has lived a very hidden life in intense prayer. When she was 6, Jesus chose her as his intimate friend and began to speak both to her heart and ears. At that time, she thought that everyone heard Jesus' voice as she did, but she remained very discreet about her own experience. Later, she heard the voice of the Father, the voice of the Holy Spirit, and the voice of Our Lady. Also from the age of 6, she has been ill with a disease which has made her suffer more and more. As a result, she became disabled, but her "heavenly companions..." continuously help her to carry this cross in peace and to unite her suffering with the Passion of Jesus. (See photo)

Georgette lives in the company of angels who help her in a very concrete manner to carry out material tasks and domestic chores, and they have done this with sometimes quite a sense of humor! More than once, they have finished off things which acute pain had prevented Georgette from getting done. Isn't that what angels are meant for?

In 1950, she received the wounds of Jesus and henceforth has been living his Passion.

I do not intend to relate here all the amazing steps of Georgette's mystical life; it would fill several volumes! But one day she went through a key event which can only bring joy to those who love Medjugorje. On Good Friday 1985, when Georgette had already offered herself up to the Eternal Father as a holocaust of Love, the Lord asked something unusual of her which would take her even further in the complete offering of herself: *Would she agree to offer her life, all her sufferings and her prayers so that the apparitions at Medjugorje be acknowledged by the Church as authentic?*

Georgette had heard about Medjugorje through Father Girard, her spiritual director. Since then she had never ceased "to work" for Medjugorje, both day and night (she only sleeps one hour). She sacrificed herself for the visionaries, the Franciscans of the parish, the local bishop and of course all parishioners and pilgrims.

During their missions in Canada, the visionaries and the Franciscans never fail to pay her a visit. Georgette belongs to their spiritual family. Her thorough knowledge of Medjugorje turns out to be deeper than that of some who were born and bred there! Yet, since her poor health glues her to her home, she cannot come to Medjugorje. What about bilocation?! For her, as with Sr. Faustina or Padre Pio, bilocation is the solution provided by God!

I am personally convinced that the extraordinary fruitfulness of Medjugorje throughout the world is partly due to such souls, who are immolated in the secret of their rooms, souls who fight against the powers of darkness to the point of shedding blood. These souls obtain the most precious victories from God's heart. Georgette is most eminently one of them.

I feel her presence every day by my side, and when I have to carry out a mission for the Gospa, her support keeps me going. We work in tandem. I know that she suffers deep agony because of the offenses perpetrated against the Queen of Peace. She suffers from the foul machinations plotted against Medjugorje; she is pierced by our indifference towards the messages, by our divisions and our slowness.

Georgette has received special insights into the fundamental role of John Paul II regarding Medjugorje. And in prayer she herself knows of the spiritual warfare that rages in Medjugorje for the salvation of the human race. She sees everything in her heart as on a mystical TV screen.

"Satan is all the more furious at me," she says, "since the Eternal Father asked me to offer to him my sufferings and to pray for the recognition of the authenticity of the apparitions at Medjugorje."

(Already well before this, Satan would never leave her in peace. He tried to suffocate her and to destroy her, using every possible means. Most of all he kept on repeating to her that she was damned, and that she had spent her whole life telling lies about herself, even to her spiritual director.)

Georgette also experiences the grace of "transverberation" (the mystical term for the piercing of the heart), as St. Teresa of Avila had.

"It is like a burning arrow of fire piercing through the heart. The pain is extremely intense. I feel my soul must never cease to give thanks while Jesus is wounding my heart. I thank him for this suffering and I offer it to him. At this moment there is a great interior joy in my soul. The greatest joy in the world cannot compare with what I feel within myself. This wound makes me resemble Jesus crucified, because I unite my will to that of the Father as Jesus did all his life, above all on the Cross.

"The Father has asked me to offer these wounds for the Holy Father, for consecrated souls, for the priests of Medjugorje and for the visionaries, so that they will be protected from their enemies, both visible and invisible, for the bishops of the former Yugoslavia, as well as for those who have recommended themselves to our prayers. I take it upon myself as a duty. Since I heard of Medjugorje, I pray and offer my suffering so that the authenticity of the apparitions may be recognized as soon as possible. I offer my wounds so that the message of the Queen of Peace may be spread in all its authenticity throughout the world.

"One day, after I had prayed that the apparitions may be recognized and that the obstacles may disappear, I saw Our Lady weeping. I was convinced that she was weeping because of the situation in Medjugorje. When I hear her weeping because of consecrated souls, her tears are sobs, like a physical pain. In the case of Medjugorje, I did not hear sobs. She was weeping profusely, but in silence, and with the dignity of a Mother and a Queen.

"Our Lady earnestly asks for prayers for the priests of Medjugorje, and also for the priests who visit this blessed place, for the pilgrims and the visionaries, so that they remain faithful to what she asks of them.

"With much insistence she asks us to pray that the Church may recognize, through the power of the Holy Spirit, the authenticity of the apparitions at Medjugorje.

"In my prayer I speak to the Eternal Father about Mary, Queen of Peace. I am convinced that this pleases him, because everything about the

Mother of Jesus consoles him. I ask him particularly that the requests and the messages of Our Lady be kept in their integrity so that they may all be presented in their authenticity and truth.

"For me, Mary is the invisible presence who gives peace to the world, and the Holy Father, Pope John Paul II, is the visible presence who asks for this peace. And this message of peace will be carried throughout the world by the messenger of peace: the Holy Father."[1]

Georgette is indeed one of the most precious gemstones of Medjugorje. When you see her in heaven, don't bother to ask her for her passport! The Queen of Peace herself will tell you what this little lady in the blue dressing gown, over there in Montreal, really means to her!

---

[1] I heard these words from Georgette herself. They are also to be found in *Mary, Queen of Peace, Stay With Us!* (©1988, Les Éditions Paulines, 250, boul. St-François Nord, Sherbrooke, QC, Canada J1E 2B9)

— MESSAGE OF NOVEMBER 25, 1991 —

"Dear children! This time also I am inviting you to prayer. Pray that you might be able to comprehend what God desires to tell you through my presence and through the messages I am giving you. I desire to draw you ever closer to Jesus and to his wounded heart that you might be able to comprehend the immeasurable love which gave itself for each one of you.

"Therefore, dear children, pray that from your heart would flow a fountain of love to every person both to the one who hates you and to the one who despises you. That way you will be able through Jesus' love to overcome all the misery in this world of sorrows, which is without hope for those who do not know Jesus. I am with you and I love you with the immeasurable love of Jesus. "Thank you for all your sacrifices and prayers. Pray so that I might be able to help you still more. Your prayers are necessary to me. Thank you for having responded to my call."

THE U-DAY PRAYER GROUP

According to what Mirjana has reported to us, it seems that it is the unbelievers...who attract the evils which afflict mankind. Good to know...since if there is no one to attract them any longer, then the evils will have less or no impact on our earth!

When the pilgrims catch sight of Mirjana, they do not expect to hear from this peaceful and radiant young woman the impressive list of today's

---

[1] Mirjana points out that the choice of the second of the month was deliberate on the part of the Blessed Mother. "People will understand why, when the secrets are revealed," she says. "That day will be very important."

"Plagues of Egypt" that are due to unbelievers. And isn't there at least one unbeliever in every family...?!

"The Gospa said that 'Evil comes into the world because there are unbelievers. Wars, divisions, suicides, drug addiction, divorces, abortions...all of this happens through unbelievers.' The Gospa does not refer to them as unbelievers: she calls them *'those who do not know yet the love of God.'* She loves them because she is their Mother, but she suffers a great deal because of them. She asks us to pray for them every day. *If you could just once see the tears running down her face because of unbelievers, you would immediately decide to pray daily for them.* Each one of your prayers wipes Our Lady's tears away. The Gospa asks for our help because 'through prayer we can change them,'" says Mirjana.

(Mirjana is extremely sensitive. She refused to see hell. Traumatized by a cursory vision of purgatory, she said to Mary, "I've had enough, I don't want to see hell.")

"Among our prayer intentions," continues Mirjana, "the Gospa asks us to give precedence to unbelievers. Praying for them means praying for our future, for the future of our children, for their security. Since 1987, the Gospa comes on the second of each month[1] and prays for unbelievers with me. She sometimes stays a long time. She taught me special prayers for this intention. Vicka knows them too. I cannot tell now what these prayers are; I will say it later."

The Gospa says that there are many unbelievers even among those who go to church. For example, there are those who attend church only out of habit, or to watch other people, and not in order to encounter God.

Mirjana adds, "How terrible it is to spend a whole life without God and find out at the hour of death that you have missed the essential. We have only one life! To help the unbelievers, the first thing to do is to love them in our hearts, then with this love, to pray for them. The Gospa does the rest. I experienced it in Sarajevo where I used to have many atheist students around. I often said to the Gospa, 'I did my part; now you do yours!'"

This call to pray for unbelievers is not taken seriously enough. May our hearts hear it today! May our share not be missing on the day when each one of us receives from God the salary for his deeds, *"... and the fire will test what sort of work each one has done"* (1 Cor 3:15).

Pilgrims from Provence (in the South of France) have fortunately undertaken to offer substantial help to the Gospa. They decided to gather in church to pray on the second of each month. They launched a U-Day tradition! A day for Unbelievers. A wonderful initiative!

From the beginning, they have noticed how pleased God was with their prayer and that he therefore encouraged them in a perceptible way, and still does:

"Here is what happened on July 2, during prayers," relates Jean-Pascal. "We had just returned home from Medjugorje. We had been shaken by the message given to Mirjana on February 2, 1990: *'I am asking for your help. Join me to pray for those who do not believe. You are helping me very little. You have little charity or love...'*

"As most people were on vacation, there were only 5 of us but we had all firmly decided to help Our Lady. So that night we prayed more than 2 hours: praise, intercession for the intention of unbelievers, etc.... Suddenly, three of us smelled a very delicate perfume, though there were no flowers around. We agreed to meet on August 2, for the same prayer, and every second of the month. On September 2, there were approximately thirty of us. After singing in tongues, one of us received a vision but didn't divulge it: Our Lady was standing among us in a magnificent robe, and water was pouring out of her heart, gushing forth onto everyone gathered there and onto the world, as if to cleanse it. The woman who saw her then noticed that many people were looking up and whispering, 'Do you hear water pouring somewhere? What could it be? There must be a leak in the building!!'"

On 2 occasions this very noticeable sound of torrents of water pouring down distracted the group. According to some it sounded like waterspouts. After the prayer, Jean-Pascal looked for the parish priest to warn him that severe flooding was threatening his church, probably a water pipe which had burst, although, oddly enough, the noise seemed to come from the *middle* of the church and not from the walls.

"That's impossible!" retorted the priest. "This church is the only one in the entire diocese that has no water supply point. Not one pipe, not even the smallest tap! It makes our life quite difficult, especially for cleaning!"

Everyone in the group saw this sign as encouragement from Heaven.

A few months later, a lady was praying in that church, waiting for the time of the U-day prayer later in the evening. She didn't realize that the priest had locked her inside. When the other members of the group found the door closed (by mistake), they started to pray in the church's square. So, the lady who thought she had been the only one to come to the meeting, began to pray fervently. She had been suffering from arthritis for a long time and couldn't raise her arms, not even to hang up her laundry. In the fervor of her prayer, she raised her arms to praise and give thanks to the Lord and, to her amazement, suddenly noticed the change: "Lord, you're healing me!"

Even today, years later, this mother of 5 children remains healed of her arthritis.

On May 2, 1996, the lady in charge of the liturgy had forgotten a hymnal in the church. Late that night, she came to look for it to prepare the choir rehearsal. The "U-day" prayer group had already left, after praying a long time for unbelievers. She was literally dumfounded with surprise and comfort when she smelled a delightful fragrance perfuming the entire church, each and every corner of it. She stayed there a long time, as if transported to heaven. "I felt so good that I could have spent the whole night there," she said.

The beautiful initiative of the U-day prayer group quickly spread to the whole region. Other small groups were formed and, today, many families devote time to prayer on that day to give a special "help to the Gospa," in communion with Mirjana and thousands of others.[2]

---

[2] Since Feb. 2, 1997 this monthly apparition is opened to all.

— MESSAGE OF DECEMBER 25, 1991 —

"Dear children! Today in a special way I bring the little Jesus to you, that he may bless you with his blessing of peace and love. Dear children, do not forget that this is a grace which many people neither understand nor accept.

"Therefore, you who have said that you are mine, and seek my help, give all of yourself. First of all, give your love and example in your families. You say that Christmas is a family feast. Therefore, dear children, put God in the first place in your families, so that he may give you peace and may protect you not only from war, but also during peace protect you from every satanic attack.

"When God is with you, you have everything. But when you do not want him, then you are miserable and lost, and you do not know on whose side you are. Therefore, dear children, decide for God, and then you will get everything. Thank you for having responded to my call."

A SATANIST ON THE HILL

Olivia is a friend of Marija's. She lived in her house in Bijakovici and shared her family and apostolic life, her most intimate joys and sorrows for many years (until 1991). She also remained by her side during the "pioneering days" when the intensity of daily life was nothing to envy and nothing short of what we read of in the *Acts of the Apostles*. During that time, Our Lady trained her children, her carefully chosen ones, intensively. The visionaries and the prayer group were hanging upon her every word because she explained everything to them in order to guide them steadily on the road to holiness. It was by a providential and unique grace that Olivia was admitted to attend the school of the Gospa.

In 1988, Our Lady began to talk to them, almost on a daily basis, about her special motherly blessing. She always proceeded in steps, as a mother would. At that time, Marija herself was going through a painful ordeal. So Our Lady conversed much with her about joy. In this supernatural joy, she revealed, little by little, the remarkable gift of her special motherly blessing. The weeks of intimate training were a preparation for the great day when she would give this famous blessing to all the pilgrims present.

This great day was August 15, 1988. That evening, tens of thousands of people covered Mount Krizevac. A grace of intense joy was flowing in every heart and that night everyone experienced true rapture in the Holy Spirit. Our Lady gave her special motherly blessing to everyone. Only Marija's little group of intimates knew exactly what it meant, but everyone had actually received it with the following task: "*Transmit it to all creatures.*" So, regardless of the stones on the way, everyone went down Mount Krizevac almost dancing, probably like the apostles did on Mount Tabor.

Together, with the prayer group, Olivia was among the first to reach the foot of the mountain. She had used a path unknown to pilgrims. A group of Germans met up with her and asked her to repeat the message, since it had not been translated into their language. As Olivia was repeating the message word for word, her eyes turned towards the hillside. She caught sight of someone coming down... He was in his 30's. His face was horribly distorted by hatred, twisted with rage, and he stared at her with his infernal eyes. This scene pierced Olivia's heart. "How could he be in such a state after having received so wonderful a present from the Gospa?!," she wondered. The aspect of this man contrasted sharply with the joy which was flowing like a river down the mountain. He walked straight in Olivia's direction. Did he intend to kill her or what...? But her heart melted with compassion for this brother, obviously possessed by the devil. She then fastened her gaze on him and in silence gave him the special motherly blessing, with all her heart and soul, begging the Gospa to fulfill her promise: May the Father bless and keep him!

The man drew near her, flung a final dark glance at her, and went on his way. Olivia quickly forgot about this incident, for that night, at Marija's, no one slept much...

The next day, as she was leaving church after the evening program, a man came up to her and insisted on talking to her then and there. It was that man again! The same one she had seen the previous night! Yet he looked different—the flames of hatred had vanished from his eyes, and he seemed peaceful now...

"Do you remember me? I wanted to ask you what you did to me last night? Tell me, did you do anything?," he asked.

"Well, yes!" answered Olivia, calmly. "I definitely did something!"

She was about to explain when the man stopped her and said:

"First let me tell you my story! You'll tell me what you did afterwards. I'm German, I'm a doctor, and I'm 30. I came to Medjugorje for the first time 3 years ago. At that time, I was involved in satanic cults, but after a week here, thanks to the help of a priest, I was completely freed and converted. I decided to stay in Medjugorje for 3 more months in order to reinforce my conversion. But I was a very proud man. Back in Germany, I asked myself how I would go and see my Satanist friends and talk to them about God, Medjugorje and Our Lady's comings, how I would manage to convert them. As a result, after a month with them, I had become worse than the whole bunch put together and they even made me the head of the group. Later on, knowing that there would be a major celebration in Medjugorje for the Assumption, I decided that I would go there too, but on a mission for Satan. I went up on Krizevac to carry out satanic rites and do evil. When I saw you transmitting the message of Our Lady, an inexpressible hatred exploded in me, I wanted to kill you! Then you turned your eyes towards me, you looked at me and at that moment I felt that something was happening because, all of a sudden, I became very confused. I passed you, completely unable to do anything, paralyzed with confusion. I went home and lay on my bed, but all night long I was unable to sleep. Although my soul and my body were given over to Satan, a totally unexpected prayer kept welling up within me: 'Oh, Heavenly Father, I know you're here, don't ever leave me again!' I couldn't stop this prayer from rising up in me, I prayed the whole night through! Early in the morning I couldn't wait, I had to go out and find a priest. I found one, Father Pavic, and I confessed everything to him. At the end, he prayed the exorcism prayers over me. But now tell me, what did you do last night?"

"You know! You just said what I did," Olivia answered.

"What do you mean?"

"Yes, for me, your story is a providential confirmation of what Our Lady has been teaching us lately.[1] Last night, she gave us her special motherly blessing and asked us to transmit it to everyone. But before this, she had explained to us the special grace granted through this blessing: the Heavenly Father commits himself to remaining by the side of the person blessed with a grace for his conversation - a grace that wouldn't have been there otherwise - until the day that person dies.

"When I saw you coming down the mountain it hurt me because I couldn't understand how someone could be so tormented by hatred after such a beautiful celebration of joy. So, right away, I put into practice what Our Lady asked us and I gave you her blessing, begging the Heavenly Father to remain by your side... That's all! That's all I did! Mary did the rest, she kept her promise. In the prayer which is in your heart now, without knowing it, you are repeating the exact words Our Lady said: *'May the Father remain by your side, may he henceforth never leave you...'*

"See! The Gospa's blessing has disarmed Satan in you, and the Father was able to reveal his love to you. What a confirmation!"

---

[1] During this "training" by the Gospa there took place a "founding" event on July 16, 1988, a month before the Feast of the Assumption; see the chapter "The Cafes of Lake Como" (June 1992).

FLASHBACK ON 1991

January 26: Msgr. Franic, Archbishop of Split, celebrated Mass in Medjugorje.

February: Vicka gave a talk in Paris and won over all the Parisians who had filled La Mutualité to the brim that day.

March 18: Mirjana's Yearly Apparition:

> "Dear children! I am glad that you have gathered in such a large number. I would desire that you gather often in communal prayer to my Son. Most of all I would desire that you dedicate prayers for my children who do not know my love and the love of my Son. Help them to come to know it! Help me as Mother of all of you!
>
> "My children, how many times I have already invited you here in Medjugorje to prayer and I will invite you again because I desire you to open your hearts to my Son, to allow him to come in to fill you with peace and love. Allow him, let him enter! Help him by your prayers in order that you might be able to spread peace and love to others, because that is now most necessary for you in this time of battle with Satan. I have often spoken to you: pray, pray, because only by means of prayer will you drive off Satan and all the evil that goes along with him.
>
> "I promise you, my children, that I will pray for you, but I seek from you more vigorous prayers and I seek you to spread peace and love which I am asking you in Medjugorje already nearly ten years. Help me, and I will pray to my Son for you."

April 11: In Zadar, conference of the Yugoslavian Bishops' Commission. A text, issued at the end of this meeting, stated the current position of the

Church: official pilgrimages (led by bishops of diocese) banned, private pilgrimages (lead by laity) authorized.

Easter: Inauguration of the Cenacolo Community in the presence of Sr. Elvira. This community welcomes former drug addicts in order to "resurrect them" through prayer, fraternal life, and work...

June 6: Discreet pilgrimage of Alphonsine, the visionary of Kibeho (Rwanda, Africa).

June 25: 10th Anniversary of the Apparitions. A huge crowd was present. Croatia proclaims its independence.

June 26: Beginning of the war. The Serbian Federal Army invaded Slovenia and Croatia.
Vicka left for Austria for medical reasons. She underwent surgery on one of her lungs. Since then her health has always been delicate.

July: Jelena Vasilj's prayer group was dissolved; Jelena left for the United States to begin studying theology at the Franciscan University of Steubenville.

August: The Franciscan Father Jozo Zovko left Tihaljina. He was appointed "guardian" of the monastery of Siroki Brieg. Father Orec, Medjugorje's parish priest, was replaced by Father Ivan Landeka.

November 10: At last, the Beatitudes Community found a home, not too far from the church! The house belonged to Bernard Ellis. Its new name: Ephesus. (See the chapter, "Let's Sleep at the Ritz!," March 1995)

December 2: Ivan received his apparition in Washington's National Protestant Cathedral: an unconditional bastion of the Reformation.

December: Father Slavko led his first "Prayer and Fasting" retreat in Domus Pacis. Through Marija, Our Lady gave a message to the 25 participants: *"Beloved, oh how easy it would be for me to stop the war if I could find more people who pray the way you pray now!"*

Jakov, on the second day of the apparitions: "Now that I've seen her, I can die, I don't mind!" He was 9.

Vicka: The smile of Medjugorje. "I have no words to express how beautiful she is," she always says.

Ivan, Marija, Jakov, Vicka and Ivanka at the site of the apparitions. Below, Fr. Slavko.

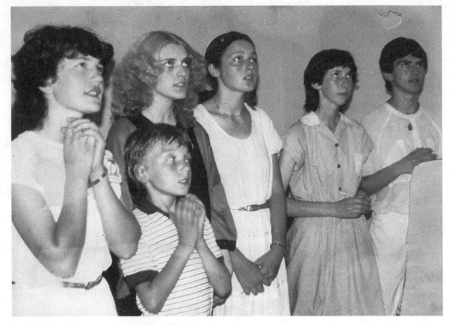

Early photo of the 6 visionaries in ecstasy: *"I don't necessarily choose the best ones,"* Mary told them.

Fr. Jozo Zovko also saw the Blessed Virgin. His charisms of preaching the Word and healing the sick bring great numbers to God.

Ivan: "I feel more comfortable with the Gospa than with you pilgrims..."

The parish has become "the confessional of the world."

Before Our Lady came, a very poor village.

Croatian soldier on Podbrdo. *Only fasting and prayer can stop wars...* said Our Lady.

The Franciscans' church at Mostar, one of the hundreds destroyed.

The crowds of pilgrims have not driven the sheep away!

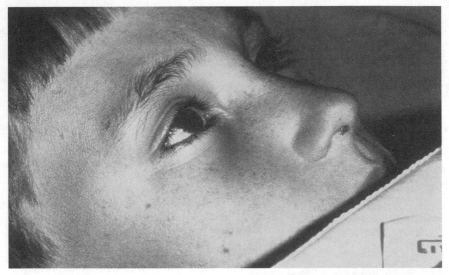

Jakov in ecstasy, 1982. *"I need you, you are important to me,"* Mary told this 10-year-old boy.

John Paul II receives those wounded in the war, led by Vicka: "Have courage, I am with you!"

John Paul II receives a Croatian group including Mirjana (at left) and Msgr. Franic (on the right). Mirjana had a 20 minute private conversation with the Holy Father. "If I was not the Pope, I would have already been to Medjugorje," he told her.

1992

— MESSAGE OF JANUARY 25, 1992 —

"Dear children! Today I am inviting you to a renewal of prayer in your families, so that way every family will become a joy to my son, Jesus. Therefore, dear children, pray, and seek more time for Jesus and then you will be able to understand and accept everything, even the most difficult sicknesses and crosses. I am with you and I desire to take you into my heart and protect you, but you have not yet decided. Therefore, dear children, I am seeking for you to pray so through prayer you would allow me to help you. Pray, my dear little children, so prayer becomes your daily bread. Thank you for having responded to my call."

MARY BOYCOTTS THE NAZIS

There were 6 children in my family. Today, each one of us serves Our Lady in one way or another. Personally, I am filled with wonder to have been sent to Medjugorje, to collaborate with Our Lady. (When I arrived, I warned her, "You chose me, didn't you? You know how I am, so it's at your own risk!") In fact, my joy was deep, and it still is. And even more so when I consider how after 8 years, the Gospa still wants me around!

However, I realize that the roots of our vocation as well as the Marian graces we receive have their roots deep in our family background. At first glance, praying the rosary together might seem to be asking a lot for a family, but what a fruitful source of blessings and protection it is for the younger generations! That my brother Bruno has been able, inexplicably, to cheat death so many times is a mystery! The others have miraculously avoided terrible pitfalls (which doesn't mean there hasn't been suffering, of course). As for me, if I told you all the stories…[1]

Let me tell you what happened to my father. He was an only son and had already lost his own father when he joined the Resistance forces in 1940. His unit comprised 10 men. After an attempt to rescue a British pilot, both he and his companions were captured by the Gestapo and deported to Germany. Thus, over a period of 3 years, my grandmother was alone and did not receive any news. Life in the concentration camps was inhumane. She knew that. But she had immense trust in Our Lady and prayed the rosary unceasingly, asking for the safe return of her son. One day, in the Camp of Hinzert, the Nazi officers ordered the prisoners to carry huge stones from a quarry for construction work on the camp. My father was so weak that he could barely stand.

So he spotted a small block and lifted it. Immediately, an SS guard jumped towards him, insulted him and placed a huge block of stone on his back. My father fell. He was unable to get up again. He knew this was the end of the line for him. The dogs would come running, and the guards would whip him. He had seen so many of his companions die like this. In his despair, he cried out to Our Lady, uttering in a whisper, "Help me!" Suddenly, as if gravity were obeying an invisible order, the stone weighed nothing! It weighed the same as a bit of confetti! My father's life was saved.

On another occasion, shortly before the Americans freed the camp of Flossenburg in 1945, the Germans decided to finish off the prisoners before deserting the camp. For this purpose, they had hit on an unusual stratagem. The SS guards gave one oat bag each to the prisoners and made them leave the camp, on foot, in Indian file. Many would fall on the way, be shot down and left in the ditch. Only a few prisoners survived. The day my father was to leave, his oat bag in hand, he called Our Lady to his rescue once more. A German soldier came and asked, "Where is the doctor?" They wanted a doctor to remain in the camp, just in case. My father was a doctor. So he remained in his cell. Shortly after, he was rescued by the Americans.[2] Out of all the members of his network, he was the only survivor.

I can still hear him talking about Our Lady sometimes when we were having a meal at home when I was a child. He was a good story-teller and at times I had to find an excuse to leave the table and hide the tears which sprang to my eyes.

The story of his encounter with my mother is also a very touching one. He met her on the first day of his return from Germany. It was another of the "master strokes" of Our Lady, because my mother had consecrated her future husband to Mary and prayed for him, even though she had no idea who he would be!

My father has now entered eternity. When Mom speaks about their first meeting, she says, "Mary Queen of Peace, thank you for all that has come from that day: Bruno, Emmanuelle, Vincent, Eric, Marie-Pia and Pascal."

So if you ask me, the Apostle John made the right choice when he took the *Gospa* into his home!

---

[1] Some of these stories are told in a one hour TV special hosted by Ralph Martin: *Sister Emmanuel of Medjugorje: Mary's Messenger*, now available on video from Renewal Ministries, P.O. Box 8229, Ann Arbor, MI 48107; Tel: (313) 662-1730. Price $15.00.

[2] It was a great joy for me to tell this story during my briefing at the Congressional Human Rights Caucus in Washington D.C. on October 22, 1997. "If you guys of the U.S. had not saved my father's life, I wouldn't be here today to speak to you about peace and life according to the Medjugorje messages!"

This briefing was broadcast on show #19 of Sister Emmanuel's TV program *Medjugorje: Our Mother's Last Call*, and is now available on video tape. (See the appendix at the end of the book for information on obtaining video tapes.)

— Message of February 25, 1992 —

"Dear children! Today I invite you to draw still closer to God through prayer. Only that way will I be able to help you and to protect you from every attack of Satan. I am with you and I intercede for you with God, that he protect you. But I need your prayers and your 'Yes'. You get lost easily in material and human things, and forget that God is your greatest friend. Therefore, my dear little children, draw close to God so he may protect you and guard you from every evil. Thank you for having responded to my call!"

MARCELLO'S MOVIE

Marcello is a young Italian man of 25 years. Although he's never been addicted to drugs, he spent a year in the Cenacolo Community (of Sr. Elvira) where, through his prayer and service, he helped former drug addicts pull through.[1]

It was during a "Prayer and Fasting" retreat led by Father Slavko[2] that he had a remarkable experience. The Blessed Sacrament was exposed in the chapel of "Domus Pacis" in Medjugorje, and Marcello had been in adoration for a long time. All of a sudden, without him even asking, the story of his life, as in a film, began to unfold before his very eyes, and with incredible accuracy. There were episodes from his childhood, from the distant past, that he had completely forgotten and that he saw afresh, from a new angle, as well as more recent scenes. Marcello was given a fresh look at his life through God's eyes.

Then the Holy Spirit revealed to him the true meaning of his life and how much he had been loved and cherished by God from the very first day even when he wasn't aware of it.

At the end of the 5-day retreat, he told us, "It was as though there were 2 categories of events: the good and the bad ones. I felt really happy about the good things, and was no longer sad about the bad events. The Lord had showed me how he had used them for good to draw me to him.

"The words kept going through my mind: *'Everything works for good for those who love God.'*[3] God had even used the evil that had been in my life to draw me to him. I was overwhelmed by the way he had managed to lead me to him, through both the evil and the good. I then understood that *love is the only thing that matters in our lives.*"

Marcello has now returned to Italy.[4] His experience is not unique. The Gospa likes her children to have such experiences in Medjugorje more than anywhere else in the world. It is as though she wants to illustrate her messages on love by real-life examples: *"May your only way be love"; "Pray with the heart, fast with the heart"; "Love can do everything."*

May these testimonies help us to focus anew on the only real goal of our lives: the love which proceeds from God.

---

[1] See the beautiful book of Fr. Slavko Barbaric on these fasts: *Pearls of Wounded Hearts*, available in Medjugorje.

[2] During these 5-day retreats, participants fast on bread and water and follow the lectures of Father Slavko. It is recommended to have previously been on a pilgrimage to Medjugorje before doing this retreat. For information write to: Zupni Ured - 88266 Medjugorje - Croatia (via Split). Fax: 00 (387) 88-651-444.

[3] Romans 8:28.

[4] The mother house of the Cenacolo Community is in Italy: Comunita Cenacolo, via San Lorenzo 35, Saluzzo. Tel/Fax: (39) 0175-46122.
There is also a house in the US: St. Vincent de Paul Farm, 5985 State Road 16, St. Augustine, FL 32042. Tel: (904) 829-6920.
There are other houses of this community in Italy, France, Brazil, Croatia, etc. These houses welcome drug addicts who wish to pull through and be helped, through a fraternal life filled with work and prayer. Hundreds of young people have already been rescued from self-destruction by this community. Many of them finally got married and started a family. (For further information, write to Italy.)

— MESSAGE OF MARCH 25, 1992 —

"Dear children! Today as never before I invite you to live my messages and to put them into practice in your life. I have come to you to help you and, therefore, I invite you to change your life because you have taken a path of misery, a path of ruin. When I told you: convert, pray, fast, be reconciled, you took these messages superficially. You started to live them and then you stopped, because it was difficult for you.

"No, dear children, when something is good, you have to persevere in the good and not think: God does not see me, he is not listening, he is not helping. And so you have gone away from God and from me because of your miserable interest. I wanted to create of you an oasis of peace, love and goodness. God wanted you, with your love and with his help, to do miracles and thus, give an example.

"Therefore, here is what I say to you: Satan is playing with you and with your souls and I cannot help you because you are far away from my heart. Therefore, pray, live my messages and then you will see the miracles of God's love in your everyday life. Thank you for having responded to my call."

WHAT ABOUT THE SECRETS?

Among the multiple speculations on the future which haunt our world, only one thing is 100 per cent sure: each and every one of us will be very surprised by whatever the Lord is preparing.

In Medjugorje, Ivanka is the visionary who has the most information on the future, because Our Lady made her fill entire notebooks on the world's

---

[1] She told me she would publish these texts some day.

future.[1] Vicka knows many things too, because the Gospa also entrusted several things to her in 1985, after showing to her her whole life (the Gospa) using words and images. Also, Mirjana knows the exact date of each secret according to what she told Father Tomislav Vlasic in 1983.[2]

I have often wondered why Our Lady, who is usually so clear and straightforward in everything she does, has felt the need to let the world know that she is telling secrets to some children's hearts.

She is smart enough to foresee that some will react with curiosity, agitation, and even anxiety. Can't she give these secrets to the visionaries without us knowing it? Many pastors of the Church feel uneasy about the secrets, and they often try to shun the issue: "Ah, if I were the Gospa, I wouldn't..." Yes, indeed, the Gospa sometimes disturbs even our pastors.

The Gospa unveils secrets because she is a mother, and a mother in a divine way. The secrets are an act of pure maternal love on her part. Among the messages that she has prepared for us, some are a little difficult for us to hear. We are not ready yet. But as a mother, she knows that the word "secret" will draw our attention, that we will look forward to the time of their revelation and attach great importance to the content of this word. When a child is bored, won't listen to anything and wriggles out of talking with you, the minute you promise to tell him a secret, his eyes light up. You excite his interest and thereby allow the opening up of a dialogue. You are then in a position to tell him the important thing he ought to know. No matter how sweet or... cauterizing that thing is!

If the messages are important, the secrets take on an importance of a different nature, an eschatological nature. Their realization might shake the world as never before. The messages are a school (and a clinic), but the secrets are directly connected to God's plan for mankind. When Father Tomislav Vlasic, OFM asked the visionaries why the Gospa had said, *"I have come to call the world to conversion for the last time,"* and also, *"These are my last apparitions on earth,"* they answered that they couldn't tell him why, because, if they did, they would reveal part of the secrets.

By revealing secrets, Mary is not only divinely a mother, she is also divinely a queen. Her eyes fixed upon God's decrees, she can see far beyond our human vision and she knows from her own experience, from her life on

---

[2] Mirjana said that the date of March 18 for her yearly apparition had nothing to do with her birthday. "Once the secrets are revealed," she told me, "it will be known why this date was so important for the Gospa. Also, the second of each month is not an arbitrary choice; there is a reason for it. It will be understood later."

earth, that God's entrusting secrets to his intimate friends is nothing new in the history of salvation. All lovers share secrets, and God is so in love with mankind! Loving intimacy with him can only attract his secrets! In Medjugorje, as in Fatima, he has chosen a very special point of impact in order to touch the earth with this loving intimacy, and this point of impact, through the 6 visionaries, is spread to the parish of Medjugorje and to the world.[3] In Christ's Mystical Body, when the hand touches something, all the limbs take part in this contact.

When I arrived in Medjugorje, I couldn't understand why the idea of these secrets filled me with joy, a supernatural joy. The more my joy increases, the more I come to understand a tiny bit of the reason behind it. Secrets make us feel secure! They show us that God is handling everything, that he is in control of the world, that he is the King, the Master of all times and that we are not orphans given over to the absurd fatalities of statisticians. It is a Heart that rules the world! My fate is in the hands of the King of Love!

What if some secrets contain chastisements (as is probably the case in the last 3 secrets given to Mirjana)? There too, praise be to God! If I had a child threatened by gangrene, wouldn't I amputate his leg to save his life? Mental cruelty? No! Active maternal love! Gangrene, plague, AIDS and despair have contaminated my sinful humanity, therefore I give praise to my God who uses his merciful genius to curb evil before my sins lead me to eternal death. I can only bless Jesus on the Cross for his unfathomable love. Isaiah said of him: "The chastisement which restores our peace falls upon him" (Is 53:5). Our peace, that's all God wants!

The idea of God as Mr. Bogeyman is a satanic invention. I only know of Jesus, Jesus crucified, who became sin to free me from sin and death. God only saves, and "chastisement" (etymologically, a father's correction) is another invention of his to offer to stretch out a last lifeline to the child who had preferred sin to Light. We are so skilled at thwarting God and his mercy that sometimes, to restore our peace, God has no other solution than chastisement. When hell is the only other alternative to chastisement ...chastisement becomes desirable.

And, while we're talking about chastisement, let's open our eyes and look around us: aren't we already smack in the middle of it? In what other period of human history have thousands of young people and children[4] committed suicide, out of agony of soul and heart just to mention one of today's plagues? When was the number of 60 million martyrs per year[5] ever reached?

This reminds me of something Marthe Robin said to a priest of my community: "The prophecy in the Apocalypse, concerning the death of two thirds of the human race, does not refer to an atomic war or any other catastrophe, but to a spiritual death." Prayer and fasting can alleviate and even prevent chastisements. (This is the case for the seventh secret in Medjugorje.)

To me, the best example of this is what happened in 1947 as France was on the brink of the abyss. The Communists were about to come to power. The whole country was paralyzed by serious strikes. A catastrophe was imminent. One morning, in Châteauneuf-de-Galaure, Father Finet opened the newspapers and immediately felt depressed.

The date was December 8. As usual, he went to the Farm to talk and pray with Marthe Robin. He described to her in detail the alarming state of the country and said in conclusion, "Marthe, France is done for!"

"No, Father!" answered Marthe cheerfully. "France is not! Because Our Lady will appear to little children, and France will be saved."

It was 10 o'clock in the morning. Father Finet left Marthe's home and went back to his work, puzzled.

At 1 p.m., that very same day, Our Lady appeared to 4 little girls in the church of L'Ile-Bouchard in Touraine (in the center of France). "*These days, France is in great danger,*" she said to them, "*Pray!*" During the following days Our Lady of Prayer taught them how to say the rosary, to pray for sinners and make the sign of the cross.

Ten days later, the strikes stopped, the Communist threat was averted, and the country was able to turn its attention to reconstruction. And to achieve this, Our Lady had found 4 little girls...and a great saint, Marthe, who offered herself day and night to God in sacrifice to ward off from her country the fruit of sin which is death.[6]

The Gospa's secret in Medjugorje? Let me whisper it in your ear: "*Prayer is the only way to save mankind*" (July 30, 1987).

---

[3] "The very first secrets will be revealed, and they will prove that the apparitions are real," said Jakov, speaking of the third secret, which deals with *the sign*. "I saw it. It is very beautiful," he added.

[4] In some schools in Quebec, parents fear for their children because each year, in each grade, children of 8, 10, or 12 years commit suicide.

[5] Abortions, during which the child experiences excruciating torture in his soul and body, each year number 10 times the number of victims in the holocaust of the Jews at the hands of the Nazis.

[6] Father Finet revealed to us that Marthe had several times prevented Communism from taking hold of France, in May 1968, among other times, when she could see what was brewing in Moscow.

— MESSAGE OF APRIL 25, 1992 —

"Dear children! Today also I invite you to prayer. Only by prayer and fasting[1] can war be stopped. Therefore, my dear little children, pray and by your life give witness that you are mine and that you belong to me, because Satan wishes in these turbulent days to seduce as many souls as possible. Therefore, I invite you to decide for God and he will protect you and show you what you should do and which path to take. I invite all those who have said 'yes' to me to renew their consecration to my Son Jesus and to his Heart and to me so that we can take you more intensely as instruments of peace in this unpeaceful world.

"Medjugorje is a sign to all of you and a call to pray and live the days of grace that God is giving you. Therefore, dear children, accept the call to prayer with seriousness. I am with you and your suffering is also mine. Thank you for having responded to my call."

THE WAR! MAJKO MOJA!

That evening...

The door opened with a bang, allowing a panic-stricken horde of women, children and elderly people to enter our chapel. It was time for Compline, the evening hymn and psalms that prepare us to spend the night in the great peace of God. However, this time, strident cries and sobs interrupted our singing. In a split second baby bottles were lined up alongside our liturgical candlesticks, diapers sought a place next to our Bibles, and the floor was covered with plastic bags crammed with a thousand things which had been hurriedly gathered together. In the

---

[1]See audio tape M9 on fasting on page 361 and 367.

corners, people were already spreading out blankets for the elderly to sit on. The news was blaring from several radios the way Croatians like it.

It was April 6, 1992 and the time was 9:30 p.m. War had just boken our in Bosnia-Herzegovina.

We had to move quickly. Bernard and Maurice took off their monastic habits in order to bring some sandbags to block the entrances to our cellar which had been converted into a chapel. The people of the neighborhood knew that our cellar was the best (but not for wine!) in the district of Bijakovici, which is why they took refuge there.

They began to examine all the different possibilities:

"If the bombs fall from the south, then it is better to put the children to bed in such-and-such a place."

"If the explosions come from the north, then we should barricade the door. But if we do, how will we get to the bathroom?"

They argued and squabbled for a while in the Croatian manner (a lot of noise, but little harm is done!) and between arguments, remembering the Queen of Peace, they would exclaim, "Majko moja!" (My mother!).

A few stunned-looking "baba's" (grandmas) were quietly praying the rosary. The children who were too young to understand were delighted that they were all going to sleep here together! It was better than being home because the opportunities for playing were multiplied 10-fold...

All able-bodied men had joined their combat units and some were already leaving for the front that night. Anguish pierced the hearts of wives and mothers: "Would he return?"

We moved several mattresses into the improvised dormitory, and mothers lay down next to their little children, on the same mattress, in the typical Croatian way.

An unpremeditated detail: it was an Orthodox Gospa (the icon of the Mother of God by Vladimir) who watched over this little world terrorized by an Orthodox enemy! A living prophecy of the reconciliation of God's children...

Later that night, the bells of the church began to peal, the signal for danger from air attack. Our guests recommended that we sleep along with them in the cellar, all stretched out in rows. But we placed our mattresses underneath the staircase of the basement, hoping to escape the constant blare...

After a long sleepless night and an uphill effort at singing the office of Lauds outside our chapel-cellar-dormitory-bomb shelter, I advised the brothers not to leave the house. I myself went over to the Franciscans for news. The situation was clear: the Federal Army led by the Serbs had begun to attack. It was only the beginning, and we had to expect the worst. Thirty kilometers from Medjugorje, Siroki-Brieg was already being bombed. And, for an airplane, 30 kilometers is no distance at all. We had to stay inside our homes.

Those who have lived through war know how this feels. In a split-second, one has to make very serious and vital decisions despite the many unknown factors involved. My neurons were firing like crazy in my head, but at the same time, deep inside, my heart remained at peace and told me that we had nothing to fear...[1]

---

[1] This is the first chapter of an article covering the war years in Medjugorje, from April 1992 to November 1993, taken from the book *Medjugorje, The War From Day to Day*, published by the Florida Center for Peace, PO Box 431305, Miami, FL, USA 33143. Tel: (305) 666-5000; Fax: (305) 668-9804.

— Message of May 25, 1992 —

"Dear children! Today also I invite you to prayer, so that through prayer you come still nearer to God. I am with you and I desire to lead you on the path to salvation that Jesus gives you. From day to day, I am nearer to you although you are not aware of it and you do not want to admit that you are only linked to me in a small way with your few prayers. When trials and problems arise, you say, 'O God! O Mother! Where are you?' As for me, I only wait for your 'Yes' to present it to Jesus for him to fill you with his grace.

"Therefore, once again accept my call and begin anew to pray, until prayer becomes a joy for you. Then you will discover that God is all powerful in your daily life. I am with you and I am waiting for you. Thank you for having responded to my call."

RABBI MYRIAM'S CREED

When I was living in Jerusalem, I had 2 very dear friends, Ruben and Benjamin. Both were messianic Jews. They came from very orthodox Jewish families. They had given up religion during their youth and had openly lived pagan lives for years, until the day Jesus revealed himself to them as the Messiah.

They both bore a grudge against the Church (due to old stuff from the past), and they thought that Catholics, although you could see their monastic habits sprinkled everywhere throughout Jerusalem, didn't really believe in God. They didn't find them " true believers," people full of Jesus and who would do anything for him, like those mentioned in the *Acts of the Apostles*. Both were upright of heart (they were "true men of Israel," Jesus would have said, "men without guile"), so they decided to be reconciled with their worst enemies and prayed to Jesus that they might encounter Catholics.

On the following morning, they bumped into us! I invited them to our house for the following Sunday. I will always remember the fire which descended upon us that evening! Like the pilgrims of Emmaus, we listened to our elder brothers in the faith as they explained to us how to see Jesus-the-Messiah in the Bible. Our hearts were burning within us. Night fell, and before their departure we prayed together for the last time. An extraordinary paean of praise came out of our mouths. Among the childish words we were saying, I can still hear the voice of Benjamin, as he expressed his joy: "Adonai,[1] I thank you for this wonderful meeting with these Catholic brothers and for the love that you have put among us. Oh Father, I praise you because you have shown me that you pour your Spirit out upon every creature, even on Catholics!"

So much for our pride!

A few years later, it was a great joy for me to see in Medjugorje the Gospa's insistence on faith, on the importance of being true believers. She loved the Creed particularly and even showed a preference for that prayer! Many parishes have replaced the Creed by wishy-washy little songs which do not proclaim the faith at all. Here again, the Gospa comes to heal us of this lethal wound. As a good and pious Jewish lady she claims: *"The most important thing is to believe firmly!"* And, *"Priests should strengthen the faith of the people!"* What a joy it is to hear the Franciscans of Medjugorje begin their homilies with: "Dear brothers and sisters, dear believers!" In a former Communist country, these words are worth their weight in gold!

In our countries, saying "I believe that..." actually means "I suppose, but I could be wrong." When we say "I believe the weather will be nice," we are reserving a margin of error for ourselves. On the spiritual level, many people say, "I believe in God, but I don't go to church." Most of the time, when they say, "I believe in God," they mean, "I know that God exists, but I don't go to church because the thought that God exists doesn't make any difference to me in my daily life. I also believe that there are constellations of stars in the sky, but so what? It's not going to change my life, is it?"

With a great sense of humor, Father Slavko compares this attitude to saying, "I am a smoker, but I never smoke."

---

[1] Adonai is the Hebrew word for "my Lord." It is the Jewish way to read the tetragram in the Bible, because the name of God cannot be pronounced. No religious Jew would ever say *"Yahweh"*!

In order to understand Mary's attraction for the Creed and her great desire to transform us into "believers," we must share with her the deep, real and biblical meaning of the words "I believe," *"ani maamim"* in Hebrew. In the Bible, the most spiritual and divine words come from the most concrete, the most incarnate realities of creation, which gives our Judeo-Christian religion a sense of what incarnation means. No, *"Ani maamim"* doesn't mean "I know that it exists." It means: "I adhere to it." It corresponds to a concrete physical action: I stick to[2] this, I form one body with it, like a sticker adheres to my car window. (If I put a sticker with "I ♥ Medjugorje!" on my car, it follows me everywhere I go. Nobody can look at my car without seeing the sticker! And when it comes to unsticking it...!)

If I say "I believe in Jesus," it means that my whole being adheres to him, that I "stick" to his whole reality, I form one body with him. I am wherever he is, I follow him wherever he goes, I get hit if someone throws a stone at him, I am embraced when someone embraces him in a word, we are ONE. If I believe firmly (if the glue adheres), then nothing could ever separate me from him. If I believe feebly (if the glue is no good), the least ordeal, the least blow will ruin the adhesion. I will be detached, and wander off by myself.

We are far from that erroneous interpretation of the word "faith" as the (correct) thought that God exists. Greco-Latin culture intellectualized the notion of faith. We must return to the origins of biblical revelation and to the genius of the incarnation. Satan, too, knows that God exists. He even knows it better than we do! He has no doubts about it whatsoever. Nevertheless, Satan does not believe in God. Satan is not a believer. On the contrary, he is the perfect prototype of the unbeliever. An unbeliever doesn't adhere, he is unstuck from God forever. (Christians should not say "I believe in Satan," but rather, "I know that Satan exists," because adhering to Satan is totally out of the question.)

Naturally, in this adhesion process, the glue is grace. And, the only way to get the glue we need is...prayer! *"Pray in order to believe firmly,"* Mary tells us.

But in the Creed, we do not only assert that "We believe in God." We also say that we believe in the different mysteries of the life of Jesus, in the different functions of the Holy Spirit, in the resurrection of the dead, etc.

---

[2] In Hebrew, the root for the word "stick to" or "adhere to" is *deveq*. The derivative *devekuth* means "fervor" (in prayer)!

When believers pray the Creed, the Gospa marvels at the creative, transforming and life-giving power of this profession of faith. Here again, let us refer to what she herself was taught when she was a child at the knees of St. Joachim and St. Anne. They taught her that when a believer confesses with his lips a reality of the faith, this reality is strengthened, and becomes a living part of him. It actualizes itself and becomes real.

So each time we confess with all our heart that "we believe in the resurrection," the entire reality of the resurrection expands in our hearts, and we become a little more risen in Christ. No, we are not reciting some old history books! We are living the resurrection! When we say, "We believe in the Holy Spirit," we allow the Spirit to pour out his gifts in full measure within us.

One day, I asked Vicka, "In your opinion, why does the Gospa love the Creed so much?"

She took a deep breath and her expression altered. I saw that she wanted to share a priceless treasure[3] with me but couldn't find words beautiful enough. Finally, she said, "But, in the Creed if you could just realize—the Father is alive! Jesus is alive! The Spirit is alive!"

Her mouth was full of the word: "ALIVE!"

Thank you, Myriam of Nazareth! You're a good rabbi!

---

[3] The prayer of the Creed is undeniably linked to peace. How does the Creed give peace? Once again, our notion of "peace" is erroneous. Mary comes to give us true peace, i.e. *shalom* in Hebrew. *Shalom* is not the absence of conflict or tranquillity ("Could I have some peace and quiet?"). *Shalom* means "fullness," "wholeness." Whoever has *shalom* is full, gratified, satisfied. He enjoys the fullness of God. The contrary of peace is not war. It's emptiness. The man who doesn't have *shalom* is hollow, empty, deprived of vitality. Naturally this empty space gives the Enemy a wonderful opportunity to introduce his own "business," i.e. hatred, envy, jealousy, all those feelings that provoke wars. "You are full of grace" is the exact definition of "You have *shalom*."

So the Queen of Peace is a Mother who wants to heal us of our emptiness. The Gospa often reminds us that God is the fullness of life and love, and that prayer allows love to grow within us, day after day, unto fullness. There is no better prayer than the Creed to lead us to fullness, to shalom, because it is only our adhesion to God which allows him to enter deeply within us.

— MESSAGE OF JUNE 25, 1992 —

"Dear children! Today I am happy, even if in my heart there is still a little sadness for all those who have started on this path and then have left it. My presence here is to take you on a new path, the path to salvation. This is why I call you, day after day, to conversion. But if you do not pray, you cannot say that you are on the way to being converted.

"I pray for you and I intercede to God for peace; first, peace in your hearts, and also peace around you, so that God may be your peace. Thank you for having responded to my call."

(Our Lady gave her special motherly blessing to all the people who were present.)

THE CAFES OF LAKE COMO

Monza, Italy, July 16, 1988, Feast of Our Lady of Mount Carmel.

At the house of her Italian friends (among whom was Paolo, her future husband), Marija saw the Gospa appearing, radiant with joy. Next to Marija was Olivia, who noticed the exceptional anointing of the apparition. Yes, something was going on!

But let's let Olivia tell us the story:

"Marija told us that the Gospa prayed a long time over each one of us (there were 6 or 7 of us) and gave her special motherly blessing to all. Then she gave a message: *This evening, my dear children, I give you a special blessing and I ask you to go out and give this blessing to all the people you meet. Go where you will find the greatest number of people, where people gather...*"

---

[1] *Grappa* is a strong, clear alcoholic drink, a type of unaged brandy.

"So, we had to find out where the crowd was! I remember that we felt like apostles who had been sent on a mission. We were overjoyed.

"We asked ourselves: "Where should we go? Where will we find the greatest number of people?" Someone suggested Lake Como. We hopped in the car and went there. The sidewalks of the cafes were crammed with people on vacation, sipping a glass of *grappa*[1] between two *gelati*.[2] Try and picture the scene: a hot summer evening, rows of cafes, parasols, lovers holding hands, tourists strolling along in their summer get-ups, etc., etc.

"We had to figure out a strategy in order to bless everyone without exception. So we spread out in a line, with our arms extended so that our fingers touched, and we began to walk ahead in this formation. Each one of us had been given a particular area to cover, so that no one would escape our eyes and consequently our blessing. You should have seen us! We were so full of the blessing that we wanted to bring it to everyone, no matter what it cost us. At times we had to slow down almost to the point of stopping because of the density of the crowd. We wanted to really look at everyone and bless them with all our heart, with all our love.

"We walked along like this, by the lake, for a long time. On our way back, a surprise awaited us: almost everyone had gone from the area we had covered! Now there were only deserted cafes with empty chairs. The waiters looked completely puzzled, pacing back and forth on the sidewalk. They usually served until 2 or 3 in the morning! They asked each other, "It's not 11 yet and everyone has gone! What's happened? Where have the people gone?"

"As for us, we had no idea, either, where they had gone. All we knew was that we had given them Our Lady's special motherly blessing. We knew that she would do something in their hearts, but it was not our business to know what she would do, or why everyone had left!

"The following day, Marija told the Gospa how amazed she was and how surprised we all were. This reminded me of the scene where the apostles returning from their mission told Jesus about the incredible things they had seen.

"The Gospa was patiently encouraging us more every day to bless people and to keep on walking on that path by her side. These days were really special!"

Olivia continued, and explained how she herself understood and lived the special motherly blessing of Mary:

---

[2] *Gelati* are famous Italian ice creams.

"Marija clearly specifies that one should make a distinction: the priestly blessing is greater. The hands of a priest have received the holy oils and his blessing brings down all the graces from heaven." Once, the Gospa told her: "*If priests knew what they give to a person when they bless, if they could see, then they would bless unceasingly.*"

The special motherly blessing of Mary is a gift, a gratuitous gift, a gift of God which passes through Our Lady as a mother. It is a true motherly gift.[3] For example, when I bless my enemies (as Jesus has asked all of us to do) with Mary's blessing, she helps me to love my enemies with a motherly heart, with her own heart.

The blessing given by the Gospa can only come out of a full heart. My heart overflows with the desire to share the gift I have received, and I only fully measure the content of this gift as I share it. This is what happened with the Satanist on Krizevac.

With the blessing, I have something to give, something of the Queen of Peace. I have received, and so I give.

Marija told us that this gift is so great that no words can describe it. It is like a mysterious reality that the Gospa reveals to us, little by little, step by step.

People sometimes ask me, "How can I get this blessing? Do I have to meet someone who has received it in Medjugorje?" This is the wrong question, because the Gospa has given this blessing to all, in her message for the world. Those who live the messages already have this gift and may pass it on to others. The real question is, "Am I giving all that I have received?" The Gospa doesn't give me a present just because it would look nice in my room as a decoration. She gives me a tool, a solution that is typically hers, in order to solve problems which, from a human point of view, have no solution. This gift is part of a whole. It leads the hearts of those who want to attend the school of the Gospa and brings them into a dynamic of love! It is just the opposite of obtaining something in order to enrich ourselves (or worse: in order to have power over other people).

Before she offered this gift to the world, Our Lady wished the prayer

---

[3] These words of Olivia's remind me of the precious moments when my mother would come and bless me at bedtime. She would trace a little cross on my forehead and I could see that her eyes were diving into the depths of another reality. She was performing a holy gesture, and my little child's heart received at that moment a "dose of pure mother love." She was fully a mother, and thereby enabled me to be fully a child. That special moment meant a great deal to me. It was like a gust of heavenly wind bringing grace into daily life, in which we sometimes suffered from communication difficulties.

group to experience it for several months and be prepared for it. This is just like her! She explained to Marija that, through this special motherly blessing, the heavenly Father committed himself to staying with the person in a special way, to help him daily in his conversion, until the hour of his death. (Of course, the Father is always close to his children, but the blessing grants something more and purely gratuitous through Mary.) She asked us to talk about this blessing and transmit it aloud only to the people who are already walking in the path of faith.[4] As for other people, we should give them the blessing with love as well, but silently.

This blessing is linked to the royal priesthood received by the faithful at their baptism. If only lay people could grasp how great their priestly vocation is! The Gospa teaches us how to live it. To really live it! In Medjugorje, she wants to reveal the extraordinary stock of graces that we should no longer bury in our closets. The world needs people who bless!

"For instance," added Olivia, "when I am in the subway, I bless everybody. Although I am a rather shy and reserved person, people come up to me. They want to talk; they open their hearts to me. We are still miles away from realizing the power of this blessing..."

Thanks to Olivia's testimony, I was able to understand what had happened to me during the first months after my arrival in Medjugorje. As I was a newcomer, totally ignorant of the Gospa's habits and ways, I had decided to spend most of my time on Podbrdo. I intended to pray and deepen my love for Our Lady. But no matter how hard I tried to pray to her, another prayer kept coming into my heart and stayed there for hours: "Father, I thank you for the gift of life." The Father, always the Father! It was great to be so much with the Father, but I felt kind of embarrassed in respect to Our Lady. I would say to her, while climbing down the hill, "Please don't feel left out... OK, I spent all my time with the Father, but it's not because I don't love you..."

Now I see clearly that she was responsible for this! Shortly after my arrival, the Gospa had given her special motherly blessing, on December 25, 1989. As a result of this, she had placed me on her lap to reveal the Father to me...

Praised be she!

---

[4] This point is of capital importance. The person involved must be absolutely free to receive it and to live it. The Blessed Mother never forces anyone's conscience, and does not bless such coercion. Moreover, she did not prescribe any gesture to accompany this blessing. So the laying on of hands is not indispensable, but the person being blessed is free to request it.

MESSAGE OF JULY 25, 1992

"Dear children! Today also I invite you anew to prayer, a prayer of joy so that in these sad days no one amongst you may feel sadness in prayer, but a joyful meeting with God his Creator. Pray, little children, to be able to come closer to me and to feel through prayer what it is I desire from you. I am with you and each day I bless you with my motherly blessing so that Our Lord may fill you abundantly with his grace for your daily life. Give thanks to God for the grace of my being able to be with you because I assure you it is a great grace. Thank you for having responded to my call."

DANAS BANK

"DANAS"? This word means "today" in Croatian. At first, it seems a rather common word, but if we take a closer look... This little word contains the greatest source of healing ever offered by the Gospa to our world which is devoid of peace.

Each month, on the 25th, Father Slavko gathers a little team of persons speaking 5 different languages, in order to translate the message.[1] First, he types the message he received from Marija in Croatian, then the work of translating begins. But even before being given the content of the message, I pick up my pad and write (in French): *"Dear children, today..."* And, most of the time, I'm right! The Gospa almost every time says: *"Draga djeco, danas..."* Why this motif from her? "Today" is her terrain of action, her center of gravity, her point of impact, her general headquarters. "Today" is when everything happens and where everything goes.

"Today" could be the name of a bank, but an extraordinary one which might work as follows: the funds would be provided by God, on demand.

---

[1] He also provides a very good commentary of the monthly message. There is a collection of them in the book *Mother, Lead Us to Peace*, available in Medjugorje.

The capital outlays would be unlimited. Whoever came and asked for a certain amount, depending on what he needed, would be given that amount, and whoever asked for twice that sum would be given twice as much, and so on. A dream of a bank! The bigger the amounts we withdraw, the more our capital increases! But there is a hard-and-fast rule in this bank: funds can only be withdrawn today, and one has to go in person. You cannot say, "Give me what you owed me yesterday," since everything concerning "yesterday" has been erased from the computer's memory. You cannot withdraw an advance on tomorrow in cash either, because the computer will display: "Tomorrow: unknown data, access denied."

This is just the way it works with the Heart of God and the Heart of Mary. If I do not draw on them now, then I condemn myself to misery. The majority of people in today's society suffer from 2 illnesses which sometimes even degenerate into psychosis. The names of these illnesses are "yesterday" and "tomorrow." They infect the soul very subtly and paralyze it progressively, until it dies of suffocation.

If you want to have life, the only teller's window open for business is the "Today" one. "Yesterday" and "Tomorrow" are conspicuous by their absence.

The characteristic symptoms of the 2 above-mentioned diseases are very easy to detect because their victims reveal the presence of their pathology in their daily conversation:

"I'll pray tomorrow." (Communication with God = 0)

"Me, dying? It's not around the corner. I'll think about it later!" (Watchfulness = 0)

"Yesterday my husband was unfaithful to me. He won't get away with it!" (Mercy = 0)

"Yesterday I already gave something to a poor person. He'd better not come back for more today!"(Charity = 0)

"Tomorrow, for sure there will be a war!" (Peace of heart = 0)

"Anyway, it didn't work yesterday so I can't imagine why it should work today!"(Hope = 0)

The victims of such diseases are stuck in "the trap of yesterday," or they invest in dreams, in "the illusion of tomorrow." They are perishing from hunger and thirst, from emptiness. They commit suicide by the thousands because of a withdrawal crisis, whereas the "Danas Bank" is open to them 24 hours a day!

Grace is given for "today." It touches, reaches and saves the reality of my life now. I can't have today tomorrow's grace, and I can't bottle today's for tomorrow.

Many newspapers do criminal work in giving space to doomsday prophets in their columns. They sow fear in people's hearts. Fear is always a symptom of the "tomorrow" psychotic syndrome. The customers of the great "Today Bank" which is God's heart can be recognized by just one symptom: "*Love.*" When I love, there is no room in my heart for fear. When I love, I make way for the future, I change the future, I build true security for my family. I am rooted in reality. I am not soaring around in the air like Peter Pan.

"Today" is the most extraordinary source of riches and surprises that I know. If I listen carefully in order to capture the grace of this day, then God joyfully reveals to me the unique plan that he has for the present moment.

My friend Karen is one of the best and most loyal customers of the "Danas Bank." She has been trained for a long time at the Gospa's school.

One day, she was invited to the States to give a talk on Medjugorje to a dozen parishes. The Gospa had shown her that she had to do it, so she gave a big "Yes." However, she was panicking because she considered her shy nature an insurmountable obstacle.

And here she was in Boston, sitting in a pew, praying before her talk. She begged Mary, "Find somebody else! I just can't do it!" Suddenly, an utter stranger tapped her on the shoulder.

"Miss, I was praying behind you. I don't know you, but Jesus asked me to tell you this: 'Don't worry about the words you will have to say. I will be with you. Just open your mouth and the words I want to say to the audience will appear before your eyes, one by one.'"

And that is exactly what happened! Karen, still shaking, walked to the microphone and saw something like a long scroll of paper rolling down before her eyes. She read one sentence out loud, forgot it immediately, and had no idea of what the next sentence would be. She depended completely on the present moment. That night, people complimented her for preparing her speech so well, for many hearts had been deeply touched. A good lesson on surrendering ourselves to God!

On another occasion, she went to the microphone with such an empty head that she couldn't even remember the 5 basic points of the Medjugorje message. However, she was full of trust and never doubted that Mary had something to say to the people who had gathered in such large numbers that evening. When she reached the mike, she was completely speechless. The silence was uncomfortably thick; she remained completely mute. Not a single word came to her mind. Peacefully, she waited. But the crowd began to wonder what was going on. They started whispering and fidgeting... For Americans, remaining 5 minutes in complete silence borders on an ontological impossibility! Karen said to Mary, "Mother! If you have no word for them, it's your choice. But, please show me how long I have to stand before this microphone!" Then Karen heard herself ask the crowd, "Are there any priests in the audience?"

Fifteen men put their hands up.

"Would you be so kind as to come up here, please?" she asked the priests.

Fifteen priests came up.

"Mother! What I am supposed to do with them now?" she begged in her heart.

The crowd wondered what on earth was going to happen. Was this Karen from Medjugorje really okay in the head? Then some words came out Karen's mouth, the very last she would have wished to have to say: "The Gospa cannot speak to you tonight. There are too many sins. You cannot listen to her voice. You must go to confession first!"

She was supposed to speak for only 40 minutes. It was 7:30 p.m. She used up those minutes to say 2 words: "conversion" and "confession." She explained these words with the help of the power of the Holy Spirit. Then she left. The following day, the parish priest, obviously overwhelmed, came to her and said, "Karen, you know what happened last night? At 1 a.m. we were still going, all 15 priests had been hearing confessions for more than 5 hours. I don't know what was up with these people, but most of them had not been to confession for 20, 30, 40 years; you should have seen the tough cookies that the Gospa sent us!"

On that night, hundreds of sinners who in most cases had come out of mere curiosity went home among the number of the just, radiant to have found their Savior again.

Just one little heart had drawn on its account with the Danas Bank; that night, this little heart had been able to give out unexpected treasures. There was enough for everybody!

— MESSAGE OF AUGUST 25, 1992 —

"Dear children, today I wish to tell you that I love you. I love you with my Motherly love and I call upon you to open yourselves completely to me, so that through each of you I may be enabled to convert and save the world, where there is much sin and many things that are evil. Therefore, my dear little children, open yourselves completely to me so that I may be able to lead you more and more to the marvelous love of God, the Creator, who reveals Himself to you day by day. I am at your side and I wish to reveal to you and show you the God who loves you. Thank you for having responded to my call."

ST. JOE CAN'T HELP IT!

At the end of October 1989, when Ephraim, the founder of the Community of the Beatitudes, decided to send a few members of his community to Medjugorje, I had to oversee every practical aspect of the operation. For that, I knew an excellent address: St. Joseph. On November 9, he received a little message from this old customer that I am for him:

"Dear St. Joe, you know how much I love you. In 9 days it will be the 11th anniversary of the day when I married your Son. So, if you were looking for a present to give me, do not look any further. Just listen:

I am leaving for Medjugorje to serve your spouse, the Gospa. She has invited me there. But you see, it would be very difficult to manage without a car. We would be inconvenienced by the least thing. Therefore, it would be really terrific on your part to offer us a car, to her and to us, a car to help the plans of peace. Of course in Nazareth you and she did without a car, but times have changed and since then you've learned how to modernize. We would need a good car, a 4-seater, solid, easy to maintain because I am not a mechanic, with a good trunk. Avoid a car with 2 doors, we get crowded in the back. A 4-door one is preferable (it is important to give him all the details). I have just enough time to make a novena before Friday. It would be really terrific if I could announce to my community in the evening that we have a car. Imagine the praise from their hearts! Also, don't go beyond the time of the novena for granting it, for we have to prepare the papers before our departure which is set for December 1st."

During the days that followed I did have my periods of doubting. A small, mean voice suggested to me, "Who do you think you are to imagine you'll receive a car for free by the 18th!... you're nuts!" But I had let everyone in the community know, and many brothers and sisters had decided to join in prayer. I decided to opt for blind trust in St. Joe's help. I had so often experienced his care!

The days went by... Friday came and nothing in sight, but in the afternoon, though, I received a letter from Sister Marie-Raphael who was to accompany me to Medjugorje:

"Dear Sister Emmanuel, you won't believe it! We got a car for Medjugorje! And the name of the donor is Joseph! He lives in Lourdes and loves Our Lady tremendously. He had promised her to give her his car, a Peugeot 305 in good condition, but he didn't know how to go about it. When he found out that I was leaving for Medjugorje with you and that a car was needed, his heart immediately lit up. He understood that the Blessed Mother wanted his car for Medjugorje. Now we have just enough time to get the registration documents ready. I'll drive over to join you in Normandy."

Guess what? The letter was dated November 9, the very day the novena began! St. Joseph had kept his promise right away, but slowed down the Post Office. He is a man of his word, he sticks to agreements. After all, we had scheduled the answer for Friday the 18th!

Since then, I can't tell you how much this car has helped Our Lady's work in Medjugorje!

A good tip to remember from this story: If you need something to serve Our Lady, ask St. Joseph and tell him sweetly: "This is not for me, it's for your spouse, the Blessed Mother. She badly needs it for her plans of peace."

For her, his heart always melts. He can't help it![1]

---

[1] Don't miss the beautiful book from Fr. Doze: *St. Joseph, Shadow of the Father*, Alba House, N.Y.

— Message of September 25, 1992 —

"Dear children! Today again I would like to say to you that I am with you also in these troubled days during which Satan wishes to destroy all that my Son Jesus and I are building. He desires especially to destroy your souls. He wants to take you away as far as possible from the Christian life and from the commandments that the Church calls you to live. Satan wishes to destroy everything that is holy in you and around you. "This is why, little children, pray, pray, pray to be able to grasp all that God is giving you through my comings. Thank you for having responded to my call."[1]

BEWARE! FAKE POWERS!

Although the church was full, everyone had noticed the lady in the fifth row continuously soaking a ton of Kleenex and who was having a hard time holding back her sobs. It had all started this morning at Father Jozo's, and since then she was inconsolable. After Mass, she grasped my arm and begged for my help. I asked her, "What's gotten you so upset?"

"This morning, at Father Jozo's, I received a *real slap in the face*! I am deeply hurt, and I just can't understand why this happened to me..."

Sobs were shaking her from head to foot and she could hardly finish her sentences. Her face was contorted with real distress. "For sure, God

---

[1] The six Precepts of the Church:

#1: "You shall attend Mass on Sundays and holy days of obligation."

#2: "You shall confess your sins at least once a year."

#3: "You shall humbly receive your Creator in Holy Communion at least during the Easter season."

#4: "You shall keep holy the holy days of obligation."

#5: "You shall observe the prescribed days of fasting and abstinence."

#6. The faithful also have the duty of providing for the material needs of the Church, each according to his abilities.

has rejected me!" she kept on saying. I tried to ask objective questions and find out what had really happened and how. That morning, with her group of pilgrims, Catherine went to listen to Father Jozo and receive his blessing. During the talk she felt captivated by the strength and the anointing of the words she heard, which confirmed her in her conviction: this Father Jozo was exceptional, probably a saint. Then she kept waiting for just one thing: the famous blessing he gives to pilgrims. That's when she would *receive something*. After all, she had come all that way to Medjugorje mainly to have Father Jozo lay hands on her. All the rest was secondary.

The pilgrims lined up in the aisle and Catherine observed Father Jozo. He would stop before them and bless them two by two, laying his hands on their heads. In a low voice, he prayed quietly, with a look of utter concentration. Catherine stood halfway down the line it was almost her turn, her heart pounded with excitement and joy. But then the inexplicable tragedy occurred: after blessing the 2 persons standing on her right, Father Jozo ignored her completely and went on to bless the 2 persons who stood on her left, missing her completely. Catherine's knees turned into jelly. He had not even looked at her! Her whole being was shaken, but still, when Father Jozo headed towards the rest of the group to bless them, she had the courage to change places and slip into the end of the line, where Father Jozo had not passed yet. But once again, the same phenomenon took place: the priest conspicuously missed her, and blessed her neighbors without paying any attention to her. "Since that moment, Sister, I am in utter despair. If Father Jozo truly is a saint,[1] then it means that God has rejected me... But tell me, Sister, you know Father Jozo well, does he sometimes refuse to give his blessing?"

"Uh... no! Except on some really rare and special occasions..."

Then the case of a man whom Father Jozo had refused his blessing to came to mind. That started me thinking about Catherine's case. "Father Jozo knows what he's doing," I said. "He is neither absent-minded nor a sadist. Now, madam, tell me very sincerely: what were your deepest intentions when you went to see Father Jozo?"

And that's how I discovered the skeleton in the closet, the bottom line. Catherine's childhood had been difficult. Her mother had always despised

---

[1] The Gospa said to Vicka, when Fr. Jozo was in prison and remained faithful, forgiving his enemies: *"He lives his ordeal in a holy way,"* (summer 1981). Of course, Our Lady never meant to canonize him before he was even dead!

her and her father was conspicuous by his absence. Catherine had struggled all her youth, trying to find her identity, her *raison d'être*. The emptiness inside her was secretly gnawing away at her and she was seriously considering suicide. Her father's death and other family events led her to meet people who knew how to "harness the energies," who had powers over other people's minds and who convinced her that she was a gifted medium and should develop this capacity. Then Catherine turned a page in her life. Through various steps of initiation and seminars in Far-Eastern countries, she was trained in the occult sciences and little by little built up a "practice" with people she "helped."At last she had found her purpose in life! — she had importance for others, people finally sought her company, asked her advice, and even praised the "positive power" she exerted over her protégés. In short, she had the feeling she existed at last.

As I listened to Catherine, the whole story became clear to me: as he often is, Father Jozo had been warned in a supernatural way. The Holy Spirit had used him to extricate Catherine from the dreadful illusion with which she had been deluding herself with for years. No need to ask her, she herself gave me the key to the events of that morning.

"So, you understand, the purpose of my visit was to receive Father Jozo's blessing..."

"But what exactly do you mean by that?"

"Well, I wanted to receive his positive energies, receive his powers of healing. I wanted to get new powers through him and thereby help my patients even more... You see, they say he is a prophet, a man chosen by God and who is tremendously gifted with powers..."

"It is precisely because he is inspired by God and often sees what lies at the bottom of people's hearts that he did not bless you..." Catherine understood that we had reached the heart of the matter and she listened to me very carefully.

"What do you mean?"

"You would have gone home just the way you came, thinking that you had reached your goal! Father Jozo acted like the prophets in the Bible. His gesture is a sign for you."

Then I explained to her at length that in the throes of her distress she had been tempted and trapped by false lights. The Gospa, in tears, had said to Father Jozo, *"You have forgotten the Bible."* Catherine had forgotten the Bible and had looked in other directions for the path to life. Without knowing it, she had thereby chosen paths that God himself calls roads to death. She thought she was living and helping life, but all she did was glorify herself, exalting her own "ego," and poisoning others. Whereas, in the beginning, she probably had the genuine wish to help other people.

"You needed that shock from Father Jozo to open your eyes! Father Jozo is not a dispenser of 'powers,' or a wizard. He is not meant to increase the power you have over other people. No, he is a servant of God, someone who is poor in spirit. He is a priest who humbly prays that the True God take hold of his children's hearts.

"Catherine, you have mistaken New Age practices for Christian living. You came here to absorb new gifts just to enhance your status with new titles, and God was waiting for you right here! He wants to give you so much more: he wants to give himself to you because he loves you immensely. That's why he wants to transform you so that you are poor in the Spirit. He wants to relieve you of all this completely shady pseudo-spiritual-esoteric hocus-pocus which is inside you and that he cannot abide. If you accept the great grace of conversion offered to you in such a striking way (which is typical of Medjugorje), then God will be able to form your life and you will become a totally new person... Then you will bear real fruits for others."

Catherine wasn't sobbing anymore, and her eyes still misty with the shadow of death slowly became peaceful.

"I had never heard anything like this before! But I feel, deep down in my heart that what you say is right, that it's true. But then, does it mean that I mustn't see people and take care of them anymore?"

"It means that, from now on, you will let God be the guide of your life. Give Christian prayer, the Bible and the sacraments first place in your life, forget your powers of divination. Little by little you will be filled with the fullness of God, and you won't even think of the power that you could have over other people. We are all meant for Glory. But Satan is shrewd, he makes us believe, even unconsciously, that glorifying our "ego" will lead us to happiness, whereas it leads to disaster. Because our "ego" is nothing but misery. No, the true Glory that awaits us, it's the very Glory of God within us. Would you accept to drop the glory of men to the benefit of the Glory which comes from God? Even considering the sacrifices you'll have to make in order to reorder your life?"

Catherine measured the enormity of the step she had to take and cried out, "But how can I find the courage to do this? My whole life has to change completely, from A to Z...!"

"Yes, Saint Paul also said it: *'It's a terrible thing to fall into the hands of the Living God!'* But this has happened to you in Medjugorje, so you should trust Our Lady! Obviously she had planned this. Now she is the one who will help you, day after day..."

Catherine agreed to make one and even several retreats to learn how to live this new life. She went to confession, and a priest, specialized in such cases, prayed for her liberation, since her mind had been distorted by the esoteric seminars she had attended. She experienced several lapses because her milieu wanted her back and the temptation was strong. Fortunately, she remains very close to Medjugorje, and thanks to the prayers of all of us, she will keep heading for the Kingdom. As to Father Jozo's blessing, she finally received it within another group, sometime after her conversion, as she knelt down to ask for the grace of being small instead of the grace of being important.

— MESSAGE OF OCTOBER 25, 1992 —

"Dear children! I invite you to prayer now when Satan is strong and wishes to make as many souls as possible his own. Pray, dear children, and have more trust in me because I am here in order to help you and to guide you on a new path toward a new life. Therefore, dear little children, listen and live what I tell you because it is important for you when I shall not be with you any longer that you remember my words and all that I told you.

"I call you to begin to change your life radically from the beginning and that you decide for conversion not with words but with your life. Thank you for having responded to my call."

BE AN ANGEL!

October 1987. After the Feast of the Guardian Angels, Marija went for a jaunt on an island off Split. Three friends went with her, among whom was a seminarian. One evening, her friends noticed how puzzled she looked after the apparition. At that time, the visionaries still used to be together for the apparition and, on that day, Marija was facing a completely new situation: receiving the visit of the Gospa on her own as a visionary. But her confusion was mainly caused by something else. "You know, the Gospa did something strange tonight," she told her friends. "She gave us homework to do! She asked us to write a letter to our guardian angel and give it to her tomorrow."

One of Marija's friends, Maud, told me, "I couldn't believe my ears! I didn't know that people could write to their guardian angel, that he liked letters! I was really embarrassed. It had been years since I had last spoken a word to my guardian angel. As a little girl, when I learned that I had an angel with me, I talked to him. But it didn't last long. And there I was, with a letter to write to him within the next 24 hours! The four of us worked industriously at our vacation homework.

When the Gospa returned on the following day, she was accompanied by little angels. Marija explained that these angels looked like little children about a year and a half old, more or less, but she didn't know whether or not they were our guardian angels. The Gospa didn't introduce them, but there were five and they gazed intently at each one of us. I personally felt strongly that my guardian angel was one of them. That evening, the Gospa invited us to make friends with our guardian angel and to turn to him for help. She told us to ask him for favors and services.

The next day, we placed our letters at the Gospa's feet. Afterwards, we burned them. Within the next few days we talked a lot together about our guardian angels. We became aware of their presence and their help. This filled us with joy, and what joy!

Each one of us started to develop a completely new dialogue with his guardian angel, and it changed our lives. All sorts of adventures began to happen to us, thanks to our guardian angels.

Here is one of them:

Shortly after our stay on the island with Marija, I spent a few days in Munich (Germany) with my friend Milona (who was also on the island with us). As we were planning our return trip from Munich to Medjugorje by car, I thought of a holy priest[1] I knew, who lived in Verona (Italy). I felt a strong urge to go and see him so that Milona could meet him. But several things made me hesitate. This detour would add a 5-hour drive to our journey, and this priest was seriously ill and therefore confined to bed, and had stopped receiving visits for some months. Moreover, we had to manage to go through 2 outside doors adjoining the Dome of Verona to be able to ring at his apartment, and on Sunday no one would open these doors to us. All the more since there is no doorbell!

Still...the intuition that we had to go turned out to be stronger than all these obstacles. This priest was so holy that just meeting his gaze imparted God in the most extraordinary way; we just had to try our luck.

We started on our way, and a few miles later we tried to call Verona on the phone, but all we got was an answering machine saying, "Father Bozio does not receive visitors, but he will answer the phone between 4 and 5 p.m." From a human point of view, our cause was doomed before it started, so we decided to put our guardian angels to work! First, we asked them to go and find Father Bozio in order to ask him if we could come, and to bring the answer back in our hearts.

---

[1] Don Bozio, deceased in 1995.

After praying a few minutes, a great joy suddenly filled us and we took it as a positive sign to start the 5-hour drive to Verona. Then, every half-hour we sent our guardian angels to Father Bozio because, according to our calculations, we would not reach Verona within the time gap when he was still available, at least according to the phone message. The angels had to carry out 2 tasks:

1. The doors : make sure that the big doors of the cloister and the convent would be open and that someone would answer Father's door.

2. Father Bozio : warn him so that he would be expecting us.

When we arrived, the first as well as the second door were wide open! We started up the stairs leading to Father Bozio's floor and, as we looked up, whom did we see? Father Bozio himself! He was standing on the last step of the staircase, watching us climb! Seeing the smile Milona and I exchanged, he said by way of welcome, "Here you are, you two who have sent me your guardian angels! Come in! I want to give you a blessing!" "This story" added Maud, laughing, "is only one example among many others!"[2]

The fact that Our Lady is accompanied by angels is nothing new in the history of apparitions. However, today we benefit from a unique grace: in Medjugorje those who see the Gospa every day, who see the angels around her, are within our reach! Vicka and Marija describe the angels in the same way (I never discussed this subject with other visionaries). According to them, angels have the appearance of humans; they have the most beautiful faces, and they are dressed in long tunics which hide their feet. Most of the time the Gospa comes with angels who look like 1- or 2-year-old children, sometimes older. They always face their Queen whom they eye greedily with a love and wonder they can't conceal. What is most striking about them is that they imitate everything Our Lady does. If she bends forward, they bend, too. If she opens her hands, they open theirs. If she speaks sadly, they become very sad. If she smiles, they smile...

Marija tells us that the slightest move of the Gospa is the purest expression of God's will; the least of her words, the smallest intonation of her voice, all of this reveals to perfection the will of God. Yet the assignment of our guardian angels is precisely to help us realize to the full the particular plan God has for each one of us. They are posted by God to our side to incline us to do God's will. When they accompany Our Lady, you can see their joy increasing every minute, because everything about her achieves God's plan. If the Gospa stays a long time, the angels cannot contain their joy, until they cannot hold it back anymore, so they start flapping their wings noisily, with more and more strength.

"For us, visionaries, watching the angels is truly instructive," says Marija. "They teach me how to imitate Our Lady and to live according to her example, how to welcome her as Queen."

In Medjugorje, sometimes, the Gospa appears surrounded by thousands of angels. I don't think that the visionaries know who these angels (or archangels?) are, exactly. I often heard Ivan saying, "Tonight the Gospa came joyful and happy, with 5 angels," or "with 3 angels." It happens mostly on major feast days, but also on other occasions.

Now, if you wish to live a particular relationship with the angel God has placed especially at your side, it's not too late! Why not write him a letter, and lay it at the feet of Mary for her visitation at 6:40 p.m.?

---

[2] In the 20th century, among those who have lived in great intimacy with their guardian angels, we should mention: Pope John XXIII, Sr. Faustina, Padre Pio, etc...

Alessio Parente, OFM wrote a wonderful book: *Send me Your Guardian Angel*, which contains the most beautiful testimonies of Padre Pio. For example, Padre Pio used to send his guardian angel to other people to help them. He also advised people, when they needed him, to send him their guardian angel.

Father Werenfried von Straaten, founder of "L'Aide à l'Eglise en Détresse" (Help to the Church in Need) also gives wonderful testimonies coming from Communist jails in which some Western Christians sent their guardian angels to comfort the prisoners.

— Message of November 25, 1992 —

"Dear children! Today, more than ever, I am calling you to pray. May your life become a continuous prayer. Without love you cannot pray. That is why I am calling you to love God, the Creator of your lives, above all else. Then you will come to know God and will love him in everything as he loves you. Dear children, it is a grace that I am with you. That is why you should accept and live my messages for your own good.

"I love you and that is why I am with you, in order to teach you and to lead you to a new life of conversion and renunciation. Only in this way will you discover God and all that which now seems so far away from you. Therefore, my dear children, pray. Thank you for having responded to my call."

THE MOST PRO-LIFE LADY

For the Croatian families of this village, the birth of a child is a great joy. The child is desired, welcomed, cherished and carried in people's arms. He brings real happiness to all and is considered a gift of God. The Gospa could not win the hearts of the local visionaries more easily than by showing them the Baby Jesus carried in her arms.

In Medjugorje, abortion did not exist. Like drugs, suicide, or divorce, abortion only belonged to other planets. The visionaries were so naive that Our Lady herself had to reveal to them certain aspects of today's evil world, so that they would become aware of it and realize how vitally urgent it was to pray. For example, she spoke to Marija about freemasonry, consecrations to Satan, secret projects to destroy the Holy Father, etc.... She showed Jelena several scenes illustrating the action of Satan and the destruction he achieves nowadays. The visionaries were completely taken aback!

Mirjana's life had been slightly different. Her parents had to leave Medjugorje shortly after they were married, to make a living in Sarajevo.

They had to survive in more than precarious conditions. They rented a tiny little room with 72 square feet of living space. Then Mirjana was born. However, the landlord warned her parents, "One more child and out you go!" Both her mother and father had to work to pay the rent, and one day they were able to move to a bigger room. Then, 8 years later, Mirjana's little brother was born.

"We were poor," remembers Mirjana. "I used to stay alone in the room during the day. My parents sacrificed themselves so much for me. They would buy 2 bananas, a very expensive fruit at the time, and would give them to me. To make sure I would eat them, they would tell me, 'We hate bananas, what a horrible fruit!' They fed me as well as they could! I received so much love from them, and never felt deprived of anything. Today I am infinitely grateful to them. I know that I would not be alive if they had given in to fear. The Communist threat was constant and there was no security whatsoever. Still, my parents trusted in God and today I thank them for having had me! And look how Our Lady guided everything afterwards no one would have guessed that I was to see the Blessed Mother one day! It is not we who decide our children's happiness!

"In order to continue my studies, I had to go to a different school, and this new school was a very difficult experience for me because many of my schoolmates didn't know God and lived very sinfully. Abortion and many other things were practiced everywhere, and I suffered a lot from all this. My apparitions had already begun, but I was not allowed to say a word about them. I was being watched and spied upon. At the first, slightest mistake my parents would immediately have lost their jobs.

"One particular morning, one of my schoolmates told me, "Today, I am going to have an abortion and afterwards I'm going to a concert." I was so shocked at her putting the death of a child on the same plane as a concert that I lost control and slapped her on the face. You know, at the time, that was like me! She slapped me back and we started to argue so loudly that we were sent to the Principal's office."

"And when Our Lady appeared to you later, did she reproach you for anything?"

"She didn't say anything about the slap, but she told me that I could change these people only through my example and prayer. I understood that I should neither lecture them nor yell at them..."

"And later on, did she tell you anything about abortion, as she did to Marija and Vicka?"

"Yes, for I often talked to her about what was taking place around me and asked for her help. She told me not to judge these women but to love them and to pray that they be reconciled with God. She told me that the father and the mother of the aborted child would have to suffer greatly. She cried a lot.[1] She said that abortion was a great sin because it is murder, that God does forgive all sins, but for this very one he requires major penance from both parents."

"And what about aborted babies?"

"She said, *'They are with me.'*"

In Medjugorje, many pilgrims (who are fathers and mothers of aborted children) have started on a beautiful path of conversion and interior healing through the reconciliation with the little being they rejected in the past. Instead of banishing his memory, they come to consider him a human person, living in heaven, gifted with a heart and a soul. They decide to reconcile with him. They ask for forgiveness from the bottom of their hearts, and develop a deeper and deeper relationship with him, as they would do with a member of the family. They give him a first name, pray to him, and pray for him. This reconciliation and the welcoming into the bosom of the family are a source of great graces for the parents, and even for the other children. Single persons who are concerned with this situation can live a similar *widening of heart*. Even if the mothers keep on suffering in a certain way, they are at peace, they are not tormented any longer or tortured by the loss of their child: they have placed it in Mary's womb.

---

[1] Sometimes Jesus asks certain souls who have offered themselves up to his mercy that they accept sufferings of reparation for the sake of abortions. Sister Faustina relates: "September 16, 1937. At 8 o'clock I felt such intense pain that I had to go to bed immediately. For 3 hours I writhed in pain, until 11 p.m. No medication helped; I vomited back up everything I took. At times I lost consciousness from the pain. Jesus let me know that in this way I was taking part in his Agony in the Garden of Olives, and that it was he who was allowing these sufferings as reparation to God for abortions. This suffering has happened to me 3 times already. I told my doctor that I had never felt such pains. He had no idea what could be causing them.

"Now I understand what these sufferings were all about, for God revealed their meaning to me... Still, when I think that I might have to bear them again, I shiver with terror. But I have no idea if I am to suffer this pain again. I leave that up to God. I will accept with submission and love all that it pleases him to send me. If I could save just one child from such murder, it would be worth all that I could suffer." (*Diary*, IV, 31)

— MESSAGE OF DECEMBER 25, 1992 —

"Dear children! I desire to place all of you under my mantle and protect you from all satanic attacks. Today is the day of peace, but in the whole world there is a great lack of peace. That is why I call you all to build a new world of peace with me through prayer. This I cannot do without you, and this is why I call all of you with my motherly love and God will do the rest.

"So, open yourselves to God's plan and to his designs to be able to cooperate with him for peace and for everything that is good. Do not forget that your life does not belong to you, but is a gift with which you must bring joy to others and lead them to eternal life. May the tenderness of the Little Jesus always accompany you. Thank you for having responded to my call."

THE MORE CHILDREN THE BETTER!

Eight o'clock. As every morning at that time, Mirjana came out of her house to speak to pilgrims. She gets up at 5 to say her rosary before her family awakens. Then she begins her day as a housewife and mother with the great peace which a heart-to-heart relationship with Mary gives. Every pilgrim scrutinizes her, because for the majority of them, seeing a visionary is like seeing a saint, or at least an exceptional reflection of God.

Mirjana shares with them the main messages and she also tells them about the role regarding unbelievers that the Gospa has entrusted her with. Her talk turns out to be simple, undramatic and brief. Like the Ten Commandments given by Moses when he came down from Mt. Sinai where he had spoken to God, the message conveyed by the visionaries is contained in 10 lines also. But such lines are enough to turn the world upside down! Then Mirjana would stop with the deep calm of someone who has said all there is to say.

One day, a man in the crowd asked, "Mirjana, what would you say to a young married woman who refuses to have children?"

"But having babies is the most beautiful thing on earth!" Mirjana immediately answered, thereby starting a wave of applause.

The man seemed quite satisfied. He had been right. Now he had his proof. He would inform the young lady. Still, he wanted more: "What if this woman is scared because the future is so dark, and it is dangerous to bring children into such a world?"

"But she has no reason to be afraid! She should entrust her children to God and to Mary. The Gospa says that we do not decide the happiness of our children. *Those who take God as their Father, myself as their Mother and the Church as their home,*' she says, *'have no reason to be afraid.'*"

"Yet, nowadays, many parents are afraid to have children..."

"The Gospa says: *'Do not be afraid to have children. You should rather fear not to have any! The more children you have, the better!'*"

The pilgrims started murmuring to one another. They did not expect such strong words from Our Lady. It was just the opposite of what is said in today's society!

"But, Mirjana, what about the secrets... We know that some of them announce hardships..."

"Do not be frightened by the secrets! Entrust your children to the Gospa and you will have nothing to fear from the secrets. Why do you think I already have 2 children and hope to have many more?"

Her argument and testimony shone like a flash in the night! It was irrefutable, stronger than all the "doomsday books" which have invaded bookstores at this end of the millennium.

While the group was leaving by the little path full of potholes and rocks, I asked Mirjana for a few more details on the subject of children.

"You know, what you have just said is a bombshell to the Western world! It goes against all the theories that powerful authorities have been imposing on us for a long time and that are drummed into our consciousness daily by the media: families break up, a child is a burden..."

"Our Lady's voice must be heard above that of humanity's gravediggers!"

"Come tomorrow!"

On the following day, while sitting in her living-room, I took notes on our conversation. Mirjana never mixes her own opinion with what the Gospa has entrusted her. She repeated to me, word for word, what she had said the day before. "Mirjana, did the Gospa ask you to get married?"

"No, I was free to make the decision. But she taught me to listen to the voice of God, to God's will in my heart. She always says, *'Pray and you will know what to do in your heart.'* Yet I never felt in my heart the desire to become a nun. Marko and I had known one another since childhood. We were schoolmates. As far as I am concerned, the Gospa never showed any other way than marriage."

"Mirjana, five visionaries out of six are married. Do you think that this is a sign of Our Lady's preference for families in this time? Should this be considered as a sign?"

"No, absolutely not! The Gospa says that both vocations are necessary within the Church and that families cannot live in the absence of priests (and religious), just as priests and religious cannot live without families. The visionaries are not examples to be imitated!"

"Yesterday you passed on very strong assertions from Our Lady. For instance: *'Do not be afraid to have children. You should rather fear not to have any! The more children you have, the better!'*"

"Yes, she did say that, and she knows why she said it. I know, too...but I can't tell you more...

"Oh...you know, too...!"

Mirjana nodded, and with a smile added, with the assurance of a strong profession of faith: "When the secrets are revealed, people will understand why it was so important for them to have many children. We are all waiting for the triumph of the Immaculate Heart of Mary!"

My heart leapt with joy because, without knowing it, Mirjana confirmed the mysterious relationship which links Fatima to Medjugorje. I looked at her and felt certain that Mirjana would see this triumph with her own eyes, in this world. Maybe she knew, too, how the triumph would come about?

"If I understand correctly what you have just said, something very beautiful will happen to all the little children the Gospa wishes us to

have?"[1]

"I hope you're not speaking for yourself! She said this for married couples!"

It was her own tactful and humorous way to make me understand that our conversation had come to an end, and that she would not add anything more. She had to prepare her children's meal, so I left her, looking forward to our next meeting.

---

[1] Listen to Sr. Emmanuel's audio cassette on this theme, *Story of a Wounded Womb*, ref. M8. (See the appendix at the end of the book for information on obtaining audio tapes).

FLASHBACK ON 1992

March 18: Mirjana's Yearly Apparition:

> "Dear children! I need your prayers now more than ever before. I beseech you to take the rosary in your hands now more than ever before. Grasp it strongly and pray with all your heart in these difficult times. Thank you for having gathered in such a number and for having responded to my call."

April 6: Serbs attacked Bosnia-Herzegovina. Beginning of the bombings. First victim in Siroki Brieg, 30 kilometers away from Medjugorje. First war fax of Sr. Emmanuel.

April 8: First Mass celebrated in the cellar of the presbytery, the church remaining closed until June 21.

May 7: Beginning of exodus of women and children. Only soldiers and elderly people remained in Medjugorje. All foreigners were requested to leave. Nevertheless, 4 members of the Beatitudes Community stayed to help. Movements of solidarity were launched: French and Italian transporters replaced pilgrims' buses by food trucks.

May 8: Two Migs tried to bomb Medjugorje, but a supernatural phenomenon prevented them from doing so. One of the planes was shot down. The pilot's testimony prompted a front page article in the Nov. 9, 1992 *Wall Street Journal*, "Forward unto Battle? Not here where the Virgin Reigns").

May 10: Two bombs missed their target next to the gas station of Medjugorje, at Tromedja's crossroads.

June 17: Father Jozo met John Paul II. "I am with you," said the Holy Father; "Protect Medjugorje."

June 24: First March for Peace, from Humac to Medjugorje (12 kms.), a German initiative. Mgr. Franic celebrated the evening Mass.

June 25: Ivanka's Yearly Apparition:
"I ask you to conquer Satan. The arms to conquer him are fasting and prayers. Pray for peace, because Satan wants to destroy the little peace you have."

August 5: French TV station, Antenne 2, aired the interview of one of the parents from Dovoj Camp. The existence of Serbian concentration camps in Bosnia began to be revealed.

September 14: Mgr. Radko Peric took over Mgr. Zanic's function as Bishop of Mostar. Only he was installed in Néum, for the bishopric of Mostar had been destroyed.

November 4: The UN peace-keeping troops arrived in Medjugorje (Miletina).

November 28: Vicka, the visionary, went to Lourdes.

1993

— Message of January 25, 1993 —

"Dear children, today I call you to accept and live my messages with seriousness. These days are the days when you need to decide for God, for peace, and for the good. May every hatred and jealousy disappear from your life and your thoughts, and may there only dwell love for God and for your neighbor. Thus, and only thus, shall you be able to discern the signs of this time. I am with you, and I guide you into a new time, a time which God gives you as grace, so that you may get to know Him more. Thank you for having responded to my call!"

NARROW ESCAPE FOR NIKOLA!

It was a Friday evening and we were preparing for the Shabbat. We had hardly started singing psalms around the table when the front door opened with a bang and the figure of our dearest Nikola appeared before us. His face was covered in grime. He had a 5-day beard and looked haggard... He had just come back from the front line in Mostar and his arm was wounded. A kind nurse in Citluk had applied a makeshift bandage which was already smeared with blood.

For the first 15 minutes, Nikola could do nothing except repeat, "Mostar is hell! Mostar is hell!" His staring eyes spoke of the horrifying visions he had seen. Little by little he described what had happened: "It was crawling with snipers," he told us, "and they were shooting right, left, and center. It was a merciless massacre! We lost several men. Myself and 2 other buddies were aiming at a Moslem position but we hadn't spotted a Moslem sniper on our tail. The guy tried to shoot us down. Fortunately, he missed his target, but the bullet went through my arm! As a result, I flung myself into a hole just in front of me but the guy kept on firing. If it hadn't been for that hole I would have been riddled with bullets! My arm was pumping blood."

"Were you scared?" I asked.

"No, when I got into the hole, my first reaction was to pray for the Moslem who had shot me. I truly felt God's protection, because my buddies had dug the hole just 2 hours earlier! Incredible!"

Indeed, the Gospel is taught to us by the poor and the humble...

Nikola, a Croatian friend brought up in France, had recently enlisted with the Croatian units in Medjugorje. You name it and he's done it! What a life story! Now he was trying hard to convert, and we had more or less "adopted" him. He knew that he was welcome in our house at any time of the day or night. His life has been anything but dull!

That winter, in order to show the Gospa that he was really *determined* to convert, he fasted for 9 days on bread and water. He then left for the front line, coming back 3 days later, stating proudly, "I really feel that I'm converted! Before, whenever I saw the corpse of a Serb at the front, I used to pray that he would go to hell. But now, guess what? I say to God, 'Lord, let him go to heaven, but stick him in purgatory at least for 100 years first! After all, he is a Serb!'"

He was perfectly serious. We gently teased him, "Nikola, do you know what Jesus said?: *For with the judgment you make you will be judged, and the measure you give will be the measure you get.'"* (Matt 7:2)

"What? He said that!" Nikola responded, flabbergasted.

Two weeks later, he returned as pleased as punch! "It's a real miracle!" he told me. "You know what? Now, when I see the body of a Serb, I say to God, 'Lord, don't send him to purgatory! Rather, let him go straight to heaven...even though he is a Serb!' Do you realize, Emmanuel, what this means for me? It has to be a miracle!"

— Message of February 25, 1993 —

"Dear children! Today I bless you with my motherly blessing and I invite you all to conversion. I wish that each of you decide for a change of life and that each of you work more in the Church not through words and thoughts but through example, so that your life may be a joyful testimony for Jesus. You cannot say that you are converted, because your life must become a daily conversion.

"In order to understand what you have to do, little children, pray and God will give you what you concretely have to do, and where you have to change. I am with you and place you all under my mantle. Thank you for having responded to my call."

A MOUNTAIN GOAT REFUSES CONFESSION

It was November of 1985, and it was pouring cats and dogs over Medjugorje. Veronika had just arrived at the Cilics' house and was finishing her dinner. Her trip had exhausted her. Tracy, a young American woman who had also recently arrived, joined her for coffee. A strong friendship developed between them. They talked late into the night.

"My roots are here," explained Veronika. "I was born in Yugoslavia, 72 years ago! Together, my husband and I tried to escape the Nazis. I was 9 months pregnant at the time. We walked and walked towards the border. In order to avoid being seen, we went through the woods. But a few yards from the border, the dogs of the SS guards began to bark. I was way behind my husband since I was having trouble walking. Then I saw him fall. The SS guards had shot him down. The dogs ran barking towards me. I was terrified. I prayed to the Gospa, asking for protection, and the dogs quietly lay down at my feet. I spent part of the night there before I could slip across the border without even being noticed! The dogs? They turned into little lambs. That very same day I gave birth to my son. Afterwards I emigrated to Australia as a refugee.

"This is the first time I have ever been back to Yugoslavia. I've always loved Our Lady, but I bear a grudge against God. I've had such a tough life! I only have a quarter of a kidney left, and I need dialysis every other day in order to survive. When I heard that the Gospa was appearing here, I decided to come and see my homeland again and to be reconciled with God. I've never been back to confession since my husband's death. I told the Gospa that I would go to her in Medjugorje and that I would make the Stations of the Cross on Mount Krizevac, to obtain the grace of a good confession.

"But I only have a few hours left! Because of the dialysis, I have to leave tomorrow for Zagreb on the 2:00 p.m. bus. What an odyssey it has been for me to get here, you wouldn't believe it! The trip took me 22 days from Melbourne! I had to stop over in Hong Kong for dialysis, again in Bombay, and yet again in Tel Aviv. I could go on! And now, I don't even have 24 hours to spend in Medjugorje. And this awful rain doesn't let up! Going up to Krizevac this evening looks out of the question..."

"Oh, but tomorrow the weather will be fine!" answered Tracy, spontaneously. "You have come such a long way, and have made such a long trip to obtain the grace of a good confession that there is no doubt that the Blessed Mother will stop the rain so you can go up Mount Krizevac!"

"Do you think so?" asked Veronika.

"I'm positive! Besides, I'll go with you. I'll wake you up at 5:00 a.m. and we could leave by 6. The weather will be nice, just you wait and see!"

Tracy aimed her faith at drying the mountains rather than at moving them!

But at 5 the next morning, it was still pouring. She woke up Veronika, who refused to hear of making the trip.

"If the rain stops by 6, I will get up. Otherwise, forget it!" retorted Veronika.

Every half hour Tracy put her nose outside the door. It was raining harder than ever. At 8 she returned to the attack.

"We really should go now," she pressed. "If we wait even more, it will be too late for you to catch the bus. It's still raining, but you'll see, the minute we're outside the sun will come out!"

Doubtful, Veronika climbed out of bed. She had her breakfast to the accompaniment of the deafening roar and gurgle of the gutters pouring their overflow onto the cement terrace. The whole project seemed a total disaster.

"As an act of faith, leave your umbrella here," Tracy gently insisted as she opened the door.

Veronika couldn't believe her eyes: the minute she set foot outside, the black clouds disappeared and the sun showed its face!

The two of them headed straight for the mountain, but Veronika was having a hard time. At the age of 72, with only a quarter of a kidney and after traveling for 22 days, climbing was tough! Tracy walked in front to help her. Suddenly, just between the first and second stations on the Way of the Cross, Tracy saw in front of her a cross radiant with light. Dazzled, she fell to her knees, and allowed herself to be filled with the presence of God, like the prophet on Mount Horeb. Her heart pounded wildly out of indescribable joy.

She looked back. Veronika was down as well, lying face down on the path and sobbing. Ten minutes passed, 10 minutes which will remain the King's secret for these two hearts. Then the shining cross disappeared, and the two women continued their climb. But, to their amazement, they didn't feel the ascent or the sharp little stones under their feet, or even the slightest fatigue. They had become true little mountain goats! Both the young one and the elderly one reached the top of the mountain in record time. At the foot of the big cement cross[1] they prayed ardently to God and went back down with the same surprisingly light step.

Tracy broke the silence to express her joy to Veronika: "Well, you made it! You've received the grace to make a good confession. We'll probably manage to find a priest around the church before you catch the bus."

"No, I don't want to go to confession!" Veronika replied, as she jumped from rock to rock. "I'm leaving straight away!"

Tracy was baffled. Several times more she offered to find a priest, but Veronika scolded her more and more. It was her irrevocable decision. She wouldn't go to confession! She was almost angry. The bus left, and Veronika was gone.

Feeling miserable, Tracy went to the church and begged the Lord to keep a firm hold on her dear Veronika. "The Evil One must have sneaked into this," she thought to herself, "especially after having been given such a sign and such a grace! How could she leave clammed up like this! I can't believe it!"

---

[1] This cross contains a relic of the True Cross. It was erected in 1933 for the nineteen-hundredth anniversary of the Redemption. The Gospa asks that people pray before this cross, and she at times appears there to pray with us. Great graces are granted at this spot.

Many weeks passed. One evening, the phone rang. It was Veronika. She was calling from Australia!

"Tracy? Oh, let me tell you! You've been praying so much for me! I want to give you a great consolation. You remember when I left Medjugorje, how I didn't want to go to confession. It took me 3 weeks to get back home, and I kept this refusal still alive within me. Something was blocking me inside. But when I reached Melbourne, just as I was going down the plane's gangway, I was struck by a deep feeling of repentance. It was so sudden! All the sins of my life flashed before me, one by one. It was so strong that I couldn't wait another minute! After leaving the airport, I ran to the nearest church, found a priest, and went to confession. What an amazing confession! Forty years of sins, of terrible sins, can you imagine?"

"So the grace of Krizevac had a delayed timing device!" said Tracy.

"And listen! There is more to it! After this confession, Jesus spoke to my heart. He granted me the grace to say the Our Father with the heart, and he asked me to spend the rest of my life praying the Our Father constantly. I received this grace and, for 3 weeks now, this prayer has been dwelling in me constantly, day and night."

"The Our Father, constantly?" Tracy asked.

"And there's more! You remember I told you how difficult my life had been since my husband died? I wanted to make it all by myself. As I was always afraid to be short, I accumulated heaps of material things. I kept hoarding everything for myself. Even my son couldn't get anything from me. Money, money, money! I just had to have more and more. There was no charity in me. After my confession, Jesus changed all this. I was given the grace to renounce material things and all my belongings.[2] I sold everything off. I gave part of the money to my son, and the rest to the poor. I sold my house and got a little room in a convent, to spend the last years of my life in prayer. After this phone call, I will be flat broke, as I decided to use my last few dollars to call you in Medjugorje. I wanted to share my happiness with you and to thank you."

---

[2] The holy Cure of Ars used to say: "When you get a rich person to open up his wallet, you save his soul!"

— MESSAGE OF MARCH 18, 1993 —
(Annual apparition to Mirjana...)

"Dear children! This is my desire: give me your hands so I can carry you like a mother onto the right path, so I can carry you towards your Father. Open your heart and let me come in. Pray, because I'm with you in your prayer. Pray and I will be able to guide you. I will take you to peace and happiness."

OH! REMEMBER THAT NIGHT?!

I came across this story completely by chance. It's one of the many stories which reveal the hidden Medjugorje of those first years: "happenings" of the heart which you don't find in books but which have knocked people off their feet, won them over, and made them the best witnesses for the Gospa. These are the people who today would do anything for her.

After evening Mass, I decided to go straight home, and so I walked towards the parking lot. When I reached the rectory, I was about to pass a small group of 3 or 4 people when I couldn't help overhearing the following:

"And can you remember that night when she kissed us?"

I recognized the happy, ringing voice of Mark, a very good friend, and then that of Draga, Vicka's cousin, and then Ivan's voice replying: "I will never forget that night..."

My heart missed a beat, because everyone who lives in Medjugorje knows that when we say "she," without stating a first name, we're talking about the Gospa. It's the local tradition. So...had she kissed them? Draga seemed full of enthusiasm, and as for Mark...he was in heaven.

I went up to him.

"I'm sorry, but I overheard some of your conversation. Tell me, seriously, did she kiss you? You don't have to tell me if you don't want to!"

And so, with Draga's help, Mark told me the whole story.

"It was on July 24, 1984. After evening Mass, I climbed up Krizevac with about 10 other young people from the village. When I got to the cross I held back a bit in order to pray, but then Draga came and asked me to join the others. Vicka had just told everyone that the Blessed Mother was going to appear during the third Our Father. We all knelt down, and when we got to the third Our Father, Vicka's voice disappeared and all we could hear was the sound of her teeth chattering.

"So I started to tell Our Lady of all the people I wanted to pray for, when suddenly, Vicka got up. We were very surprised, because the apparition was still taking place. We got up, too. Then Vicka stretched out her right arm and, still staring at the cross, put her arm round the waist of the person closest to her. I wondered what on earth was happening, but did not have the slightest idea!

"After standing next to Vicka for a little more than a minute, the girl went back to her place. Then Vicka got hold of a second person and did the same thing with all of us, one at a time. I was the fourth. Vicka held me firmly. We were standing in front of the cross. Various questions went through my mind: Was I supposed to see something? Or someone? Was I supposed to do something? Since I didn't get an answer, I prayed a Hail Mary and then surrendered myself completely, thinking, 'If I'm going to receive something, I'm ready. If I'm not going to receive anything, I'm still ready.' At that moment, I was filled with indescribable sensations of joy and peace. Returning to my place, with that peace, it seemed as though my heart wasn't big enough to contain it all. I said to myself, 'I want to keep this happiness forever...'

"Meanwhile, the others were taking their turn with Vicka. When everyone had finished his turn, we prayed 4 Our Fathers and Glory Be's, and Vicka talked with the Blessed Mother for a little while. Then she said out loud, 'Ode,' which means: 'She's going.'

"After the apparition, Vicka told us what had happened. She had presented each one of us to the Gospa, who had not only blessed each one of us individually, but had also kissed us!

"Before walking down the hill, we prayed 3 Our Fathers and Glory Be's for unbelievers and one for us.

"That sense of joy and peace stayed within me for more than one year. It was as though heaven was in my heart! Every time I prayed, every time I went into a church, every time I saw a statue of Jesus or Mary, I could feel that happiness. In the evening my jaw sometimes ached from having smiled so much.

"The years have passed and I don't feel it in the same way now. Sometimes I find it hard to pray. But I tell myself that every Hail Mary I say is a kiss from me to the Gospa..."

— MESSAGE OF MARCH 25, 1993 —

"Dear children! Today like never before I call you to pray for peace, peace in your hearts, peace in your families and peace in the whole world, because Satan wants war, wants lack of peace, wants to destroy all that is good. Therefore, dear children, pray, pray, pray. Thank you for having responded to my call."

TORN BETWEEN TWO LOVERS

Sarah was at the end of her rope. After 16 years of marriage, she arrived in Medjugorje with her husband in 1991. Sarah was in love with 2 men at the same time. She couldn't sleep, and the pain she felt because of her torn heart exhausted her even more. For 2 years the passionate love which had re-emerged for an old friend never gave her a break. Yet she loved her husband deeply, but did not understand how she could love 2 men at the same time and in such different ways.

She had found her faith at the age of 18. At that time Jesus was everything to her, the meaning of her life and the source of her joy. But when she turned 23, her heart was lit on fire with a ravenous and passionate love for a married man with children. She lost control and lived an intense relationship with him until the day he lost interest in her. She was broken-hearted. Still, she got over it, and married Bertrand, who shared her faith and had the same vision of life as she had. True love united them, a different kind of love, but a very deep one.

However, 20 years later, although the "married man" had kept only distant, but friendly, ties with Sarah, they met, and their tête à tête turned out to be overwhelming. Obviously the man had changed, and an uncontrollable passion suddenly burned within Sarah. The extinct volcano became active once again, now more than ever! Temptations assaulted her mind and body and they peaked when the man suggested they could spend a weekend together.

"Okay, it will be a deep spiritual encounter and I will respect you," he told her when she spelled out her wishes before accepting the invitation.

But Sarah was not fooled. True enough, she wished to bring this man closer to God. But there was no point in denying it, she also dreamed of being in his arms. The prospect of a weekend aroused deep anxiety within her. After postponing the meeting several times, she finally canceled it. "The Lord protected me," she told me later.

But the passion still raged within. Day and night she "lived with him." She remembered each word of his. She visualized his eyes and trembled at the sound of his voice.

The Evil One was turning this into an obsession, harassing her relentlessly. He kept on suggesting that letting herself go with this man would be *no big deal* and that it would be the most *natural* thing: "You already knew him and loved him once, what difference will it make to do it one more time? Okay, you swore not to betray your marriage, but *this* is different. He is an old and very dear friend of yours. You will be able to talk to him about God! And, if you happen to have a physical relationship together, well, it won't be that bad since it will be really nothing new..."

These thoughts plagued her, even in prayer.[1] Sarah was deeply troubled, all the more since she knew deep within that this weekend was not the will of God. She had to admit the truth: she was not capable of seeing this man without committing adultery. She definitely wanted to see him and save him at any cost, but God was asking her to renounce this because he had a completely different plan.

Was it mere coincidence that all of a sudden the relationship with her husband worsened? Some of his faults began to get on her nerves, and a professional setback forced Sarah to go back to work. Things could not have been much worse!

However, Sarah did have *one* thing in her life, something extraordinary, something which saved her and that she had known from the age of 18. She summed it up humbly in 3 words: "I've always prayed."

"In the darkest hour of my ordeal," she said to me, "I cried out to Mary. During the night, although I doubted I would ever find peace again, I kept on praying. Disappointed hope made me very sad, and I doubted whether Mary could heal the wounds of my heart. Before this ordeal, I had already begun to live Our Lady's messages in Medjugorje, and for 5 years I had been praying the rosary. My husband had always prayed the rosary, but alone, for at the time I had no interest in it. I though it was a rather dull and stupid prayer. But, as Mary spoke about the peace of the heart and peace in the family, I held onto these words although I couldn't remember what the peace of God felt like..."

Sarah arrived in Medjugorje with her husband in a state of utter confusion:

"I brought this tumultuous experience I was living to Mary in Medjugorje. On the way back, I wondered what graces she could possibly have granted me, for no remarkable event had occurred during my pilgrimage. We had ended our stay with the consecration to Mary during Mass on the last day. But as the weeks went by, I discovered that I was a totally different person. I was at peace! I had never before in my life felt such a peace. I had surrendered my passion and my daily concerns to God through Mary. All the grievances which had accumulated in my married life had vanished. For a long time, there had been something in my love for my husband which had been hurting me like a thorn, something I couldn't cope with. Now, I accept my husband as he is, and I love him just the way he is. The insurmountable barrier has disappeared. Even the permanent state of anxiety within the very depths of my life is also a thing of the past. I am happy!

"Since Medjugorje, we have been praying the rosary very faithfully, and our children have followed too. Our family is united and I am constantly amazed at the depth of harmony between us. God did the best thing: he brought my husband and me closer together.

"And what about my passion for the other man? That bond has been broken as if by itself.

"I feel fine and I sleep easy. Mary has given me her peace!"

---

[1] Concerning Satan's plan to tear apart and destroy families, listen to Sister Emmanuel's cassette *Story of a Wounded Womb*, ref. M8. (See the appendix at the end of the book for information on obtaining audio tapes).

— Message of April 25, 1993 —

"Dear children! Today I invite you all to awaken your hearts to love. Go into nature and look how nature is awakening and it will be a help to you to open your hearts to the love of God, the Creator. I desire you to awaken love in your families so that where there is unrest and hatred, love will reign and when there is love in your hearts, then there is also prayer.

"And, dear children, do not forget that I am with you and I am helping you with my prayer that God may give you the strength to love. I bless and love you with my motherly love. Thank you for having responded to my call."

GO AND RAISE THE DEAD!

My job does not consist in rummaging through the trash cans of Medjugorje (at every corner and always full to overflowing!) in order to expose whatever is ugly. On the contrary, like a pearl diver, I want to bring what is marvelous out into the open so that a beautiful thanksgiving prayer may ascend to God.

However, this selectiveness in my reports doesn't mean we are naive, or see this village through rose-colored glasses. In Medjugorje, things can be rosy, blue, or red, but they can also be black.

The other day, Karlo, Vicka's cousin, was remembering his childhood.

"As a child, when I walked home through the streets at dusk," he told me, "I could hear every family praying the rosary. My steps were in rhythm with the Our Fathers and the Hail Marys coming from each window. Today, if I walk along the same way, all I hear is the sound of the television programs. How sad! We haven't recognized this time of visitation. The situation is serious."

Father Jozo himself often observes how television has replaced prayer in families. "Islam and Communism tried for centuries to destroy people's fervor, and they failed," he said. "But money did it in 10 years!"

These 2 comments echo the Gospa's cry: Do not abandon prayer! Indeed, if you do, there is no hope! Without prayer, our hearts register a flat EKG as regards love.

At the beginning of the apparitions, the Gospa gave the visionaries some very interesting insights concerning the realities of heaven and purgatory.

In heaven, the saints have very personalized relationships of love. They know each other in the full light of God, soul to soul, and they communicate in a way which is unknown here on earth. Each chosen one knows who has prayed for him while on earth, or while he suffered in purgatory. The Lord allows the elect and his *benefactor* to have an eternal and special relationship within the Mystical Body. If today I say these simple words: "Father, bless James who faces hardships," James and I will have a kindred spirit of love in heaven, forever. These few words and the grace that they have poured out upon James will remain an inexhaustible source of wonder and joy in his heart, for his degree of glory will have been increased by this grace. When we are in heaven, we will know with accuracy the smallest sacrifice, the least prayer that someone has made or said for us (among men, but also among angels). We will enjoy all kinds of favors from God, and we will know who obtained them for us, how, when and at what expense![1] We will come to understand the astounding and infinite value of the least prayer. The splendor of the Communion of Saints will unfold before our eyes.

Souls which do not pray cannot decide by themselves for conversion, to forsake a particular sin, to be self-denying and to practice charity, to be detached from money, to forgive an enemy, etc. Such souls are in a way lifeless. According to St. Catherine of Sienna, they are one of the "dead children in the womb of the Church." However, my prayer can obtain for these souls the step towards the good that they cannot make by themselves. One day, such a soul will make a good decision and save his very life. But

---

[1] Generally (but not systematically) the souls in purgatory know who is praying for them on earth. If we pray for a soul who is already in heaven, God uses our prayer for another soul who will be eternally thankful to us. We may expect many surprises!

who will have obtained this grace for him? The answer will be known only in heaven.

In this way, within the very heart of the Beatific Vision which will be our eternal joy, the happiness of the chosen ones will consist partly of the interwoven threads of love and gratitude existing between them. A wonder of the Mystical Body!

When someone renounces the world and commits himself to prayer, he chooses to specialize in a wonderful profession: raising the dead! I have often wondered why nobody obeys this clear commandment of Jesus; *"Raise the dead!"* Where is the present-day Lazarus who cries out: "I was dead for 4 days when someone said to me: 'rise up!'?" Of course, Jesus does not want us to go into cemeteries and scream, "Come on, everybody! Make a move! Wake up!" That's not the point.

In Medjugorje, Mary gives me the key to this commandment: each prayer of mine will touch some paralyzed soul and raise him up. When I reach heaven, he will leap like a deer towards me and we will embrace joyfully, because that man who was dead has returned to life. I also will learn that if I did not sink while I, too, was in the depths, it is thanks to someone who prayed for me.

Sadly enough, preferring television to prayer[2] prevents us from hearing the cries of the dead. Who will rescue them?

It is Satan who wants to make couch potatoes of us, consumers of emptiness, surfing maniacs.

In Medjugorje, church attendance grew poorer and poorer when Santa Barbara[3] was broadcast during the hour of Mass. Santa Barbara? Really? Well, not the saint!

There certainly is a St. Barbara in heaven. But I suspect this saint is constantly whispering in our ears: "Don't make the wrong choice! Don't choose the wrong happiness! Click the off button, turn off the TV! Unplug it and get up! Go and raise the dead!"

---

[2] The visionaries told me that the Gospa never said we should throw our TV sets away (she never said we should keep them either!). But she often invites us to turn them off, especially during the novenas which precede major Feast days. Once again, she leaves us free to decide everything out of love and not out of constraint.

[3] The soap opera, nonsense which glorifies what the Lord rebukes: the fascination of money, the arrogance associated with wealth, impurity, and lust for power.

— MESSAGE OF MAY 25, 1993 —

"Dear children! Today I invite you to open yourselves to God by means of prayer, so that the Holy Spirit may begin to work miracles in you and through you. I am with you and I intercede before God for each one of you because, dear children, each one of you is important in my plan of salvation. I invite you to be carriers of good and peace. God can give you peace only if you convert and pray. Therefore, my dear little children, pray, pray, pray and do that which the Holy Spirit inspires you. Thank you for having responded to my call."

A NORWEGIAN CONQUEST

Denis Nolan remembers:

"It was a terribly cold evening in the university town of Notre Dame, Indiana. However, the weekly TV show on Medjugorje, in which I invited viewers to join me in praying the rosary the following week at 'Fatima Retreat Center,' had been recorded a month earlier on a beautifully sunny day. As it happened, it wasn't possible for us to meet inside the Centre on the arranged evening. So, we had to pray outside! I was concerned at the thought of possible pneumonia cases. It had been snowing and people would have to kneel in front of the Gospa's statue for a long time. But nothing stops the Children of Medjugorje! Come rain, hail, or snow, the prayer group would go ahead as usual!

Just at that moment, a woman arrived by taxi. Feeling awful about not having warned people about the cold weather, I offered to run her back into town after the meeting. She gratefully accepted.

On the way back to town, she told me her story:

"My husband and I, along with our daughters, arrived in Notre Dame 6 months ago. We come from Norway. My husband was doing some research at the University. When we first arrived, I was shocked at the statues of the Blessed Mother dotted all around the campus. It seemed like idolatry to me, even sacrilege! A month after our arrival on October 6, 1991, I noticed a book in the campus bookshop with Our Lady of Medjugorje on the cover. I picked it up on an impulse and started reading it. I couldn't put it down. I bought the book and read it in one go. From start to finish!

"I read through the night, and the following morning I made my way to the Basilica of the Sacred Heart. I had barely put my nose in the door, when I heard a priest talking about the rosary. In that instant I became absolutely convinced that all I had just read on Medjugorje was true! I rushed to Corby Hall, the priests' lodgings and knocked on the door. The Superior answered. I tried to explain to him what was happening within me. However, I suspect that as I was talking so quickly and vehemently, I terrorized the holy man! When he finally understood what I was saying, he asked me *the* question: 'Okay, so what do you want? Do you want to become a Catholic?'

"'Yes,' I immediately replied."

Gurti Blomberg was received into the Catholic Church at Easter the following year. Her enthusiasm in serving the Gospa and in spreading the messages of Medjugorje is endless. She's written to the Norwegian Catholic press, reproaching it for not having published a single line on Medjugorje. She's even sent them an account of her own experience so they can publish it. She would often rent a VCR, carrying it home on her bicycle, just so her family could watch a video on Medjugorje!

---

[1] Only 2% of Norwegians are Catholic.

[2] The Gospa has a really soft spot for Protestants...

I met a famous Anglican psychiatrist who led a deep prayer life and lived close to Christ. He came to Medjugorje to inquire about Mary's apparitions which were a question with him. He was cautious about the devotion to Mary, fearing that it might be an obstacle on the path towards Jesus. He was therefore on the lookout upon arrival in the village.

I met him the evening he got here. With tears in his eyes, he told me: "I heard Jesus' voice as I was going towards the church. He said to me, 'I myself asked my Mother to come here. She draws all the people here and brings them to me. All generations shall call her blessed.'" The next day he received the same word. Since that time Our Lady has become for him a spring board to Jesus.

Another time I brought a Swiss Protestant pastor to see Vicka. Hearing her say that Mary had cried because we (Catholics) had forgotten the Bible, he found that he could only sympathize with the Mother of God. "In that case," he said to me, with a grin on his face, "She's one of us!"

Gurti has now gone back to Norway. She openly declares that her purpose in life now is to convert Norway to Catholicism.[1] She sings in the parish choir, and every Friday a small group led by the parish priest gathers together to pray the rosary.

Gurti tells everyone about the wonderful things the Gospa does. This isn't always easy, since a large proportion of her relations are anti-Catholic. However, things are happening around her. Heaven, seeing her confidence, grants miracle after miracle!"[2]

— Message of June 25, 1993 —

"Dear children! Today I also rejoice at your presence here. I bless you with my motherly blessing and intercede for each one of you before God. I call you anew to live my messages and to put them into life and practice. I am with you and bless all of you day by day. Dear children, these are special times and, therefore, I am with you to love and protect you; to protect your hearts from Satan and to bring you all closer to the heart of my Son, Jesus. Thank you for having responded to my call."

I COULDN'T KNEEL!

It's always a delight for me to meet Father Albert Shamon (from New York), who has the most mischievous sense of humor. We love to share our latest jokes together and update our collection! The quality of his theology and his deep attachment to the Church are well known throughout the United States. One day, he decided to form his own opinion once and for all about the reported apparitions in Medjugorje. He made the best possible decision; he opted to go and see for himself![1] (That's being a good shepherd!)

He tells about his first day:

"A bit apprehensive, I decided to carry the Blessed Sacrament on me, as a priest would on sick call. I felt that if these apparitions were from the devil, the presence of Our Lord would raise a holy war with him!

"When I arrived, a large crowd had already gathered at the door leading to the room of the apparitions. I thought I would never be able to

---

[1] This was also the case with Fr. Svetozar Kraljevic, a Croatian Franciscan residing in the US. He tells the story of his fantastic adventure in *Pilgrimage*. Available from Paraclete Press, Orleans, MA 02653. Tel: 1-800-451-5006.

get in, but the Franciscan who guarded the door noticed me and beckoned. He held back the crowd and told me to enter. I attributed this privilege to the Blessed Sacrament which I was carrying.

"The room was packed to the rafters. Even though I was pushed against the wall, I was content just to be there. Marija and Jakov, escorted by Father Slavko, came and knelt in the doorway, and they began to pray the rosary. They stopped at the third Sorrowful Mystery. Father Slavko came into the room and cleared a spot for the visionaries. That was fine, because everyone in front of me had been removed, and I found myself right next to Marija!

"The moment of the apparition came, and at a gesture from Father Slavko everyone knelt. Everyone except me! I tried to kneel, but somehow my knees locked. I was embarrassed that I couldn't kneel, so I bowed low in order not to attract attention. That evening, when I concelebrated Mass, my knees were fine.

"The second night, I decided to try my luck once again,[2] and stood before the door. The same Franciscan hailed me and told me to go into the apparition room. I thanked Jesus, whom I was still carrying, for this unusual favor. I went in, and again, when Our Lady appeared, I couldn't kneel! I tried and tried again, but in vain. Once again, I had to bow low.

"Still carrying the Blessed Sacrament, I was allowed to go inside the apparition room a third time. As my knees still locked, I asked Our Lady to tell me why. She seemed to say, 'I do not want my Son to kneel before me.'

"I left Medjugorje convinced of the authenticity of what was happening there."

---

[2] For obvious reasons of fairness, it is unusual to be allowed more than once to attend an apparition.

Several booklets of Fr. Albert Shamon are recommended: *Three Steps to Sanctity; The Power of the Rosary; Let the Holy Mass Be Your Life; Pray the Creed Prayer at Medjugorje; Monthly Confession — Remedy for the West*. Available from The Riehle Foundation, PO Box 7, Milford, OH USA 45150-0007. Fax: (513) 576-0022.

— Message of July 25, 1993 —

"Dear children! I thank you for your prayers and for the love you show towards me. I invite you to decide to pray for my intentions. Dear children, offer novenas, making sacrifices wherein you feel the most bound. I want your life to be bound to me.

"I am your Mother, little children, and I do not want Satan to deceive you, for he wants to lead you the wrong way, but he cannot if you do not permit him. Therefore, little children, renew prayer in your hearts, and then you will understand my call and my live desire to help you. Thank you for having responded to my call."

HE WAS JUST LIKE JESUS

Francis was born in December 1980 in Glasgow, Scotland. His parents soon discovered that he was impulsive and quick-tempered, though extremely appealing. At the age of 5, while he was playing outside, he was run over by an ice-cream van.

Francis' little body was severely damaged, and he was disfigured for life. A long way of the cross began for the little blind boy, who dreamed of jumping and running after the birds, but, most of all, of seeing the face of his mother once again. One of his kidneys was removed, as it had become cancerous. Margaret, who had been his sponsor at Confirmation, visited him every day either at home or at the hospital and talked to him about Jesus. He learned to pray, and his parents sometimes caught him talking to Jesus, using the deeply moving words of a love relationship. Still, day by day, Francis' condition grew progressively worse. The cancer became general, and, in spite of frequent chemotherapy sessions, death overshadowed the little boy.

It was then that his parents took him to Medjugorje. Francis was 6. Strangely enough, although he was in great pain, the young boy never complained. Margaret never so much as left him for a single second during their visit to Medjugorje, except during the rosary and Holy Mass. At those times he was placed in the care of Nora, Marija's friend. His parents, very humble folk, didn't venture to ask to attend an apparition. At that time, in July 1987, the Gospa appeared in a tiny little room of the rectory, and everyone had to wait their turn if they wanted to attend.

During these days, Nora kept Francis on her lap throughout the rosary. They would sit under a tree because of the scorching heat. As Francis couldn't see with his eyes, he wanted to see with his hands so that he could *feel* the expression on people's faces. As the rosary began in Croatian, Nora translated each word to Francis. Soon, though, she sensed that this little 6-year-old darling would be the one who would teach her how to pray, as he knew quite a lot about Jesus.

"But you don't know how to pray!" he said suddenly.

"Okay, Francis! Then you will have to teach me how to pray the rosary."

"Do you want to know how Jesus prayed the rosary?"

"Well, yes... Did Jesus pray the rosary?"

"Yes, of course, the Child Jesus prayed the rosary!" (It sounded like: "How could you possibly not know that at your age?!")

"But how could he say the rosary? These words are the words that the angel spoke to his mother!"

"But the angel only repeated what he had heard! In heaven, God speaks like this to Mary! All that the angel did was pass on what he had received from God!"

Nora remained silent, to let the little boy pray in his own way.

"Hail Mary, full of grace...," he said, ever so slowly. He stopped, full of joy. Suddenly a cry full of wonder burst from his lips: "Oh Mummy! Of course you are full of grace; you are full of Me!"

Nora understood from this joyous outcry that Jesus himself was celebrating *his* Mother. God himself was saying: "Hail Mary, full of grace!" The Father had spoken to Mary, and the Child Jesus repeated the words that he had heard the Father say.

Francis grew more and more bewildered by Nora's lack of knowledge, but he continued with the prayer. He whispered, "The Lord is with you... Oh Mummy, do you think that I would ever leave you?"

All Nora could do was remain silent and hold back her tears.

That was how Nora and Francis prayed the rosary. Then, out of the blue, the authorization came for him to join the visionaries for the apparition, and he went to the apparition room. Nora, who remained outside, prayed, convinced that Francis would return healed. Her faith was so strong! All she could do was give thanks in advance for the gift of healing.

Shortly before Mass, Francis left the rectory and was handed over to Nora once again. She gave him his favorite spot: on her lap, as always. Still, she soon noticed that the child was squirming more than usual. Nora realized that he had not been healed. She said nothing, as she was speechless with sorrow.

"Don't you want to know what Our Lady did when she came?" Francis asked.

"Well, yes!" Nora replied. "What did she do? Tell me!"

"Well, she came and then I was healed!"

Francis felt Nora's face with his fingers and detected her disappointment.

"All you think about is the body!" he said reproachfully.

"OK, Francis, then tell me more," Nora asked. "How have you been healed?'

Francis relived the scene of the apparition and joyfully explained to Nora: "You know, the Gospa had only been there for a second when I opened wide my heart, and I forgave the truck driver!"

Nora was dumfounded. Francis had never talked about his accident, his operations, or his sufferings. Had the truck driver been burdening his heart? He had been keeping this to himself over all these months?

With a smile of pure angelic joy, he exclaimed: "Now I'm free! Free! You know what I told Our Lady to thank her? I said, 'Mummy, I accept all my suffering but, in exchange, I ask you to free all the people who come here, just as you have freed me.'"

Francis was aware that he was dying of cancer. Nora remained silent and thought, "Now, for sure, he is going to die."

Then the young boy drew himself close to Nora's ear as if to share a wonderful secret.

"Yes, that's it, I'm going to die," he whispered.

What joy there was in his face! Although Francis was only 6, his happiness lay in the fact that his heart had been healed and he now had the freedom to love!

From that day on Francis sowed the love of Jesus wherever he went. The testimonies of other people could fill a book. Here are four of them:

Francis was not always easy-going. Sometimes, when frustrated, his face would go red with anger and he would stamp his feet and kick whatever was around. His mother wouldn't say anything to him, as she didn't want to add to his burden. In Medjugorje, however, the Gospa taught her a lesson or two. For example, she was not helping her little Francis by reacting like this. She had to scold him sometimes, gently but firmly, in order to help him mend his ways.

A few days after their stay in Medjugorje, back home, she asked Francis to put away one of his toys. She left the room. Francis was reluctant to do as he was told. Suddenly, she heard him stamp his feet and rebel. Remembering the words of the Gospa, she took a deep breath and headed straight for his room to scold him, when she heard: "Get behind me, Satan! You know that I have chosen to be good!" He calmed down and, noticing his mother standing in the doorway, he told her with a smile, "Mum? Did you ask me to do something? I'll do it right away!"

From that day on, his fits of anger disappeared completely. His mother knew that in Medjugorje, Francis had made up his mind: "*I choose holiness.*"

The second story happened a few months later in Fatima. Francis' parents still hoped for a physical healing. While the little group of pilgrims was making the Stations of the Cross with him in the beautiful park outside the shrine, Francis disappeared. His mother looked everywhere for him and found him just off the path, where the life-size statues of the angel of Fatima giving the Holy Eucharist to the 3 little visionaries stand. These statues, made of stone, are surrounded by protective fences. The mother couldn't believe her eyes: Francis was perched in the arms of the angel and was having a lively conversation with him! How did he end up there? (Remember, he was blind!)

"Francis! What are you up to?"

"I'm talking to the Angel of Peace, Mum..."

How did he know that this was the Angel of Peace? His friends helped him down. A little later, Francis' mother discreetly asked him, "What were you discussing with the Angel of Peace?"

"You know, Mum, there are sometimes secrets between the soul and God!"

The third episode was at the Children's General Hospital in Glasgow, where thousands of little ones suffer and die. Francis had been taken there because of the advanced stage of his cancer. However, when his parents came to see him, the youngster couldn't be found! This little blind boy, drawn and scrawny, crippled, and suffering indescribable pain, had disappeared into the other wards. He had pulled out all his tubes and intravenous drips, everything which held him prisoner and kept him from going from one room to another, and went to the bedside of other little patients. What was he doing? What was he telling them? If you got close, you could hear Francis speaking to them about Jesus, using words that only a little martyr could use. He consoled these little children and asked them to offer all their sufferings to Jesus so that there would be no more sin in the world.

The fourth episode took place on September 15, 1988, at Marija Pavlovic's home in Medjugorje. The telephone rang and Nora picked it up.

"Oh, Francis! Is it really you?" she asked.

"Yes, Nora. Is Marija home?" said the little voice. "Please tell her to ask the Gospa a favor for me, tonight when she comes. I would like Mary to promise me something: When I get to heaven, I wish she would give me the title of *Guardian Angel of Abandoned Children.* Okay?"

Our darling little Francis[1] departed to join the Father 17 days later, on October 2, 1988. It was the Feast of the Guardian Angels.

---

[1] See two photos of Francis.

— Message of August 25, 1993 —

"Dear children! I want you to understand that I am your Mother, that I want to help you and call you to prayer. Only by prayer can you understand and accept my messages and practice them in your life. Read Sacred Scripture, live it, and pray to understand the signs of the times. This is a special time. Therefore, I am with you to draw you close to my Heart and the Heart of my Son, Jesus. Dear little children, I want you to be children of the light and not of the darkness. Therefore, live what I am telling you. Thank you for having responded to my call."

THE ELECTRONIC APPOINTMENT

Paris, France, May 1994. My friend Bernadette P. had arranged for me to give a talk in St. Leo's Church in the part of town where I used to live when I was younger.

Three minutes before I was due to begin speaking, I found myself in that inescapable and awful situation: I had to check both the height and the volume of the microphone; adjust the lectern and put the book of messages on it in such a way that it wouldn't slide off; invite the people squeezing in at the back of the church to come forward; remind the parish priest of the correct pronunciation of the word "Medjugorje" for his introduction; realize that the woman who was supposedly in charge of the flowers hadn't arrived yet and reassure the other woman who had given her this responsibility; keep a low profile so that I wouldn't catch the eyes of all the dear friends in the audience and rush towards them to say hello; and get the first few words ready in my head for the kick-off and receive in my heart Our Lady's anointing, without which every single word would be dead and empty...

This was the moment that Francois chose to turn up, grab my arm and start pleading: "Sister, Sister! I've got to talk to you right now, it's incredible, Sister, I've got to tell you what happened, Sister, you're not going to believe it! I've got to tell you..."

I had never seen him before. Even though I didn't know him, I could never forget him because no stage make-up artist could have created a face like the one before me. All the physical and psychological suffering in the world were concentrated in this person, straight out of I don't know what drama. An unspeakable anxiety had devastated his face.

"Excuse me, but I have to begin in 2 minutes!"

"It can't wait. Oh Sister, let me tell you, I don't even know what's going to happen or what I'm doing here tonight..."

"If you don't know now, you'll find out very soon, during the talk!"

"What are you going to talk about?"

"Fatima and Medjugorje."

"What's that?"

"That's exactly what you're going to find out!"

He was shaking from head to toe and was preventing everyone from getting near me. He'd taken a little electronic address book out of his pocket and thrust it in front of my eyes so that I could read what was on the screen.

"What do you see, Sister?"

His hands were just as pale and scrawny as his face.

"I promise you I'll read it at leisure after the talk. Come and see me right here. But for now go and sit down over there and listen carefully to every word I'm going to say: there will be some messages for you!"

For just an instant his eyes lit up and I slipped away.

My time for the talk was strictly limited to one hour. People's souls, what a colossal stake! I knew that the audience was peppered with folks who seldom set foot inside a church, because I'd said to my friends, "Get the unbelievers to come. They're the ones I'll be talking to." In a word, I had one short hour before me to get them to discover and love God... I tried to do my best in spite of my deficiency. I did it with joy.

As expected, my little man was waiting for me just as I had finished my talk, brandishing excitedly his computer address book.

"Sister, you promised me..."

After a few brief chats with other people, I sat down behind a column with Francois. I had kept him for last, guessing that this story would be very, very unusual... His anxiety had diminished visibly, but I could tell from his restless manner of speaking that he was still terribly stressed inside.

"I listened carefully to it all, Sister! I would never have thought that all that could happen. I loved the whole story, and now I understand why I had to come here. I'm just overwhelmed!"

While he was talking, I scrutinized his poor ravaged face. His hair, permed and dyed blond, his carefully plucked eyebrows and the gold ring in his left ear only served to underscore the misery on his face. "Maybe I'm talking to someone who's dying?" I thought. "He's so skinny!" He was actually shaking. Could it be some virus that was sapping him?

"I've been through a terrible time, Sister. I was living with someone who died from AIDS 2 weeks ago. I loved him so much that I couldn't live without him. All day long, I keep asking, "Where is he? Where is he?" I call to him. I know it's stupid, but he was my friend and now I don't have anyone! Yesterday I grabbed my address book to look up a number and what did I see on the screen? An incomprehensible message which I hadn't written! I read it and read it again. I couldn't figure out how these lines could have been written because I always keep the book on me. Here, take a look for yourself, Sister."

I looked at the screen and saw, "Tuesday, May 17, 8 p.m., St. Leo's."

"But that's tonight's talk!" I said.

"Yeah, but how did it get on the screen? You tell me! When I saw that, I said to myself right away, It's him; it's my friend who's sending me a message. I know it's him, he's going to meet me somewhere.' But "St. Leo's" meant nothing to me. I went through everything, I checked if there was a subway station by that name, a hotel, a restaurant...but nothing! Then someone said to me, "St. Leo's" might be a church, it's the name of a saint... But no one had heard of this church. So I went into the church in my neighborhood and the person at the reception looked in a little book and told me, It's in the 15th district, near La Motte-Picquet.' So that's how I got here tonight, without knowing what I was going to find..."

I swallowed hard, tried to collect my thoughts and kept silent for a moment while I called upon the Lord. But Francois wouldn't allow me 5 seconds.

"So what should I do now, Sister?"

This question reminded me of something in the *Acts of the Apostles*, when the people ask Peter, on Pentecost, "What must we do?" Francois was hanging on my every word, like a child under a spell, or rather like a casualty of love who has just heard about a way out and is awaiting the magic word that will propel his life from hell into heaven. That evening, that person was me!

I had to tell him quickly something very clear and simple. The church was still full, but I could hear the clanging of keys and knew that the doors would soon be locked.

"It's very easy," I said to reassure both him and myself. "You go and buy a Bible and the collection of Our Lady's messages right now at the stall over there. You plunge right in, reading it every day, and you start praying just as I explained this evening. The Blessed Mother herself will guide you through her messages in the book. Then, as soon as you can, you come to see us at Medjugorje. You'll see how your heart will open up there, and you'll find great peace."

"But where is it? How do I get there?"

"Go and see the lady over there at the back. That's my friend Genevieve who organizes pilgrimages. She'll give you all the details you need."

"It's incredible how good I feel just being here with you all. You have the light with you. Now I understand. It must have been my friend who wrote the message so that I would come here and learn about all this."

"Your friend, or maybe...Our Lady, perhaps? She's your mother. She wanted you to get to know her... But I tell you, it's the first time that I've known her to send a message by computer!"

I left for Medjugorje the following day and, 3 months later, I saw Francois in a group of pilgrims. His appearance had already changed completely; he wasn't shaking, and his cheeks weren't so hollow. A kind of serenity had settled over him. He had joined a prayer group, found his faith, and started to live the sacraments, in his own way. Grace was at work, clearing a path in him through the staggering, pain-filled map of his past, through the trials of a childhood and youth which only divine mercy could describe. I don't know what has become of him today, not even whether he is alive or dead.

Francois, if the Lord has called you back to him, help us from heaven to bring to the heart of God all those who have suffered like you. If you are alive, I want to tell you that your little sister at Medjugorje prays for you every day and would love to hear from you!

— MESSAGE OF SEPTEMBER 25, 1993 —

"Dear children! I am your Mother and I invite you to come closer to God through prayer because only he is your peace, your savior. Therefore, little children, do not seek comfort in material things, but rather seek God. I am praying for you and I intercede before God for each individual. I am looking for your prayers so that you accept me and accept my messages as in the first days of the apparitions. Only then, when you open your hearts and pray, will miracles happen. Thank you for having responded to my call."

CAN A PROTESTANT SEE OUR LADY?

I have to say it: Barry is a tough cookie (Our Lady loves those cookies!). His wife Patricia? A treasure of sensitivity whom I suspect of praying all the time, judging from the profound radiance which emanates from her. She used to leave her native England often to recharge her batteries in Medjugorje and to entrust her husband to the Gospa. How marvelous it would be if he too could one day discover the joy of living with the Living God!

Although he was baptized a Protestant, Barry didn't believe in God and was proud of doing without him. However, there was an old memory buried deep in his heart: once, when he was young and going through a very hard time, he had prayed to God: "Send me a good wife!" Some time afterwards he had to stop his car near a strange house because of a mechanical problem. The young woman who answered the door bowled him over so strongly that he married her 3 months later! He forgot to thank this mysterious God who had so promptly rewarded him with such a happy marriage. There was only one problem: Patricia was a Catholic. Barry did all he could to destroy her faith, but realized quickly that he was on slippery ground.

But, in her 40's, Patricia found herself worn down from a spiritual isolation that was too much for her, in an England that had become materialistic and jaded. It was then that Medjugorje saved her from going off course, and offered her something she didn't dare hope for: to be bathed in the heart of God in a place where heaven comes down to earth every day! Talking with her, I was amazed by her unshakable trust in Providence. She was utterly convinced that all her relatives would convert, at a time to be decided by God. Then war broke out in Bosnia-Herzegovina.

On the evening of January 1, 1993, Barry and Patricia were watching television and heard the appeal launched by the *Medjugorje Appeal:* 30 drivers were needed for relief trucks carrying tons of supplies to Bosnia. Without knowing that Patricia knew Bernard Ellis, a Jew who had converted at Medjugorje and the key person in this organization, Barry took up the challenge and announced to his wife that he wanted to take part in this adventure, especially since he had his first class license. Patricia couldn't believe her ears! Bernard had planned that some of the trucks would go to Medjugorje, others to Zagreb.

Two weeks later our "scoffer," accompanied by his wife, made his entrance into Medjugorje at the steering-wheel of his truck! All he cared about was getting the supplies to the refugees. On the very first night, his services were called upon. In the morning, he got back to his bed-and-breakfast room at the foot of Mt. Krizevac and looked for his wife, but the bird had already flown. Barry walked out onto the terrace and saw the church, down in the valley. His eyes were drawn to the 2 spires pointing up to the sky and, strangely enough, he felt an irresistible pull towards this church. He had only one thought in mind: "I have to go into this church and say a prayer." He couldn't figure himself out: say a prayer? Him? The dyed-in-the-wool atheist? Was he going nuts? But the urge was irresistible. Barry set off and walked calmly to the church. There was one problem: what prayer would he say? He only knew two: the Lord's Prayer, which he had learned at school, and the Hail Mary, which he had ended up knowing by heart because he had heard his wife so often teaching it to the children. Which one would he choose?

Once inside the church, he saw that it was cleaning time, and he settled himself discreetly in the last pew. He decided to say both prayers, and stayed there in silence for 5 minutes. Then he decided to go and clean out his truck. A Franciscan priest, Father Svet, saw him and gave him his rosary beads. Later on, he went back to his room. Since Patricia still hadn't come back, he thought he would take a little nap. As the light was so bright, he drew the covers over his face, but then a bluish light began to dazzle him. He thought that the bedspread must have fallen off his face, so he pulled it up again. Still the bluish light grew brighter, filling the whole room. Barry began to think that this was rather weird. Then an even brighter light, pure white, appeared in the blue and came closer and closer to him, growing before his eyes. What on earth was going on?

"The white light was completely clear," Barry explained, "and there she was. It was Mary, the Mother of God! I could see her. I knew that it was she. The blue light changed into beams radiating out from her. How beautiful she was!

"I wasn't scared at all. I watched her, fascinated. I knew who it was there before me. Then she raised her hand and waved at me. She didn't say anything. Then she left. I sat up to look around the room. A scent of roses wafted through the air, and I felt throughout my whole being, even in my body, an unimaginable peace. All I could do was repeat, 'Why me? Why me? What have I, a rough diamond, a half-civilized country lout, done to deserve this?' I kept thinking of all the terrible things I'd done in my life, and in spite of all that, Mary had appeared to someone like me!

"Soon afterwards Patricia came back, and I told her everything. She was ecstatic! She wanted me to become a Catholic overnight! She invited me to go to Mass with her. In church, I continued to think: 'Why me?' When it was time to go up for Communion, Patricia suggested I should go with her to receive the priest's blessing. If I crossed my arms over my chest, it would be clear that I could not take Communion. The priest, nonetheless, forced the host into my mouth, and I was obliged to receive the Body of Christ. I was so overwhelmed that tears were rolling down my cheeks. You should have seen this big tough guy crying like a baby! What a day! On the way back, I met a pilgrim who said, 'I've always been a Catholic. I come here a lot, but I've never seen or felt anything!' But I was there for the first time, me, who had never put a foot inside a church, and in one day I had managed to: 1) go inside a church; 2) say a prayer; 3) be given some rosary beads; 4) see the Blessed Mother; and 5) receive the Body of her Son Jesus!

"Back in England I decided to go to Mass with Patsy, and little by little I discovered prayer, prayer from the heart. I continued to help in the humanitarian convoys for Bosnia, and once we even had Ivan the visionary with us between London and Medjugorje! At the moment of the apparition,

---

[1] A prophecy of Pope Leo XIII known throughout the United Kingdom goes: "When England comes back to Walsingham, the Blessed Mother will come back to England." Mary appeared in Walsingham in Norfolk in the 11th century and showed a vision of her house in Nazareth. Thanks to Barry and Patricia Kelly (among others), crowds gather there for weekends of prayer in communion with Medjugorje. General details of pilgrimages may be obtained from the Rev. Director, Pilgrim Bureau, Friday Market, Walsingham, Norfolk, England. Tel: 011-44-1328-820217.

we all knelt down in the truck. Deep inside me, I still had a burning desire to see Our Lady again.

"Some time later, Bernard asked me if I would drive a coach to take pilgrims to Medjugorje. So I swapped my load of groceries for a load of brothers and sisters. On the way, we stopped in a hotel close to Slovenia. Right after dinner there was a power outage. I went up to my room to find my flashlight, and when I came back down into the hall I felt an urge to sing a hymn to Mary.

"The whole group started to sing with me, and we then began to improvise a prayer which was taken up by the whole hotel! At that moment Our Lady appeared once more to me, just as in Medjugorje, with that blue halo around her. I was the only one to see her. I realized then that I still hadn't done anything for her or for God, despite having received so much grace. Once Mary wants something (or someone!), she doesn't give up! I felt she was calling me closer to her and to her Son Jesus. I had to make a commitment to her. So I decided to ask to be received into the Catholic Church. Patricia found me a marvelous sponsor from whom I took instruction.

"I went on driving pilgrims to Medjugorje for some months, and Patricia was helping as well. I had a secret wish that some of 'my passengers' might be granted the joy of seeing the Blessed Mother, and my prayer was soon answered: 4 pilgrims saw her on Podbrdo.

"I was received into the Church on Easter 1995. Ever since, the Lord has called Patricia and me to work for him in our own parish and our diocese, where the shrine of Walsingham is located.[1]

"Mary set about bringing all our relatives to her Son. Our 2 sons, as well as various relatives who formerly had been atheists, have converted. She has already reconciled several couples whose marriages were in trouble (brothers- and sisters-in-law), and we have great hopes for the others.

"As for me, I'm part of a team which helps people who intend to become Catholic. I'm ready to do whatever the Lord and his Mother want of me, and, little by little, I'm growing in their love.

"And my dream? That the whole world might discover the Blessed Mother!"

— Message of October 25, 1993 —

"Dear children! These years I have been calling you to pray, to live what I am telling you, but you are living my messages a little. You talk, but do not live, that is why, little children, this war is lasting so long. I invite you to open yourselves to God and in your hearts to live with God, living the good and giving witness to my messages. I love you and wish to protect you from every evil, but you do not desire it. Dear children, I cannot help you if you do not live God's commandments, if you do not live the Mass, if you do not give up sin. I invite you to be apostles of love and goodness. In this world of unrest, give witness to God and God's love, and God will bless you and give you what you seek from him. Thank you for having responded to my call."

I WAS AN ABORTED BABY

Joyce S. is a highly respected woman in San Francisco. As the leader of one of the oldest prayer groups in the city, she is known for a deep faith, and love for the Church and the Holy Father, and she's filled with love for the Gospa, her Mother. I know her well and admire her.

Medjugorje turned her life inside out. Now, she can't meet anyone without talking about the extraordinary power of the rosary. Responding to an interior call from Our Lady, she helped found and coordinates one of 12 Medjugorje Centers for Prayer in the San Francisco Bay Area. These Centers encircle the city like Mary's royal crown of 12 stars. They offer constant prayer to recapture for God the hearts of all those who live in the beautiful Bay Area of St. Francis, but have sadly fallen under the power of darkness.[1] In fact, San Francisco suffers grievously from the active influence of Satan, and the Blessed Mother is on the lookout for "good vehicles" to defeat the "evil one" who threatens her children.

One day Joyce was particularly exhausted after having just returned from a long trip to Rome and Medjugorje. She had made the pilgrimage with her husband, their 12 year old son and two priests to seek healing for her husband's progressive illness. Immediately upon her return, she was invited to speak at Holy Redeemer Church. (Since this parish reaches the greatest number of AIDS victims with the gospel, Joyce knew that most of her audience would be gay or lesbian.)

While she realized that a huge crowd would be expecting her, just the idea of getting into the car for the long drive was exhausting, much less "getting up" for several hours of witnessing. Her husband didn't want her to go alone, and he was unable to accompany her. Just then her friend Denis called: "If there's one place in the world where Satan has a control," he said, "it's San Francisco. Satan doesn't want the people there to hear about the Blessed Mother and Medjugorje, for your words will open their hearts to her and they will rush for protection under her motherly mantle. I beg you, don't give up! Don't quit!"

That's all she needed! Joyce was determined to go. She couldn't keep from sharing the good news of Our Lady's coming today in Medjugorje!

Joyce was the same age as Mary when the Blessed Mother stood at the foot of the Cross, and she considered Mary her best friend and, better still, her confidante. The two women obviously understood each other. That night, when Joyce spoke, the words which came from her lips were not only very tender, but also mysteriously powerful. In the audience, people were pulling Kleenex after Kleenex out of their pockets.

At the end of the evening, a young man, visibly moved, went up to Joyce to tell her what had happened to him while the video of Medjugorje was playing. Tears were streaming down his cheeks.

"I was an aborted baby," he told her. "I don't know how or where I was born. I was thrown into a trash barrel in a hospital parking lot. A man who was passing by heard me crying. He looked all around to see where the cries were coming from, and finally he opened the trash barrel. He was horrified. I was covered in blood, yet very much alive. He took me home with him, wrapped me up as well as he could, and looked after me for several days. Then he decided to keep me and raise me. He applied for the right to adopt me and this was granted.

"So I grew up with this man, a homosexual, and with his friends who lived there. At no time in my childhood was I touched, dressed, fed or even kissed by a woman. I never knew the motherly warmth of a woman. I didn't know

[1] Listen to Joyce's beautiful testimony on cassette, available from Resurrection Tapes, 3927 E. Lake St, Minn, MN 55406 • Tel: (612) 721-7933. Ref. 94ND03.

the love of a mother. I grew up in this atmosphere, and once I had become a teenager, I too was a homosexual, as though this way was the normal one. What else could you expect?

"A few years ago, I began to discover the gospel through some people who belonged to the Episcopal Church. They welcomed me, and one day I decided to become a priest in their Church. On the day of my ordination, I was standing with some other candidates, ready to go up to the altar to be ordained. All went up, except for me. In spite of myself, I was unable to move. It was as though someone's arms were holding me back, preventing me from taking that single step forward. I wasn't ordained, and ever since I've been asking myself why I didn't go forward. What could possibly have been holding me back on that day?

"This evening, while I was watching the video, I was absolutely overcome. When we saw the young visionaries in ecstasy, I could feel a woman's arms around me, .loving me. I was being surrounded with love, an indescribable love. I was convinced that there was a woman behind me. Captivated by the video and unable to take my eyes off the screen, I felt again these arms around me. It was so overpowering that I could hardly bear it! I could have died of joy. My whole body was shaking and I couldn't stop crying. The warmth and love of the embrace were so strong!. I turned around to see who it was, but there was no one there! Then I heard a woman's voice saying, 'Dan, I love you. You belong to me.' For the first time in my entire life a woman's arms were around me. I had found my Mother's love! Then, in a flash, I understood why I hadn't been able to go forward for my ordination. It was she! She had stopped me because homosexuality is not of God. First of all, I had to renounce this. I had to ask for forgiveness..."

Joyce listened to Dan's story as if she were listening to her own son. She could hardly hold back her tears. She understood why she had to fight so hard in order to come that evening... She realized that this child had been a victim even before he left his mother's womb. He was a victim of our society. Just talking about the apparitions of the Blessed Mother in Medjugorje was enough to save him from the power of Satan over his life.

"Joyce, how do I become a Catholic?" Dan asked.

Today, San Francisco is one Catholic richer, and there is one more soul nestled under the mantle of the Gospa. And not just anyone! Mary had been waiting for this one for a long time, ever since he was wailing in the trash barrel! Yes, she had been waiting to wrap her arms around him, to draw him close to her motherly heart. All the more so, because today Dan is preparing for the priesthood in the Roman Catholic Church.

— Message of November 25, 1993 —

"Dear children! I invite you in this time like never before to prepare for the coming of Jesus. Let little Jesus reign in your hearts and only then when Jesus is your friend will you be happy. It will not be difficult for you either to pray or offer sacrifices or to witness Jesus' greatness in your life because he will give you strength and joy in this time. I am close to you by my intercession and prayer and I love and bless all of you. Thank you for having responded to my call."

VICKA'S SECRET

One morning I was supposed to pick up Vicka at her house and leave for the States with her, along with Don Dwello from New York. At the last moment, Don said to me sadly, "Vicka is sick. She's not coming. Her sister told me that we will have to leave without her..."

"What?" I replied, shocked. "She was in great shape yesterday!"

"She came down with it last night. I went to visit her with Ivanka P. She was in bed and she was in great pain, her arm paralyzed and her hand completely blue. She told me that it might get better during the night, but actually her younger sister told me this morning that it had gotten worse."

Nine days later, I returned home from my trip to the US where I'd been witnessing to Our Lady. When I arrived at Vicka's house I found her hanging out her laundry with a huge smile on her face.

"So you're cured?" I said. "And you let me go off all alone to America! When did you feel better?"

"Only this morning! I got up and everything was fine! I've even been able to talk to a group of pilgrims; you see, it's all over!"

"This morning? So you were sick for a whole week, exactly the amount of time we were supposed to be away on mission! How do you explain that the sickness lasted precisely the same amount of time?"

"That's the way it is!" (typical expression among the local people). "The Gospa had her plan: you were supposed to talk, and I was supposed to suffer. She's the one who decides!" (The Gospa, evidently, had not consulted the 5,000 Americans in Pittsburgh who would have definitely preferred it the other way around!)

"And what was wrong with you, exactly?"

I shouldn't have expected a logical explanation from Vicka about her health...

"Oh, no big deal! See, it's gone! Until it comes back again... That's life!"

She laughed and changed the subject.

Sam, an American pilgrim and dentist, wanted to make sure she got a thorough checkup, however, and he asked me to point out to her the seriousness of the situation. This I did.

"You're going to see one of the best doctors in the USA. He'll carry out some tests and keep you under observation for a while, and that might save your life. One never knows, you might have something serious... Okay, you'd be happy to go to heaven right now, but we poor things hope to hang on to you for a long while yet!"

"I don't know...we'll have to see...let's wait a bit..."

Coming from Vicka, that means "Forget it!" Then an idea came to mind.

"But, Vicka, your health and strength belong to the Gospa, don't they? Therefore she's the one who should decide. Why don't you ask her what to do?"

"Oh, you're right," she said gratefully, as if the thought hadn't occurred to her. "I will."

Two days later, Vicka let me know the reply from above: "It isn't necessary," the Gospa had said.

Okay, fine! If the Gospa herself is ruining our attempts to get Vicka medical treatment...

As far as I know, no one has yet explained the mysterious secret that hovers over Vicka; there might be more surprises in store for us yet!

Let's go back to 1983-1984. Vicka had a very serious brain disease. I can still hear Father Laurentin's sorrowful announcement: "She's going to die." She was suffering so much that she would lose consciousness for several hours at a time, almost every day. Her mother, pierced by the sight of her daughter suffering so much, said to her, "Have an injection to kill the pain. You can't go on like this…"

But Vicka replied, "Mother, if you knew how many graces my suffering obtains, for myself and for others, you wouldn't talk like that!"

After a long calvary, the Gospa told her: *"On such and such a day you will be cured."* Vicka wrote about this prophecy to 2 priests so that they'd have it written before the prescribed day, which was in a week's time. Indeed, Vicka was cured on the given date. She acquired from this experience a very deep understanding of the mystery of suffering and its fruitfulness.

I remember a personal anecdote. I was translating Vicka's words for a group of pilgrims when she quoted a message of the Gospa about suffering: *"Dear children, when you are in pain, when you have an illness, a problem, you think* 'Oh, why is this happening to me and not to someone else?' *No, dear children, don't say that! Say, rather,* 'Lord, thank you for the gift you are giving me!' *For when suffering is offered to God, it attracts great graces!"*

And the intrepid Vicka added (on behalf of the Gospa), "Say this as well: 'Lord, if you have other gifts for me, I'm ready!'"

The pilgrims went away deep in thought, with plenty to meditate on. As for me, that very evening someone said something hurtful to me while I was walking towards the church for Mass. I got so upset that I had to struggle hard in order to follow Mass with all my heart, rather than obsessing constantly over this remark. As I received Jesus in Communion, I offered my pain to him. Suddenly Vicka's words came to mind, and I prayed, "Lord, I thank you for the gift you've given me! Use it to spread lots of graces! And if you have more gifts for me… (I took a deep breath so I could keep going) I…I…, please wait a little bit before you give them to me!!!"

Vicka's secret is that she does not keep a tally when she says "Yes" to the Lord. Her assents are never measured. Like the children at Fatima, she has seen hell, and hasn't the slightest inclination to haggle when it comes to the salvation of souls. When one day the Gospa asked the visionaries, *"Which of you is willing to sacrifice himself for the sake of sinners?"* Vicka was the first to volunteer. "All I ask of God is his grace and his strength to keep me going," she says.

We need not look any further for the reason why Vicka embodies the joy of heaven to all who come in contact with her. In an interview for an American TV show,[1] she exclaimed, "But you don't realize how valuable your sufferings are in the eyes of God! Don't rebel when suffering comes. You only get angry because you're not really seeking the will of God. Once we seek God's will, the anger disappears. Only those who refuse to carry their cross are rebelling. But you can be sure that, if God gives you a cross, he knows why he's giving it, and he knows when he'll remove it from you."

For Vicka, a small corner of the veil was lifted. She knows what she's talking about.

---

[1] Available from Children of Medjugorje, (see the appendix at the end of the book for information on obtaining video tapes).

— MESSAGE OF DECEMBER 25, 1993 —

"Dear children! Today I rejoice with the Little Jesus and I desire that Jesus' joy may enter into every heart. Little children, with the message I give you a blessing with my Son Jesus, so that in every heart peace may reign. I love you, little children, and I invite all of you to come closer to me by means of prayer. You talk and talk but do not pray. Therefore, little children, decide for prayer. Only in this way will you be happy and God will give you what you seek from him. Thank you for having responded to my call."

HOW TO OVERCOME INFERTILITY?

February 1995. Rèmi and Claire, who live near Paris, had 2 crosses weighing heavily on their hearts: Rèmi had been unemployed for 3 years; consequently, his wife had to work to put supper on the table. And, despite all the possible courses of treatment, the medical diagnosis was unequivocal: they would not be able to have the second child they had been dreaming of for 6 years. For their type of fertility problem, as they were told by doctors in Paris, their last hope lay in test-tube fertilization.

In addition to this painful situation, people around them were mocking their attitude with innuendoes and here and there a superior smile. Rèmi and Claire in all simplicity explained their wish to remain faithful to the Church's pronouncements on procreation and genetic manipulation. They wouldn't diverge from the Pope's teachings for anything in the world. They would rather be pointed at and considered "old fogies" by those who think that man is smarter than God when it comes to creating new life. Besides, they had seen several marriages ruined subsequent to artificial fertilization, because these attempts had not only been unsuccessful, but also humiliating and ruinously expensive.

Rèmi grieved to see his wife long so for maternity. When they got married, hadn't they hoped to have lots of children? They couldn't help thinking, "There are so many abortions each day,[1] and people like us who want to have many children can't have them! Won't our little Inez ever have the brothers and sisters she dreams of?"

Their grief was intense and deep. But one year later Claire confided to me: "United in faith, we entrusted our distress to the Lord, and, through the intercession of the powerful Blessed Mother, we asked him to have mercy on us and to answer our prayer. Just as we were calling for help, we thought of Medjugorje. Our finances were at rock bottom, and everything seemed to be against us. We decided that Rèmi (who was out of work) would go alone, since I couldn't get away.

"A pilgrimage was leaving to be there for the Feast of the Annunciation. On March 25, while Rèmi was flying off to Split, I learned that I was pregnant! I had conceived approximately when we had made up our minds (the check was dated February 25). Unbelievable, but true! Our prayer had already been answered before Rèmi left, and he spent the pilgrimage weeping for joy and thanking Mary. Our little girl was born in November; we called her Marie-Laetitia, *Mary's Joy*!"

Claire's story is only one of a very long list. We have stopped counting the miracle babies who can boast they saw the light of day thanks to a pilgrimage to Medjugorje! As for Marija and Vicka, the visionaries, if you get them going on this subject, they have an inexhaustible series of examples, each one more touching than the last (get some Kleenex...)! It's not by pure chance that the Gospa was carrying her newborn baby in her arms in the first apparition on the hill on June 24, 1981. Just like Jesus, she has come for life!

---

[1] Let me share with you a great joy: some planned abortions that failed. On the Feast of Mary Queen of Peace (in June 1995), a child escaped death. When one of my talks to French pilgrims was over, a young man came over to me, visibly distressed. "Where can I find a telephone?" he asked. He'd taken to heart the Gospa's message on life, children, abortion...

"My girlfriend's going to have an abortion in 2 days' time because I said to her, 'Go ahead!' I've got to call her and explain these messages, and we'll keep the baby! That's what she wanted, actually... It was my indifference which made her give up the baby. She didn't feel strong enough to bring it up on her own. But now I want to save this little life and love it!"

We have seen how the Mother of God brings her children back to life and frees them from sins of which they were unaware. This lad's eyes opened up and he kept on repeating to me, "I didn't realize!" (See the appendix at the end of the book for information on obtaining audio tapes.)

However, not all couples with infertility problems come back from Medjugorje with their problem solved. As Mary said several times at Fatima,[2] *"I will heal some, but not others."* It's the same at Medjugorje.

Why?

I'm fond of the following simple words from Father Emiliano Tardif, who also is repeatedly confronted with this *"Why?"* Indeed, during Holy Mass, some sick people are cured and others are not.

"We are brought up against the mystery of the love of God. Whereas it's true that the Lord only heals some, it's also true that he offers us all lasting healing: eternal life where there will be no sickness, no bereavement, no tears. We are granted healing gratuitously, but who are we to ask God why he healed this person and not another? We're not healed because we deserve it; it's a gift from God."

I've seen it with my own eyes: no woman who comes to Medjugorje and begs for the grace to be fertile leaves sterile. One is given a child whom she'll carry in her fleshly womb, another is given a different kind of motherhood which is no less real and concrete. The Blessed Mother doesn't float around with her head in the clouds! No! Our Lady will wink at her and talk to her heart. She will soon make that woman realize the wonderful motherhood planned especially for her. Mary will whisper, *"You see that little one over there, who belongs to me but has no one to love him or talk to him? You see that youngster? You see that life falling apart?... I put them in your hands."*

Because, once a woman really takes Mary's hand and starts to see the world the way Mary sees it, she discovers that an unsuspected fruit of love is germinating in the depths of her heart. Then, at the sight of every human being on earth, she can say to herself, "That's my child!"

The Mother of God's womb is within her!

"I want you to love everyone on earth with the same love as I have for you," the Gospa said.

---

[2] See Sister Lucy's account of the events of Fatima: *Fatima, In Lucia's Own Words*, ed. Fra Louis Kondor, SVD, Vice-Postulation Centre, Apartado, 6, P-2496 FATIMA Codex, Portugal.

FLASHBACK ON 1993

January: Cardinal Glancy of Sydney invites all the bishops of Australia to give a warm welcome to Ivan and Father Slavko during their apostolic mission which attracted more than 100,000 people.

February 2: Major tour of Brazil by Marija, with Father Orec.

February: The press focuses upon the scandal of the rape of thousands of women.

April 11: Wedding of Jakov to Anna Lisa Borozzi, from Mantua (Italy) at Medjugorje. They will live in Medjugorje.

April 28: The French national newspaper Le Monde ran the headline: "Medjugorje, zone protected by the Blessed Mother" (p. 4).

June 25: Ivanka's annual apparition. The Blessed Mother was crying and showed Ivanka some terrible visions. Then she left this message:
"Open your hearts to my Son so that he may guide you on the right path... Be messengers of peace."

July 2: First soldier from Medjugorje killed on the front: Ilija Barac, 20 years old.

September 8: Wedding of Marija with Paolo Lunetti, an Italian. They honeymoon in France, and live in Monza, near Milan.

November 7: First visit by Ephraim, founder of the Community of the Beatitudes. This pilgrimage begins the foundation of the "Communion of Mary, Queen of Peace" (BP 24, F-53170 Saint-Denis du Maine, France).

November 9: Destruction of the old bridge in Mostar, the last of its 18 bridges.

1994

— MESSAGE OF JANUARY 25, 1994 —

"Dear children! You are all my children. I love you. But, little children, you must not forget that without prayer you cannot be close to me. In these times Satan wants to create disorder in your hearts and in your families. Little children, do not give in. You should not allow him to lead you and your life.

"I love you and intercede before God for you. Little children, pray. Thank you for having responded to my call."

WITH MARY, DEFEAT SATAN

When Marija still lived at her parents' house in Medjugorje, many pilgrims came to see and to talk with her, especially Italians, since Marija spoke their language very well. (She received the gift of this language from the Gospa in April 1983, on her birthday after the apparition.)

A young Italian woman, suffering from *possession*, had come to stay in the village for a few days. Everybody rejected her because her behavior was deeply disturbing. She had in fact, among other things, made a pact with Satan, and participated body and soul in Black Masses and other such sacrilegious activities, to the point that she was possessed by the Evil One. Marija, who saw the Mother of all Mercy every day, agreed to extend her hospitality to the young woman, as she could clearly see that she had come to Medjugorje to seek peace and healing.

Over the period of a month, life in the Pavlovic family changed dramatically. The disturbances caused by the demon which gripped and tortured the girl were indeed quite spectacular. However, Marija reacted without losing her calm. Although she was surprised by what was happening, her peace and her kindness never left her.

At that time, an Italian priest was also staying at Marija's. Naturally, there were rumpuses between Satan and "priesthood"! For example, one day, the priest decided to pray discreetly for the young lady (it was impossible to pray in front of her without infuriating her!). While she was in her room, he silently blessed her from the other side of the door and traced a sign of the cross in the air. She flung open the door and yelled: "Stop torturing me!" (I'll spare you her exact vocabulary!)

On another occasion, a friend of Marija's sat by her side to comfort the young Italian woman who lay on the floor, tortured within herself. Marija's friend prayed to the Gospa in her heart and asked her to come to console and bless the girl. At that very moment the young woman startled as if burned with hot coals and shouted, "Stop your dirty prayers!"

Nevertheless, Marija had done the right thing. Her perseverance and open hospitality, her patience and the prayers of all finally overcame the Abominable. Within a month he loosened his grip and the young woman was freed. She left in peace for her home country.

The age-old hatred which brings Satan and Our Lady into conflict is a tangible reality in Medjugorje. In the book *Medjugorje, the War Day by Day*, I related what had happened to Jelena on the eve of August 5, 1984 (2000th birthday of Our Lady). I was dumfounded when Jelena told me some messages concerning Satan which were given by the Gospa to the small core of persons who lead the prayer group. Our Lady said to Jelena, who was in her early teens, *"One day, Satan went to see God.*[1] *He asked him to hand Medjugorje over to him; in exchange for this, he would renounce the rest of the world."*

Jelena added, "Of course, God refused! The Gospa wanted to show us the central importance of Medjugorje in God's plan today for the salvation of the world. This message must be set in context."

---

[1] This is reminiscent of the Book of Job.

I was puzzled, although I never doubted the young girl's honesty. She always reported the messages given to her with sobriety and surprising accuracy. So I went to see Father Tomislav Vlasic who had been spiritual guide to the prayer group. The Gospa had said to the visionaries, *"He guides you well."* But concerning the message which had been given to Jelena, he confirmed it for me and even added, "There's nothing surprising about this! We are still far from understanding the plans of God through Medjugorje. The Gospa herself often said, *'You do not understand my plans!'"*

He also confirmed another message that contained a harsh reality and was given by the Gospa to Jelena: *"Satan and his angels have left many places on earth to come and settle in Medjugorje to ruin my plans."*

The Gospa keeps warning us against Satan, who is active, who wants to destroy us and who is strong as never before. She does so in season and out of season. Like a good mother, she tirelessly reminds us of the weapons that Jesus has given us to defeat Satan: fasting and prayer are two of them. For our protection, she recommends holy water.

In Canada, a priest told me that he truly believed in Medjugorje when, after a pilgrimage to the village, his parishioners began to fast. "As a parish priest, I tell you that when it comes to fasting, no matter how hard you try, people won't take it lying down! Not even one of us priests could have convinced anyone in our parishes to fast! Now, when the parishioners come back from Medjugorje, without our saying a word to them, they fast! Twice a week, at that! Medjugorje has transformed our whole parish! There is absolutely no doubt in my mind: it can only be Our Lady who appears there!"

A well-known exorcist, who lives in Rome and is a personal friend of the Holy Father, came to Medjugorje. I asked him what, in his opinion, after 23 years of office, was Satan's major plan today.

"It's the destruction of families," he answered. "In Australia, I have seen people organizing themselves as 'Worshippers of the Devil.' They worshiped Satan in order to destroy families. I saw it with my own eyes! It's at its worst in Europe, where more and more organizations seek to destroy marriage. Look at the Parliaments. Who respects marriage? All the laws legislate against it!"

This priest calls Our Lady "the world's most powerful exorcist." She was appointed by God himself. According to this exorcist, there are several ways to release and free those who are tormented by demons. He advises lay people to take the tormented into a church before a statue of Our Lady (blessed according to the rite of the Church) and to pray the rosary with them there. He has often seen how powerful the Mother of God is in defeating Satan in the hearts of people.

He has also experienced the effects of prayer before the Blessed Sacrament. You take the tormented person before Jesus and ask them to look at him in the Eucharist. At first, they will refuse and start fidgeting. They will close their eyes. However, if they look at Jesus, they will be saved. The next most important thing is to keep in contact with the person and help him to fulfill his longing to know and to love God. (Exorcism formulae are reserved for priests. It would be dangerous for unprepared lay persons to directly confront Satan.)

Another witness of Medjugorje told me: "Medjugorje? It's Mary's heel! It's the place where she crushes the head of the serpent."

Of the 6 visionaries, only Mirjana has seen Satan face to face; he appeared to her just before Our Lady came. She was scared. He looked handsome and attractive, but his eyes were red and full of hatred. She told me that she didn't wish to speak about him now, but would do so later. "We all wait for the triumph of the Immaculate Heart," she said.

I cannot hide the fact that Marthe Robin herself said to the French philosopher, Jean Guitton, "Lucifer is always in a rage. But when Our Lady appears, he cannot do anything against her. Our Lady is so beautiful, not only her face, but her whole body. As for him, he can imitate everything. He even imitates the Passion. But he cannot imitate Our Lady. He has no power over her. When Our Lady appears, if you could see him tumbling down, you would start laughing!"

Why is Satan in such a rage over Medjugorje? Just remember that with each apparition, each coming of Our Lady, Satan loses a little more of his power.

"This is why he has become so aggressive," the Gospa explained to Mirjana.

The faithful can say the prayer to Saint Michael the Archangel which Pope Leo XIII recommended to be said after Holy Mass:

"Saint Michael the Archangel, defend us in this day of battle. Be our safeguard against the wickedness and snares of the devil. May God rebuke him, we humbly pray, and do thou Prince of the Heavenly Host, by the power of God, thrust Satan down to hell and with him all the wicked spirits who wander throughout the world for the ruin of souls."

In 1995, Pope John Paul II also recommended that this prayer be recited after Holy Mass.

There is another powerful prayer which invokes Mary as Queen in charge of the angels, which Pope Pius X gave his imprimatur to on June 8, 1908:

"O exalted Queen of Heaven, Supreme Mistress of the Angels, who from the beginning has received from God the power and the commission to crush the serpent's head, we pray thee humbly, send down thy holy legions, that they, under thy command and power, may pursue the spirits of hell, everywhere wage war against them, defeat their boldness and thrust them into the abyss of hell."
"Who is like unto God?"
"O kind and tender Mother, thou shalt ever remain our love and hope."
"O divine Mother, send thy holy angels to defend me and cast away from me the cruel enemy."
"Holy angels and archangels, defend us, protect us! Amen."

— Message of February 25, 1994 —

"Dear children! Today I thank you for your prayers. You all have helped me so that this war may end as soon as possible. I am close to you and I pray for each one of you and I beg you: pray, pray, pray. Only through prayer can we defeat evil and protect all that Satan wants to destroy in your lives. I am your Mother and I love you all equally, and I intercede for you before God. Thank you for having responded to my call."

THE MOST DELICIOUS DINNER!

Bernadette had 8 children, and they were still very little when war broke out in 1939. Tragedy arrived when Oliver, her husband, was captured by the Nazis in 1940, deported to Germany and sent to a concentration camp.

All alone to feed and raise her children, Bernadette was worn out from work and grief, all the more so that she never heard a word from her husband. Day by day she grew more despondent, and only her deep faith in God kept her going. Of course she feared the worst for her husband: was he dead? tortured? a starving skeleton in a bunker or deep in a dark cave somewhere?

In 1943, at the end of her rope, she hears about Marthe Robin and the retreat center called the Foyer de Charitè [Home of Charity] in Châteauneuf-de-Galaure, which was still being built at that time.[1] So she makes up her mind to go see Marthe, and sets off on a long journey by train, changing trains at several different stations because she lives hundreds of miles from the mystic. She puts all her hope in this visit, because, as she said to herself, only a saint of that caliber could help her. During the long ride in the train she thinks about what she would say to Marthe, what she would ask her. Poor Bernadette, who was weighed down by the hundreds of domestic chores and worries of her daily life, the cooking, the laundry, the cleaning, and of course the constant money worries, never could find the time for the long periods of inner recollection and prayer that she longed for!

She hungers and thirsts for God. So she will ask Marthe how to pray in the midst of all the obstacles that her daily life presents, and she will use this retreat to plunge deeper than ever into God.

Exhausted but full of hope, she reaches Châteauneuf and signs up to see Marthe (there was a list of people on retreat who wanted to see the mystic). On the very first day she is called up to "The Farm," for 10 minutes with the holy woman. On the way up she rehearses the words of her questions and is ready to pour out all the distress of the past 3 years of separation from her husband without any news of him. She goes into the room, her heart pounding, and it's dark as night in there. The minute she sits down on the little chair next to Marthe's bed she introduces herself, and before she can get a word in, the mystic starts asking her about her farm, her children, the meals she manages to put on the table, her housework—in a word, exactly what she did *not* want to talk about! And not a word on prayer. The 10 minutes fly by, and then suddenly, just before Bernadette has to go, out of the blue Marthe cries: "Oh, I know what you must do! Go right home, and the minute you get there, set the table as pretty as for a party and cook a delicious dinner for your children!"

This is a hard blow for Bernadette, who recites the Hail Mary that ends the meeting in a dull and lifeless voice.

Crushed with disappointment, she packs her bags and goes back the way she came, waiting for hours in the same train stations, and wondering why she ever invested so much in a trip that was so frustrating. If only she had been able to spend those 5 days on a real retreat! But even that was more than she could hope for. Clearly, it is her fate in life to scrub pots and give up forever the deep spiritual life that she longs for! She thinks to herself: "What a waste, to take such a long trip to go see such a great saint, only to hear that what I have to do is cook good meals! And when I don't even have the money to buy the ingredients!"

But Bernadette does as the holy woman told her to do, and scrapes together the best meal she can in order to make a party. And the children sit down at the table with her.

All of a sudden, while they are eating, the doorbell rings, and the door opens. It is her husband, home from Germany! He's alive!!

"Oh, by chance we've prepared a delicious dinner!"

---

[1] These centers have spread throughout the English-speaking world. In the US: Fr. Matthew Bradley, 74 Hollet St., North Scituate, MA 02060. Tel: (781) 545-1080.

— Message of March 25, 1994 —

"Dear children! Today I rejoice with you and I invite you to open yourselves to me, and become an instrument in my hands for the salvation of the world. I desire, little children, that all of you who have felt the fragrance of holiness through these messages which I am giving you, will carry it into this world, hungry for God and God's love.

"I thank you all for having responded in such a number and I bless you all with my motherly blessing. Thank you for having responded to my call."

ANY TRICK IN THE BOOK...

Let's not be afraid of slipping messages of the Blessed Mother into our letters.

Once, a French pilgrim told me that he was going blind subsequent to glaucoma and an unsuccessful operation. He was very depressed the day he received a picture of the Gospa in the mail. It had these words on it: "*If you knew how much I love you, you would weep for joy!*" Being in such pain, he cried out from the depths of his heart, "Then show me your love now! I'm hurting so much!"

Within the next hour, his sight returned to normal, and his choroid detachment problem disappeared completely! This brother came to Medjugorje to give thanks, all the more since his healing had also brought about the conversion of his family, who were tough cookies! See what great good a mere message can do!

You never know where the Gospa's next conquest will be, or what stratagem she is going to devise in order to reach those of her children who might never be reached by the Church. To reach her goal, anything goes! A friend of mine who leads pilgrimages related this story to me:

"Mrs. N. lived near Paris. One day, as she was bored and feeling at loose ends, she went with some friends to an amusement park. She stopped at a "fish tank" where, instead of catching fish, you catch a small surprise gift package. The woman grabbed a fishing rod and tried her luck. What would she get? She hooked a tiny, flat, hard package. It was a tape on Medjugorje![1] She had gotten "Prayer Obtains Everything," along with a list of pilgrimages to Medjugorje. Puzzled, she wondered what on earth Medjugorje could be. When she got home she listened to the mysterious tape, and Our Lady touched her so deeply that she experienced a real falling in love. By the time she called a friend of mine to join a group of pilgrims, her life had already radically changed through the Blessed Mother, and a joy she had never experienced before now filled her life.

Yes, an imaginative heart with an active hand had placed a little cartridge of love at an amusement park stall. Only in heaven will he find out whom the Gospa had chosen to receive it![2]

---

[1] Tapes on Medjugorje may be obtained from Children of Medjugorje, (see appendix).

[2] The messages of the 25th are published in Medjugorje newsletters and magazines, but you can get them immediately by calling the phone numbers in the back of the book. They are also on the Internet (see appendix for information on obtaining the monthly messages).

— MESSAGE OF APRIL 25, 1994 —

"Dear children! Today I invite you to decide to pray for my intention. Little children, I invite each one of you to help my plan to be realized through this parish. Now I invite you in a special way, little children, to decide to go along the way of holiness. Only this way will you be close to me. I love you and I desire to conduct you all with me to paradise. But, if you do not pray and if you are not humble and obedient to the messages which I am giving you, I cannot help you. Thank you for having responded to my call."

TONIGHT THEY MAY TOUCH ME!

Marija loves to tell this story, because it signaled a profound change for the entire village of Medjugorje.

It is August 1981, a "hot" summer in every sense of the word - the hot wind that is blowing is no hotter than the brain fever of the Communist militia. And not only that, but there are mysterious "fires" lighting up the sky over the hills where the apparitions take place, and they disappear without a trace when people go up to investigate! The children say that they are "supernatural fires," signs given by the Gospa. But how far is this all going to go? And what about the cross up on Krizevac mountain that everyone has seen turning and dancing...? Now it's completely gone and in its place is a huge bonfire! The village talks of nothing else. And the militiamen are muttering: "All of this is making us Communists look like fools! What the heck is going on?!"

"Your Gospa," they tell the visionaries, "why is she against us? She wants to destroy us!"

"*There the atheists have got it right,*" Father Jozo thinks quietly (he'll have opportunities to tell it publicly later). And anyway he isn't far wrong: the Gospa has come to free our people from the Communist yoke. She has heard our prayers and she has a plan for destroying the Empire of the Lie and bringing the captives back to God. Didn't the demons also tremble when Jesus came to cast them out? *"What have you to do with us, Jesus of Nazareth? Have you come to destroy us?"* (Mark 1:24). Yes, the Communists are right on the mark: our Gospa is stronger than they are...

In any case, there is no way to silence the visionaries, despite the formal order that they had received to say that they had seen nothing, that it was all a tissue of lies, and that from then on their lips were buttoned up. But nothing doing! And Vicka is the worst. Even though she was ordered to stay home and fade out of sight, she goes up on the roof of her house and shouts out the latest messages of the Gospa in those decibels she is famous for- she doesn't need a loudspeaker. There is nothing in the world that would make Vicka shrink from the mission that the Gospa entrusted to her and the other five: *"Tell the people..."*

The militiamen guarding her house are at their wits' end. Some even are converted when the voice of their Mother pierces the sometimes weak armor of their hearts. But these are quickly sent away to Zagreb or Sarajevo, or to prison.

Since the visionaries refuse to shut up, the militia decide to put the hill off limits to the people. They put ropes up at the foot of Podbrdo mountain so the crowds can no longer go up for the daily apparitions.

But the Gospa is a "wise virgin": she had foreseen the verdict and she reorganized her plans, taking into account those of her sons, the militiamen.

"Tomorrow," she tells the visionaries, "I will appear to you in Gumno's field. Tell the villagers to come with you."[1]

The moon is high in the sky already when the Gospa appears to her children around 10:00 p.m.

"Today, all those who want to can come and touch me," she tells the visionaries.

"But how can they?" answer the children. "How can they touch you when they can't even see you! We're the only ones who can see you!"

"Bring them over to me yourselves, and that way they will be able to touch me."

---

[1] See the TV programs (which are available on video- see appendix): *"Be reconciled!,"* and *"I desire reconciliation among you and more love, like brothers"*

This is news! The visionaries are dumfounded, but they do as she says.[2]

The villagers are stupefied and overjoyed, and, guided by the visionaries, they put their hand on the Blessed Mother's shoulder, on her head, her veil, or her arms... Every one of them feels her actual presence, although they can neither see nor hear her. Some feel something warm when they touch her, others something cold, something like an electric current, but indefinable... The level of emotion is astronomic, unforgettable!

During this entire unbelievable scene the visionaries notice that some dirty stains are beginning to appear on Mary's robe. The spots get bigger and bigger, and soon the robe is really getting dirty. And the Gospa's face is beginning to look sad...

Hold it! this isn't normal! And the visionaries are getting upset.

"Gospa! Your robe is all dirty!"

"Those marks are the sins of the people who are touching me," she answers humbly.

Like all children, the visionaries are bossy. And what is more, they are Croatian, and they are madly in love with their Queen. The things of God are holy, and must not be dirtied!

"Stop touching the Gospa!" they holler at the villagers. "Stop it!"

At that point the Blessed Mother tells them of the necessity for confession, for everyone. "There is no one on earth who does not need to go to confession at least once a month," she explains.

A man cries out, "Let's all go to confession to purify ourselves!"

That evening an ocean of sinners flows into the parish, a tidal wave so monstrous that poor Father Jozo thinks he has bats in his belfry! He has to call in his colleagues from neighboring parishes so that all the confessions can be heard. That evening the compassion and mercy of heaven flow like a river through the village. The meaningful act of the Gospa, in its surprising simplicity, had touched her children's hearts more deeply than all the long speeches in the world.

Since then, Medjugorje is never short of sinners seeking forgiveness, and has rightly earned a new name for itself:

Medjugorje? The confessional of the world!

---

[2] In those days their degree of ecstasy was doubtless not the same as today, for they still had a certain awareness of the exterior world during the apparition.

— Message of May 25, 1994 —

"Dear children! I invite you all to have more trust in me and to live my messages more deeply. I am with you and I intercede before God for you, but also I wait for your hearts to open up to my messages. Rejoice because God loves you and gives you the possibility to convert every day and to believe more in God the Creator. Thank you for having responded to my call."

FRANJO'S FRUSTRATION

My friend Franjo is a man with a finger in every pie, and he runs his show with great skill! Sometimes he's working hard in the fields, sometimes he's welcoming pilgrims into his home; he remains even-tempered and in good spirits. When the Gospa made her first entrance into his village, he was still in his teens, and he understood that through her his life would never be the same again.

Franjo isn't easily taken for a ride. He never had enough to eat as a child, and it was a tough struggle just to survive, for him and his family. He takes his time and checks things over before taking up anything new, no matter how appealing it might seem.

One evening he opened his heart to me and offered one of the most moving stories from the village. Here it is:

For a month now (since the second day of the apparitions), the village has taken on a new rhythm. Everyone goes to church every day, and at that time it isn't unusual that something happens...

One evening, Franjo feels really uncomfortable. Before evening Mass, his relatives and neighbors are gathered in the little lane which leads to the church, staring at the sky, obviously enraptured by some strange phenomenon which they are contemplating with unmitigated joy. They let out gasps of surprise and wonder. Everyone can see something—except

Franjo! No matter how hard he stares in the same direction, nothing in sight!

Back home that night everyone stays up late, describing every last detail of the phenomenon. The sun had started to dance, sending out beams of different colors in such beautiful hues that they were beyond description. It plunged towards the little group, then rose again, like the pulse of a heart, and sometimes the silhouette of a woman could be seen next to it. Franjo listens to this tale with a somewhat strained smile as he realizes that he is the only one not to have seen it. How frustrating! He felt so singled out. Why not him? Did the Gospa have something against him?

The following day the same thing happens at another curve in the path, and once again Franjo is the only one not to see it. So he withdraws into himself, looking back over his life, scrutinizing it in the light of the gospel. He then comes across some sins which he'd never confessed. This triggers some interior warfare. Will he have the courage to go to a priest to tell him all that awful stuff? The extraordinary grace of light bestowed upon the village through the Gospa's apparitions eventually wins out; Franjo goes to confession, tells the whole story, frees his conscience of everything that had been weighing on it.[1]

That evening, for the third time, the small group stops dead in its tracks next to the church: the sun is dancing again! And this time a glorious cross is visible as well! Franjo raises his eyes timidly, and...he can see it! Everything is as clear as day! He gasps with the others, and his heart leaps for joy.

"Franjo," I later asked him, "how do you explain that?"

"Confession, Sister! It's Confession!" he replied humbly but with assurance.[2] "My sins were stopping me from seeing. After confession, the veil fell from my eyes..."

---

[1] The holy Curè of Ars spoke of confession with great realism. Some of his penitents didn't dare tell some of their sins at confession. They felt ashamed, and preferred to hide them carefully. He could sense it (like Padre Pio, who could read souls). During a homily he declared: "The sins that we keep back will all be brought to light on the last day, in front of all. To hide your sins well, confess them!"

[2] For those who still lack courage, read the little book by Fr. Slavko: *Give Me Your Wounded Heart*, available in Medjugorje.

— MESSAGE OF JUNE 25, 1994 —

"Dear children! Today I rejoice in my heart in seeing you all present here. I bless you and I call you all to decide to live my messages which I give you here. I desire, little children, to guide you all to Jesus because he is your salvation.

"Therefore, little children, the more you pray the more you will be mine and my Son, Jesus! I bless you with all my motherly blessing and I thank you for having responded to my call."

TWO CONTRACTS FOR HAPPINESS

Jelena Vasilj studies theology at the Angelicum, the Dominican University in Rome. She always impresses those who listen to her by her wisdom and depth. To my question, "What is the Gospa teaching you these days (through your inner locutions)?" she answered, "God is present in every aspect of our lives, even in our slightest daily actions and in the most material and apparently insignificant things. Every second, he gives himself completely. We are wrong to assign time slots to our relationship with him, or to schedule our times of receptivity. Naturally, we have to dedicate special time to him, but let's not fail to be open each and every second. We will be enriched by this constant gift of himself, and the briefest moment will become immensely valuable, as it was for Our Lady who lived in a state of permanent communion with him on earth."

Jelena is now 25 years old. As of yet she still has to decided what she will do with her life.

"What matters," she says, "is that I live completely in the present moment. I do not worry about the future, because it rests in God's hands. Whether I will get married or not is not important to me, because God completely fills my heart. I do know that all women are called to motherhood: to give themselves in love. For a woman, it's the most beautiful gift. However, there are many different ways to live this motherhood, not just in the flesh. Mary teaches me how to be a mother of souls even when I have my nose in a book! The world does not understand this, though it is dying because of the lack of motherhood."

Abandon yourselves to God? It's the safest deal!

I was recently stunned by another type of "contract." First, let me tell you what happened:

One day, a large crowd had gathered in Marija's courtyard. Her friend and translator, Kath, could barely find enough space next to her. As Kath's eyes swept through the crowd, she was struck by a face which stood out sharply from the others. This face was so bright that it radiated like the sun piercing the mist. What joy! An inexpressible joy shone from this face, so much so that Kath had trouble concentrating on the translating. She couldn't keep her eyes off him. Never had she witnessed such joy before! Yet this man stood humbly leaning against the wall, and there was nothing about him that was otherwise remarkable.

As soon as Marija had finished, Kath dropped her like a hot potato, leaving her in the midst of the "dear" pilgrims, hungry for photos, autographs, and everything else that could serve as a souvenir. She headed straight towards the "sun" that was shining next to the wall. He was actually very small, a tiny little priest, and so old that he could have belonged to another century!

"Please excuse me, Father, if I'm being nosy, but I would really love to know what makes you so radiant with joy. You must have a secret...," Kath asked.

The priest was Italian. She looked at the expression in his eyes. Despite his advanced years, he had the innocence of a little child.

"I'll tell you, ma'am," he answered. "I am 95 now. But at the age of 5, I discovered with great sadness that people were always complaining. They would complain for trifles, and find 100 good reasons to feel frustrated, and this shocked me as a child. I also felt that Jesus was saddened by this. I wanted very badly to console him, so I decided to make a contract with him. I promised him that during the first 100 years of my life, I wouldn't complain once. On the contrary, I would thank him for everything, for the good and the not-so-good, but above all I would always celebrate the gift of life. And you know, ma'am, I must say that I've kept my promise! During all these years that I've spent celebrating life, no evil could ever touch me; I've avoided all demons!"

"Incredible! But since you are now 95, your contract will come to an end soon!" Kath exclaimed, smiling.

"Well, yes, I've thought about that, too. But it's okay; I told Jesus the other day that I was ready to renew the contract for the next 100 years of my life!"

— Message of July 25, 1994 —

"Dear children! Today I invite you to decide to give time patiently for prayer. Little children, you cannot say you are mine and that you have experienced conversion through my messages if you are not ready to give time to God every day. I am close to you and I bless you all. Little children, do not forget that if you do not pray you are not close to me, nor are you close to the Holy Spirit who leads you along the path to holiness. Thank you for having responded to my call."

APPARITIONS ON THE HILL

The 80's were the Golden Age of night-time apparitions on the mountain for the prayer group of young people from the village, with Marija and Ivan leading the chorus, of course. One day these two decided to spend the evening in prayer with a few other young people. Their purpose? To thank the Gospa for her apparitions. This splendid initiative had already been taken 2 or 3 times when, one night, out of the blue, the Gospa appeared on the mountain to the 3 visionaries present. She wanted to thank them and show them how much it meant to her that they came like that to give her thanks. (We just do not realize how touched the Blessed Mother is by our slightest spontaneity with her.)

She promised to come back at night, on the mountain, to help with their formation as a prayer group, and this is how the group of Marija and Ivan got its start. The Blessed Mother told them the number and the names of the members: they were to be 16, counting Ivan. Vicka often joined the group along with her sister Ana, her brother-in-law Nedjo, and some others, and they became the pillars of the group, which was still led by Ivan.

Three times a week this group prayed for at least 2 hours, sometimes on the mountain at Krizevac, sometimes at Podbrdo. The Blessed Mother appeared to the visionaries at the end of the meetings. Then Ivan would pass on the instructions of his Heavenly Shepherd. The place and the time of each meeting was settled the day before by the Blessed Mother when she appeared to Ivan in the daily apparition. At times the Gospa asked Ivan to hold the meeting in a house, and not on the mountain, warning him that the militia was lying in wait up there in the hills.

Winter and summer, in all sorts of weather, these young people answered Mary's invitation. Neither the freezing wind of December nor the torrential downpours of March kept the Gospa's fans from climbing up into the hills in the middle of the night! Often she would arrange with the visionaries to invite the pilgrims to join the group, which still happens today. Sometimes 10's of thousands of people swarm over the mountain — it's awe-inspiring.

Mary's purpose was not to open up the group in order to reach as many young people as possible, as a measure of modern efficiency! No, not at all: once again she demonstrated the truth that her thoughts are not our thoughts. She wanted to form her own "commando unit," trained over years in her school: if the village gave 16 saints to the Church through this little group, this would be true efficiency as God sees it!

In the early 90's, after I arrived in Medjugorje, I understood right away that this group cobbled together by the Blessed Mother was a central and major element of the Gospa's secret plan for Medjugorje, and certainly one of the most beautiful. It was an absolutely unique event in history — a humble reality, perhaps, for Ivan is naturally very shy, the group is made up entirely of young people from the village (and not all come every time, since some are married and can't always be present), the singing is, well, *amateur*, there is no priest present, the meeting is never announced to the pilgrims in the church, etc.

Poverty and simplicity reign, as, for instance, in the pain in your knees when you have to kneel on sharp pebbles, fidgeting between the feet of your neighbor in front, the umbrella of the lady to your left, and the backpack of the grandpa on your right! But the Gospa is so happy to see us gathered around her, our Mother! *"I am happy to see all of you here this evening in such great numbers,"* she often tells us.

The Gospa is happy, but we are in paradise. Nowhere else have I ever sensed so vividly the closeness of heaven, its atmosphere, its scent, its quality, that indefinable *something* that transports us out of time and space and plunges us into the plenitude of God. This is the real, authentic Medjugorje, untouched.

One episode that I find particularly moving:

One evening Vicka was standing in for Ivan, who was in America. She had bounded up Krizevac mountain like those good guerrilla fighters of Herzegovina that she is descended from, and there she was at the foot of the cross, talking with the Gospa during the apparition. She had asked me to translate the message for the pilgrims, so I stayed next to her and could see everything with ease. The conversation was going along fast and furious (I can't reproduce here Vicka's expressions and gestures, but they can be seen on video). This lasted for some 20 minutes. When Vicka gave the message in Croatian, it boiled down to just one sentence: *"Dear children, when you are at home, pray the Joyful Mysteries in front of the crucifix, and pray for my intentions."*

I said to Vicka: "Is that all? But the Gospa told you much more than that!" Her answer just enchanted me: "First she prayed, and then she gave the message. After that, *abbiamo parlato delle cose nostre* (we talked about our things)."

What "things" did she mean? I didn't want to pry, but I know that after 15 years of daily apparitions, the visionaries and the Gospa are extraordinarily close. Vicka is the most "peasant-like" of the group, and some could look down their noses at her, with her limited vocabulary and above all her outrageous grammar. But the Queen of Heaven takes pleasure in talking with her about everyday things, and, who knows, even about the "Daily News" of heaven!

She loves her, so badly that she needs to!

— Message of August 25, 1994 —

"Dear children! Today I am united with you in prayer in a special way, praying for the gift of the presence of my most beloved son in your home country. Pray, little children, for the health of my most beloved son, who suffers, and whom I have chosen for these times. I pray and intercede before my Son, Jesus, so that the dream that your fathers had may be fulfilled. Pray, little children, in a special way, because Satan is strong and wants to destroy hope in your heart. I bless you. Thank you for having responded to my call."

A BREAKFAST WITH JOHN PAUL II

Rome, November 24, 1993. All the bishops from the Indian Ocean Regional Episcopal Conference[1] had breakfast with the Holy Father, for their "*ad limina*" visit. Here are a few excerpts from their conversation:

Question (from the bishops):

From a spiritual point of view, how do you see the sequence of Marian apparitions especially since the apparitions to Catherine Labouré in Paris (rue du Bac) and the ones in La Salette and Lourdes, until Fatima?

Answer:

When I visited Ali Agça in jail, he told me, "I cannot understand how a professional killer like me who never misses his target, could miss you. Which of your feasts were you celebrating on that date, what happened?"

I told him it was the feast of Our Lady of Fatima. Then, he said, "It was her, then, she interposed herself!"

---

[1] The I.O.R.E.C. includes the islands of Mauritius, Rodrigues, La Réunion, Seychelles and the Comoro Islands.

I consider this sign in the light of the faith and as an intervention of Mary at this moment in history.

Question:

You must know that opinions diverge concerning the consecration of Russia to Our Lady. Some people consider that this consecration requested by Mary in Fatima has been done, whereas others consider it has not.

Answer:

I did consecrate Russia to Our Lady and I asked the bishops to join in this. Naturally, for reasons of form and understanding, I did not mention it explicitly, but the consecration has been done. Sister Lucy (the visionary) so agrees.

Question:

Regarding the third secret of Fatima itself, newspapers reported that during your trip to Austria you affirmed that it would be useless to reveal it... knowing that parts of the planet were about to disappear and that in the political context of the time (the USSR/USA conflict) some would make political use of it?

Answer:

During general audiences, I heard Americans shout several times, "Consecrate the USSR to the Heart of Mary!" The political use would have been obvious...

Question:

Then, only conversion with the rosary as the weapon (cf.: Austria) will do, and it is the reason why in *Dives in Misericordia* you ask to implore the divine Mercy, even if mankind today deserves a new "Flood" on account of its sins, just as in the past Noah's generation deserved it.[2] Therefore, we understand that considering today's sins, only God's immense mercy will save us.

Answer:

This comes from Sister Faustina,[3] a Polish mystic who had a great devotion to the Heart of Jesus. *The most important thing is indeed conversion with the support of Mary.*

---

[2] See Gen 8:15.

[3] In 1938 Sr. Faustina learned from Jesus that **"out of Poland will arise the spark that will prepare the world for my last coming."** The reference to the Polish Pope is obvious here (cf. § 1731 of her *Diary*).

Question:

As in the message of Medjugorje?

Answer:

As Urs von Balthasar put it, Mary is the Mother who warns her children. Many people have a problem with Medjugorje, with the fact that the apparitions last too long. They do not understand. But the message is given in a specific context, it corresponds to the situation of the country. The message insists on peace, on the relations between Catholics, Orthodox and Muslims. **There, you find the key to the comprehension of what is happening in the world and of its future.**

❊   ❊   ❊   ❊

Many priests and bishops wonder whether they should let witnesses to Medjugorje speak in their churches or not. That was the case for Archbishop Felipe Benites (Asunción, Paraguay), who was confronted with the eventuality of a tour by Father Slavko in Latin America in October 1994. On the occasion of a stay in Rome, he solved his problem in the best way: he asked the Pope himself. The latter answered him right away: "Authorize everything which concerns Medjugorje."[4]

There are some who question whether the words of the Holy Father quoted in the booklet Medjugorje: *What Does the Church Say?* are true, but it shouldn't be a problem. In our community we have a golden rule: we check with the person involved each unconfirmed word that we hear about him! In this present case, John Paul II is still alive and so is Archbishop Benites. It would be rather unscientific to express and publish a dubious reference without consulting them beforehand.

On the subject of the Holy Father, I'd love to share an anecdote which touched me deeply. As each visionary bears in a special way one aspect of

---

[4] I was able myself to verify this position of the Pope on November 15, 1996, when he gave me and 30 others a private audience. When he came to me, he gave me a gesture of blessing in the air, as he had done for the others. I said to him, "I have been living in Medjugorje for 7 years, and my mission is to spread the message of Medjugorje through books, cassettes, TV programs, and talks everywhere in the world. Is it possible..." As I spoke, his expression grew radiant, he raised his hand immediately to my forehead and said, "I bless you!" Then he looked with joy at my book for children *(Children, Help My Heart to Triumph!)* and the book on Medjugorje *(Medjugorje, the War From Day to Day)*, and he gave me a third blessing! Several Polish ministers were present, but I was alone in receiving 3 blessings, (see photo, after May 25, 1996 message).

the intercession for the world, Marija was entrusted with the job of praying for priests and consecrated souls. Since the very beginning of the apparitions, she has developed a very deep love for the Holy Father,[5] coupled with a burning desire to see him. She kept on saying to everyone (including to the Gospa), "I want to see the Pope!"

One day, as John Paul II was being welcomed by thousands of people in Latin America, the Gospa presented Marija with a unexpected gift during the apparition: she showed her the Pope and Marija saw him "for real," talking to a crowd. Once out of ecstasy, she described the scene to one or two close friends, quoting what she had heard the Pope say on the assassination attempt of May 13, 1981 that had taken place in Saint Peter's Square.

The next day, one of them happened across a newspaper article: on the front page, the picture corresponded to the description given by Marija the day before, and the headlines quoted the very same words of the Pope she had reported.

Sometime later, she had the opportunity to see the Pope in Parma (Italy) along with a group. He recognized her, came up to her, and patted her cheek saying in Croatian, "Budi dobra!" (Be good!).

---

[5] Marija makes no secret of the fact that for years now she has offered her life for the Holy Father (as Vicka has done for sinners). On April 1, 1997, her birthday, the Gospa appeared to her for a much longer time than usual, and of course she kissed Marija on the cheek, as she always does on birthdays. Marija seized the opportunity to renew the offering of her life for the Holy Father, putting it in Mary's hands. Marija was less than 6 feet away, and I saw her face, absolutely radiant. Then she explained to us that this offering had special meaning those days when John Paul II was coming for the first time to her country (Sarajevo, Bosnia-Herzegovina). She told us that the Gospa wants us to pray in a very special way for the Holy Father.

— Message of September 25, 1994 —

"Dear children! I rejoice with you and I invite you to prayer. Little children, pray for my intention. Your prayers are necessary to me, through which I desire to bring you closer to God. He is your salvation. God sends me to help you and to guide you towards paradise, which is your goal. Therefore, little children, pray, pray, pray. Thank you for having responded to my call."

DYING IN MEDJUGORJE, DYING WITH THE HEART!

When they see that they are getting old, some smart alecks ask Our Lady to let them die in Medjugorje. Fortunately she does not grant their wish! Think of the awful headache for the Croatian host, and what a drag for the guide of the group! Actually, an elderly priest did collapse next to the altar in the church and probably ended up finishing his Mass in heaven. And I also know a little grandma who had barely set foot in the village when she departed this life in her sleep. But these occurrences are rare, though, and they are definitely not advised! (No chance of being buried on Apparition Hill and rising there on the Last Day, since a pilgrim's body is immediately taken to Split!)

Dying in Medjugorje is not what matters. As a "native Parisian," I lament as much as anyone else the inhumane way the dying and the dead are treated in our Western cities. But if each and every one of us took this to heart, we could greatly improve the situation. Among us are perhaps mayors, parish priests, doctors, medical examiners, and even people employed in funeral parlors. In our prayer, the Gospa will inspire each one of us with specific changes necessary in each profession so that everyone will be able to "die with the heart," and families will be able to "live their mourning with the heart."

Here in Medjugorje, the Croatian people have kept alive a beautiful tradition. As soon as a person dies, someone runs to inform the parish priest, and the bells toll for the departed one. A priest immediately comes and administers the last rites, "conditionally," if the person has not received them prior to his death. When the bells ring, the villagers pray for the departed. Once they find out who that person is, they visit the family and help with the funeral arrangements. During evening Mass, the priest announces the death, and the congregation prays for the deceased, who is buried the following day at 3:00 p.m.

During the 24 hours preceding the funeral, the deceased is waked in an open coffin at his home, so that everyone can pay his last respects. People pray the rosary continuously, and holy water is sprinkled repeatedly (which is recommended by the Gospa). Along with their parents, children are also present, as here death is not hidden from them. When Marija's father died, Marija heard her 4-year-old niece say to her 3-year-old cousin, "You know, one day we also will be just like Grandpa. It's the same for everyone: we are born, we get big, we go to school, we get married, we have babies, we become grandfathers, and then we die and go to heaven with God. That's how it goes!"

Sometimes there are some deeply moving scenes. During the 24-hour watch, each member of the family comes and opens his heart, expressing his love and his grief to the deceased with complete spontaneity, out loud. All the mourners talk to him as if he were still alive, uttering their most sublime confidences. They give their best to him before their final farewell. They not only express their pain, but also their gratitude for all the good the deceased has done. They even thank God for giving and then taking him back, in the hour he has chosen. The Gospa has said, *"Here, I have found true believers."* The way they face death is a good example!

They close the coffin only when the priest returns for the burial. Once again, he prays with the family. Then a long procession winds through the streets, praying the rosary in rhythm with the march towards the cemetery. All those prayers are of great value to the deceased! As the coffin is lowered into the ground, some people weep loudly, releasing their sorrow. Mass offerings are collected by a relative of the deceased. And then back to life, everyday life, for one needs to struggle on in order to survive. It's all so healthy!

Being close to nature, hence to the Creator, Croatian people are not subject to depression in the face either of life or of death, but rather they say, "Bogu hvala!" ("Thanks be to God!").

We know that the greatest help we can offer to the departed is to celebrate a Mass. There is no greater act of love in the world than this. But why wait until someone is buried before having a Mass celebrated for him? If this person converts before he dies thanks to this Mass, then he will enjoy a greater glory in heaven, for eternity! We have only our short time on earth to determine our degree of glory in heaven, for *"at the eve of life, we shall be judged on our love."*

Many sick people come to this "new Lourdes" that is Medjugorje, and indeed recoveries abound here: even advanced cancers, AIDS, etc. But again I weep over the spiritual abandonment endured by our sick in our home countries. Sometimes they end up in Medjugorje as if to try their luck, their ultimate chance of being healed, after months of medical tests, hospitalizations, unsuccessful surgery, painful relapses, etc. Most of the time their suffering has been terrible. And if I ask them, "Have you received the sacrament of the sick?," the majority answer, "Well, no... I wasn't told anything about that!"

What a crying shame! How many healings has this negligence prevented from taking place? All the sick cannot come to Medjugorje, but they can all receive this sacrament of the sick. Why wait until a person is on the verge of dying before offering this sacrament to him, when it can heal him as soon as the symptoms of the sickness appear?[1]

This sacrament will also help the sick person to live his "passage" peacefully if no physical healing occurs. At that crucial moment when an eternity is at stake, God does everything to attract this soul to him, but the Accuser might also intervene. He will use his best wiles to make this soul lose all its trust in divine mercy, and close the gates of heaven before him. (His suggestions would go: "It's too late for you! After all that you've done, how dare you think for a minute that God will forgive you? It would be too easy!" etc., etc.)

Many families are unaware of the spiritual warfare experienced by the dying.[2] At this point the best way to show him your love is to call a priest, pray a long time and very fervently at his bedside, help him forgive his enemies, and warn him tactfully that he will soon appear before God. This is the only way you can be useful to him.

In Medjugorje, the families of the dying often arrange to have the rosary prayed non-stop at the bedside of the sick person, because no one better than Mary can keep watch to protect a soul and soften his heart. Isn't it she who crushes the head of the Serpent?[3] If the dying person is far away in the hospital, this vigil can be organized at home. Still, even in Medjugorje, I was sometimes saddened by the sight of relatives who spent more time gathered around a bottle of raki (a strong local alcoholic drink) or a dish of food to comfort themselves, rather than interceding powerfully at the dying person's bedside. As Jesus pointed out to Martha, in the house of Lazarus, the duties of hospitality can be excessive and get in the way of true love.

How do you die with the heart? By living with the heart![4]

---

[1] When she lived the Passion, each week, Marthe Robin saw Jesus teaching his apostles after he had established the Eucharist. According to her, Jesus spoke for a long time about the different sacraments they would be administering, Holy Mass, the forgiveness of sins, etc., and he showed them how to prepare the blessed oil for the anointing of the sick. How poignant were the words he used to describe the greatness and the dignity of the priesthood to them! Jesus also explained the different uses of holy oil, the prayers they were to say while they applied it, on which parts of the body it should be applied, and on what occasions it should be used. Jesus described it as an efficient remedy against the diseases of the soul and of the body, which could be used in extreme cases in which the Eucharist couldn't be applied, but also as a spiritual cure which could only be administered by a priest, who would accompany each anointing with the most consoling prayers, asking forgiveness for the sins the patient has committed with his 5 senses. He told them that all those who received this heavenly remedy would be protected, body and soul (see the beautiful prayers which accompany the rite). Jesus also spoke to them about all sorts of graces for the sick person, his relatives and his home. If the person is not healed because God has decided otherwise, he will be able to depart this earth without anxiety, without fright, and, for his passage into the next world, he will have received all the help that the Holy Church can give him.

[2] Some saints have spiritually assisted the dying. Sr. Faustina relates in her *Diary* (ß 1797): "Today the Lord came to me and said; '**My daughter, help me to save souls. You will go to a dying sinner, and you will recite this little rosary. In this way, you will obtain for him trust in my mercy, for he is already in despair.**'

"Suddenly I found myself in a strange cottage where an elderly man was dying in great torment. All about the bed was a multitude of demons as well as the family, who were crying. When I began to pray, the spirits of darkness fled, with hissing and threats directed at me. The poor dying soul became calm and, filled with trust, rested in the Lord.

"Instantly I found myself again in my own room."

[3] Prayers to the Archangel St. Michael are also highly recommended. Here is a famous one: *"St. Michael the Archangel, defend us in battle; be our safeguard against the wickedness and snares of the devil. May God rebuke him, we humbly pray, and do thou, O Prince of the Heavenly Host, by the power of God, cast into hell Satan and all the other evil spirits who prowl through the world seeking the ruin of souls. Amen."*

"Most Sacred Heart of Jesus, have mercy on us! Immaculate Heart of Mary, pray for us! St. Joseph, pray for us!"

[4] In Medjugorje, no visionary is afraid of death. Vicka said, "Dying is nothing, it's like going from one room of the house to another, or even from one corner of the room to another." Remember that, like Jakov, she saw heaven with Our Lady...

In 1986, the Gospa told Jelena, *"If you abandon yourselves to me, you will not notice the passage from this life to the next. You will start living the life of heaven on earth."*

— Message of October 25, 1994 —

"Dear children! I am with you and I rejoice today because the Most
   High has granted me to be with you, to teach you and to
guide you on the path of perfection.
"Little children, I wish you to be a beautiful bouquet of flowers
which I wish to present to God for the day of All Saints.
   "I invite you to open yourselves and to live, taking the saints as
an example. Mother Church has chosen them, that they may be
an impulse for your daily life. Thank you for having responded to
my call!"

A PAL FROM HEAVEN

Our community (of the Beatitudes) has a beautiful tradition which
actively strengthens its ties with the Church in heaven. On the eve of each
new year, we ask a particular "protector" saint to choose each one of us for
the coming year. Actually, it is the saint who chooses us, and not the other
way around! He has the responsibility of taking good care of us
throughout the year, he will protect us, guide us on the right path, and
reveal to us his particular charism.

Beforehand, someone wise has chosen a number of saints. The name
of each saint is written on a piece of paper along with a quotation from or
about him. Each person also receives a prayer intention inspired by this
saint. To find out which saint has chosen us, we gather to pray, we call
upon the Holy Spirit, and then we pass around a basket filled with those
little papers carefully folded. The name of a saint is written on each,
together with a quotation from or about him. Each person picks out one of
them. And then we share and rejoice together about the saint that has been
given to us.

Seeing how much these saints take their commitment to heart is
amazing, each one according to his own personality! When someone isn't

acquainted with the saint he has drawn, what a great opportunity to discover him and let this saint teach him! If he already knows a little about him, then it's an opportunity to discover new aspects of his life and take him as a companion on the road of life.

Obviously, it is the saints who choose us and not the other way around. Like everything that comes from above, how reassuring!

We have gladly extended this tradition to our visitors, friends, and family members, and each eagerly anticipates being given a saint for the year. Once more, we can only marvel at the workings of divine Providence, since, most of the time, this new companion has achieved wonderful things for his "protégé" before the end of the year. Examples are countless! I will never forget a particular woman who had drawn a paper marked Sr. Faustina, in our chapel in Medjugorje. Her eyes opened wide, and she appeared a little disappointed to have drawn a name completely unknown to her. Yet, back in France, she bought a book on *Sr. Faustina* and it was like a lightning bolt! The entire message on divine mercy was a vital discovery for her.

The following year, she came back to Medjugorje and told me, "Sister, without the help of Sr. Faustina, I would never have pulled through this year's events. She took me by the hand and with her my life has changed dramatically. I wonder how I ever managed without her before! Jesus is now completely alive for me!"

This tradition has spread far and wide, and we have learned that in some families, parishes, or prayer groups a little basket is passed around during New Year meetings!

Why not in your family? To make it easy for you, I have presented a few names of saints in the next few pages. This way, you can copy them and cut them out. It's only a model to start with; each of you may add the saints he knows,[1] and thus enrich the heavenly assembly he will offer his nearest and dearest!

To be sure, Our Lady, Queen of all saints, is thrilled by this concrete and very personalized way of increasing our communion with the saints,

---

[1] The names chosen must be only those of persons who are dead (and not those of holy persons that we admire who are still alive). They must be recognized by the Church, canonized, blessed or venerable, or have their case introduced in Rome (such as Charles de Foucault, Marthe Robin, etc.).

because second only to the Bible, she recommends that we read the lives of the saints. In the story of the personal troubles, struggles, problems, and even failures of the saints, each one of us can recognize his or her own story. How did the saints manage to live in holiness through all these quite human circumstances?

For Our Lady, holiness is not just another nebulous, distant and out-of-reach theory, but a victory of love applied to each moment of our day, no matter how insignificant it may seem. By connecting us to the saints, those wonderful companions, she once again heals our lack of heart. Just as she wove the seamless tunic of Jesus on earth, she keeps on weaving every thread that links her children in heaven and her children on earth; she is weaving the Church to come. To do so, she has no other thread than love, and no other canvas than her heart.

Dear saints, please, make yourselves at home in our hearts!

Saint Peter the Apostle

"Lord, you know everything,
you know that I love you."

Pray for the Holy Father and the Vatican

Saint Mary of Magdala

"And a woman in the city, who was a
sinner, having learned that he was
eating in the Pharisee's house, brought
an alabaster jar of ointment. She stood
behind him at his feet, weeping, and
began to bathe his feet with her tears
and to dry them with her hair. Then
she continued kissing his feet and
anointing them with the ointment"
(Luke 7:37ff.)

Pray for the conversion of sinners

The Curé of Ars

"There are some who weep because
they do not love God! But I tell you,
those people do love him!"

Pray that priests may be holy

Saint Seraphim of Sarov (Russia)

"The true goal of Christian life is the
acquisition of the Holy Spirit."

Pray for a new Pentecost of love

Saint Margaret Mary

(of Paray-le-Monial)

"I beseech you, take up your home
in the Sacred Heart of Jesus."

Pray for those who are tempted

Saint Helen

"O innocent Jesus,
your Cross is my cross."

Pray for children who are tortured

The Blessed Sister Faustina
(Poland)

"You will do great things if you
abandon yourself entirely to my will:
'...not what I want, but what you
want.' If these words are spoken from
deep within the heart they bring the
soul instantly to the heights of
holiness" (Jesus to Faustina).

Pray for souls tempted by Satan.

Marthe Robin (France)

"I give you thanks, Jesus, for you
take us as we are and you offer us to
the Father as you are."

Pray for vocations to the priesthood

Blessed Sister Faustina (Poland)

"Your wretchedness sinks in the
ocean of my Mercy."

Pray that confessionals be full

Saint Simon of Cyrene

"It is the Cross that bears you, not you
who bear the Cross"
(the Curé of Ars)

Pray for the dying

Saint Theresa of the Infant Jesus

"In order to be at peace in suffering all you need is to want what Jesus wants."

Pray for those who are about to die

Saint Michael the Archangel.

"Satan is powerful, and that is the reason why I seek your prayers for those in his power, that they might be saved" (message from Mary at Medjugorje)

Pray for those who do evil.

The Holy Family of Nazareth

"Do not be afraid to take Mary as your wife, for the child conceived in her is from the Holy Spirit" (Matthew 1:20)

Pray for the unity of couples.

Saint Theresa of the Infant Jesus

"Truly I tell you, just as you did it to one of the least of these who are members of my family, you did it to me."

Pray that abortion ceases

Saint Maximilian Kolbe (Poland)

"What is essential is not to accomplish a great deal according to our own lights, but to be in the hands of the Immaculate Virgin."

Pray that Mary Immaculate may reign in

Saint Joseph

"You shall love the Lord your God with all your heart, and with all your soul, and with all your might" (Deuteronomy 6:5)

Pray for the Jewish people

Saint Bernadette

"My weapons are prayer and sacrifice, to my dying breath. At death the weapon of sacrifice will fall away, but that of prayer will follow me to heaven."

Offer sacrifices to Mary for her intentions

Saint John the Evangelist

"O open heart of Jesus, devoured with such a pure love, into your wound I place my wounds and my lack of love" (Ephraim)

Pray for those in despair

Saint L.-M. Grignion de Montfort

"The more the Holy Spirit finds Mary in a soul, the more he becomes active and empowered to produce Jesus Christ in that soul, and that soul in Jesus Christ."

Pray for Our Lady's intentions

Saint Dominic Savio (Italy)

"Just as you did it to one of the least of these who are members of my family, you did it to me" (Matthew 25:40)

Pray for consecrated souls

Mary Queen of Peace

"I need you. You are important to me" (message of Mary in Medjugorje).

Pray for Mary's plan in Medjugorje.

Charles de Foucault (of France)

"My Father, I abandon myself to you. Do with me what you will."

Pray for the conversion of sinners

Saint Gertrude

"I desire my close friends to follow me by showing greater affection for their enemies than for their benefactors, because they will derive incomparably more benefit from it." (Jesus, to the saint)

Pray for your enemies.

Saint Mechtilde

"All those who love my gifts in others will receive the same merit and glory as those to whom I have granted those gifts." (Jesus, to the saint)

Pray for the underprivileged

Saint Catherine of Genoa

"Dear children, I ask you to pray every day for the souls in Purgatory. In this way you too will acquire intercessors who will be able to help you in life" (message of Mary in Medjugorje)

Pray for the souls in purgatory.

Joseph-Benedict Cottolengo

"Exercise charity, but do it with enthusiasm. Never be called twice, be ready. Interrupt any other activity, even the most holy, and hurry to help the poor."

Pray for those who are sick in body and heart

Saint Bernadette

"You want to pray like a saint; I invite you to pray like a pauper."

Pray for those who are discouraged.

Saint Nicodemus

"I have come for the sake of the lost sheep of the house of Israel."

Pray for the enlightenment of Israel.

Saint Vincent de Paul.

"You have as much need to be compassionate as the poor person has need of your compassion."

Pray for compassion.

The Curé of Ars

"My children, the power of a pure soul over God is beyond belief; such a soul obtains for Him all it wants."

Pray for priests

Saint Francis of Assisi

"I know Jesus poor and crucified, and that is enough for me."

Pray that Jesus be loved

Saint Theresa of the Infant Jesus

"One cannot trust too much in the power and mercy of God, and one obtains from him all that one hopes for from Him."

Pray for the holiness of families

Saint John Bosco

"The young are my very greatest hope. But many youths seek happiness in just those things where one loses it" (Mary in Medjugorje)

Pray for the young

Saint Anthony of Padua

"We spread the love of God by loving as he loves."

Pray for non-believers.

Child Jesus

"Whoever receives one such child in my Name, receives me." (Matthew 18:5)

Pray for an end to abortion.

Saint Benedict

"This message of mine is for you, then, if you are ready to give up your own will, once and for all, and armed with the strong and noble weapons of obedience, to do battle for the true King, Christ the Lord."

Pray for vocations to the monastic religious life.

Saint John the Baptist

"He must increase but I must decrease" (John 3:30)

Pray for the prophets of our day

Saint Catherine Labouré

"My child, the Cross will be despised, thrown on the ground, and the Lord's side will be opened again" (Mary to St. Catherine)

Pray for the enemies of the Church

Francisco of Fatima

"I think of God who is so sad because of so much sin! It makes me very sad. I offer him all the sacrifices I can. If only I could comfort him!"

Pray for children

Saint Veronica

"It is your Face, Lord, that I seek!"

Comfort Jesus through adoration

Saint Dominic

"My God, what will become of the sinners? My God, have pity on sinners!"

Intercede for those of hardened heart.

Jacinta of Fatima

"Tell everyone that God grants us graces through the Immaculate Heart of Mary. We should ask her for them."

Pray for the triumph of the Immaculate Heart

— Message of November 25, 1994 —

"Dear children! Today I call you to prayer. I am with you and I love you all. I am your Mother and I wish that your hearts be similar to my heart. Little children, without prayer you cannot live and say that you are mine. Prayer is joy. Prayer is what the human heart desires. Therefore, get closer, little children, to my Immaculate Heart and you will discover God. Thank you for having responded to my call."

JUST FOR FUN

Her folks tell a little 6-year-old girl about heaven, purgatory, and hell. She understands perfectly: After death, you go to one of these 3 places, and it is very important to pray hard so that everyone chooses to go to heaven.

The next day the subject is brought up again at home, and she announces: "Well, I always pray for 3 things!"

"And what are they, honey?"

"Well, that nobody goes to hell when they die; and I also pray that everyone who is in purgatory gets out fast and goes to heaven..."

"That's only 2 things; what's the third?"

"The third thing is I pray that everybody who is in heaven gets to stay there!"

✤ ✤ ✤ ✤

Vicka told me that she had seen Jesus in his 30's in 1982; he came with the Gospa. I asked her some questions about this apparition:

"What color is Jesus' hair, what color are his eyes?"

"His hair is light brown, wavy, and with a part in the middle, and his eyes are light brown too."

"His eyes are light brown? fantastic! Just like mine!"

At this she looks me straight in the eyes, and after careful consideration she concludes: "No, they're much more beautiful than yours!"

* * * *

Vicka doesn't put up with much, and when people push her buttons she can explode! Before her illness her reactions were sometimes too strong, almost violent. Now she is patience incarnate.

In 1981 when the Communist authorities were persecuting the parish in 100 different ways, the visionaries were summoned to Ljubuski for more psychological tests. The authorities wanted to find out if these kids were "normal" or not.

They were seated at a table, and each found at his or her place a sheet of paper with the picture of a square table with only 3 legs. The question the authorities asked them was: "What is this table missing?" Marija wrote her answer carefully: "It is missing a leg." All the other children answered similarly, except for Vicka; she was so furious that they were being treated once again like idiots that she snatched up the piece of paper, scrunched it into a ball and threw it across the room. As for the stream of words that escaped from her lips, nobody ever dared to repeat them to me.

But this humiliation turned out to be fruitful: the other day Marija, laughing, told some pilgrims: "In our village we are the only ones to have medical certificates declaring that we are normal!"

* * * *

Lucy (4 years old) and her brother Vincent (5) are at Mass, listening quietly to the prayers. Suddenly Lucy turns to her big brother and asks, "Vincent, what does 'Lord have mercy' mean?"

Her big brother, who is proud of his superior knowledge of religion, lets her know her question is naive.

"It means 'Kyrie eleison,' dummy!"

"Oh! I see," answers his little sister, completely satisfied.

* * * *

One evening Providence had us all gathered around Marija in a little committee, and she began to tell us about some things from the past.

"In the early days we (the visionaries) were almost always all together for the apparition, except for Mirjana who was staying in Sarajevo. But I have to say that we all dreaded it when Vicka was with us, because...

"This is what usually happened: the Gospa would appear and she would greet us, then she would stretch out her hands over us in blessing, and only then could we talk to her. So, always in the same order, Ivan would begin by saying: 'I recommend to you all the special intentions of the pilgrims who have come and also the sick and the needs of all the other people.'

"Ivanka then spoke up, saying 'I recommend them to you too.' Then Jakov said, 'I do too,' and then I said the same thing, 'I do too.' Then it was Vicka's turn, and she launched into an endless monologue, telling the Gospa in great detail about all the intentions she knew about... 'I recommend to you the Italian lady who came this morning; her son is very sick, you know, he's almost dying and his wife is very depressed. On top of that they don't have any more money and can't make the last payments on the house, and the owner is trying to kick them out... It would be wonderful if you could cure this man, because then his wife would get better too, and who knows, maybe then he could find work again... I also recommend to you Iva who is 94 now and can't see clearly any more. She needs help because yesterday she fell and made a gash in her knee, I was just passing and you should have seen all the blood, poor thing, an old lady all alone like that, couldn't you do something, especially seeing that she prays a lot, it's not like someone who...'

"So you see," went on Marija, "As soon as Vicka got started we knew that the rest of us would never get a word in edgewise. The apparition was almost over and we hadn't had a chance to say anything at all to the Blessed Mother.

"Now one day, when the same thing was happening as usual, Vicka was telling the Gospa about a very long-winded intention and she was talking very fast. In the middle of a sentence she stopped a second to take a deep breath, and the Gospa instantly jumped on the chance to interrupt her with 'Oce nas,' the beginning of the Our Father that we always ended the meeting with. And the rest of us jumped in with 'who art in heaven,' while Vicka let out the gasp of air that she had just taken in order to go on with her story..."

Oh yes, there's a lot of humor in heaven! Some of us may find that reassuring.

✻✻✻✻

Here is a Medjugorje riddle:
 Why hasn't the Gospa ever appeared to Father Slavko?
 Answer: She tried, but as soon as he saw the 3 flashes of light
 he exclaimed, "No photo! Only prayer!"

— MESSAGE OF DECEMBER 25, 1994 —

"Dear children! Today I rejoice with you, and I am praying with you for peace: peace in your hearts, peace in your families, peace in your desires, peace in the whole world. May the King of Peace bless you today and give you peace. I bless you and I carry each one of you in my heart. Thank you for having responded to my call."

VICKA, THE ONE AND ONLY!

Vicka is appreciated in a special way not only among the villagers, but also among the pilgrims. In all weather, summer and winter, she goes out under the grape arbor of her family home and tirelessly delivers the Gospa's most important messages to the pilgrims of all nations. She brings to everyone who has contact with her a taste of that heavenly joy that she drinks in from the source, as she serves non-stop the intentions of her beloved Gospa.

Since her serious illness (she was later miraculously cured), Vicka is on a different schedule for the apparitions, for the Gospa appears to her at a different time from the other visionaries, usually a little earlier, and for a longer time. Sometimes when her day is going to be particularly long or she must leave on a trip, Our Lady appears to her very early in the morning.

Her availability and warm welcome are legendary, but, paradoxically, no one else is present at her apparitions that she receives in private, like her cousin Jakov. And why? That I can't tell, for if you ask her such a (useless!) question, Vicka, like the good Croat she is, just answers with a smile: "That's the way it is!"

However, the other day she surprised me. I was coming down the hill, and since her place was on my way, I stopped by to see if she was home and to ask her something. I found her deep in conversation with a Croatian woman who was going on and on interminably about her problems, with Vicka only managing to get in: "I will tell the Gospa" from time to time in a tone of voice that said plainly, "That's enough now." My appearance was a godsend. I asked her: "Has the Gospa invited the pilgrims to join Ivan's prayer group tonight?" (When Ivan is away Vicka sometimes takes over this group.)

"No, not tonight," she said, with a gesture of her arms that showed she knew she was disappointing me.

At that I took her hands and played the comic, acting like my heart was broken: "Oh boy, the Gospa doesn't love us any more, she wants to get rid of us! She hasn't invited us for several weeks now, she's tired of us; maybe we won't ever be invited again!"

Vicka burst out laughing and said: "Hold on a minute, I have a surprise for you!"

Since this was just after Christmas, I was sure she was going to give me a box of candy brought by one of the pilgrims, a kind of candy the Croatians don't like very much. But no, she beckoned to me to follow her up the hill and we went into her parents' house, upstairs, in the *upper room*. Then I understood: it was almost time for her apparition, and she wanted me to stay. I couldn't believe it! This was the first time she spontaneously invited me like that.

"Vicka, I never expected anything like this, it's a fabulous Christmas present!"

"Oh," she said with a twinkle in her eye, "I like to surprise people too!"

We started to pray the rosary in the middle of the most indescribable clutter of stuff: all around the statue of Our Lady of Lourdes were piled bags of rosary beads to be blessed, medals on chains, statuettes of all sizes and colors and for all tastes, wedding announcements, snapshots from all over the world, crucifixes, "St. Josephs," "St. Ritas," "little" and "big" Theresas, "Padre Pios," Bibles, and in particular entire heaps of letters, letters of love and supplication addressed to the Gospa containing stories of every imaginable human suffering, all cast down at the feet of the Blessed Mother. (Every time the Gospa appears she blesses religious objects and prays with the visionary for the special intentions of the pilgrims.)

Vicka picked her way easily through all this stuff—after all, this was her domain—but I had to really be very careful where I stepped lest I knock over and smash a "Child Jesus" hidden on the floor.

At the end of the rosary Vicka stood up in front of the statue next to which the Gospa was going to appear, and began the 7 Our Fathers. In a fraction of a second her face lit up with an indescribable smile, and her glowing eyes were fixed on the vision of the one who had just appeared. She fell to her knees instantly and the thud of her knees caused me to wince for her... The ecstatic experience began and lasted in the guise of a very animated conversation for 17 minutes. It was as if Vicka was just bursting with all the intentions she had stored up in her heart to tell her beloved Mother. I almost wondered how the Gospa could get a word in...!

Filled with happiness, I closed my eyes to welcome into my heart, like Vicka, the Visitation that Our Lady was offering me that day in such a special way; I was overwhelmed once again (you never get used to it!) to see the most ineffable heavenly realities coming down to meet and embrace our lowly human existence in its humblest aspects. She is here, actually here; she has torn open the heavens to come to this little meeting today in the Ivankovics' house, and this freezing messy room instantly becomes a holy Mt. Tabor. Our wretched hearts are turned into palaces of joy and celebration!

"The Gospa blessed us," Vicka tells me after the apparition, "and she prayed with us. She asks us to pray for her intentions, and in particular for a special plan she is working on."

"What did her face look like?"

"Joyful, it was joyful!"

We go our ways in silence, for we each need to savor in the depth of our hearts, privately, the happiness that the Mother of Our Lord has given us by coming all the way down here to us.

A number of sick persons are to taste this happiness tonight, for before her day is over Vicka still has her long rounds in the village. She has surprises in store for the suffering as well!

FLASHBACK ON 1994

March 18: Yearly apparition to Mirjana:

"Dear children! Today my heart is filled with happiness. I would like for you to find yourselves in prayer every day, as today, this great day of prayer. Only thus can you proceed towards true happiness and true fulfillment of body and soul. As Mother, I want to help you in this. Allow me to do so. I am telling you again to open your hearts to me and allow me to lead you. My way leads to God. I invite you that we may proceed together because you see for yourselves that, with our prayers, all evils are destroyed. Let us pray and hope."

March 25: Bishop Hnilica celebrated in Medjugorje the 10th anniversary of the consecration of the world and of Russia to the Immaculate Heart of Mary.

April 15: Ivan takes part in a humanitarian convoy between London and Medjugorje. He had apparitions before several "unbelievers" and some Protestants.

May 2: Vicka goes on a mission to Canada. In Quebec, she has an apparition in the church of Saint Roch, before 2000 people, breaking off with her custom of welcoming Our Lady in solitude.

May- June: In Medjugorje, filming of the movie *Gospa*. (Not really a success...)

July 14: Birth of Michael Lunetti, first child of Marija Pavlovic-Lunetti.

July 17: Wedding of Milka Pavlovic, Marija's sister. Milka *saw* Our Lady on the first day of the apparitions.

August 24: Ivan gathers 7000 people in Beauraing (Belgium). For this occasion, Bishop Léonard testifies to his faith in the apparitions at Medjugorje.

September 11: Pope John Paul II visited Zagreb. (He could not go to Sarajevo.) Marija had her apparition in the cathedral, discreetly.

October 23: Wedding of Ivan and Laureen Murphy, in Boston (USA).

December 6: Cardinal Vinko Puljic comes to Medjugorje, for humanitarian reasons, on behalf of his city, Sarajevo.

December: Father Jozo is released from his duty of "guardian," and begins extensive preaching tours over the world.

1995

— MESSAGE OF JANUARY 25, 1995 —

"Dear children! I invite you to open the door of your heart to Jesus as the flower opens itself to the sun. Jesus desires to fill your hearts with peace and joy. You cannot, little children, realize peace if you are not at peace with Jesus. Therefore, I invite you to confession so that Jesus may be your truth and peace. So, little children, pray to have the strength to realize what I am telling you. I am with you and I love you. Thank you for having responded to my call."

I WAS COVERED WITH ACNE

This message reminds me of the story of Patrick D., who, at the time, lived his life far from Medjugorje and far from God too, much to his wife's despair. Although he had gone through all the usual steps for Catholic children: Baptism, First Communion, Confirmation and Marriage in the Church, "nothing had clicked." He explains: "Things were at a perfect standstill. God left me alone, and I ignored him too." His wife's piety got on his nerves more than anything.

In January 1994 he attended a conference on Medjugorje in Versailles (not far from Paris). He was curious and skeptical, but secretly hoped to get more information concerning humanity's future, for he had heard about the famous "10 secrets" the visionaries had received. He was totally disappointed! The Sister who spoke (guess who!) did not say a word about the secrets.

"Nevertheless, grace had seeped in and had already deeply transformed me, although I was still unaware of it." Patrick went back home carrying a book of the messages and 2 tapes on Medjugorje.

"So, I read the messages and afterwards everything changed," he later wrote to me. "In the face of all the things that Our Lady does for us, I, in return, wanted to respond to one of her major requests so that she would at least get something from me, too. Therefore, I decided to go to confession. Sister, I won't tell you how many horrors the priest had to listen to from me on that day! I coughed up 30 years' worth of sins! This confession brought about many changes in my life, and I learned to pray and to say the rosary. To my wife's great astonishment, I joined a prayer group (whereas, before, the very thought of such a thing made me sick!). I began to attend Holy Mass, not only on Sundays, but also very often during the week, not just walking, but running to get there! During each Mass, I felt a great joy in the depths of my heart.

"But I must say that after my confession, something spectacular happened to me. For more than 9 years I had been plagued by a skin disease. I suffered from infectious acne; my skin was very infected. My face and chest were completely covered with pimples. They were not just spots, but actual pustules! If one pimple happened to clear up, another one would soon replace it. Therefore my face was full of scars. Doctors had me trying one treatment after the other, but all in vain. After the sacrament of reconciliation, my lesions one by one all disappeared, without trace (except for a few scattered scars that are still visible).

"At work, my colleagues were wondering what 'healer' I was seeing.

"'Did you go to a new dermatologist?'

"'Yes, I went to the best!'

"I consecrated myself to Our Lady. The hatred I used to feel for other people completely vanished.[1] We now pray together as a family, and once a week we open our home for a prayer group. Even if there are sometimes spiritual struggles, I now experience wonderful moments, and I cling to the Gospa just like a child who has found his mother again."

---

[1] The holy Curé of Ars stated, "The saints did not all start out well, but they all ended up fine!"

— MESSAGE OF FEBRUARY 25, 1995 —

"Dear children! Today I invite you to become missionaries of my messages, which I am giving here through this place that is dear to me. God has allowed me to stay this long with you, and therefore, little children, I invite you to live with love the messages I give, and to transmit them to the whole world, so that a river of love flows to people who are full of hatred and without peace. I invite you, little children, to become peace where there is no peace, and light where there is darkness, so that each heart accepts the light and the way of salvation. Thank you for having responded to my call."

A TIME TO EMBRACE

It's 4 o'clock in the afternoon and I'm pacing around in the little bedroom that my American friends have fixed up for me in their house near the University of Notre Dame. I've sat down before my pad of paper a dozen times to try and write a few lines, and then I get up again in disgust, because my head is completely empty. I can't pray, I can't read, I can't write, and I'm so hopeless that all I can do is repeat over and over, as I think of Mary, "She has never abandoned me...she has never abandoned me...she is not going to abandon me tomorrow..."

Tomorrow I have to speak in front of 5,000 people on prayer; my name is printed on the program, so there's no help for it. They're so happy to see me again... If they only knew what a mess I am! The Lord is allowing me to be tried like this, to be incapable of feeling anything spiritual. I know this too shall pass, but when I have to get up on the stage in a state like this, it's just horrible! It's almost time for supper and then night will fall, and I still haven't found anything interesting to say.

My friend Denis bursts in all excited: "Sister! I've found a great message on prayer, you have to quote it, it gives the heart of the Gospa so well!" The problem is that he has already passed me a dozen such passages to quote, each more beautiful than the last. I have a stack of them, but I'm just as dead inside because I still haven't found the whole point of what I am to say. I scribble a few lines that strike me as dull as dishwater. My brain and my poor paralyzed neurons I'm sure would come out as an absolutely flat EKG.

I go to bed but I can't sleep, dreading all night long that awful moment when my worst enemy will tell me it's time to get up, the signal that now I must face the lions.

Nine o'clock. This is it. I go on at 9:30am, after we pray the Joyful Mysteries. I'm dry as a desert, dry and frozen like the Siberian steppes. I try blackmailing the Lord one more time: "If you don't help me, 5,000 hungry souls will go on starving. And these are YOUR children. But if you anoint me, think how many hearts you will sweeten!" I know deep in my being, despite my deep funk, that he can't refuse.

When my turn comes and I'm given an introduction in which I am praised to the skies the way Americans do, I look at this crowd in the midst of thunderous applause,[1] and their trust and expectation move me deeply. So I take the microphone in a state of pure faith that the Gospa is holding my hand.

The words come without too much trouble, and after about 20 minutes I start to tell about an episode in my personal life from the time before my conversion, in order to illustrate the first degree of prayer. When I tell about the surprise call to follow him that Jesus sent me when I was 25, my heart begins to swell and I am almost suffocated by a crushing feeling of love that stops me in my tracks. My throat is stuck; I can't get out a word. My eyes fill with tears, tears of love to be sure, but tears that keep me from going on. For a number of interminable seconds there is only silence, and of course this unplanned silence just rivets the attention of the 5,000 listening hearts in the audience even more. What is passing through here? I know: it is God who is passing through the auditorium. His outpouring of love fills the assembly, and time is suspended. I want to go down on my knees to adore, and I have to grab the lectern because the overwhelming joy that grips me could make me lose my balance.

Bit by bit I get my breath back and a few words come out: "I'm sorry... I'm sorry..." Then I pick up my thread of thought about prayer again, and am able to finish.[2]

Naturally, when I am done everyone rushes over to me to tell me that the best part of my talk was when I couldn't speak!

Later, when I am moving away from the crowd in order to pull myself a bit more together, I bump into a German woman who is making wild gestures to me: "I prayed that I would meet you! I have something to tell you!" She tells me that she had been in the audience, and while she was quietly listening to me, she saw Jesus come over towards me and take me in his arms. And the closer he held me, the more I was unable to speak. This lasted a few minutes, the length of time that I couldn't go on. Then he showed me his Cross and said something to me.

I look at this woman I had never met before (only my friends knew her), and I only half pay attention because I am suspicious of visions; one often has to take things people say with a grain of salt, so I prefer not to take these private revelations at face value unless, of course, they only confirm what I have already been shown previously by the Lord. And the words she said Jesus had spoken to me were word for word those he had been putting into my heart for the past 3 weeks and which kept coming to me as I prayed, like a rhythmic groundswell, a wave beating again and again on the shore.

"Oh, did he really say that?"

"Yes, and he seemed really happy."

Since these words were exactly those I had heard and I had told no one what inhabited my heart, I was inclined to believe the rest of what she had seen in her vision.

Now, that evening when I was at last alone with the Blessed Sacrament, I thanked Jesus, but I also scolded him a little: "*Please* don't play that trick on me again, in front of crowds! There is a time and place for embracing!" But, yes, I know, God is God, and he will go on doing what he wants, and when he wants...

---

[1] I relate this episode because many in the audience have absolutely no idea what preachers and other witnesses to the Gospel actually go through personally. It's good that the curtain be lifted a little so they can see what goes on behind the scenes, and pray for the fragile instruments that we are!

[2] On tape: *Prayer Obtains Everything*, ref. M7, (see the appendix at the end of the book for information on obtaining audio tapes).

— MESSAGE OF MARCH 18, 1995 —
(Annual apparition to Mirjana...)

"Dear Children! As a Mother, for many years already, I have been teaching you faith and love for God. Neither have you shown gratitude to the dear Father nor have you given him glory. You have become 'empty' and your hearts have become hard and without love for the sufferings of your neighbors. I am teaching you love and I am showing you that the dear Father has loved you, but you have not loved him. He sacrificed his Son for your salvation, my children. For as long as you do not love, you will not come to know the love of your Father. You will not come to know him because God is love. Love, and have no fear, my children, because in love there is no fear. If your hearts are open to the Father and if they are full of love towards him, why then fear what is to come? Those who do not love are afraid because they expect punishment and because they know how empty and hard they are. I am leading you, children, towards love, towards the dear Father. I am leading you into eternal life. Eternal life is my Son. Accept him and you will have accepted love."

LET'S SLEEP AT THE RITZ!

The following story could cause jealousy if its main character weren't the Gospa! However, it is the Gospa indeed, so it can bring nothing but happiness!

I have noticed that my readers remember concrete stories best of all. Among those which struck people the most, the story of St. Joseph and the car was always number 1 on the charts! (see the chapter dated August 25, 1992, *St. Joe Just Can't Help It*) However, it is one thing is to read a nice story which happened to other people, and another to experience it personally!

As a matter of fact, that story contributed a great deal to increasing devotion to St. Joseph. The number of cars (all kinds of them) he happily provided for people is beyond count! Today, I receive testimonies from all over the world which naturally contain innumerable details on the cars obtained by his intercession. Each time I receive one, I take the opportunity to stand before his icon and tell him with a knowing look: "Well done, St. Joe, keep it up!" St. Joseph loves being thanked. A good thing to know!

Well, it's nice to have a car, but what if you don't have a home?

Medjugorje is well equipped to accommodate pilgrims, but it's a terrible headache when it comes to staying for a long time, because prices are amazingly high. Friends had helped us out by lending 2 campers, where Maurice and Bernard, our brothers, lived. Cécile and I were renting a room. The four of us shared the kitchen with a Croatian family. Consequently, no privacy was ever possible. No Shabbat on Friday evenings, no Resurrection vespers on Saturdays, no visitors...it was like the early days when we lacked far more than we had; when only sheer grace cemented the stones of the spiritual building that was to be constructed. Besides the cramped quarters of our camping premises, it was the cold that we suffered most from, because neither the campers nor the Croatian house were heated.

With a smile, Maurice remembers those mornings when he had to break the ice in his bucket before washing his face, while Bernard, playing St. Francis, hastily thanked God for our brother frost! As for me, as I never had any affinity with brother frost, I thanked God rather for the coming of spring which would deliver us from it! I must acknowledge that below a temperature of 50°F, my brain freezes, making any attempt at intellectual work simply impossible. Nevertheless, Cécile, my roommate, had good fun each night seeing me dressed as an Eskimo before going to bed. Indeed, I was looking *slightly plump* because of the many sweaters I had put on! At least laughing keeps you warm.

However, after 2 winters spent this way, it was enough. We had to make a change and find a place more fit for our mission. In the summer of 1991, I subtly began to pave the ground on the Gospa's side — I knew that appealing to her kind heart would lead us somewhere.

"Dear Gospa," I said to her, "you do know that we cannot spend a third winter like this. If the brothers fall down, the consequences would be terrible. Moreover, I am convinced that you too would like us to be more numerous. But where could we possibly lodge the newcomers? We have no chapel, no place for community gatherings... Imagine how happy your Son would be if we could invite people to our prayer services!" The more I spoke to her, the more I was convinced, deep in my heart, that things were going to change and that we should get prepared. For sure, this inner movement was not mine, but the Gospa's.

Towards the end of August, I said to her resolutely, "Dear Gospa, it's high time for us to find a house! From tomorrow on, I will make inquiries locally about possible rents until someone offers me a reasonable price."

As I really dreaded this prospect, I added, "The problem, you see, is that it will take an awful lot of time. You know how Croatian families are — you love them in such a special way. I won't be able to drop in without staying for a long time and having a cup of coffee, a glass of raki, etc. If I take French leave too fast, people will think I'm rude. Well, so what... But is it okay with you that the time I could spend praying is greatly cut into with all these visits? But if there is no way I can escape them, well then..." I started mentally to go through the nearby houses. What about the house of the little baba,[1] just in front? Not enough room. Anka's? Too expensive. Bosilko's? We would have no privacy. What about the Ritz? This thought brought a smile to my face: we had baptized our neighbor's house "the Ritz" in comparison with the freezer we were living in. This place was one of Medjugorje's ritziest, most "upscale" houses—always warm, with a modern kitchen and a warm cup of coffee always waiting for you there, rooms with a view of the mountains, sunlit wooden balconies, a tastefully furnished interior, etc.... In a word, it was the height of luxury! Whenever we felt discouraged by the cold, taking turns we would look for any excuse to say, "I have to drop over to Milona's," just to accumulate some heat for the rest of the day and be comforted... We could dream of the Ritz, because it was crammed full. All year long, besides Milona, bunches of young American, German and Irish girls swarmed there non-stop. So, there was no space for us.

On that day, I told the Gospa, "I can't see any way out, help me! I am *begging you*, this is taking forever..."

Instantly, a quiet and crystal-clear answer resounded in my heart: "Don't do anything, leave it in my hands. You just pray." It wasn't an inner

---

[1] Baba means "grandmother" in Croatian.

locution, but the inspiration was so strong that I felt overjoyed. The process was clear, and I followed it without a second bidding. I immediately threw all my projects in the trash, and my mind was instantly freed from this heavy worry. I was floating in such total confidence that it was just as if...we already owned a house!

August passed, and nothing happened. September passed, and nothing happened either. October passed, nothing! I remained as peaceful as ever. In early November the weather was still mild, but the cold of winter could have hit us any time.

Sometimes I like to joke with Our Lady. We have developed a certain kindred spirit—naturally, after all, she's my Mother! In those days, I began to tease her: "See how obedient I am? I didn't do anything about the house, just because you are in charge of it. It's such a great relief for me to know that you are handling it. By the way, did you notice that it's almost All Saints Day? Oh, I'm just saying this to remind you that November is already here..." I smiled at her, and I knew very well that she was smiling back at me.

On November 8, when the war had been raging in Croatia for months, some rather alarming rumors that the war could well penetrate even as far as here started to circulate. We had already heard reports of all sorts. They are the kind of rampant weeds that grow very fast in Medjugorje; for this reason, we were not the least shattered by this latest one. Nevertheless, before our flabbergasted eyes, the inhabitants of the Ritz suddenly exploded: in less than 24 hours there was not a soul left in the house!

Then a glimmer of light flickered in my poor little brain. In 15 minutes, I wrote a fax to our friend, Bernard Ellis, the owner of the Ritz, to let him know that his house was empty and to ask him to provide sanctuary for the four of us. "We could spend the winter in your warm house until something else comes up..." Less than 2 hours later, I received 2 pages by fax from England. Bernard sounded very enthusiastic! He said he was honored we would stay in his house! (Bernard comes from a Jewish family. When he had once heard us singing verses of the Bible in Hebrew in a Jewish melody, his heart had skipped a beat and, from that day on, we had developed a strong friendship.)

"It's a real blessing for Sue and me," he wrote, "that you are able to come live and pray in our house." Shortly after receiving this wonderful news, the strangest kind of move took place! There was no need to pack everything in boxes or suitcases: we just took all our belongings, walked the 20 feet that separated our former house from the Ritz, and placed our items directly on the shelves. Six years later, they are still there!

Would you like to know what I told the Gospa? I don't want to disclose a secret, but the conclusion of our conversation can be heard by everyone: "Dear Gospa, living with you is really great! You're definitely the best at swapping things. You take our worries and our needs and give us your intentions in exchange. If you think of any other deal like this...here I am, you can count on me!"

Two days after we settled in, our joy knew no bounds. Something obvious struck me, and I shared it with my brothers and sisters: "Do you remember the crosses we had to bear before we came to live here?"

"Yes, of course, how could we not?!"

"The Lord is good. Since he has delivered us from those crosses, he will certainly offer new crosses to us. He cannot leave us without a cross to carry, it would be tragic."

Two or three weeks later, Cécile took me aside and told me, "About the new crosses... I think they have arrived."

She was right. We had all noticed it. Jesus had visited the Ritz and he had provided us with crosses to bear. Silently, he had fulfilled the need of our hearts. Of all the gifts we had received, this one was the greatest.

Five months later, the war broke out in Bosnia-Herzegovina.

— Message of March 25, 1995 —

"Dear children! Today I invite you to live peace in your hearts and families. There is no peace, little children, where there is no prayer, and there is no love where there is no faith. Therefore, little children, I invite you all to decide again today for conversion. I am close to you and I invite you all, little children, into my embrace in order to help you, but you do not want it and in this way Satan tempts you, and in the smallest things your faith disappears. Therefore, little children, pray and through prayer you will have blessing and peace. Thank you for having responded to my call."

I HAD A DREADFUL HABIT

The Gospa is a real mother: she is no chicken when it's time to cleanse our hearts of the most degenerate, decaying deposits which secretly poison us and which, from the viewpoint of heaven, must give off an unbearable stench—the stench of sin that several saints, like Catherine of Sienna, could actually smell to the point of fainting. Some saints were sent reeling by such reeking smells. At the final hour, when every shameful corner of our lives is revealed in the full light of day...ouch! We'd better clean them out before that day, now while we still have time! For this job, Our Lady is the priest's perfect assistant.[1] First, she's excellent at identifying the problem and, second, like a good therapist, she does not stop there.

William's testimony[2] isn't the worst I've ever heard, far from it. (The fact that I wear a veil sometimes prevents me from publishing the worst!) But you only need to multiply William's hidden weakness by 5, 10, or 100, to understand to what extent the most holy and pure Mother can intervene

---

[1] She said, "Dear children, I ask you to make sacrifices, but I am happier still when you renounce the sin that dwells within you."

[2] Published with his agreement.

in our lives to restore the faded beauty in each of us.

For William, the habit was so deeply ingrained that it had become a reflex beyond his control. It was stronger than he: as soon as he saw a woman, his eyes would immediately focus on her breast, in order to take note of its shape and assess its dimensions.

Having heard, in a talk given behind my house at Medjugorje, that Our Lady comes to earth on a daily basis precisely to help us break with evil, an idea began to take shape in his mind. Encouraged by the story of my own healing, he asked the Blessed Mother to help him, and resolved to do the *24 Hours of the Gospa*.[3] He promised Mary, as a gift to her, to make an effort to change, even though he didn't really believe he could do it. As he explained to me humbly, he would give up this "nervous tic" for 24 hours. He succeeded almost effortlessly, and ever since has been renewing his commitment with a happy heart—he is free.

"Thanks be to God and to the Gospa," William wrote to me, full of joy at having become a new man. Then he added, "I ought to tell you, Sister, that I am 74."

Well... better late than never!

---

[3] This is explained in the audio cassette *Prayer Obtains Everything*, ref. M7, (see appendix).

— MESSAGE OF APRIL 25, 1995 —

"Dear children! Today I call you to love. Little children, without love you cannot live, neither with God nor with your brothers. Therefore, I call all of you to open your hearts to the love of God that is so great and open to each one of you. God, out of love for man, has sent me among you to show you the path of salvation, the path of love. If you don't first love God, then you will neither be able to love your neighbor nor the one you hate. Therefore, little children, pray and through prayer you will discover love. Thank you for having responded to my call."

FORGIVING WITHOUT MORPHINE

My Mexican friend Helga is doubly blessed: her heart is on fire and her common sense is surprisingly efficient. It was inevitable that one day she would end up at Medjugorje! But I'll let her tell her own story:

"After a novena to Padre Pio,[1] some friends gave me the fare for a pilgrimage to Medjugorje in September 1989. A dream come true! Medjugorje is really the antechamber of heaven! When you get there, you really feel like you have come home, to your true home.

"During the climb up Krizevac for the Feast of The Glorious Cross (September 14), surrounded by 10's of thousands of people, I experienced the love of Jesus in an altogether supernatural way. I could feel how much he had loved us during his Passion, and that the more he suffered, the more his love for us poured out of his heart. It seemed to me that his heart had finally burst because it was overflowing with love, even before it was pierced by the lance of the Roman soldier.

---

[1] A good technique to try for those who can't afford the pilgrimage...

"The day of departure came, but I couldn't accept the idea of leaving Medjugorje: I wanted to stay for the rest of my life! I wandered sobbing behind the church, begging Jesus to let me stay. But his own words came strongly to my mind: *'He who, having set his hand to the plow, looks back, is not worthy of the Kingdom of God.'*

"Once back in Mexico, I wanted to live to the full the graces that I had experienced in Medjugorje. I decided to do everything just as in Medjugorje: I began to pray the 3 parts of the rosary every day, to go to confession regularly, to prepare carefully before receiving the Eucharist, to fast on bread and water on Wednesdays and Fridays, to read the Bible, and to adore the Blessed Sacrament. In a word, I started living the messages!

"I also wanted to read everything that dealt with Medjugorje, and that's how I found out that, to my surprise, in Jelena's prayer group Our Lady had given a commentary on the Our Father. "You don't know how to pray the Our Father," she had said. Then she recommended that they pray only the Our Father for a whole week, so that they would learn how to pray it with the heart. When they started doing so, each youngster realized that some lines of the Our Father stuck in their throats: they just couldn't put their whole heart into them. For example, some of them couldn't pray, "Thy will be done," wholeheartedly. Others had trouble with 'Forgive us our trespasses as we forgive those who trespass against us...'

"This story moved me so deeply that I decided to live the same experience for a week, starting the next day. But, to my amazement, I found out that I wasn't even able to pronounce the very first words of the Our Father with the heart. No matter how hard I tried, I wasn't able to call God my Father. I began to ponder, and I remembered that because of my parents' divorce, my father hadn't been present by my side when I most needed him. Very soon I experienced a strong anger against God, who had deprived me of a father, and I said to him, 'How can you ask me to call you "Father," when I don't even know what it is to have a father?! You know all too well that Daddy left us when I was 6, and that I barely know him, since he remarried and has never shown any interest in us.'

"For an entire week I continued to level accusations at God, but towards the end of the week I was able to begin forgiving him. First, I forgave God for having let my parents get divorced. Then I asked him for the grace to forgive my parents for not having tried hard enough to save their marriage, and finally the grace to forgive my father for having abandoned us.

"The next day at Mass, I could not believe my ears! The gospel reading was precisely the one where Jesus teaches his apostles to pray, telling them: 'When you pray, say "Our Father..."' In the car going home I felt an irresistible urge to shout at the top of my voice and with all my strength, 'Our Father! Yes, you are also my father, my cherished Papa, my heavenly Dad, I love you, I love you tremendously! Please, forgive me for never having called you *Father* before, as I'm doing now, with all my heart!'

"I cried my eyes out, and begged God my Father to let me see my earthly father again; not to let him die before I could tell him that I loved him and forgave him for having left us. I asked God to give the same grace to my sisters.

"Five years later, I learned that my dad had cancer, and that his condition was critical. My sisters and I went to visit him, and continued to do so for 3 months. We asked each other's forgiveness, and my dad even asked my oldest sister to tell our mother how much he hated himself for the suffering he had caused her by leaving. He begged her to forgive him. On each visit I talked about God and the Blessed Mother. My dad was scared of dying and couldn't face the idea of not getting better.

"In the last stage of his cancer, my dad was in terrible pain and had to take morphine 3 times a day. Getting the morphine, however, wasn't easy. We had to obtain a special prescription from a doctor each time.

"One Saturday my dad had no morphine left, and my sister wanted to get some. Both his doctors were away for the weekend, and there was no way to get hold of a prescription.

"My dad was crying with pain. I suggested that we pray. He said he'd forgotten how (I should point out here that all my family are Lutheran except for me; I became a Catholic in 1985). I told my dad that first of all we should ask God's forgiveness. He replied that he'd never stolen anything or killed anyone!

"'But Dad, tell me, have you always loved God with all your heart, and have you loved your neighbor as yourself?'

"'Uh...no! But who does?'

"'Well then, Dad, you must ask God to forgive you.'

"He agreed, and we prayed together for God's forgiveness. We told God that we couldn't understand the reason for all this suffering, but that we offered it up for my dad's and the world's salvation. After an Our Father, my dad said to me, 'Please ask your Catholic friends to pray for me. Tell them to ask God to call me to him. I feel very tired and now I'm ready to die.'

"For the next few days Dad had no pain at all. Without morphine! He died very peacefully the following Friday, and the Lord allowed me to stay at his bedside right up to the last moment.

"A great sadness filled me, nonetheless.

"'My heavenly Father,' I said one day to God, 'Oh, if only my earthly father had told me, just once before he died, that he really loved me...'

"A few minutes later, while I was talking on the phone to my editor's secretary, someone came on the line, a very dear friend who was the same age as my dad, and he said: 'My little child, I just wanted to tell you how much I love you!'"

— Message of May 25, 1995 —

"Dear children! I invite you, little children, to help me through your prayers so that as many hearts as possible come close to my Immaculate Heart. Satan is strong and with all his forces wants to bring the most people possible closer to himself and to sin. That is why he is on the prowl to snatch more every moment. I beg you, little children, pray and help me to help you. I am your mother and I love you. That is why I wish to help you. Thank you for having responded to my call."

WHEN IT HAS BECOME IMPOSSIBLE...

Coming across insurmountable obstacles on the way when we form human plans is hard enough to cope with. But, when our plans seem to be inspired by God and designed to glorify him, we cannot understand, and we feel forsaken. Or worse, we develop a suspicion that God secretly does not finish what he begins and therefore we had better give it all up.

One of my friends had received a vocation to the priesthood, and had generously answered YES to Jesus. He was certainly both good-hearted and smart. After some time an avalanche of problems fell down upon him, to the point that his very decision to become a priest soon became unachievable. He would find a brick wall in front of him, a barricade on his left, an obstacle on his right. In a word, everything seemed to conspire against his vocation. Even the principal of the seminary turned him down. He began to have doubts, persuading himself that he wasn't up to it. The call, though, was still biding in his heart of hearts, inescapable.

He knew Marthe Robin,[1] who had confirmed his vocation. One day he visited her, and gave her the news that he would never be a priest, for everything hampered this plan (except for his heart!), and the situation was such that he could not take a further step in that direction.

Marthe experienced great intimacy with Our Lady, who used to visit her each week when Marthe lived the Passion. Marthe replied to my friend with these unforgettable words: "When something has become humanly impossible, then it behooves the Most Blessed Mother Mary to obtain it for us!"

Today my friend is a priest, and I can even say that he is an exceptionally good one!

<hr>

[1] Marthe Robin (1902-1981). French lay mystic and stigmatic (see photo after May 25, 1996 message). Paralyzed from the age of 26, Marthe consecrated herself to Jesus, reliving his Passion every Friday. For 50 years she took no food or drink except the Eucharist. Marthe lived the Passion. Marthe founded the Foyers de Charité (Homes of Charity). Her cause for beatification is now before Church authorities in Rome. (See the book *Marthe Robin, the Cross and the Joy*, by Rev. Raymond Peyret, available from Alba House, NY, Society of St. Paul, 2187 Victory Blvd., Staten Island, NY 10314. N.B.: There are good books on her in French. Good translators are needed!)

— MESSAGE OF JUNE 25, 1995 —

"Dear children! Today I am happy to see you in such numbers, to see that you have responded and have come to live my messages. I invite you, little children, to be my joyful carriers of peace in this troubled world.

"Pray for peace so that as soon as possible a time of peace, which my heart waits impatiently for, may reign.

"I am near to you, little children, and I intercede for every one of you before the Most High. I bless you with my motherly blessing. Thank you for having responded to my call."

NOW! AND ON THE DOUBLE!

During my stay in Paris, the Gospa had not really planned to give me any time to rest! The minute I arrived I got an earful of the still-secret story of what she had just done there... How can I refrain from passing it on to you?

It happened last January. The Mother Superior of the Sisters of Charity picked up the phone. A male voice resonated in her ear. It sounded like a long distance call, and the man had a strong foreign accent. It was an urgent message from the Archbishop of Recife in Brazil. After so many years of duty at the Rue du Bac, the Superior should have been used to that kind of telephone call, but nevertheless her heart skipped a beat, and she had to catch her breath to answer the Archbishop. He said he had all the evidence in hand, the whole file, and could guarantee that the story was true...

The story? It had happened 3 weeks earlier. A Brazilian woman landed in Paris. She had insisted on making this long trip because, for some time, her motherly heart had been broken with sorrow and she had heard that at the Rue du Bac Our Lady often did great favors for those who came to implore her help. She brought little Sandra along with her. She would take her to the Rue du Bac and ask for a miracle. She would place her in the armchair where Our Lady herself sat when she appeared to Catherine Labouré, and then, for sure, something would happen. She would have a mother-to-mother talk with Mary. She would cry out to her: Sandra was only 5, and they said her disease was incurable. She couldn't stay like this: what kind of future could she hope for with a paralysis like this? Mary would see her distress, and she wouldn't let her leave without doing something.

Mother and daughter went through the big archway of the convent entrance, and at the far end of the courtyard they reached the Chapel of the Miraculous Medal.[1] They went in.

A huge crowd was praying there. The mother recognized the place she had so often marveled at on postcards, and walked slowly towards the choir. She knelt down and prayed with her little girl. She had spotted the armchair. Unfortunately, it was surrounded by a rope, and couldn't be reached! But, for Brazilians as for Oriental people, protective barriers are not necessarily an obstacle! And little Sandra hadn't come all this way to touch the armchair with her eyes only!

There had to be a way. At precisely that moment some Sisters began to busy themselves arranging something near the altar.

"Sister, please, let my little girl sit on the armchair!"

"I'm sorry, Madam, but I can't let you, because then everybody would ask to do the same thing, and it's not possible..."

The mother's heart was crushed at this refusal. The armchair was part of her plan, of her pilgrimage! She had to find a solution.

Shortly afterwards, she noticed that the Sisters had gone away. An idea then struck her pained heart, and she whispered to her daughter, "Listen to me carefully: squeeze under the rope and, as fast as you can, crawl your way under the armchair. Once you are underneath, use your hand to touch the place where Our Lady sat, and then come back here. But now! On the double!"

The little girl was off without being told twice. As fast as her cruel handicap would allow her, she crawled to the armchair on all fours, but instead of obeying her mother's orders, she laid her cheek on the chair's velvet seat for a long moment. Her mother was dumbstruck. Then the little girl came calmly back.

"Why did you do that?" scolded the mother. "I told you only to go under the armchair and as quick as possible!"

"But Mommy," answered the child with a radiant smile, "it was the LADY who told me to lay my head on her lap!"

Back in Brazil, the child was completely cured. Such a to-do was made about this story that the Archbishop of Recife had wished to warn the Sisters of Charity, Rue du Bac, personally. On his desk he had all the medical files and enough documents to assert that this healing couldn't be explained from a strictly human point of view.

At the Rue du Bac, don't expect the Sisters to be surprised! "You know," they would tirelessly say, "here there are miracles every day!"

---

[1] In 1830 Our Lady appeared to Catherine Labouré in the chapel of the convent of the Daughters of Charity, in the Rue du Bac in Paris. During the first apparition, Mary came and sat in the armchair placed near the altar, and had a conversation with the little Sister who was kneeling before her. It was during the second apparition that Catherine Labouré was given the message to have the "miraculous medal" struck.

— MESSAGE OF JULY 25, 1995 —

"Dear children! Today I invite you to prayer because only in prayer can you understand my coming here. The Holy Spirit will enlighten you to understand that you must convert. Little children, I wish to make you a most beautiful bouquet prepared for eternity, but you do not accept the way of conversion, the way of salvation that I am offering you through these apparitions. Little children, pray, convert your hearts, and come closer to me. May good overcome evil. I love you and bless you. Thank you for having responded to my call."

ARE YOU TIRED OF ME?

It seems that not everyone can truly understand, or even simply *desire* to understand, the comings of the Gospa. For the friends of Medjugorje, there is of course the wound of the negative position of the bishop of Mostar,[1] but there is also the painful shock of hearing people sometimes say, "What! she is still appearing? Hasn't that been going on a for an awfully long time!"

When little Jakov asked her in 1981, "Gospa, how much longer are you going to keep on appearing to us?" she answered, "Are you already tired of me?"

There are also some who believe in the apparitions of Medjugorje, but who are uncomfortable with the persistent daily frequency of Mary's comings.

---

[1] See *Medjugorje: What Does the Church Say*. In this book you will find all the texts and declarations concerning the position of the Church regarding Medjugorje. It's a must! Available from Queenship Publishing Co., PO Box 42028, Santa Barbara, CA, USA 93140-2028. Tel: (800) 647-9882; Fax: (805) 569-4374. Price: $ 3.00.

Monsignor Brandt, the archbishop of Strasbourg (in eastern France), who is favorable to Medjugorje (he let me speak in one of the large churches of his diocese), said to me one day in October of 1993, "Sister, there's something that bothers me about Medjugorje: Isn't the fact that the Blessed Mother has been coming every day for so many years a lack of sobriety?"

I bounced on my chair (which I guess you're not supposed to do in the presence of a bishop!) and couldn't keep myself from blurting out: "Father, if your son had been in an accident and was in the hospital in a coma, hovering between life and death, wouldn't you stay by his side day and night until he pulled through?"

"Oh, I see—Medjugorje is a sort of Intensive Care Unit!"

And that's exactly what it is.

"No, dear Gospa, we're not tired of you! Keep on appearing to us! We need you so badly, you are our Mother, and because of your comings, millions of your children are taking heart again. Please don't be offended by our cold response, it's part of the sickness of heart that you want to heal!"

One day Marija confided in me: "You know, yesterday, when the Gospa came, I grabbed her dress and pulled on it, pleading with her: 'Don't abandon us, keep coming for a very long time!' I didn't want to let go."

Father Daniel-Ange (a noted French speaker) puts it very well when he talks about the crucial importance of these apparitions today: "Look at Medjugorje! We are seeing our future unveiled in these apparitions; I get to see what I can look forward to! I know that some day I will see the color of Mary's eyes, I will give her a big kiss, I will caress her cheek... So I am not jealous of Vicka, because I know what is waiting for me, in a few days, or hours, or weeks... What she sees is my future!

"The apparitions have an eschatological, prophetic role; they show us that our true home is in the other world, and our whole goal in life is to see God and to have a glorious body like Mary the Mother of God. The role of the apparitions is of enormous importance in a world entirely withdrawn into itself, where people live with their noses to the pavement, shut off from everything that is truly meaningful. So, with Medjugorje, wow! at last! We can breathe again, the sky opens wide...!"

For the past century hasn't Lourdes done more for the faith of the people than all the "rationalistic," scholarly books of some theologians?

And today Medjugorje is coming again to the rescue, and this time the danger our world is in is not only very serious, it is *mortal* danger!

Why should we let our hearts shrivel from an excess of rationalism, this subtle banana peel that trips up the arrival of Grace? Is there any hard and fast doctrine of the Church that says that the Mother of God *can't* come to see her children every day? Long ago the Pharisees thought that Jesus was excessive. And the same attitude is found today. But the simple folk know Who is talking, Who is filling our hearts with good things, Who is healing us, and above all, Who is showering us with love every day? Long ago the Pharisees thought that Jesus was excessive.

The visionaries of Medjugorje know this, and they live these realities with humility. They respect their bishop and pray with sincerity for him. Here priests are venerated as holy men.

One day when the 6 visionaries were visiting Bishop Zanic on his feast day,[2] Marija said to him, "Monsignor, you know we pray a lot for you!"

"Yes, but you pray for me the way one prays for a sinner!"

"No, Monsignor, we pray for you the way we pray for our bishop!"

Many pilgrims are sad that their parish priest does not believe in the apparitions of Medjugorje. But this situation is changing bit by bit. As soon as one of these priests agrees to come on a pilgrimage, the cause is won, for just a few hours hearing confessions in Medjugorje suffice to make him understand what is going on deep in the hearts of his penitents, and to see how exceptional it is. Those who, back in France, wouldn't be caught dead in a confessional here are breaking down in tears of joy. Since the day they were ordained, our priests haven't seen anything like it.

There is another way to win them over. Marija likes to tell the story:

"I met a priest in France who was against Medjugorje and had lost his faith in his vocation long ago. Some of his parishioners prayed hard that he would allow the adoration of the Blessed Sacrament and the rosary. But he wouldn't allow it. So they decided to put into practice this message of the Gospa: 'May your only way be love.'

"One day the aristocrat of the village asked the priest if she could come clean the church and put flowers on the altar. He said okay. In no time at all this priest was confiding in this woman, without either of them ever mentioning Medjugorje by name. Little by little, other persons came to help in the parish. Then the priest allowed them to have a prayer meeting in the church. Next, with so much peace in the hearts of these helpful people, he allowed an adoration service, and then the rosary... They could at last live the messages! Nowadays this priest is the spiritual father of the young people and of the whole village. He has a prayer group connected with Medjugorje.

"What often is a stumbling block for priests," went on Marija, "is the fanaticism of some people. The priests feel they are being judged badly if they don't do this or that of the things the Gospa asked for. But if you have a humble, loving, and helpful attitude, then the Gospa herself brings down all barriers. For example, in Baton Rouge (Louisiana), I know of a parish that was empty. Today there are so many people that they have 24-hour adoration. You know how this happened? It was entirely thanks to one couple who had come back from Medjugorje..."

---

[2] In most Catholic countries one celebrates not so much a person's birthday as his or her "name-day," the feast day of the patron saint whose name was given to the person at baptism.

— MESSAGE OF AUGUST 25, 1995 —

"Dear children! Today I invite you to prayer. Let prayer be life for you. A family cannot say that it is in peace if it does not pray. Therefore, let your morning begin with morning prayer, and the evening end with thanksgiving. Little children, I am with you and I love you and I bless you and I wish for everyone of you to be in my embrace. You cannot be in my embrace if you are not ready to pray every day. Thank you for having responded to my call."

THE AMAZING VICTORIES OF THE ROSARY

My friend Denis Nolan was teaching religion at St. Joseph's High School, near Notre Dame (Indiana). Gifted with a wonderful heart, the heart of a child, he quickly won the affection of his students for, in his classes, he would always relate a lot of anecdotes from his personal experience or that of some close friends of his, showing how alive and active Jesus and Mary were in day-to-day circumstances. I wouldn't bet on his students having turned into perfectly studious theologians, but I am sure that they have all become enthusiastic Christians amazed by their God, as well as excellent witnesses.

Useless to say that when Denis came back from Medjugorje his students were given an account in due form of his pilgrimage, followed by immediate practice in all the good things given by the Gospa: they all decided to pray a decade of the rosary before each class. Soon, the fruits of grace and blessing started to pour down over the students. This transformed even more Denis' classes into a forum of exchange on the wonders of the Living God. Many students from other courses would convert, and everything concerning Medjugorje started to spread like wildfire. Protestants, Jews, and even atheists asked for rosaries![1]

In October 1987, Denis left again for Medjugorje, and on his first day back at school, one of his students shared, "When you were gone, Mr. Nolan, we prayed a decade of the rosary before each class. The substitute teachers didn't want us to. (They thought we just wanted to use up class time). They wouldn't lead us in it, so we led it ourselves. A few days ago, as we went around the room mentioning prayer intentions beforehand, I said out loud, 'May God protect my brother Brian.'"

(Denis later asked her, "Why did you pray for your brother?" She answered that one day during a lecture, he had mentioned, "If you don't have anything to pray for, pray for members of your family." So she had simply gotten into the habit of praying for her brother.)

"The next day, my brother had a business meeting with a lady at the Ramada Inn in Indianapolis. An unforeseen circumstance came up just before the meeting that would make him 10 minutes late. Ten minutes before the appointment time, he called her and asked if she wouldn't mind his being 10 minutes late. She replied, 'All right.' Ten minutes after the time set for their meeting, as he was driving into the parking lot of the Ramada Inn, he saw a jet plane crash right into the room where the lady was waiting for him. She was killed immediately."[2]

Denis added, "How fortunate this fellow was to have a sister who had made a habit of putting him under the mantle of Our Lady each day when she prayed the decade of the rosary before class! His parents later told me that he acknowledged that his sister's faith had saved his life. (Our Lady's call at Medjugorje had deepened her faith and incited her to pray the rosary.)

And there is more! Denis related to us:

"One day, another student (Linda F.) shared with us that, a month earlier, her father had come to her bedroom to inform her that he and her mother were getting divorced. Linda, a senior, decided, along with her brother, a sophomore, to go to the basement each night and pray the rosary. She told me that one week later her father had come again into her bedroom to say that they wouldn't divorce. The following week, she announced that he had gone to Mass with the rest of the family for the first time in 10 years! The week after that she confided in me that their family life was happier than it had ever been. This all had come from the fact that she and her brother were praying the rosary every night putting the whole family under the Blessed Mother's mantle!"

---

[1] Denis told me, "In a desk in the Theology Department office, a drawer was filled with rosaries. In the previous 11 years I cannot remember a student or a teacher ever taking one of them. After hearing of the report of apparitions of Our Lady in Medjugorje, not only did all the rosaries get taken, but in the next 2 years, I was never able to get my hands on enough rosaries to fill the demand of all the students who wanted them!"

[2] This accident was talked much of in the newspapers.

— Message of September 25, 1995 —

"Dear children! Today I invite you to fall in love with the Most Holy Sacrament of the Altar. Adore him, little children, in your parishes, and in this way you will be united with the entire world. Jesus will become your friend, and you will not talk of him like someone whom you barely know. Unity with him will be a joy for you and you will become witnesses to the love of Jesus that he has for every creature. Little children, when you adore Jesus, you are also close to me. Thank you for having responded to my call."

WHEN JESUS MAKES WAVES

Denis Nolan was raised on a ranch in California. A heavy-set 46-year-old man, father of 8 children, he isn't a dreamer, but rather someone with both feet firmly on the ground.

One day he was wondering what could be more beautiful, more affecting in our poor ravaged world than the loving visitations of the Mother of God in Medjugorje each and every day. The answer wasn't long in coming, during a pilgrimage.

On that particular day, Denis attended evening Mass. He was crammed in tight between 2 Croatian women who were singing out their faith at the top of their lungs, and who raised their hands towards Jesus the moment he appeared on the altar during the consecration.

Denis also raised his eyes towards the altar, and suddenly he could see waves radiating, flowing from the host. The waves came pulsating from the Eucharist, slowly spreading throughout the entire church. When they reached him he could actually feel their impact. With each new wave he was knocked somewhat off balance. His body reeled from the shock of the love of Jesus. The waves continued in a gentle and regular rhythm like those of an ocean during calm weather.

After Mass, Denis undertook a discreet investigation among the other men of his group.

"Did you notice anything special during Mass?"

"Yes! Waves were radiating from the consecrated host. I could actually feel it when the waves hit my body, and was knocked off balance. But I thought that surely I was the only one seeing them, that Jesus wanted to touch me with his real presence. So you felt it as well?"

During the week of his pilgrimage this experience repeated itself each time Denis attended Mass or prayed before the Blessed Sacrament. The waves filled the whole church (or the Adoration Chapel) — nothing escaped their impact. That particular week, a small group of pilgrims all experienced the same grace.

Denis had his answer, and in his joy he couldn't help sharing it with everyone: the greatest gift offered in Medjugorje is not the apparitions, it's the Eucharist![1]

"*Adore my Son,*" the Gospa tells us. "*Unceasingly adore the Blessed Sacrament. I am always present during the adoration by the faithful, special graces[2] are then being received*" (March 15, 1984).

And once again, she did not refrain from speaking with more than words. For Denis, for his friends and so many others, she ever so slightly lifted a little corner of the veil.

---

[1] The apparitions and messages show that Mary wants us to focus on Jesus, and Jesus in the Eucharist. The fact that she appears 20 minutes before the evening Mass is significant: her coming prepares us to receive infinitely more than her own presence.

The teaching which she has given to the prayer group on fasting is similarly enlightening. The fasting she appreciates most is when we renounce sin. "*Reject sin!*" she says. This allows us to receive Jesus with a purified heart. However, the Gospa has never talked of fasting on bread and water as a sacrifice, the visionaries tell us, and this surprises us.

On the other hand, if Mary has chosen to have us fast on bread and water on Wednesdays and Fridays, this is to prepare us to receive the Eucharistic bread. She restores to us the idea of bread as *the* basic life-giving food. The Wednesday fast spares us the distraction of other forms of food which appeal to our external senses: we are therefore dependent on bread. In this way, when Thursday arrives (a day that she wants us to live each week as a Holy Thursday), we are prepared to receive another Bread, the one that comes from heaven.

If Mary asks us to fast on bread and water on Fridays too, it is in order to give thanks to God for the Living Bread given to the world on Holy Thursday. In a certain way, she leaves us with bread alone, as if to prolong in us and protect the gift of the

Eucharistic bread, distancing ourselves from other foods which distract our hearts from it. In this way, the great gift of Holy Thursday is set like a jewel in the gold clasps of these 2 days of fasting. We should note that Our Lady has never associated fasting with the memory of the Passion. It is, rather, a joyful celebration of bread!

This shows that the center of our lives is really Holy Mass. Seen in this light, it is easy for us to understand why fasting is such a powerful weapon against the demons.

[2]Sister Faustina wrote in her *Diary* published in 1987 by Marian Press (§ 319, 320, dated August 9, 1934): "Night adoration on Thursdays. I made my hour of adoration from 11 o'clock till midnight. I offered it for the conversion of hardened sinners, especially for those who have lost hope in God's mercy. I was reflecting on how much God had suffered and on how great was the love he had shown for us, and on the fact that we still do not believe that God loves us so much. O Jesus, who can understand this? What suffering it is for our Savior! How can he convince us of his love if even his death cannot convince us? I called upon the whole of heaven to join me in making amends to the Lord for the ingratitude of certain souls. Jesus made known to me how very pleasing to him were prayers of atonement. He said to me, *'The prayer of a humble and loving soul disarms the anger of my Father and draws down an ocean of blessings.'*

After the adoration, half way to my cell, I was surrounded by a pack of huge black dogs who were jumping and howling and trying to tear me to pieces. I realized that they were not dogs, but demons. One of them spoke up in a rage, 'Because you have snatched so many souls away from us this night, we will tear you to pieces.' I answered, 'If that's the will of the Most Merciful God, tear me to pieces, for I have justly deserved it, because I am the most miserable of all sinners, and God is ever holy, just and infinitely merciful.' To these words all the demons answered as one, 'Let us flee, for she is not alone; the Almighty is with her!' And they vanished like dust, like the noise of the road, while I continued on my way to my cell undisturbed, finishing my *Te Deum* and pondering the infinite and unfathomable mercy of God."

— MESSAGE OF OCTOBER 25, 1995 —

"Dear children! Today I invite you to go into nature, because there you will meet God the Creator. Today I invite you, little children, to thank God for all that he gives you. In thanking him you will discover the Most High and all the good things that surround you. Little children, God is great and great is his love for every creature. Therefore, pray to be able to understand the love and goodness of God. In the goodness and the love of God the Creator, I also am with you as a gift. Thank you for having responded to my call."

LITTLE FLORENCE

Those who see Our Lady with their own eyes are not so rare among the pilgrims. It would be a shame not to take advantage of these testimonies to illumine one of the most touching characteristics of our Mother's personality. Whom does she choose? Among the children who come here by the thousands, drawn by her, all tenderly loved by her, who is given the privilege of seeing her? Only the facts themselves can answer this question, and one of the most beautiful answers I know, the most radiantly evangelic, is the story of little Florence.

Little Florence Majurel, who lives in Montpellier (in the southwest of France), was 16. She was a Down's Syndrome child, and could barely talk. On the evening of August 15, she went with her mother to the Blue Cross, at the foot of Podbrdo, for Ivan's apparition. Two thousand people started to pray in silence. When Ivan's ecstasy began, the little girl started to smile while staring at a particular spot near the cross, and said, "Mom, what's that?" (she doesn't know how to say "Who is that?").

Her mother, guessing that something special was happening, began to watch her. Florence nodded several times as if trying to repeat something she was being taught; then she started to clasp her hands together and gently intertwine her fingers, something she had never been able to do before. She was still smiling when she blew 3 kisses with her hands, like children do to say goodbye, just before the end of the apparition.

Then her mother asked her, "What did you see?"

"Our Lady," Florence answered.

"And what was she like?"

"B'ooful!"

The next day, for the first time in her life, Florence spontaneously said "Hail Mary, full of grace" (and no more), whereas up until then she had never been able to say these words of the prayer. Now she could pray 2 out of 3 words of the Hail Mary.

One more test still needed to be carried out. As Florence is not able to name the different colors, her mother placed 6 pieces of colored paper in front of her and asked her to point out which one looked like Our Lady's robe. Immediately, Florence put her finger on the gold-colored paper. To test her further, her mother showed her the yellow paper and said, "I rather think it was this color." But Florence got angry: "No! This!" she said, pointing again at the gold paper. Her mother was deeply moved, for on special Feasts like August 15, Easter, or Christmas, the Gospa appears in a golden robe.

What a lovely gift for Florence and for all those who are so often despised by the world! What a beautiful example of the unfathomable tenderness of God for the smallest, the most vulnerable of his children! And what a wonderful response given by heaven to modern medicine, which so quickly arranges the abortion of their tiny lives because of their handicap, whereas these innocents often atone for the sins of the very people who exclude them. They are temples of the Living God, and through the honor she gave to Florence, the Gospa wants to honor each and every person with a handicap.

— MESSAGE OF NOVEMBER 25, 1995 —

"Dear children! Today I invite each of you to begin anew to love, first of all, God who saved and redeemed each of you, and then the brothers and sisters near you.

"Without love, little children, you cannot grow in holiness and cannot do good deeds. Therefore, little children, pray without ceasing that God reveals his love to you. I have invited all of you to unite yourselves with me and to love.

"Today I am with you and invite you to discover love in your hearts and in the family. For God to live in your hearts, you must love. Thank you for having responded to my call."

THE PATTER OF LITTLE FEET

Francois-Joseph just turned 6—he is both my nephew and my godson. Each night his parents pray with him while he sits in his bed before going to sleep and, in accordance with the school of the Gospa in Medjugorje, they bless him. During prayers, there is a time to spontaneously thank God for the beautiful things which happened during the day, and to make his requests, such as, "Bless Mr. So-and-so who is sick," etc.

That evening, everything seemed to be normal and the parents left the child, leaving the door which communicates with their own room half open for the night, as usual. Ten minutes later, they heard the sound of 2 little feet walking on the wooden floor. They expected him to walk into their room and ask for a last-minute cuddle or something like that. But no! The little feet suddenly stopped, and the parents discreetly peeped around the doorway to see what was going on.

The child stood before the little altar that he had himself decorated with a cross, a tiny statue, some flowers (wilted, to tell the truth), pictures (some of which were in dubious taste), and other religious items which he had collected from here and there... He held in his arms the little puppy given to him 2 days before and for which he had developed an unconditional love. He pressed it against his heart, almost smothering the poor animal which had managed to put its head on the child's shoulder in order to breathe, a truly touching sight.

Then the little boy addressed to God a prayer which came from the bottom of his heart:

"Lord, bless my little puppy, just as you blessed the Child Jesus in Mary's womb!"

— Message of December 25, 1995 —

"Dear children! Today once again I rejoice with you and I bring you the Baby Jesus, so that he may bless you. I invite you, dear children, so that your life may be united with him. Jesus is the King of Peace and only he can give you the peace that you seek. I am with you and I present you to Jesus in a special way, now in this new time in which one should decide for him. This time is the time of grace. Thank you for having responded to my call."

HE BLEW OUT THE CANDLES!

Little Loïck was only 6 years old, but his heart was already tormented by uncontrollable fears and a sense of insecurity. His parents did not get along well, and the child could feel this lack of peace, which went deep into his psyche: it took his mother almost 2 hours every night to soothe his fears and get him to fall asleep. A couple who were friends of the family, Loïck's godmother and her husband, offered to take him to Medjugorje, together with a group of other children. It would be a long journey from the west of France, but everything had been organized to make sure that the kids had both fun and edification. There would be good times and good praying too!

One evening in Medjugorje, Loïck went up to his godmother, his little face completely lit up: "Godmother, godmother! You know what? Well, during prayers, Jesus, he came to see me! I saw him for real, and he had 2 candles. He showed me the candles, they were lit and you know what? He said, 'Loïck, can you see these candles?' And he blew them out, both of them. And he said, 'You saw how I blew out those candles? Well, just like I blew out the candles, I blow away your fears.'"

The change in Loïck became obvious that very evening: he was filled with a great peace. From that moment on he would fall asleep as soon as his head hit the pillow, like a baby in its mother's arms.

The next day, he went to see his godmother. He could hardly contain his joy. That afternoon, she had taken the children to the exposition of the Blessed Sacrament, and they had thus been able to pray for some time, while from time to time she led them in a little meditation they could easily understand.

"You know what? During the adoration Jesus spoke to me in my heart! He said: **'Make the sign of the cross often and make it well! Whenever you see a cross, make the sign of the cross.'"**

His godmother understood then that Jesus, who had healed little Loïck's heart of a torment which was too much for him to bear, had also shown him the shield he could use to ward off the evil of the world and its Author from coming to trouble him again. At the age of 6, Loïck had been given peace and a simple way to keep it safe in his heart: the sign of the cross.

As often happens in Medjugorje, the children were able to be present at an apparition. There were no other pilgrims with them that day, and the Gospa took this opportunity to give Ivan a special message for them. According to Ivan, she was very happy to see the children there, and she blessed each of them individually. In the message, she asked the children to bless their families, now that they themselves had been blessed. Each of them was to pass this blessing on. She also added (for the benefit of the accompanying adults): *"Continue to bring children!"*

Little Magali (who was almost 12) was present at this apparition. This little girl had always been overly attached to her mother, to the point of not tolerating the least separation from her, even for a moment. Girl Scout camps, school, vacations were a torture to her, and made her cry her eyes out. As she grew older, it became more and more of a handicap.

During the apparition, she did what her godmother had suggested, and presented her earthly mother to Mary, while asking her, the Gospa, to truly become her Mother. She told her, "I choose you for my Mother!"

When they got back home, even though the "earthly mother" had no clue whatsoever that this request had been made, she phoned the godmother to express her surprise.

"I hardly recognize my daughter!" she exclaimed. "She has become quiet, sweet, and independent. She doesn't cling desperately to me anymore. Something must have happened!..."

Indeed, something had happened! In Medjugorje Magali had experienced a great liberation; she had placed herself in Mary's womb.

FLASHBACK ON 1995

February: Father Petar Ljubicic leaves Medjugorje, to everyone's great sorrow. He goes to Switzerland, where he will take care of Croatian people in Zurich.

Father Jozo goes on mission to France. He is welcomed in several churches in France, including Chartres Cathedral. In Paris, he meets the papal nuncio, who is very open-minded about Medjugorje.

February 2: A statue of Our Lady from Medjugorje (brought back by a priest to a family in Civitavecchia, Italy) weeps tears of blood. Analyses are being carried out.

March 18: Yearly apparition to Mirjana.

March 23: Vicka takes 310 invalid soldiers to Rome. They meet the Pope, (see photo after the *Flashback on 1991*).

April 2: The people demonstrate in front of the residence of Bishop Peric at Mostar, to ask that the Franciscans might keep their parishes.

April 6: Cardinal Kuharic and Doctor Radic (Vice President of Croatia) visit the Pope in Rome to invite him to Split. John Paul II replies that he would like to go there, as well as to Maria Bistrica and to Medjugorje. (*Sloboda Dalmacija*, April 8, p. 3)

April 15: Four young people from the Cenacle Community are baptized during the Easter vigil in Medjugorje. They have risen again from drug addiction.

May 10: Monsignor Lagrange, Bishop of Gap (France) comes to Medjugorje, followed by Cardinal Wamala (Uganda) and by Cardinal Margéot (Mauritius).

June 15: The American pilot Scott O'Grady, whose airplane had been shot down over Bosnia, tells the press that he owes his life to the Blessed Mother of Medjugorje who appeared to him during his 6 days of hiding in the war-torn region of Banja Luka, before being rescued.

June 17: Monsignor Grillo, Bishop of Civitavecchia (Italy), enthrones the statue from Medjugorje and invites the faithful to honor it: "This grace comes to us from Medjugorje," he declared in his sermon (at the beginning of February, the statue had wept tears of blood while he was holding it, in the presence of 3 witnesses). Father Jozo concelebrates Mass with him in front of 3,000 people.

June 25: Yearly apparition to Ivanka. Our Lady asks that we pray for families because Satan wants to destroy them. She also invites us to be messengers of peace.

July: A new community, "The Precious Blood," settles in Medjugorje. The founder, Guglierma, is Italian.

The first 4 homes for orphans are inaugurated close to Medjugorje, under the patronage of Father Slavko. Each one is financed by a particular country. For information: Father Slavko, Zupni Ured, 88266 Medjugorje, Bosnia-Herzegovina. Fax: (387) 88 651 444.

July 29 & 30: Marija and Father Tardiff are in Monza stadium (Italy).

August 9: Inauguration of the "Casa San Giuseppe" located between both hills, a place for retreats with Father Jozo. Marija sometimes has her apparitions there. For information on retreats, contact by Fax: (387) 88 651 768.

August 30: Vicka accompanies 1,000 war orphans to Rome for an audience with John Paul II, in the Basilica of Saint Peter.

October: Jelena continues her theology studies in Rome, (see photo after May 25, 1996 message).

October 15: Ivan and Laureen have their child in Boston, Kristina Maria. They live sometimes in Medjugorje, sometimes in the States (Boston).

October 17: All the bishops of Bosnia-Herzegovina are summoned to Rome by John Paul II, to talk about peace.

1996

— MESSAGE OF JANUARY 25, 1996 —

"Dear children! Today I invite you to decide for peace. Pray that God will give you true peace. Live peace in your hearts and you will understand, dear children, that peace is the gift of God. Dear children, without love you cannot live peace.

"The fruit of peace is love and the fruit of love is forgiveness. I am with you and I invite all of you, little children, before all else, to forgive within your own family and then you will be able to forgive others. Thank you for having responded to my call."

MY MOTHER'S WOMB WAS A TOMB

"Without love, you cannot live peace"? But what if my mother's womb was a tomb, if my life is rooted in complete "non-love," am I condemned to be deprived of peace forever?

That Sophie ended up in Medjugorje was a miracle. This charming 40-year-old English teacher told me her story with enthusiasm. She kept on saying, "It's amazing, really amazing!" The truth is that, in her life, neither God nor Satan has been idle...

For Sophie, the disaster began as early as her conception: her mother didn't want the pregnancy. When she was told that she was expecting twins, her rejection was even more violent. At birth, the disaster continued: Sophie's twin brother was stillborn. From that moment on Sophie felt inside her both the death caused by the absence of love and an emptiness in her human relationships: her first counterpart, her very first love was dead! She grew up without God and without human closeness.

At the age of 20 she got married because she was pregnant. Yet another failure: she felt unable to love, and so did her husband. Their life as a married couple was a disaster: they were like 2 walls crashing into each other, and falling to pieces. She got divorced. Her little girl, Claire, started down the same tragic path of a lonely childhood. Hoping she had found a better man, Sophie remarried, and then realized to her horror that things were not better, but worse! She was stifled by a sense of "non-identity," and she was unable to communicate with her husband. Their relationship was caught in a vicious cycle of "anger-accusation-bitterness." Once again, Sophie was surrounded by the impenetrable wall of "non-love." But an even worse event triggered her real descent into hell: as she was giving birth to a baby boy, she relived the drama of the death of her twin brother, feeling all the guilt she had inherited from it. She realized that, just like her mother's, her own maternal womb was empty, there was no life in it, there was no love.

In her despair, she even forced her body to reject life. After the delivery, she developed a lethal disease which the doctors describe as "auto-immune," i.e., a self-destructive process. Her antibodies, designed to ward off the attacks of disease, had turned against her own body to destroy it from within. Her body was at war with itself, because her heart was filled with death. She came across a poem by Paul Eluard: "Thank you, Mother, for having created me!" It made her scream! She hated her life so much!

Collagenosis, rheumatoid polyarthritis, anemia...the wheelchair loomed on the horizon, probably to be followed by a slow death accompanied by terrible suffering. And there she was, her body hardened and drugged by strong medications.

Naturally, like anyone who doesn't know the Savior, she found herself a quack-savior. He was expensive; you had to supply him with locks of your hair every 3 weeks, but he had a picture of Jesus Christ in his office, so "the man couldn't be all bad...," she told herself. Indeed, the progress of the disease was arrested...

But inevitably, like all diseases cured by quacks, the pain stopped in one place, only to start somewhere else. It got worse. The man introduced Sophie to esoterism and occult practices. Fascinated, Sophie started to practice automatic writing every day.

"My hand was not in my control, I just *had* to write!" she told me later.

She went to every back-street bookstore in Paris to buy New-Age type books, and devoured them greedily. She took up yoga, and soon went on to practice the "opening of the chakras." Terrible fears invaded her, assailing her day and night without warning. She was paralyzed with anxiety as never before.

One night, as she had just been taking down a demon's dictation (sincerely believing that it linked her to "cosmic energies"), she came to herself with a start, sweating and mortally frightened. Then she saw Satan. He was standing next to her and stretched his ugly black hand towards her. It was ghastly! For the first time in her life, she uttered the name of God, and called on him to come to her rescue. It was her first prayer from the heart!

To her surprise, the Lord answered her plea and made her feel his presence. Sophie understood then that this God was *living*, he was *good*, and he was *peace*. Her life changed completely.

She began to pray every day, and discovered the Catholic faith. Later, she came to understand that esoterism and Christian life do not mix, and she made her choice to walk with Jesus, the true Savior, who doesn't play deadly tricks to destroy her.

"What about Medjugorje?" I asked.

"It's amazing! Jesus gave his Mother to me!"

"Tell me about Krizevac...that rebirth you experienced."

"I was making the Stations of the Cross with my group. When we reached the thirteenth station where Mary receives the body of Jesus in her arms, Brother Cyril asked me, 'Sophie, can you read the meditation of Father Slavko?' Without thinking, I answered yes, and started to read."[1]

I saw Sophie's eyes brimming with tears. Her voice began to quaver.

"So I read; but when I reached a certain passage, suddenly the nightmare returned. I broke down and wept; someone else had to take over the reading. Mary was waiting for me here, at this thirteenth station. The

---

[1] *Pray With the Heart*, by Fr. Slavko Barbaric, OFM. Available in the States from Franciscan University Press, Steubenville, OH 43952, or at Medjugorje.

passage went: 'Mary, I pray to you especially for abandoned children who do not know the warmth of a mother's lap. Please, be a mother to them, give them back the will to live! Mary, I pray to you for the mothers whose wombs have become the graveyards of life, for they have either killed or abandoned their children. Restore them to life too! Let the mother's wombs come back to life, and do not let any of them become the grave, but rather the cradle of life!'

"In a split second, I had touched the root of all my sufferings: my mother's womb had been a grave! My life had begun in a place filled by death! I had not received life!

"And the meditation continued with this message: *'Dear children, I have already told you that I have chosen you in a special way, just the way you are. I am your mother and I love you all...'*

"So, Mary became my mother—my root, the womb where I take shape. The most amazing thing of all is that everything happened so quietly. I felt a soft breath, something very gentle, and it was done. I expected a jolt, but no! Before these Stations of the Cross, I was an orphan; afterwards, I had found my other Mother. That's it, it happened very gently. I now have great peace, an incredible peace!"

Then Sophie added, whispering as if not to awaken a child: "And now I can say with all my heart, '**Lord, I thank you for having created me!**'"

— MESSAGE OF FEBRUARY 25, 1996 —

"Dear children! Today I invite you to conversion. This is the most important message that I have given you here. Little children, I wish each of you to become a carrier of my messages. I invite you, little children, to live the messages that I have given you over these years. This time is a time of grace. Especially now, when the Church also is inviting you to prayer and conversion. I, also, little children, invite you to live my messages that I have given you during the time since I appear here. Thank you for having responded to my call."

A LITTLE GLUE AND LOTS OF LOVE

Veronica was 40 and her life was a mess. "Basta! Enough is enough, life is too cruel!" Her decision to commit suicide was irrevocable. As she was walking alongside a row of cars parked on the street, feeling very depressed, she caught sight of a note stuck on a windshield. She went over and read: "Message from the Blessed Mother Mary in Medjugorje."

She felt as if she had just landed on another planet.

"...Little children, do not fear, for I am with you, even when you think that there is no way out and that Satan reigns. I bring peace to you. I am your mother and the Queen of Peace. I bless you with the blessing of joy so that God may be everything to you in your lives. Thank you for having responded to my call."

She read and read again, and then once more. It seemed as if she were drinking from an invisible spring. She savored each word slowly, and her heart began to beat again, completely freed from that morbid preoccupation with death! Later, Veronica tried to find the road leading to

Medjugorje, that unfamiliar and bizarre name. So, one day, she ended up at Medjugorje... to give thanks! That's how we got to know her story in detail.

The Gospa is looking for helping hands; she needs them! But once she has got hold of them, she uses them relentlessly; they serve as a release valve for her immeasurable motherly love, which she can hardly contain and which cannot conceive of anything but saving souls. The car's owner has never heard about Veronica's story. But he knows that he offered up his hands and heart to the Gospa, by sticking her messages[1] onto his car, among other things![2]

---

[1] See the book *Medjugorje Day by Day*, by Richard Beyer. A passage from the gospel and a daily meditation follow a message from Medjugorje, for one year. Available from: Ave Maria Press, Notre Dame, IN 46556. Price: $ 9.95.

[2] We've made your task easier: to enable you to spread the messages, here's a list that you can Xerox. You can also start a lovely tradition: when you have guests or when you are celebrating a Marian Feast in your prayer group, xerox these and then cut them out and when the prayers are over, have everyone pick out a message from the basket.

Dear children, you are absorbed with material things, but in the material you lose everything that God wishes to give you. I call you, dear children, to pray for the gift of the Holy Spirit. (4.17.86)

You do not know, dear children, how great my love is, and you do not know how to accept it. In various ways I wish to show it to you, but you, dear children, do not recognize it. Dear children, accept me in your life. (5.22.86)

Dear children, today I am calling you to holiness. Without holiness you cannot live. Therefore, with love overcome every sin and with love overcome all the difficulties which are coming to you. (7.10.86)

Dear children, in the place where you live, act with love. Let your only instrument always be love. By love, turn everything into good which Satan desires to destroy and possess. Only that way will you be completely mine and I shall be able to help you. (7.31.86)

Dear children, I thank you for the love which you are showing me. You know, dear children, that I love you immeasurably, and daily I pray the Lord to help you to understand the love which I am showing you. (8.21.86)

Dear children, without you I am not able to help the world. I desire that you cooperate with me in everything, even in the smallest things. Let your prayer be from the heart and surrender completely to me. (8.28.86)

Dear children, you are forgetting that I desire sacrifices from you so I can help you and to drive Satan away from you. Therefore, I am calling you again to offer sacrifices with a special reverence towards God. (9.18.86)

Dear children, today I wish to call you to pray daily for the souls in purgatory. For every soul prayer and grace is necessary to reach God and the love of God. By doing this, dear children, you obtain new intercessors who will help you in life. (11.6.86)

You know that I love you and that I burn out of love for you. Therefore, dear children, you also decide for love so that you will burn out of love and daily experience God's love. Decide for love so that love prevails in all of you, but not human love, rather, God's love. (11.20.86)

Dear children, I beseech you, surrender to the Lord your entire past, all the evil that has accumulated in your hearts. I want each one of you to be happy, but in sin, nobody can be happy. Therefore, dear children, pray, and in prayer you shall realize a new way of joy. (2.25.87)

Dear children, I am calling every one of you to start living in God's love. Dear children, you are ready to commit sin, and to put yourselves in the hands of Satan without reflecting. I call each one of you to consciously decide for God and against Satan. (5.25.87)

I want each one of you to be happy here on earth and to be with me in heaven. That is, dear children, the purpose of my coming here and it is my desire. (5.25.87)

Dear children, Satan is very strong, and therefore I ask you to dedicate your prayers to me so that those who are under his influence may be saved. Sacrifice your lives for the salvation of the world. In heaven you shall receive the Father's reward which he has promised you. (2.25.88)

Little children, do not be afraid, because I am with you even when you think there is no way out and that Satan is in control. I am bringing peace to you. I am your Mother, and the Queen of Peace. (7.25.88)

Dear children, I am calling you to complete surrender to God. Let everything that you possess be in the hands of God. Only in that way shall you have joy in your heart. (4.25.89)

Little children, rejoice in God the Creator because he has created you so wonderfully. Pray that your life be a joyful thanksgiving, which flows out of your heart like a river of joy. (8.25.88)

Dear children, I want you to comprehend that God has chosen each one of you, in order to use you in a great plan for the salvation of mankind. You are not able to comprehend how great your role is in God's design. Therefore, dear children, pray so that in prayer you may be able to comprehend what God's plan is in your regard. I am with you in order that you may be able to bring it about in all its fullness. (1.25.87)

I am calling you to Consecration to my Immaculate Heart. I want you to consecrate yourselves as persons, families, and parishes so that all belongs to God through my hands. (10.25.88)

I do not want anything for myself, rather all for the salvation of your souls. Satan is strong, and therefore you, little children, by constant prayer, press tightly to my Mother's heart. (10.25.88)

It is necessary to pray much, not to say, "If today we have not prayed, it is nothing serious." You must strive to pray. Prayer is the only road which leads to peace. If you pray and fast, you will obtain everything that you ask for. (To Jelena, 10.29.83)

The important thing is to pray to the Holy Spirit that he may descend on you. When one has him, one has everything. (10.21.83)

When you go to Mass, your trip from home to church should be a time of preparation for Mass. You should also receive Holy Communion with an open and pure heart, with purity of heart and openness. Do not leave the church without an appropriate act of thanksgiving. (10.84)

Pray, dear children, so that God's plan may be accomplished, and all the works of Satan be changed in favor of the glory of God. (2.17.85)

Pray, little children, for the health of my most beloved son who suffers, and whom I chose for these times. (8.25.94)

Dear children, this evening I pray that you especially venerate the Heart of my Son, Jesus. Make reparation for the wound inflicted on the Heart of my Son. That Heart is offended by all kinds of sin. (4.5.84)

I urge you to ask everyone to pray the rosary. With the rosary, you will overcome all the troubles which Satan is trying to inflict on the Catholic Church. Let all priests pray the rosary. (6.25.85)

Pray for the outpouring of the Holy Spirit on your family and on your parish. Pray, and you shall not regret it. God will give you gifts by which you will glorify him till the end of your life on this earth. (6.2.84)

Dear children, I still need your prayers. You wonder why all these prayers? Look around you, dear children, and you will see how greatly sin has dominated the world. Pray therefore that Jesus conquers. (9.13.84)

Dear children, today I call on you to read the Bible every day in your homes and let it be in a visible place so as always to encourage you to read it and to pray. (10.18.84)

Dear children, today I call you to live the words this week: "I love God!" Dear children, through love you will achieve everything and even what you think is impossible. (2.28.85)

Dear children, today I wish to call you to pray, pray, pray! In prayer you shall perceive the greatest joy and the way out of every situation that has no exit. (3.28.85)

When you will suffer difficulties, and need something, come to me. (1983)

Give me all your feelings and all your problems! I wish to comfort you in all your trials. I wish to fill you with peace, joy, and love of God. (6.25.85)

Dear children, today I call you to place more blessed objects in your homes and call everyone to put some blessed object on yourself. (7.18.85)

Dear children, today I call you especially now to advance against Satan by means of prayer. Dear children, put on the armor for battle and with the rosary in your hand, defeat him! (8.8.85)

Dear children, I want to tell you that the Cross should be central these days. Pray especially before the crucifix, from which great graces are coming. (9.12.85)

I, as the Mother, wish to call all to holiness so that you can bestow it on others. You are a mirror to others! (10.10.85)

Today, I call you to start working on your hearts. Now that all the work in the fields is over, you are finding time for cleaning even the most neglected areas, but you leave your heart aside. Work more and clean with love every part of your heart. (10.17.85)

Dear children, I am calling you to the love of neighbor and love toward the one from whom evil comes to you. In that way you will be able to discern the intentions of hearts. Pray and love, dear children! By love, you are able to do even that which you think is impossible. (11.7.85)

Dear children, again I call you to prayer with the heart. If you pray with the heart, dear children, the ice of your brother's heart will melt and every barrier shall disappear. (1.23.86)

Dear children, I wish to call you to a living of Holy Mass. There are many of you who have sensed the beauty of the Holy Mass, but there are also those who come unwillingly. Let your coming to it be a joyful one. Come to it with love. (4.3.86)

— MESSAGE OF MARCH 25, 1996 —

"Dear children! I invite you to decide again to love God above all else, in this time, when due to the spirit of consumerism one forgets what it means to love and to cherish true values. I invite you again, little children, to put God in the first place in your life. Do not let Satan attract you through material things but, little children, decide for God who is freedom and love. Choose life and not death of the soul.

"Little children, in this time, when you meditate upon the suffering and death of Jesus, I invite you to decide for life which blossomed through the Resurrection and that your life may be renewed today through conversion, which shall lead you to eternal life. "Thank you for having responded to my call."

COLETTE'S MINISTRY

"Advanced breast cancer."

Professor Joyeux put down the report of Colette's tests and informed her husband, Chris, that Colette had to be operated on, as soon as possible.

This was a big shock for her family and for the Community of the Beatitudes[1] to which she belonged. Colette was a young and beautiful woman, so full of life and energy...

After the operation, a long and painful calvary began for Colette.

---

[1] This is a lay community founded in 1973 in France by a married deacon, Ephraim Croissant. Today there are 65 foundations throughout the world. For information on their communities write to, among other addresses:
Community of Beatitudes, 2536 rue Immaculée- Conception, C.P. 123, Saint-Ours, JOG 1PO, QC, Canada. Tel: (450) 785-2220; Fax: (450) 785-3523.
Cty of Beatitudes, care of Lyons, 64 Middlepark Road- Stockburn, Christchurch, New Zealand. Tel: (643) 351 45 23; Fax: (643) 351 45 02.

Metastasis had reached other organs. She got weaker every day. In February 1994, she and Chris decided to do something crazy: they came to Medjugorje, in spite of the critical state of Colette's condition. She could hardly stand up. In Medjugorje a severe sore throat made things even worse, and she had to stay in bed for 6 of the 8 days she spent there. She, who had dreamed of praying on the mountains and who wished to meet Vicka! She offered everything to Mary, without complaining.

But a surprise was waiting for her: Vicka had been told about the situation, and she came hurrying to Colette's room. She prayed over her for a long time with her usual simplicity. While she whispered blessings in Croatian, she kept smiling encouragingly at Colette. As she left the room, she kissed her and said, "Don't worry, the Gospa is always with you!"

We, who were still ignorant of God's plans for our lives, which are so much more beautiful than our own, we all expected Colette to be healed, and were disappointed to find out that her state was rapidly getting worse.

Colette's sufferings became unbearable, in spite of all the treatments offered by modern medicine. Nevertheless, she amazed everybody. She was so incredibly peaceful and joyful, even during the hardest moments of her race toward death. Since her trip to Medjugorje, she had been totally immersed in Our Lady's blessing: it even seemed that this grace was growing deeper every day, and it transfigured Colette's face.

"After Vicka's prayer, the Blessed Mother has never left me, not for a second," she once said to me. "She, herself, taught me how to suffer in communion with Jesus, like her, and you won't believe me if I tell you that the more I suffer, the more I feel intimately united to Jesus. The times of the worst sufferings are also the most deeply joyful to me. I feel a truly divine joy which I cannot describe to you. I feel within me his own joy in saving souls. It's extraordinary! Seeing me like this, a poor sick thing lying in a bed, no one would believe that I am the happiest woman on earth!"

July 1995: the end was close. Her poor ravaged body could not hold out much longer. Her family came to rally around along with all those who love her, and they whispered the usual things in her ear: "Colette, when you get up there, don't forget..." Colette was preparing herself to leave with Mary, peacefully, like someone who in her life had given all she had, and more.

A few months earlier, during an adoration (she had the Holy Sacrament in her room), Jesus had shown her what her arrival in heaven would be like. She saw the elect bursting with joy as she walked in, dressed in a magnificent white dress. She was the most beautiful woman, the unique one, and Jesus came and took her in his arms, and they started to dance, dance, dance...

But July 1995 was not the time chosen by God, because, against all (medical!) odds, Colette did not depart, and regained new, supernatural energy. What could have happened?

On the verge of death, she had a "visitation" from Marthe Robin (see photo), who asked her whether she was willing to live a little longer in order to extend her ministry as a soul "crucified by love,"[2] to help her brothers and sisters in her community. Colette had scarcely heard of Marthe Robin, but this visit was the beginning of the amazing collaboration of these two souls. Hadn't Colette offered her illness and her life for her brothers and sisters in the Community?

Tangible signs of this compassion towards souls were soon visible. Over the days that followed, Colette experienced such an intense compassion towards everyone that she hardly recognized herself. It wasn't her! Deep down, inside each heart she saw, as if on a screen, everybody's wounds, and in every detail the circumstances which caused these wounds. She saw, heard, and felt even the words and the secret thoughts of the parents at the moment of the child's conception. She saw the child in its mother's womb, the baby's extraordinary awareness of love in spite of its microscopic size, and she sensed how this tiny little being had felt every lack of love, the conflicts, the impurities, and in some occasions even rejection by its parents. The baby is conscious of everything, and oh so acutely!

Colette sobbed with grief, but the tears that flowed were not hers; she felt it was Our Lady who cried within her in front of these hearts tortured and torn even before they were born. It was the Blessed Mother Mary who cried to see the twisted and unfortunate directions taken later by the child because of its very first and deepest wounds.

Then Colette began to practice a ministry which had never been seen before: in prayer, she told people what God showed her[3] and the precise moments when, as a child, they had refused life, refused God, refused love,

---

[2] This is the term Jesus used to explain her vocation and mission to Marthe Robin: *"You will be my little (soul) crucified by love."* (1929)

[3] This charism comes under the charism of science and prophecy, as can be found in the Bible. For example, the prophet Nathan went to see David and told him, on behalf of God, what he had done, in order to obtain his conversion (2 Sam 12:1-15). Of course, this has nothing to do with "divination," in which the person uses photos, coffee grounds, pendulums, tarot cards, etc. as props to consult the spirits. They actually consult evil spirits, (not the Holy Spirit!).

as if trying to protect themselves against the rejection of which they were the victims. But seeing is one thing, healing is another! What could not be achieved in 20 years of psychoanalysis, i.e., putting someone back on his feet, Colette, as an instrument of God, could do after meeting the person once or twice.

The compassion of Jesus and Mary overflowed from her heart like a torrential river, and the healing began.[4]

Only God knows how many resurrections took place in Colette's room. We went to see her, and behind her smile, her sense of humor, her joy and her patience, we would see Mary, we found the Mother of our lives, the Mother who took us to her heart and gave us a new taste for life and the true identity we had lost.[5]

Eight months later, on March 2, 1996 (the first Saturday of the month), Colette entered into heaven at last. In her dying moments, her husband Chris was by her side with two of their children and a Sister of the Community. Colette was no longer able to speak, but she could still hear. At her bedside they started to pray the rosary. Before praying the last Glorious Mystery, the coronation of Mary in heaven, Sister Catherine said to Colette, "Colette, you may go now! They're all waiting for you up there!"

And Colette quietly stopped breathing; she left them at that very moment.

Today, she keeps on working among us, only in a different way. She makes herself available to all those who request her help. Fortunately, as she knows that we always need to see with our own eyes, touch with our own hands, and hear with our own ears the most beautiful things of God, she had scarcely reached heaven when she started to talk to other hearts, prepared by God, in order to take over her unbelievable ministry.

Yes, if we carefully water and tend the graces we receive in Medjugorje, the Gospa makes them grow and bear fruits such as this. What a promise this is for all of us! For Colette did not do anything but receive the blessing of Our Lady in good soil.

---

[4] I myself benefited from this charism. In fact, for 30 years I had been unable to sleep without taking pills, and I suffered from terrible insomnia. Colette saw that this was not due to physical causes, but was the result of spiritualism seances which I had taken part in when I was younger, before my conversion. "The Evil One has entered that way, and he still has an impact on your sleep. He is trying to exhaust you and destroy you that way," she told me. "He is furious that you have been called to bring Jesus and Mary to those who he intended should never hear of them." Colette prayed, and in 2 months both the insomnia and the pills were a thing of the past.

[5] Colette exercised her ministry with the consent of her spiritual director, who verified the authenticity of the graces received.

— MESSAGE OF APRIL 25, 1996 —

"Dear children! Today I invite you again to put prayer in the first place in your families. Little children, when God is in the first place, then you will, in all that you do, seek the will of God. In this way your daily conversion will become easier. Little children, seek with humility that which is not in order in your hearts, and you shall understand what you have to do. Conversion will become a daily duty that you will do with joy. Little children, I am with you and I bless you and I invite you to become my witnesses by prayer and personal conversion. Thank you for having responded to my call."

ONE OF COLETTE'S FRUITS

"A sinner my mother conceived me,"[1] Fabienne kept on repeating to herself, "but my Mother was conceived Immaculate." She heard this phrase in Lourdes in October 1994, and ever since then she did not stop turning it over and over in her heart. She had the confused feeling that a great truth and a life buoy were hiding behind this simple phrase.

Fabienne was 25 years old. She was sick and tired of suffering; her inner turmoil never ceased. She hadn't found her identity. She had the painful feeling of being a fake, and the fact that she suffered from a complete lack of self-confidence spoiled all her relationships. Being looked at frightened her, and her pathological timidity altered her behavior. "As unsociable as one can be," she said, describing herself bitterly. Fabienne's diagnosis was right on the button: she had built a fortress around herself.

She grew to know Colette over several visits. The very first time they prayed together, Fabienne wondered, "Why was Colette talking so much about St. Jerome? And, by the way, who on earth is he anyway?"

---

[1] Psalm 50.

The "Blue Cross," a specially holy place of apparitions; many miracles have taken place here.

Mirjana receives her annual apparition on March 18, 1991: *"Attend Mass once a month for those who do not know God's love yet,"*

Mirjana, Marko, and little Marija. *"Satan wants to destroy your families,"* Our Lady told her. *"The best weapon against him is to say the rosary as a family."*

Fr. Svetozar and Vicka in Montreal with Georgette Faniel, a soul-mate of Medjugorje.

Marija. She receives the monthly messages for the world. The Gospa told her, *"I give you my love so that you can give it to others."*

Jelena. She was 12 when Our Lady asked her to found a prayer group. Her beauty and her witness touch many young people.

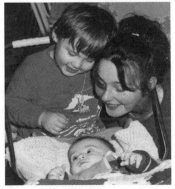

Fr. Slavko tirelessly explains the last message.

Ivanka and her 2 oldest children. The most hidden of the visionaries. The Gospa has told her the future of the world.

John Paul II blesses Sr. Emmanuel 3 times for her mission of spreading Our Lady's messages from Medjugorje (Nov. 15, 1996).

The sick and the crippled make the climb. All of them come down happy, some cured.

Mother Teresa strengthens her ties

The parish prays the rosary on Podbrdo. Fr. Petar is the one who will reveal Mirjana's 10 secrets.

Patrick Latta and his friend Wayne Weible in Medjugorje.

Denis Nolan, responsible for beginning the Medjugorje Conferences in the US in 1989. Now 200 take place each year. His last contribution: 52 TV programs on Medjugorje.

Francis just before his death; he said yes to holiness at Medjugorje.

Christian and Colette Estadieu with Vicka in 1988. Their testimony has saved hundreds of families from breaking apart.

Francis, "Marija's darling," before his accident.

Colette a month before her death in March 1996. "The Gospa is always with you," Vicka told her.

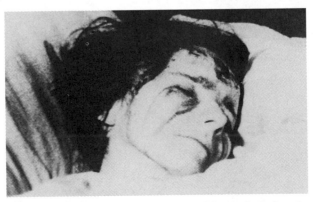

Marthe Robin, the French mystic who died 3 months before the first apparition.

"St. Jerome," Colette told her, "had given everything to the Lord but his sin."

"How could a saint possibly not confess his sin?" Fabienne wondered, puzzled. "And what does this have to do with my own problem?"

On Colette's advice, Fabienne decided to go to Medjugorje. Upon her return, things gathered momentum. While praying, Colette saw Fabienne "in an amniotic sac, refusing to get out of it." She knew only 2 things about Fabienne: her parents had lost a 2-year-old little girl, and Fabienne had been deeply desired and was born a year after the baby's death. Then the Lord revealed everything to her, and she got to the bottom of it. Fabienne had actually been desired by her parents but not as a second child, unique and special: they wanted her to *replace* their first daughter. They wanted back the child they had lost. Colette went even further: she explained to Fabienne that in her mother's womb she had rebelled against her parents because of this; she had refused to be born, she had said no to life. Besides, she had also refused to be a girl.

As soon as Colette told Fabienne what she had lived and suffered in her mother's womb just after she was conceived, Fabienne experienced a deep healing immediately. (Colette always thought about these healings in the hours of utter exhaustion, which was a wonderful comfort when her ministry to help souls demanded more and more from her.)

One week later, Fabienne was about to leave again for Medjugorje. Colette called her and suggested, "Once you get there, go and find a priest to confess this sin."

Fabienne was totally dismayed... What a weird idea! How could she explain to a priest that she had sinned in her mother's womb by refusing life?

"You'll go and see Father Slavko," said Colette. "He will understand."

"I'm going... I'm not going..." Fabienne struggled a lot within herself during the journey. In Medjugorje, the Canadian priest who celebrated Mass on the first day declared in his homily, "As the Lord asked of St. Jerome, let us also offer him what he wants most: our sin!" Fabienne couldn't believe her ears; her spirit eventually saw the light, and she could understand why this phrase kept coming back to her: "A sinner my mother conceived me, but my Mother was conceived Immaculate." It was now her turn to do what the Lord had asked of St. Jerome.

So she went to Father Slavko with her confession, and it allowed her inner healing to be fully achieved. Forgiveness and mercy opened up the gates of her heart, and a total acceptance of life poured in. After all these terrible years spent in a dark tunnel where she lived like a zombie, and begrudgingly, Fabienne finally felt the joy of seeing the hand of God upon her. She became aware that he now could achieve the divine plans he had for her, that she was worthy. She knew in her heart that she had been created, loved, and chosen in a unique way. All the trouble caused by the feeling of having to replace someone else vanished completely.

Fabienne finally realized that she had been born of God and that the true source, the true roots of her life, were much more firmly entrenched in the Father's maternal womb than in her earthly mother's. She was discovering her Creator! She began to breathe differently, and the most tangible sign of her healing was obvious to everyone: Fabienne the recluse, the inaccessible, the ever surly one, had become an understanding young lady, full of compassion and peace, so that meeting her is now a real treat.

There were 2 things that Colette didn't know about Fabienne. Would you like to know them?

1. That very year she had received St. Jerome as her protector.[2] (She had found it weird: an almost unknown saint!)

2. Nine months had passed between the day when she had immersed herself in the motherly waters of Our Lady in Lourdes (you know those freezing pools...) and the moment when, in Medjugorje, she experienced this rebirth, this new birth through Colette's prayer.

Among the people who have been helped by Colette, Fabienne's case is far from being the most extreme, if you consider all the children who have not been desired by their mothers, or even have had to face total rejection. Much deep despair is rooted in these wounds, as well as much chronic anguish and psychological blocking, which become real handicaps. But God has prepared a work of his mercy for each misery of ours, and he has hidden it in the Immaculate Heart of his Mother... Now, make the most of it!

---

[2] See the chapter, *A Pal From Heaven*, (October 1994).

— Message of May 25, 1996 —

"Dear children! Today I wish to thank you for all the prayers and sacrifices that you have offered to me, during this month which is dedicated to me. Little children, I also wish that you all become active during this time, that is through me connected to heaven in a special way. Pray in order to understand that you all, through your life and your example, ought to collaborate in the work of salvation.

"Little children, I wish that all people convert and see me and my Son, Jesus, in you. I will intercede for you and help you to become the light. In helping the other, your soul will also find salvation. Thank you for having responded to my call."

KIDS TEACH US SACRIFICE

I am proud of children, because when the Gospa invites them to offer prayers and sacrifices, they are the first ones to respond, and how they apply themselves!

In April 1992, when I got wind of the existence of concentration camps in the north of the country, I had to do something, anything... I wanted to go there, and I wanted to tell the whole world about this horrible scandal...but it would only have added one more death to the list.

Therefore, I prayed to the Gospa, begging her to use me in another way. She didn't waste any time! A few days later, as I was finishing a time of adoration, I snatched up a pen to put down all the things that were

---

[1] See in the book, *Medjugorje, The War Day By Day*, p. 79: "Children Will Overcome Hatred."

surging up in my heart. So, with Vicka's collaboration, a very special operation was born: "Little children, save Medjugorje!"[1] Through it thousands of children heard Our Lady's call to help her stop the war and the rise of evil, through their prayers and sacrifices. Only in heaven will we learn of the miracles obtained by these innocent hearts to prevent our world from sinking into complete horror.

However, during that war, our practical means were very limited, and carrying out this project was very difficult. Besides, "Medjugorje" and "sacrifices" are words that do not please everyone among our catechetical authorities! Therefore, I made a deal with the Gospa: "The day you want to launch another 'Children — SOS,' you can definitely count me in... But, next time, we could use Fatima as the main story, so that no one gets an attack of hives when reading the word 'Medjugorje.' We will ask for the imprimatur to avoid hearing that proposing sacrifices to children is a federal crime against freedom."

Two years later, the moment had come! As she knew that I didn't have much time, Mary herself provided all that was needed! The best possible artist offered her services, a Cardinal granted the imprimatur in 24 hours... In short, the book[2] was ready a little before the "month of Mary." And what did Mary tell the children that very month of May 96? *"Today, I wish to thank you for all the prayers and sacrifices..."*!!

Since then, I have been receiving their colored drawing books from the children who have finished their novena for Mary. Your heart melts when reading what they offer, give, or ask for. You will find a few unedited quotes from them in the chapter, "We'll Get Those Five Million Little Ones" (February 25, 1997).

Little Oliver received the book just 9 days before his First Holy Communion. His parents then suggested he make the novena as preparation for that day. Therefore, every day, Oliver chose a sacrifice to offer, but his 4-year-old brother didn't think it was fair that only his brother could enjoy such a privilege!

The younger boy finally threw a tantrum, crying, "What about me? What about me? What is my sacrifice for the day?" He was given a few

---

[2] *Children, Help My Heart To Triumph*! For children between 6 and 13. Drawings by Pascale Nouailhat, 56 colored pages. Available from Saint Andrews Publications, 6111 Steubenville Pike, McKees Rocks, PA, 15136. Price $10.

ideas which he immediately put into practice. Just like his brother, he put his heart so much into it that the parents began to feel a little excluded. "What about us...?"

So they decided to follow in the footsteps of their sons in their adventure with the Gospa, and the whole family experienced a great renewal in their relationships.

Shortly after, little Chrystelle, 7, taught every one of us, with one sentence, a deeply mystical and theological lesson about spiritual warfare. She ended her novena and said to her mother, "Mommy, now I know how to consecrate myself to Mary: it's easy! I give her my heart, and she gives me her Immaculate Heart! We sort of swap!"

"Great, honey!"

But a thorny problem came to Chrystelle's mind: "But what if I do something naughty? What will happen then?"

She thought it over for a minute, then the light came: "I know! If a naughty idea comes to me, it will see the Immaculate Heart and it will immediately run away!"

— MESSAGE OF JUNE 25, 1996 —

"Dear children! Today I thank you for all the sacrifices you have offered me these days. Little children, I invite you to open yourselves to me and to decide for conversion. Your hearts, little children, are still not completely open to me and therefore I invite you again to open to prayer so that in prayer the Holy Spirit will help you, that your hearts become of flesh and not of stone. Little children, thank you for having responded to my call and for having decided to walk with me toward holiness."

HEY, AREN'T YOU FROM JERUSALEM?

Medjugorje could easily be taken for a town around Safed or Cana, the countryside looks so much like the Galilee: the same vegetation, the same stunning white light that one finds in the Mediterranean lands, the same gentle valleys tumbling over with briars, fig trees, grape vines and pomegranate trees, and not last those inevitable stones, the nightmare that haunts the farmers of Israel even today. The Blessed Mother of Nazareth would feel right at home, which she certainly wouldn't in, say, Norway!

But the startlingly biblical atmosphere of the apparitions of Medjugorje doesn't derive, ultimately, from these exterior similarities between the landscape of Herzegovina and that of Israel. It comes from the person of Mary, her demeanor, her prayer, her bearing, her attitudes, and even her choice of words. Her entire being embodies the biblical woman from the royal family of King David.

Rita F., Father Slavko's American assistant, celebrated her birthday the other day. As a special treat, Marija invited her to be present at the apparition in her little chapel, and Rita brought a rose for the Blessed Mother. Now Marija did not know that Rita was of Jewish background. Our Lady appeared, and after reciting the Magnificat that always followed the apparition, Marija described to everyone what had just taken place. She smiled mischievously and said:

"This evening the Gospa greeted us and blessed us, and looked right away at the rose. She really liked it! But then she started to pray in her mother tongue, and I didn't understand a thing!"

Rita's friends understood the gift that this represented, in particular Bernard Ellis, our English friend from a very observant Jewish family, who was there at the time.

"She spoke in her native tongue because she felt at home!" I said, to make him happy.

Bernard had tears in his eyes: that very morning he had asked God for a sign that the apparitions in Medjugorje were really and truly the Mother of the Messiah. This sign was even more than he had hoped for!

Our Lady speaks perfect Croatian; so why speak in her native tongue,[1] which could only upset her little Marija who wouldn't understand a word?

Our translations do not always faithfully reproduce the original meaning.[2] We are, in fact, far removed from the meanings of the original words spoken by God or by the angels, words that were rich from the intensive formation over 3,000 years of the People of the Book, and which bear deep within them the inviolate meaning of the Heart of God.

It gives us such great joy to see that Mary uses in her messages the very words of the Bible, of Revelation! But they lose so much of their resonance in our hearts and souls when they are translated into English and other modern languages, since the equivalent word does not have the same associations or the same root meaning.

The following Hebrew words that Mary used in her June 25 message, words for conversion, holiness, and heart are good examples that we may consider:

Conversion: The Hebrew root of this word that is found throughout the history of the people of Israel (and therefore the history of our souls) could scarcely be farther from the connotations of our modern word, with all that

---

[1] Mary's mother tongue was Aramaic, but she most probably also spoke Hebrew.

[2] In June 1996 His Holiness John Paul II declared that the English-language "Hail Mary" does not give a true sense of the real greeting of the angel Gabriel, which is full of a joy that the English does not convey.

dreary procession of negative notions like renunciation and superhuman effort. The Hebrew word *teshuva*, which means "return," quite the contrary is redolent with positive and comforting connotations of return from exile. Back home at last, at last!

So the exile has finally returned to his beloved homeland, to his loved ones, to the house where he was conceived by his parents, home where life is good and love prevails, home to his roots, the spring of his being. He has endured the privations of being far from home and family, in dire need, in poverty both of heart and body as a slave among barbarian peoples; and here he is finally reunited with his beloved family and friends, he reclaims his patrimony, and he is safe once again—his cup runneth over.

At Medjugorje Mary tells us that her most important message is conversion. Well, of course it is! If I do not dwell in the heart of the Father (John 1:18) with Jesus, I am a dead man!

"The world is far from God, and that is why there is no peace," she tells us, and, *"I have come to bring you closer to the Heart of God"*—and so she does.

Holiness: For most Christians, this word evokes dread and shrinking away, with its connotations of renunciation morning, noon, and night, renunciation and more renunciation! Whereas we want only to breathe free, to live, to live it up! Look at those poor saints in their caves, suffering like animals...agonies of soul and body. Nope, not for me! We want to enjoy all the good things of life, we want to be happy!

And who do I think I am, anyway?! Holiness is out of reach for me, way out of reach! Do you think I am going to perform miracles, levitate, multiply the loaves and the fishes? You're nuts! That stuff is for rare individuals, special persons born in holy water. But I'm just normal, like everybody else. And anyway it would just lead to pride to think that a nobody like me could become a saint. And why not Abraham Lincoln, while I'm at it?

"Dear children," said Mary to the prayer group, *"I know that many of you are afraid of holiness..."*

Kadosh, "holy," means *"set apart"* in Hebrew, as in God dividing light from darkness, as in separating the wheat from the chaff. I am "holy" when I am not "of the world," although I am *in* the world. I have been "set apart" by baptism, in order to belong to God. For it is he who gives me a share in his holiness, for he alone is holy.

The Gospa asked Jelena's group *not to imitate the other young people who run after pleasure.* Far from signifying some sort of deprivation, this counsel, quite to the contrary, implies the notion of abundance: Why squander mindlessly the precious treasures of my inheritance by dealing with the Thief, the Liar, the Murderer, when by choosing holiness I can have everything of God's, since I am part and parcel of him? At Medjugorje the Gospa offers everyone who is afraid of holiness the most magnificent reassurance: Not only is the saint not "sent to bed without dessert," but she possesses in her heart all the fullness of love. And isn't that what everyone yearns the most deeply for, with a piercing, aching longing, deep within? *"Without holiness you cannot live!"* she says.

I often quote the following words of Mary when I speak with young people: *"You are unconsciously putting yourselves right into the hands of Satan,"* she said; and I add: "Do you want to know the fastest way to put yourselves in the hands of Satan? It's easy! Just do what everybody else is doing, it's foolproof. But on the other hand, if you follow the teachings of the Gospel and the words of Our Lady, that is also a foolproof way, you'll be in the hands of God and you will obtain all that you seek. If you live in holiness, the world, which is famished for God, will be powerfully drawn to you, people will ask you, like those young Communist atheists asked Mirjana in Sarajevo: 'We see that you have something that we do not have: a certain peace, an inner happiness... We want that too! Tell us what your secret is!'"

Heart: "Thou shalt love the Lord thy God with all thy heart..." *Levav*, "heart" in Hebrew, includes both the good and the bad impulses. This verse from Deuteronomy quoted by Jesus means that in your heart there is both flesh and stone. No human heart is only one or the other. Still, it is one or the other that is dominant, either the flesh, or the stone. God transforms the stone into flowing water. Love God with your whole self, and, little by little, he will change into living flesh what is still stone within you. That is what Mary means in this message.

Oh, but it looks like I'm writing a 2nd book on all those Hebrew root words! I must refrain myself...but not you! Never again let yourself read the messages thinking: "Oh, how colorless, tasteless, odorless...! No! Find among your priests or pastors one who can unlock for you the treasures of the Bible; someone who can reveal to you the extraordinary depth of meaning in even the slightest iota! And when you have a chat with Our Lady of Lourdes, Our Lady of Fatima, Our Lady of Guadalupe, Our Lady of Czestochowa, Our Lady of Paris, go ahead and ask her:

"But, wait, Madam—aren't you from Jerusalem?

— MESSAGE OF JULY 25, 1996 —

"Dear children! Today I invite you to decide every day for God. Little children, you speak much about God, but you witness little with your life. Therefore, little children, decide for conversion, that your life may be true before God, so that in the truth of your life you witness the beauty God gave you.

"Little children, I invite you again to decide for prayer because through prayer, you will be able to live the conversion. Each one of you shall become in simplicity similar to a child who is open to the love of the Father. Thank you for having responded to my call."

A TOY SHE COULDN'T RESIST!

For the filming of our television programs on the messages,[1] Marija and Paolo had let us use their house. With a professional American film crew under the direction of Denis Nolan, we installed our studio in the tiny chapel where Marija receives her daily apparitions when she stays in Medjugorje. Blinding spotlights had therefore replaced for a short time the soft, celestial and uncreated light which accompanies Mary when she visits this *upper room*.

Ruzka, Marija's older sister, did the cooking for us, and we soon became good friends. I was delighted to see the perfect understanding, the kindred spirit, between Mark, a movie-maker from Hollywood, and this Croatian woman who has spent all her life serving, helping others, and working hard to survive: a true Martha of Bethany with, in addition, the heart of Mary. Ruzka, to me, is the deeply moving portrait of the biblical

---

[1] For information on these television programs (now also available on videotape) please see the appendix.

woman who knows how to keep the *Shalom* in the home: her heart set on God, her feet firmly planted on the ground, her hands in diapers and her face always cheerful, come what may. Nothing escapes her, whether concerning people or material things. She treasures all these things in her heart and sometimes, when she feels confident, she lets out gems which are more precious than gold. Her company heals me from the last Parisian viruses still clinging to me! Moreover, she is one of the most reliable witnesses to the first months of the Medjugorje events, as the humble people of the visionaries' families saw them.

One evening, as she was preparing the strongest coffee I ever tasted, she spontaneously shared her flashbacks about the pioneering days of Medjugorje when policemen and false brothers made their lives a misery, and when the village was showered with the most sublime graces.

"One night," she said, "I was in the church, and there were so many people that some of them were crammed into the choir. I was standing 3 feet away from Father Jozo. Suddenly, during the rosary, his face changed and reflected the greatest surprise. For a few minutes he stared at something slightly above the crowd, towards the gallery, and stood gaping, fascinated. I could see the expression on his face very well, and I knew that something was happening. Then he bent his head and remained thoughtful, absorbed.

"After the prayer, since I knew him well, I asked him: 'What did you see?' He looked at me and didn't say a word; he was determined not to answer my question. As for me, I knew that he had seen the Gospa. I knew my sister; I knew how one looks when seeing the Gospa. Only later did he say that the Gospa had been present like a Mother among her children, her people, and that she had been praying with us. From that day on, all his doubts left him and he protected the visionaries."

Later, the conversation came round to Bishop Zanic.

"I was here when he came after the first apparition. He spoke for a long time with the visionaries. I remember that evening clearly: we were in the church, he formed a ring with his thumb and forefinger (she imitated the gesture) and in a firm, convincing voice he said to the people: 'The visionaries are not lying, they are telling the truth!,' and he repeated insistently: 'Istina, istina!' (the truth, the truth!). He was even shouting!"

"But what about you, Ruzka, did you believe at once?" I asked.

"Yes, immediately! You know in your heart when something is true. I don't see anything, I don't hear anything, but I do know she is here. My little Ivana saw her, though! At that time, no one could control the crowd; it was almost impossible to manage all these people, and the poor visionaries were tightly squeezed — we were afraid that they would end up being crushed in the crowd!

"I had come to the apparition with Ivana, who was only 18 months old at the time. I held her in my arms, high up, so that she would have enough air. Unwillingly, pushed by the people surrounding Marija, I found myself almost exactly where the Gospa stood, about 5 feet away in front of the visionaries. That's when the strangest scene took place. Little Ivana climbed up on my arm, and, with her hands, she tried to grab something. She was pulling this invisible thing with all her weak little strength, but she wasn't able to seize it. A priest from Split was standing close to her and observed her little game, fascinated. He burst into tears.

"After the apparition, Marija said that the little girl had also seen Our Lady, and that she had been playing with her 12-star crown, trying to catch it, which made the Gospa laugh merrily.[2] As for the priest, he explained that he had not believed in the apparitions, and had come to prove that they were fake. But Our Lady had just given him an undeniable sign. In tears, he kept saying, 'A child cannot lie.'

"This priest became a great defender of Medjugorje."

Ruzka added that, at that time, the crowd was bristling with Communist spies, and that no one could say anything without running huge risks. But her little Ivana had spoken in the name of everyone, louder than any declaration from bishops or theologians!

To convince those in doubt, the Gospa had chosen a little child!

---

[2] There is a very beautiful book on the Gospa as related by Marija: *Marija and the Mother of God*, by Heather Parsons. Available in Ireland for £ 4.95 from: Robert Andrew Press, Blanchardstown, Dublin 15, Ireland. We also recommend: *A Light Between the Hills* by the same author (a best-seller), available from the same publisher for £ 4.95.

— MESSAGE OF AUGUST 25, 1996 —

"Dear children! Listen, because I wish to speak to you and to invite you to have more faith and trust in God, who loves you immeasurably. Little children, you do not know how to live in the grace of God, that is why I call you anew to carry the Word of God in your heart and thought.

"Little children, place the Sacred Scripture in a visible place in your family, and read and live it. Teach your children, because if you are not an example to them, children depart into godlessness. Reflect and pray and then God will be born in your heart and your heart will be joyous. Thank you for having responded to my call."

THERESA'S SWAP

Picture a tiny, 53-year-old woman, a small farmer from Brittany (in northwestern France), a believer even before she was born, coming to Medjugorje on the trip of her lifetime. That's Theresa. It took a case of absolute necessity to extract her from her village and throw her at the feet of the Gospa: Theresa suffered from a grief as wide and deep as her motherly heart. For 3 years, her son-in-law had been fighting constantly with her daughter and criticizing his wife's family, calling them "sanctimonious bigots." He would state openly that he didn't believe in God, and had no intention whatsoever of laying himself open to that load of rubbish. Theresa then left for Medjugorje to entrust the whole situation to Mary, while, on the same day, her daughter Vera had an appointment with a lawyer to begin divorce proceedings.

During the long journey by coach, Theresa chewed over all these sorrows in her heart. The thought of her granddaughter, Harmony, being torn between Dad and Mom was unbearable. They argue and talk about divorce right in front of her! As for Harmony, all she dreams of is to have a little brother or sister!

Once in Medjugorje, Theresa heard about the "deal" which can be made with Our Lady.[1] So she decided to abandon her problem and her pain to the Gospa, and she told her: "You take care of Vera and her family, and, as for me, I will take care of your intentions."

Once this deal was concluded, she went to the Blue Cross and prayed fervently for all those whom Mary recommended to our prayers: unbelievers, young people, sinners, priests, those without peace of heart, etc. On that first night, a phone call informed her that her daughter had canceled her meeting with the lawyer, for she wanted to give her marriage one last chance.

The days passed, and each night, after the evening prayer service at the parish, Theresa would escape and go up to the Blue Cross where at considerable length she confidently interceded for the Blessed Mother's intentions.

Back in France, she was told to her great amazement that her son-in-law was a totally different man! Her daughter related that one night around 10 p.m. he was watching TV from his bed and suddenly called to her: "Vera, come quick! Look! There's a big blue cross above the TV set, can you see it?"

Vera couldn't see anything, but her husband insisted: "Look harder, there it is, I see it!"

He was all shaken up with fear. A rationalist like him!

Theresa told her daughter that she knew that Blue Cross well! In Medjugorje, every night, she had been praying before it at this very time of the evening.

The Gospa had indeed upheld her end of the bargain: she had taken care of the son-in-law, while Theresa took care of her intentions!

Since then (this happened in June of 1995), Vera and her husband have found their way back to the Church. They both received the sacrament of reconciliation, the first time in 10 years for Vera, and in 20 years for her husband... Every day the family prays together, and little Harmony has wonderful news to tell: she's expecting a little brother for this fall!

---

[1] It was the world-famous pilgrim, Albert, who had inaugurated in Medjugorje those exchanges with heaven, about which Jesus had already spoken to Catherine of Sienna: "You take care of my business, I'll handle yours." Albert's beautiful story is related in the audio tape *True Consecration to Mary* (see appendix).

— Message of September 25, 1996 —

"Dear children! Today I invite you to offer your crosses and suffering for my intentions. Little children, I am your mother and I wish to help you by seeking for you the graces from God.

"Little children, offer your sufferings as a gift to God so they become a most beautiful flower of joy. That is why, little children, pray that you may understand that suffering can become joy and the Cross the way of joy. Thank you for having responded to my call."

MYRIAM, YOU'RE JUST LIKE ME!

Winter 1991. Terminal stage. Eugenia is doubled up with pain on her bed. Successive chemotherapy treatments have exhausted her, but were unable to arrest the lung cancer that is eating away at her without mercy. In the little house in the suburbs of Paris, her children and grandchildren go on with life, but for her, the encounter with the God of her forefathers grows nearer every day. And she's not really crazy about the prospect!

Eugenia was born in Blida (Algeria), of a long and distinguished Jewish line counting many rabbis and men of prayer, faithful pillars of the local synagogues where the Sephardic liturgy mixes smoothly with the calls of the muezzins. Her mother Rachel educated her in the purest Jewish tradition but, to tell the truth, Eugenia has only kept up the simple exterior observances. Nothing in the world could make her forget to celebrate Yom Kippur (the Day of Atonement), or to light the Shabbat candles at dusk on Friday evenings, or to place the Shabbat bread, braided by her own hands, on the table.

Still, apart from all this, Eugenia prefers not to think about this God whom she hardly knows, and who might demand hours of prayer from her while there is so much to do in the house! She has had to struggle hard to survive, which had not contribute to the mellowing of her difficult temper. She is an early bird who has spent her life serving, and who must live out her last days in a suburban town near Paris as an immigrant, looked down upon by everyone.

Her heart is secretly tortured, because one of her sons is in a center for handicapped persons. The cup she must drink is bitter indeed, despite the loving care of her other son, Paul, who has kept her home with him and shares her lot.

December cold has settled over Paris: Christmas is coming soon. Little Esther, Paul's 6-year-old daughter, declares to anyone who will listen that there is no way Grandma will soon be buried, because she will get well. "Childish imaginings!" the family thinks.

In a corner of the living room an icon of Mary sits imposingly, for Paul married a Catholic, Eliane, and the mixture of religions does not bother anyone. However, this icon caused some trouble recently when Grandma Eugenia looked at it. She was fretting over Paul, who was desperately looking for a job, so she couldn't refrain from crying out to the icon: "Myriam, you're just like me, you're a mother and you're Jewish! Help my son Paul!"

Then she distinctly heard a crystal-clear voice behind her: *"Don't worry, I will stand by your son!"*

Eugenia turned around, but...no one was there! The voice was female, young, and so divinely sweet that it was almost unbearable. She was overwhelmed with puzzlement, happiness, and fear as well. She ran to the kitchen to see if someone were there, but there was no one home! She was alone, so..."Myriam" had to be the one who had spoken to her! The icon then began to give off an extraordinary fragrance- rose? jasmine? Eugenia didn't know what to say. The perfume lasted a long time, perceptible to all who entered the room.

Paul had a successful job interview. Against all odds, he was hired as a commercial engineer. When he came back home that evening, he rejoiced: "It's incredible, listen! During the meeting, we smelled an inexplicable perfume, something very delicate, between rose and jasmine... Well!... Here, too! It's the same perfume!"

Little Esther didn't miss a word of the grownups' conversation. She venerated the icon, and developed her own secret relationship with Our Lady. When she claimed that grandma Eugenia would recover, she knew what she was saying. In fact, shortly before Christmas, Eugenia was cured. The doctors couldn't find any trace of her cancer left, and, what's more, she could eat a horse!

One night in January Eugenia spat up blood. It was very scary. She called out to "Myriam" for help once again. This time, the icon came all by itself into her arms at 4 o'clock in the morning, and was spattered with blood, while Eugenia heard the same heavenly voice coming from the icon: *"Don't worry, it's nothing serious!"*

On her way to the hospital, she had no idea of the shock she would receive upon hearing the radiologist tell her: "It's nothing serious, don't worry, it's just a tiny blood vessel which ruptured."

On the following Friday, Eugenia asked Paul to translate the Our Father into Hebrew so that on Shabbat, that evening, everyone could pray it.

The bond that grew up between "Myriam" and Eugenia was very mysterious, but so strong that Eugenia changed in a spectacular way, in just a few days. This practical woman, always busy with something, who used to be so good at making people's lives a misery, became an angel of patience, goodness, and joyfulness. She learned the Hail Mary and prayed it unceasingly.

She woke up in the middle of the night with this persistent prayer. She kept praying until dawn, before a new day began for this typical Jewish grandmother, always eager to help, to console and intervene. Whenever a problem or a sorrow arose, she would exclaim "Mommy!" and have a secret conversation with "Myriam" to obtain from her everything she wanted. She knew how to wind herself around her heart: hadn't she touched her deeply once when she told her, "You're just like me, you're a mother, and you're Jewish!"? Since then, "Myriam" obviously had to give in!

Eugenia had no Christian culture whatsoever, and she accepted all these events with the innocence of a child. As I was in her town, she came with her relatives to hear a talk of mine on Medjugorje in January 1995. It caused quite a stir in the family, who suddenly realized that "Myriam" was explaining the faith in this little village of the former Yugoslavia! "We have to go there!" they thought.

Eliane was the only one who could make it, and Eugenia candidly gave her daughter-in-law a piece of advice: "Over there, you'll surely find out the explanation for what has been happening to me. You'll be able to explain it all to me when you get back! Oh, if only I could go there myself!"

From Medjugorje, Eliane brought back a statue of Our Lady that Eugenia kept in her room. She even moved her bed so as to face it. She could feel her presence and talk heart-to-heart with her. Favors and graces of all kinds then started to rain down upon the household! Each day, at dusk, Eugenia would declare gently but firmly, "Let's pray!" The whole family would then kneel before the statue from Medjugorje and pray the rosary for the intentions of the Queen of Peace. Often, as Eugenia is used to speaking her mind and not making a mystery of her relationship with "Myriam," she would cry out, "She is here, she is here! Can't you see her?!"

With Medjugorje, Eugenia understood a secret that was quite new to her: the fruitfulness of suffering. After all, if "Myriam" means "ocean of perfume" in Hebrew, it also means "ocean of bitterness," doesn't it? The Immaculate *and* Sorrowful Heart of Mary revealed itself little by little to Eugenia, whose strong maternal streak had expanded to encompass the whole world of sinful and suffering humankind. She, so possessive at other times, so centered on her own children, began to take on the the the desire to save each and every person on earth and, speaking of "Myriam," she would say, "She suffered a lot more than I do!" Crucifixes fascinated her. They reminded her of her other son, crucified and humiliated.

She fell ill again with cancer in her other lung, but she bore her pain in a totally different way. She often had to remain under an oxygen tent and, during this last calvary, she displayed true heroism. She never complained! On the contrary, her face was transfigured. When her family gathered around her, she loved to sing: "Child Jesus, O King of Love, I trust you, I offer my heart to you, come and dwell in it, always keep me by your side!"

Neighbors and friends would come out of her room radiant with joy from the light they had found in her. Even priests came to see her and asked: "Pray for me, pray for my parish!" She promised to do so, and everyone left pacified, enriched and with deeper inner beauty.

Eugenia departed this life in great peace on June 5, 1996, at the age of 81. She was buried according to the traditional Jewish rite, to which a few Our Fathers, Hail Marys and other invocations to the Child Jesus were quite successfully added.

Two motherly hearts had met, understood, and loved each other, that's what this story is all about...[1]

---

[1] Little Esther was baptized and has the same charisms as her grandmother. She will disclose her own secrets herself one day. I don't think I am betraying any confidences by saying that "Myriam" brings her a mixture of happiness and martyrdom, because when she revealed herself to this 6-year-old child, she entrusted to her this weighty mission: "*The rosary that I taught you to pray, now go and teach it to your schoolmates.*" Little Esther did so, but was soon crucified by the children's mockery, the parents' accusations, and all kinds of persecutions from the teaching staff. Would the child of immigrants cause a revolution in this state school which is so proud of having evicted God? In tears, Our Lady told Esther: "*If they knew how much I love them! Tell them! The children should pray for France!*" Nevertheless, a few children believed her and formed a little rosary group that is still very active, connected to the local parish.

— MESSAGE OF OCTOBER 25, 1996 —

"Dear children! Today I invite you to open yourselves to God the Creator, so that he changes you. Little children, you are dear to me. I love you all and I call you to be closer to me and that your love towards my Immaculate Heart be more fervent. I wish to renew you and lead you with my Heart to the Heart of Jesus, which still today suffers for you and calls you to conversion and renewal. Through you, I wish to renew the world. Comprehend, little children, that you are today the salt of the earth and the light of the world. Little children, I call you and I love you and in a special way I implore you: convert! Thank you for having responded to my call."

THE TREE PAID THE PRICE!

What happened in New York is a perfect illustration of the extraordinary power of humility. The holy Curé of Ars extolled it: when asked which was the greatest of the virtues, he replied, "Humility!"

"And the second greatest?"

"Humility!"

"And the third?'

"Humility!..."

All right, but now we need some concrete examples.

There is one that brings me to my knees whenever I talk about it. One day, one of my friends, Karen, asked Marija, "When the Gospa is there before you, how does she look at you? How do you feel about the way she considers you?"

Marija smiled and collected her thoughts for a few seconds, as if reliving the apparition again in the depths of her heart and searching for the right words. Then, in her soft, clear voice, she replied, "When the Gospa comes, when she looks at me, I have the feeling that, for her, I'm the one who is the Queen of Peace, and that she is totally amazed at having the privilege of coming to visit me."

"What!! Would you say that again?!"

"Yes, that's it; she's amazed at the privilege that God has granted her..."

"But it should be the other way around!"

"That's the humility of the Gospa!"

Karen was left speechless.

Some time later, she was invited to speak about Medjugorje in a large church in mid-town New York, the Church of Saint Pius X. Naturally, crowds of people flocked to hear her. It was already dark, on a clear summer's night.

Karen embarked on a magnificent description of Our Lady according to what she had heard from the visionaries, for whom a little corner of the veil is lifted every day. She spoke of our Mother's humility, quoting, of course, Marija's astounding words given above.

"The Gospa is the most powerful of all creatures against Satan, because she's the most humble..."

Then she stopped suddenly, smiled, and added: "Satan won't be happy with what I'm going to tell you, I warn you, because it's something he can't conceive of or imitate, or accept... Here it is: in the Kingdom, Mary is the least of all creatures..."

The instant the last word had left her lips, a hellish rumbling reverberated throughout the church, making it shake right down to its foundations. The power went out, and they all waited in darkness, with no microphone. Speechless with fear, everyone was still for a while, and some wondered if the end of the world had come! Then they heard a gentle laugh and the quiet voice of Karen saying, "You see, I told you. He doesn't like it at all that Mary is the least!"

The priests brought flashlights to check out what had happened, and it took half an hour before light was restored so they could resume the prayer meeting. The prayers were somewhat agitated, but, as never before, they came from the heart! Outside, a few yards from the nave, an enormous plane tree lay on the ground, split in two, black as coal. It had been struck by lightning. Lightning? But there was no rain, no storm, and no flash of lightning that evening: stars were twinkling like chandeliers in the New York sky. I wasn't there to see, but maybe they even danced in honor of their Queen!

On the subject of Our Lady's humility, let me tell you a final anecdote: one member of the prayer group in Medjugorje had a secret habitual practice. Since he lived fairly near the visionaries, he used to leave a little note for the Blessed Mother every day on the very spot where the apparition was to take place. It was often just a few simple loving words, since he had very little time to write. Sometimes he would just draw a little heart on a scrap of paper, but he always did something.

One day he broke off this lovely custom because the great numbers of pilgrims were taking up all his time, and a week went by without one single love note from him. He told himself, "Anyway, my little messages aren't worth much, who am I to dare think the Queen of Heaven pays any attention to these pathetic scribblings of mine? She can see my heart, and that's what matters..." However, on the ninth day, he left 3 or 4 lines in his secret hiding place just before the apparition was due to take place, without anyone knowing. When the apparition was over, Marija went looking for this brother, with a questioning look.

"Zeliko, come here..."

"What is it?" asked Zeliko, swallowing hard.

"The Gospa looked very happy during the apparition! She asked me to give you this message, but I can't understand it: *'Thank you for your letter, it gave me great joy. For the past eight days, I've missed your letters so much!'* That's what she told me to tell you."

Zeliko beamed with happiness and remained speechless for a good while!

Such is the sublime Mother that Jesus has given each one of us! Who could ever fathom the divine tenderness of her heart? Who could conceive of even a fraction of her joy at the slightest free offering from us?

Dearest Gospa, the day when Jesus told me: *"Behold your Mother!,"* he gave me more than heaven and earth and all they contain. He offered me his most precious treasure!

And my joy at having you, who could ever take it away from me?

— Message of November 25, 1996 —

"Dear children! Today, again, I invite you to pray, so that through prayer, fasting and small sacrifices you may prepare yourselves for the coming of Jesus. May this time, little children, be a time of grace for you. Use every moment and do good, for only in this way will you feel the birth of Jesus in your hearts. If with your life you give an example and become a sign of God's love, joy will prevail in the hearts of men. Thank you for having responded to my call."

LITTLE MARIO'S MASS

Rita is sitting on our sofa, in Medjugorje, and she is crying a lot, almost unable to tell me her incredible Way of the Cross. She has a modest and shy nature, and she would certainly have preferred to keep silent, but I assure her that her story will help other couples. So, out of sheer love, she recalls each step of her past.

Rita is Flemish, from a little Belgian town, and has a strong physical build. She was affectionate, beautiful, and never ill until she became pregnant.

"My first child was stillborn, at 8 months of pregnancy," she explained. When they announced it to me, my heart broke with grief, especially since I was not able to see my little daughter, who weighed 5 pounds.[1] I had several friends who had also given birth, and I was constantly seeing pictures of babies. As for me, I did not have anything, not even a picture, not even the least souvenir! The doctors diagnosed a placental insufficiency and a series of other problems."

The nightmare was to continue for Rita and would be renewed 6 times: 7 babies died inside her womb or at birth. And each time, a new medical treatment was prescribed to try and protect these little lives. However, the medication was harmful to the mother and entailed secondary effects such as weight gain. Each pregnancy provoked a new emotional shock, a new dagger in Rita's heart.

Then she discovered Medjugorje through her friend Anne-Marie, and decided to go on pilgrimage. There, she relearned prayer, which she had abandoned since her early youth. Her faith grew progressively stronger, and she began to look upon God as a friend, an ally, a Father. From the depths of her heart, she asked him for a child (who would live), saying the words which mark the difference between non-conversion and conversion: "Lord, may your will be done and not mine!"

She went back to Medjugorje 4 months later, and Vicka promised to pray so that a child might be granted to her. She went to Tihaljina, and that day Father Jozo offered to bless the whole assembly. The pilgrims got in line and received the laying on of hands on their heads. When he came up to Rita, knowing nothing of her suffering, Father Jozo blessed her, but unexpectedly laid his hands on her belly and prayed quietly for a long time before he went on to the next pilgrim. What Rita did not know is that she was 4 weeks pregnant! This pregnancy was as difficult as the previous ones but...the little boy was born fully alive! Rita gave him the name of Mario in thankfulness for Our Lady. Her joy knew no bounds.

Today the little boy is 8 years old. He just recently learned here in Medjugorje the miracle his birth, and the meaning of his name. His mother told us that since he was 4, he would play the Mass for long hours. He would put together carefully chosen white sheets, some utensils, some picture books whose pages he turned solemnly, and murmured prayers of his own, snatches he remembered from church and expressions arranged, invented, and enriched with his little vocabulary. To say that the angels kept a straight face while listening might be pushing it...!

And no way was he going to forget an important element of Mass: the active and praying presence of the congregation: lions, giraffes, leopards were dragooned into making the responses. Nor did they escape 1, 2, or even 3 moralizing homilies. At Communion time, the whole menagerie was facing the altar and the boy would go religiously in front of each little cuddly toy, each little soldier, each airplane pilot to give him Communion.

And his mother adds with the characteristic tenderness of those who have suffered a lot,

"I never understood, sister, why he was giving Communion to some and not to others...?!"

"Maybe he thought that some of the faithful had not gone to confession for too long a time!!" I said.

Rita smiled and added, "What will this child become? Each day I entrust him to Mary. His father has left the house. I am alone and in bad health…"

"But now, Rita, you have thousands of friends who will support you in prayer."

"You know Sister, Our Lady of Medjugorje led me to her Son Jesus. I realize that in my joy, as in my suffering, I can rely on them. They give me more help than anybody!"

— MESSAGE OF DECEMBER 25, 1996 —

"Dear children! Today I am with you in a special way, holding Little Jesus in my lap, and I invite you, little children, to open yourselves to his call. He calls you to joy. Little children, joyfully live the messages of the Gospel, which I am repeating in the time since I am with you. Little children, I am your Mother, and I desire to reveal to you the God of Love and the God of Peace. I do not desire for your life to be in sadness, but that it be realized in joy for eternity, according to the Gospel. Only in this way will your life have meaning. Thank you for having responded to my call."

EVEN GOD PLAYS HIDE-AND-SEEK!

Every year the visionaries of Medjugorje wait impatiently for Christmas Eve, for on that special night they get to see the Infant Jesus. And each year I ask one of them for news of the Child. This year Marija tells us that the little Jesus was cuddled in the arms of his Mother as peaceful as a lamb, and was looking at her with love. How was he dressed? Actually, he didn't seem to have clothes, but rather was wrapped up in the golden veil of his Mommy.

On some Christmases the Child Jesus sleeps as soundly as a dormouse, but on others he is wide awake and looks with eyes round with astonishment at everyone present, one by one. "Natch," says Vicka, "he is discovering the world, like all children!"

But the Christmas none of us will ever forget was in 1981, the "first Christmas."

"At the beginning of the apparitions," tells Marija, "since we were still a little awkward and intimidated, the Child Jesus wanted to put us at ease. When his Mother prayed and spoke with us, he stayed snuggled in her arms out of sight. But suddenly he raised his little arm and started playing with the edge of her veil, like babies do.

"Then slowly and timidly he peeked out from the veil, and then his whole head appeared and he looked straight at us. He smiled and then ducked back behind the veil. Then he appeared again, looked at us, and then hid again. We realized that he was playing hide-and-seek with us! He started to play this game a third time, which absolutely delighted us. This time, after smiling at us, he winked, which moved us deeply. A baby can't look and smile like that. But we understood that it was really God who was there before us..."

We must add that Marija took good note of this mischievousness, and began to imitate her Master before her friends. Now this didn't go down too well among these traditional Croats! Young ladies just do not wink! So Marija boasted laughingly: "But I learned that from the Child Jesus!"

One cannot exaggerate the value of this immersion in simplicity[1] that Medjugorje has to offer us. Our poor Western brains are so crammed with excessive information, drowning in piles of paper, our hearts dried out by an intellectualism that only ends up confusing everyone and leads more to the nuthouse than to illumination. Oh, how I love to immerse myself in this simplicity! It's so healing!

The visionaries have remained children, and I can still hear Marija tell us the following episode:

"It was in the early days of the apparitions. The Communists had picked us up to put us through endless interrogations in Ljubuski. We were treated very badly, they gave us nothing to eat or drink and tried to frighten us in 100 different ways, threatening to put us in prison or in a psychiatric hospital. We were exhausted. But we didn't give in, and finally they let us go.

"When the Gospa appeared to us we all told her about our horrible day and explained everything that had happened to us in great detail, everything our interrogators had done, everything they said. She paid great attention to everything we told her and stayed almost a whole hour until we had finished our story. Then when we were done she comforted us and smiled, saying: 'I was there with you and I saw everything!' So we realized that she had listened to us purely out of love, because she knew it all already. As our Mother, it was a joy for her to see us open our hearts to her with so much trust, knowing that she would share the pain and fear with us."

O Medjugorje, what a school of child-like simplicity you are for us!

That story reminds me of something Jesus said to Sister Faustina:

"My daughter, they tell me you have a lot of simplicity; so why do you not tell me about everything that concerns you, even the slightest details? Tell me about everything; it gives me great joy."

"But you know everything, Lord."

"Yes, I know everything, but that is no excuse. Talk to me with the simplicity of a child, because I have an ear that listens and a Heart that hears you, and I like to hear you talk to me." (*Diary*, § 920)

— FLASHBACK ON 1996 —

January 15: Mirjana's and Father Slavko leave for a mission in La Réunion and Mauritius.

January 24: Birth of Francesco Maria, second child of Marija and Paolo.

January: Father Jozo's apostolic tour in Italy, supported by Cardinal Piovanelli of Florence. Father Jozo meets 13 cardinals and bishops in favor of Medjugorje.

March 18: Mirjana's yearly apparition:

> "Dear Children! On this message, which I give you today through my servant, I desire for you to reflect a long time. My children, great is the love of God. Do not close your eyes, do not close your ears while I repeat to you: Great is His love! Hear my call and my supplication which I direct to you. Consecrate your heart and make it the home of the Lord. May he dwell in it for ever.
> "My eyes and my Heart will be here, even when I will no longer appear. Act in everything as I ask you and lead you to the Lord. Do not reject from yourself the name of God, that you may not be rejected. Accept my messages that you may be accepted. Decide, my children, it is the time of decision. Be of just and innocent heart, that I may lead you to your Father, for this, that I am here, is His great love. Thank you for being here!"

March 17 – 20: Annual meeting of the Medjugorje leaders at Tucepi.

April–May: Filming of the 52 television programs: *Medjugorje, Our Mother's Last Call, With Sister Emmanuel.* These programs are now available (in English) for all channels from Children of Medjugorje- see appendix.

June: Mirjana has a miscarriage. She says: "Lord, you gave me a child; you took it back, I thank you..."

June 6: The French newspaper *La Croix* headline: "The Vatican confirms that the Medjugorje pilgrimages are forbidden..." This major error had repercussions abroad. No erratum was ever given; thousands of people cancelled their pilgrimages.

June 21: Jose Carreras' concert. President Tudjman (Croatia) takes the opportunity to come to Medjugorje.

June 25: 15th Anniversary. Ivanka's yearly apparition. Our Lady asks us to pray for all who are under Satan's influence.

End of July: Ivan leaves for the USA for 7 months.

July 31: International Youth Festival.

August 1: Jelena's prayer group starts up again. It had been interrupted since 1991.

August 21: Because of the increasing amount of false information spread about on Medjugorje, Dr. Navarro Valls, spokesman of the Holy See, makes an official declaration to specify once again the position of the Church.

September 5: Birth of David-Emmanuel, second child of Jakov and Anna Lisa.

September 21: Father Jozo is in charge of the Eucharistic adoration evening in preparation for the Holy Father's arrival in Reims (France).

November 1–20: Father Jozo is on mission in 7 countries of Latin America: Puerto Rico, Panama, Costa Rica, Nicaragua, Honduras, El Salvador and Mexico. On the 15th, he speaks to 7,000 gang members from Mexico.

November 14–15: Extraordinary meeting of the Franciscans of Herzegovina with their Father General, in Mostar. An attempt is made to calm down the "Diocesan- Franciscan conflict."

November 15: Ephraim (Founder of the Community of the Beatitudes), his wife, and Sister Emmanuel meet with John Paul II in Rome concerning Medjugorje (see note 4, in the chapter *Breakfast With John Paul II*, August 25, 1994. Also see photo.).

1997

— MESSAGE OF JANUARY 25, 1997 —

"Dear children! I invite you to reflect about your future. You are creating a new world without God, only with your own strength and that is why you are unsatisfied and without joy in the heart. This time is my time and that is why, little children, I invite you again to pray. When you find unity with God, you will feel hunger for the Word of God and your hearts, little children, will overflow with joy. You will witness God's love wherever you are. I bless you and I repeat to you that I am with you to help you. Thank you for having responded to my call."

DOES PROVIDENCE STILL WORK?

I have a clue for those who are worried about the future!

Better than Greta Garbo, Holy Providence is "The Divine" par excellence. She has her own ways, and I will define her 2 main assets as "Love" and "Humor." Providence is full of surprises and extremely resourceful! She is so good at taking care of her lovers that each of them thinks he is the happiest man of all. But then how come Providence has so few of them?

The problem is that rare are those who know her address, and even fewer are those who live there. Would you like a hint? Nothing is simpler: if you have never met her, and if you are drifting along at random, you need to make a sharp turn from where you are, yes right there! You are almost there, her house is really close! But be careful you need to follow the user's guide step by step. You will be tempted not to turn radically because you will find other enticing signs along the way, especially if you like wide roads. Avoid them!

For example, avoid this really busy avenue called Clinging Avenue. At first, you will think that Maximoolah Boulevard is very appealing, but don't go down it. The shops are enticing, but they only sell anti-anxiety medication. A very crowded main thoroughfare is Paranoid Promenade. Run away from it, it is full of toxic gases! You're wasting your time, the pedestrian mall Dreamland Street is a dead end. Lastly, the world-famous Worry-wart Way will lead you to the Everglades. All this will not take you to the Divine One. Her street is lowly and unpresuming, and it is easy to miss it. It's on Trusting Terrace. That is where she lives—it's a private house, and on her gate you will read: *"Abandon yourself."* It's here, come in, make yourselves at home: she awaits you as the Messiah…

Once you are in, the surprises won't stop!

An incredible feeling of security will fill you, and this will be the first surprise. Then, little by little, your old links with Maximoolah Boulevard, Paranoid Promenade, Dreamland Street, Worry-wart Way, etc., will fall off your shoulders like old stinky rags you will not want to wear anymore. The Divine will introduce you to an unknown world; you will be in your element, like a fish in water. You will taste an extraordinary freedom. The Divine has such intelligence, knowledge, and know-how, as well as a sensitive heart, that she deals easily with the most hopeless situations, even the most tragic ones, of her lovers. No one can resist her!

At Medjugorje, the Gospa would not have been able to hide her address without running the risk of antagonizing Jesus. That is the reason why she keeps reminding us of the key steps along the way in this divine itinerary:

"Always abandon your burdens to God and do not worry." (10.11.84)

"God will give you great gifts if you abandon yourself to him." (12.19.85)

"Abandon yourself to me so that I can guide you completely. Do not be concerned about material things." (4.17.86)

"Surrender yourself to God [1] so that he may heal you, console you and forgive everything inside you which is a hindrance on the path of love." (6.25.88)

"I am calling you to a complete surrender; let everything that you possess be in the hands of God." (4.25.89)

"Abandon your worries to Jesus. Listen to what he says in the Gospel: 'And which of you with taking thought can add to his stature one cubit?'" (10.30.83)

"Be confident and rest in joy. Goodbye, my beloved angels." (11.26.81)

The messages of the Gospa are full of these words of wisdom, road signs on the journey of life, and if they are so little followed it is because unfortunately the other itineraries offered by the world flash their strobe lights... And whatever shines...everybody (or almost) grabs, and gets swallowed up! But it doesn't shine for very long. Who can measure the havoc wrought in hearts, souls, psyche and even bodies by these Maximoolahs and Worrywarts??! Who can describe the mortal sadness, the emptiness and the secret disappointment?!

---

[1] A couple from my Community met Marthe Robin in 1977. She told them that abandoning themselves to God was the solution to their problems.

"But Marthe, what if we *can't* abandon ourselves?"

"Well, you just have to."

She was fond of saying: "Abandonment is watchful, active, attentive to the most secret and most intimate requirements of God. In abandonment the Good Lord does not leave us alone. It means belonging to him."

She also said, "It doesn't mean just giving what you have, but giving down to the very roots of one's being, which comes from the Father and goes to the Father. One cannot just give what is extra, a share, even a large share of our life, our actions and apostolate, but one must give the very substance of one's being. To abandon oneself is to reach the pinnacle of what God requires of us." (Quoted by P. Pagnoux in *Marthe Robin*, 1966.)

Armelle was living peacefully with her husband and children. The devil hates this. Therefore, he decided to show her one of the prophecies of doom and gloom which he enjoys so much and that abound in seamy bookstores. As usual, he hissed his forecast of the day of the "great crash." The trap worked perfectly, and the lady, although a good Christian, started worrying. Obsessive thoughts haunted her. She absolutely must prepare for the worst, for the security of her family. And there she went, making plans to stock up on provisions. The most important item was fuel, for heat, light, and cooking. So what did she do? Well, she bought 30 big bottles of gas. But where can she store them? They'll have to go in the garage; so what if the car gets parked outside. One day goes by, 2 days, and all peace goes out the window.

Not content with having embraced the demon Maximoolah, she flirted with Worrywart. By day, she bit her nails, with a glazed stare. By night, she feared that a cigarette butt would set all the gas bottles exploding and the entire house would go up in flames. The horror movie continued. She became dangerously tired because of her sleepless nights. Her distractedness irritated her husband and kids, and because of her anxiety, she snapped at everybody... In a word, the devil had won: in 3 weeks, the quiet atmosphere if the family had changed into a nightmare. There was water in the gas! A family was so vulnerable, it could be destroyed so quickly!

But there was a happy ending. A Medjugorje pilgrim talked about the Divine One to our friend, and she changed course and decided to trust in Providence. The wreck of this home was avoided in the nick of time.

My wonderful American friend, Cathy, has a totally different story. She is 47 years old, she has 8 children, and since her marriage to Denis, she joyfully exploits the treasures of Divine Providence. Both of them work really hard for the Gospa, and they are top quality instruments for Mary's work. When Cathy tells me a story, I never know whether to cry or laugh. So you want to hear about her latest adventure?

She decided to adhere literally to Mary's request in her message of August 25, 1996:

"Dear children, <u>listen</u>, because I wish to speak to you and to invite you to have more faith and trust in God..."

Before Christmas, delighted to have the chance to enjoy a little break, she went into her room to pray. As she was closing the door, she sensed in her heart that God was asking her to go out and do her shopping. It was not her choice, because it was rush hour. However, because of her decision, she obeyed this interior urging, and went out despite what it cost her.

She found all the items she needed and headed for the check out counter. As she stood in line, a lady slipped in ahead of her and took her place. Cathy chose to keep the peace, and prayed in silence. When it was her turn at the register, an employee went up to her and said, "Congratulations, ma'am, you are our fiftieth customer! You are the winner of our big promotional lottery! Everything in your cart is free!"

She thanked the Lord with a smile of complicity, especially since she had entrusted to him her money problems. She congratulated herself on having listened to this inspiration and above all, on having obeyed it![2]

At first, people have a tendency to fall in love with the Divine One because she (Holy Providence) is so good at taking care of money problems.[3] But She has plenty of other tricks up her sleeve, as you will see from the ending of this glorious story—for example, her genius in arranging human encounters.

Cathy may have gone dragging her feet to the department store that day, but she came out floating! She reached her car in the parking lot, put everything in the trunk, and avanti! Home! But the Divine One had not had her last word (actually, she never says her last word, you'd better realize that right away). As she drove straight home, Cathy sensed another interior inspiration:

"You need to go to the bookstore."
"But Lord, that's across town!!"
"The bookstore.."

---

[2] Cathy prays a lot every day, which allows her to enter more easily into this sort of "conversation with God." Jesus said to Sr. Faustina: **"Try to live meditatively, so that you can hear my voice which is a murmur; only the meditative souls can hear it."** (*Diary,* § 1778)

[3] Helen Call works in an office in the US. She tells the following story: "When I first heard about Medjugorje, it was like a bolt of lightning. I knew in my heart that I had to go there. But I hadn't the foggiest notion where to find the money.

Once again, because of her promise, Cathy adjusted her course and went to the bookstore. She prayed, thinking: "We'll see!" When she entered the store, she spied a good friend whom she hadn't seen in a while. After a happy greeting her friend confided her story to Cathy.,

Jane was unpeaceful. At 45, she was pregnant with her seventh child, and not everyone seemed to think that this baby was a good idea. In America,, as in many developed countries, children are not desired, and people can say cruel things about large families. Jane was very upset by the difficulty that seemed to surround this pregnancy..

"You understand, I'm 45!"

"Yes, I understand!" Cathy exclaimed joyfully. "When I was 43 I was expecting my *eighth*! And you can't imagine how much joy he gives to all of us! Our entire family had been blessed by this little boy!"

That day, Jane's spirits soared, and the negative voices that discouraged her were silenced. Jane welcomed the future with her new baby with renewed peace and joy! This is also the work of Divine Providence, to spread the peace of God everywhere!

---

[3] (continued)

In March 1996, while I was working on the Internet, it occurred to me to see if there were any websites on Medjugorje. There were tons! I read Sr. Emmanuel's report where she quoted a pilgrim as saying 'If you don't have the money, ask the Gospa and she will get it for you!' I felt such a powerful pull to Medjugorje at that moment that I promised myself (and God!) to go. Then I prayed for the money I would need. A travel agent told me what I'd have to come up with: $1500 dollars! This was expensive, but I felt an indescribable calm and certainty. The same day my boss called me and said, talking about the IBM project I was working on, 'I think we could get a bonus for you; you should apply for it.'

"'How much do you think I could get?' I asked her.

"'Maybe as much as $5000 dollars!' she said.

"'No, I only need $1500.'

"'Ask for the $5000 anyway.'

"After going through all the steps, the file came back to us and the award granted amounted to $1500 dollars! My boss was very disappointed, but for me, it was like a wink from heaven! I had received exactly the amount I needed for the trip, to the dollar! Thanks to the Divine!"

— Message of February 25, 1997 —

"Dear children! Today I invite you in a special way to open yourselves to God the Creator and to become active. I invite you, little children, to see at this time who needs your spiritual or material help. By your example, little children, you will be the extended hands of God, which humanity is seeking. Only in this way will you understand that you are called to witness and to become joyful carriers of God's word and of his love. Thank you for having responded to my call."

WE'LL GET THOSE FIVE MILLION LITTLE ONES!

Allison is 5 years old. Her mother, Mary MacDonell, who lives near Chicago, is a friend of mine and she often teases me because her daughter knows all my tapes on Medjugorje by heart. She quotes in full whole passages to her mother, and even reproduces my mistakes in grammar (OOPS!). Allison once asked her mother, "Mommy, is there a Saint Allison?"

"No, sweetheart, unfortunately, I don't think there is one."

"Then Mom, I'll be Saint Allison!"

Since then, Allison has been working hard on the project of becoming a saint, and never misses a single opportunity offered by Providence. When the book *Children, Help My Heart To Triumph!*[1] was published, her mother read it to her. The little girl wouldn't let her stop before the very last page; she was drinking in each and every word of it! When they had finished reading the book, her mother suggested doing something else, but Allison insisted, "No, Mom, let's start praying and making sacrifices right now!"

[1] Available from Saint Andrews Productions, Pittsburgh, US. Fax: (412)787-5204.

Mary has experienced conversion, thanks to Medjugorje. Her past life was more gloomy than full of light, and she is acutely aware that prayer saved her life. She agreed: "Of course, darling, but what do you think we should start with?"

"Come on, let's go to my room!"

Allison's bedroom looked like any other American child's bedroom: chockablock with all sorts of toys and other stuff. Allison's eyes lit on her beloved dolls. She grabbed her favorite one, held it out to her mother and said, "Let's give this doll to Kate!" (her younger sister). "And let's give that one to Don!" (her brother, Donald).

Then so calmly and joyfully that her mother was deeply moved, little Allison took her favorite things one by one and allocated them to children she knew. "This is for so-and-so, and that one goes to so-and-so." She was a whirlwind, clearing out the room! Mary could hardly hold back her tears.

This was only the beginning of Allison's sacrifices. At times Mary would say to me, "I wonder what God has in store for her..." In the meantime, Allison's family takes delight in her funny remarks.

The other day Allison went with her mother to church and, for the first time, saw incense burning before the exposed Blessed Sacrament.

"What's this, Mommy?"

"It's incense, love. You see, just like our prayers, it goes up to heaven. Did you notice how it smells?"

"Oh, Mom, the incense goes into my heart!"

"No, sweetie, not into your heart; it goes up to heaven."

"But Mom, that's where heaven is, in my heart!"

Padre Pio (the Italian Capuchin friar) could see the invisible. The more closely he identified himself with Christ in his body and his soul, the more he discovered, to his wonderment, the beauty of children and the paramount role they are called to play in these times when the majority of mankind has lost the trail of God. Padre Pio loved to repeat: "Children will save the world!" When he saw that his journey on earth was coming to an end, he called a young friar whose soul, he sensed, was a fiery soul.

"Andrea," he said, "listen to me carefully: 5 million children would be enough to save the world. When I am gone, I want you to form groups of children. Have them pray, teach them how to make sacrifices. Let them all consecrate themselves to the Immaculate Heart of Mary. It's now the most important thing to do."

Then, with humble means, Father Andrea began to raise a small army of praying children in the spirit of Fatima. He gladly acknowledges that the circles most receptive to his calls are the Medjugorje groups. During a major Medjugorje conference in the States,[2] he shared with us Padre Pio's words about children, and said, almost shouting, "I already have 1 million kids, but where am I going to find the missing 4 million?"

What if we, in the English-speaking world, were to decide to offer to God 1 or 2 million kids? If we consider all the various blunders that we have made over the last decades (the terrible laws we have enacted, among other things), maybe it wouldn't be such a bad idea after all!

The Gospa invites us to *"open our hearts to our Creator and become active."* Well, I have good news for her—our little sweeties, for their part, are very active!

We receive endless streams of coloring books in which the children have colored in their "victories" after offering prayers and sacrifices. Here are a few lines culled from their prayers:

"I was nyce to my bruther for the day." (Katie, 9)

"I made my bed without beeng told when I didnt want to." (Sally, 8)

"Thank you Jesus for switching the lyte on for those who are in the dark!" (Violaine, 7)[3]

"Mary, Im allwayz skared of everything. Pleeze help me get over my feer, I hold out my hand to you, giv me yours, I have to lurn how to swimm." (Aurore, 10)

"Lord and Mary, help your poor siner!" (Blandine, 11)

"I know I'm a pain in the neck, so, just for you, I will try to make you happy. I'm not saying that I will sukceed, but, for you, I will try!" (Mathias, 10)

---

[2] Cassettes from this conference are available from: Resurrection Tapes, 3927 E. Lake St., Minneapolis, MN. Tel: (612) 721-7933. *Consecration of the Innocents*, ref. 94ND06.

[3] Without realizing it, this little girl is expressing here the pleading of the Gospa for those who have not experienced the love of the Father. On March 2, 1997, Mirjana tells us that Mary wept throughout the entire apparition at the Blue Cross. *"Illumine all those souls that are in darkness,"* she said. *"Pray for those for whom life on earth is the most important."*

"Mary, stop the wars of the wurld, make all peeple love each other, the whites, the blacks, the yelows...and even the Indeeans!" (Emilie, 9)

"I ate peaz even thow I hate them." (Billy, 6)

"I wish that some day my Dad would finuly understand the life of JEZUS." (Coralie, 9)

"Mary, help the peeple who are nuts." (Manon, 8)

"Dear Mommy, you are everyting to me, you are my boss, my hevenly Mother, my mistical rose..." (Marie, 8)

"Mary, I love you and you must no it because the love I have for you is larger than ennything, most of all make war stop when peple fite it's dumb." (Audrey, 9)

"Heal my asma, my left eye and my teeth, so that I remayn in good helth forever after. I pray that Jesus heels my mother, so that she can folow the Mass better, and also that Daddy and Mommy won't alwayz be mad at eech other." (Amélie, 8)

"Heal me from my lyce, my nits, and my bad thowts; I pray for my father to want to go to Mass; may the Holy Spirit continyou to dessend on Sonia." (Christel, 8)

"I understand yor sufering when you saw, with your own eyes, your Son dying on the Cross; Mary, keep families from fighting and Satan from bothering them!" (Isabelle, 11)

"...and now since I want you to forgive me even though I know you don't hold it against me, I make this act of consekration to you: Mary, today I give you my hart and I take your Imaculate Hart within me so that it teeches me how to love the way you love. Sined, Your faverite daughter, Jennifer."(age 10)

"Lord, give joy to famlees who have no food, so they will be ful." (Jean, 8)

"Mary, I know that my Daddy will come back, but please, help me to hold on until his retern! With this noveena, which I hope will pleese you, I present my hart to you. Camilla who loves you so much." (age 10)

"I didnt eat candy for a day." (Patty, 11)

"I put things bak where they belonged after use." (Benjy, 10)

"I made meal time plezant." (Ellen, 11)

"I ate my vegtible soop in beaf broth." (Zach, 9)

"Dear Mary, as you can see, I am thrilled to start my novena. Mommy says that Jesus and you are everywhere on earth at the same time. Is this true? If I pray with all my heart, will I go to heven? Could you help me stop sinning? I hope that your answers will be YES to all these questions.

Will I see you one day? Am I bothering you? If so, you don't have to read my letter but I continue with it because I'm sure that you'll read it!" (Myriam's letter)

No one on earth will ever be able to measure the impact of little Jacinta of Fatima on God's plans. She was only 6 when Our Lady invited her to make sacrifices for sinners. In today's catechesis, who dares encourage children to venture into the way of sacrifice, or show them the inexpressible power it has over the heart of God? Many adults project onto their children their own burden of unbelief. Still, more and more parents are grasping the Gospa's hand and teaching their children. Here are some of the sacrifices offered by their little angels:

"I put up with pane; I continyood the novena although I was discoriged." (Florian, 7)

"...the suferings my family costs me when they fite..." (Amandine, 7)

"...playing tag with Claire, I agreed to be It even tho it was her turn." (Mary, 10)

"I didnt call for Mom to go to the bath room and I went on my own." (Edward, 6, shortly after an operation)

"I didn't watch Baywatch, I went to Mass instead." (Julie, 10)

"I didn't get Roland wet when he was dry." (Marie, 9)

"Help me pleese so that I don't fall by the wayside and stop making sakrifices." (Maud, 9)

"I neel and make the cross with my arms." (Blandine, 11)

"My sakrifiss is to blow my noze ofen." (Amélie, 8)

"I did some extra home work in my bath; I cut Grandmas hedge insted of playing." (Thibaut, 10)

"I didn't make a sene to get a whole stick of gum; I didn't rest too much when the others were werking." (Agnes, 10)

"I brusht my teeth; I found the botle kap." (Lucie, 7)

"I didnt hitt my sistr." (Jean, 8)

"I let Anthonee opin the pakage of sawsages; I let him take his bath ferst; I helped him find the pensil sharpner." (Melanie, 8)

Yes, some children become so committed that they sometimes open the eyes of their relatives. Matthew is a 7-year-old boy who attended an Adoration Group for Children organized by a priest I know for a whole year. At the beginning of the following year, his mother pointed out: "You already go to Sunday school; why would you want to go to that Children's Adoration Group too?"

"Mom, why don't you understand? In Sunday school, I get to know Jesus, and in the Adoration Group, I learn to love him!"

During our "children's missions," we ask the youngest ones to close their eyes and look deep inside their hearts to find a present to offer to Mary before the end of the day. When we ask, "Who found something to give?" nearly all of them raise their hands and shout, "Me! Me!" We have a tough time making sure that the meeting doesn't turn into a contest of self-sacrifice! Children are quicker than we are to understand the things of God. They haven't had the time to become immune to the Holy Spirit; what's more, they can't calculate really well yet...

Teachers of religion sometimes tell us with tears in their eyes, "After this mission, we will never be able to teach catechism the way we used to..." (They did not expect the children to get so deeply and easily involved in prayer and sacrifice.)

Indeed, I think that during those mission days, well before sunset, the Gospa lets herself into the hearts of the children and exults over all the marvels she finds and puts in her treasure basket... Ready for the next collections?

— MESSAGE OF MARCH 25, 1997 —

"Dear children! Today, in a special way I invite you to take the cross in the hands and to meditate on the wounds of Jesus. Ask Jesus to heal your wounds which you, dear children, during your life sustained because of your sins or the sins of your parents. Only in this way, dear children, will you understand that the world is in need of healing, of faith in God the Creator. By Jesus' Passion and death on the Cross you will understand that only through prayer you too can become true apostles of faith; when in simplicity and prayer you live faith which is a gift. Thank you for having responded to my call."

STORY OF A WOUNDED WOMB

The chapel of the Oasis of Peace is already full to bursting. Although it is a tiny place, that doesn't keep the Italian pilgrims from pushing their way in, their eyes closed to whoever might be in the way! Anything to get in! Outside, hordes of people are hanging from the window sills, peering in at the "happening" of the day...

Marija Pavlovic-Lunetti is kneeling on a step in front of the altar, gazing slightly upward. Her lips barely move, the expression on her face is intense and serious; no doubt, tonight is a special evening indeed, the Gospa is staying much longer than usual.

The date is April 12, 1997, and we are in Medjugorje, at 6:45 p.m. At exactly the same time, in Sarajevo, the Holy Father is ending his visit to the city's devastated areas before making his way to the cathedral. Marija stands up, and instantly our friend Tim aims his heavy video camera at her and zooms in on the scene. Although he doesn't yet realize it, he is actually immortalizing an incredible story that is about to come from Marija's lips, a story that the Blessed Mother will use to unveil and heal the secret despair of so many women.

Marija positions herself close to the tabernacle, and just seeing how cheerful she is, you can tell that she is about to speak from an overflowing heart. Today is a big day: "It's the first time the Holy Father comes to my country," she had said that morning. "Many people advised him not to, but he wanted so badly to make it that despite his physical weakness, he would have come on foot! He is coming as a bearer of peace in the midst of those ruins."

Not long before she had seen his face on TV as he caught sight of that capital city shattered by the bombings and marked by death.

Marija continued: "Yesterday, the Gospa prayed with me for him. She asks us to pray a lot for him, for his health...he is her most beloved son! Tonight, the Gospa was joyful, she greeted us and blessed us all with her hands extended..." In the audience, rich and poor alike have the same expression, have one ear and one heart, for they know that Mary has heard the cry in the depths of their heart, and has looked down upon them. They all hang on every word, every sentence, waiting for just one message from Marija, even the slightest fragment from heaven that will help them change their life. How beautiful are these faces riveted to the Invisible, as if lifted out of all that weighs them down!

Then Marija tells about Mary's love for the Pope, about Sarajevo being destroyed...and then, out of the blue, she embarks on *the* story...

A deeply wounded woman came and opened her heart to Marija: "I'm coming to you because I don't have the courage to see a priest — I don't dare go to confession. You won't believe it, but I've had 8 abortions! I'm afraid the priest will be angry at me and throw me out of the confessional. But you, Marija, I'm sure you can do something: please, ask Our Lady to help me! I'm so profoundly depressed that I can't sleep at night, I suffer too much. My husband was opposed to life, you know. We were broke. Now I can't have children anymore. Will you tell the *Madonna* about me?"

Marija has always been active in making people love and protect life. She listened to this woman with love and entrusted her to Mary that very evening. Our Lady prayed for her and then she amazed us once more with the extraordinary hope she puts in us, her children, especially when everything looks hopeless from a human standpoint. She replied to Marija,

"From now on, it is she who will be a carrier of life for others!"

This woman became reconciled with God and went to confession on Marija's advice. The mercy of God so transformed her heart that, today, she testifies with great effect to this healing of her whole being[1] (including her sleep!). She is at peace with God and greatly enjoys the gift of life. She goes to see women who are considering having an abortion, even to the hospital where she had her own, in order to share her experience with them and persuade them not to kill their child. She is having considerable impact! She explained to Marija: "I do everything I can to win over these mothers. First of all, I pray, then I tell them my story and the anguish I used to have in my heart." She added, "Life is so short, I have to hurry now, I have to rush! Not only on behalf of my own children, but also for those who are threatened by abortion."

This is the way Mary wishes to act in each one of us. Moreover, far from taking offense at our deathly wounds, she transforms them into sources of life. Better still, Jesus and she are actually drawn by our wounds! If only we would offer to Jesus all the evil accumulated within us, he would heal us through his own wounds, forever glorified.

When Mary our Mother looks at us, does she see our sins, all the foul stains in even our voices and eyes? Does she feel disgusted, she the Immaculate One? No!

---

[1] God chose the Hebrew language for the instruction of his people for thousands of years. He used the most earthy, physical words to express the most sublime spiritual realities. Even today, a Jew will use the Hebrew word for uterus, womb, to say "mercy" (*rahamim*, in the plural). What a wonderful image!

When I sin, God does not punish me from behind some judge's desk, but rather he feels what a mother feels in her womb when she sees her child drowning—all she can think of is saving him at any cost. This is the true meaning of mercy: a womb that creates life bit by bit, day after day, in secrecy—a haven of love, a home, a place where the child is cherished! (The Hebrew verb derived from the root *raham* means "to cherish.") And if I stray far from this home, God suffers and cries from the divine depths: "Come back!" And when I do return to the motherly womb of the Father, he lavishes me with all the treasures of closeness with him. The word *misericordia* in Latin (*miserere* and *corde*) is also rich in meaning, but it doesn't express the maternal dimension of mercy that God gave in the original Hebrew.

Among the 13 names for God in the Bible (and the name defines the identity), we find "the Most High," "the Eternal One," "the Almighty," but we also find "*Harahamim:*" the "Merciful," or better, the "One who carries in the womb" (Exod 34:6, at Sinai).

When the Blessed Mother looks at us, her glance pierces the opaque layers of our darkness to contemplate the divine stamp buried deep down, where no evil can reach and where the splendor of the Creator radiates more brightly than the sun. Contemplating this radiance she is in awe, she burns with love. She immediately saw in that woman, our sister and our friend, the divine seal: *"She will be a carrier of life!"*

Who dares ask the Mother of Mercy to change the prescription of her glasses?! To readjust her vision? We know well that in the midst of the thousand and one voices of our subtle accusations, it is the Mother who is the only one to have seen clearly because she has seen the beauty and the greatness.

Some friends of Medjugorje had asked me to give a few talks in California. When I got to San Francisco, I noticed that the streets were attractive, posh, squeaky clean, but devoid of children. Dead streets! I cried for help to the Gospa, begging her to put in my heart the words that her motherly heart had in store for the people I would meet. What I had to say would be aimed at a society which legalizes thousands of abortions (even up to the ninth month of pregnancy under the misleading term of "therapeutic abortion"). The answer came without delay. I then grabbed the first occasion of speaking in public and transmitted the inspiration I had received in prayer:

"Satan rages against human life, he wants to destroy it at all costs and to wipe it off the map forever. Don't give in to him! In the spirit of Mary at Fatima as well as at Medjugorje (where she invites us to consecrate ourselves as individuals), I suggest that all people of the female sex consecrate their "motherly womb" to her Immaculate Heart. What does it mean?

"For example, married women can say, "Now I offer you this part of my body; henceforth it is yours. May everything that might happen there serve your plans and God's will. From now on, you'll be the one who decides how many children will be conceived there and be brought to birth. Protect this precious place from all impurities, all diseases, everything that might prevent you from realizing your desires. Let it be the reflection of your incomparable motherly womb. Bless in advance all the children to be born, bless those who have already come to life there. Heal me of the consequences and wounds of all that may have displeased you. If this place has been touched by death (from miscarriage or abortion[2]), heal my whole being from the damage, and welcome into your motherly womb the little one I have lost. Dearest Mother, let everything I have be yours, as you too gave me all that is yours."

A child, a girl or an unmarried woman can make this consecration, with variations, of course. A girl commits to Mary's care her future as a mother and the potential for life she has within her, so that it may develop according to God's grace, be protected from any violent aggression, and never shelter sin. A woman who suffers from being single and not being a mother can adjust her consecration, adding the dimension of the secret martyrdom she may live. This martyrdom itself can bring thousands of people back to true life, in the economy of salvation. As for grandmothers, they have plenty to consecrate: both their past and their descendants.

Of course, husbands too can take part in this consecration. It's highly recommended! In San Francisco a man had asked his wife to have her tubes tied after the birth of their second child. He came to me with tears in his eyes saying that they would now do everything medically possible to enable her to conceive. One couple also stated, "This consecration had the effect of a liberation for us. We had been afraid of life, of the future. Now there is a fresh joy in our marriage, we are open to life. May Mary give us all the children that God has planned for our family!"

The barometer of happiness goes up when a man respects and honors a woman's womb. Firstly, he can be grateful for his mother's womb, thanks to which he was born. This leads him to revere his wife's womb, those of the women he knows, and his own daughters'... Blessings abound when men pray with all their hearts that women may resemble the Mother of God, the most beautiful of all women, and not the appalling magazine models! In the case of painful situations (that often entail innocent victims), when consecration between spouses is not possible, the Gospa tells us in prayer what to do; she shows each one, case by case, the wonderful fecundity that God has prepared especially for each person.

---

[2] A 40-year-old woman once told me: "When I was 20 I had an abortion. After that I wanted to get married, but it never worked out. Now I have a skin disease, and I've gained so much weight... But since my conversion, Mary has given meaning to my life. I joyfully offer all my sufferings, my loneliness and health problems, so that no woman chooses abortion. Every new day is another occasion to work for Jesus and for life."

The other day, I met my little Paul near the church. He is 7 months old. He was sitting enthroned in his stroller, blissfully happy in the middle of the crowd. His father hailed me: "Sister, look at this child! He owes his life to the Gospa! You know, we were at a talk on the messages you gave last year in Lisieux..."

"What do you mean?!"

"Yes, my wife and I had kind of 'stopped having children,' but after Lisieux, we said to Mary that she could use us to give life; and a year later, little Paul was born!"

I observed the baby with tenderness. Indeed, he was very special... I patted his hand and all of a sudden he graced me with a radiant smile, one of the most beautiful (toothless) smiles I had ever seen on a little one's face, a portrait of perfect joy. I immediately fell in love with Paul, and the following days, I kept on looking for him...but in vain. His parents had returned to France...

Little Paul, when you grow up, try to find me! Maybe you'll help the Gospa proclaim to all the world that the remedy against our culture of death is consecration to her Immaculate Heart. And you will be just the right person to say: "Entrust your fertility to Our Lady, she seeks motherly wombs to place there and bless all the children that the Father dreams of bestowing upon both earth and heaven!"

— Message of April 25, 1997 —

"Dear children! Today I call you to have your life be connected to God the Creator, because only in this way will your life have meaning and you will comprehend that God is love. God sends me to you out of love, that I may help you to comprehend that without him there is no future or joy and, above all, there is no eternal salvation. Little children, I call you to leave sin and to accept prayer at all times, that you may in prayer come to know the meaning of your life. God gives himself to him who seeks him. Thank you for having responded to my call."

SHE PULLED THE PLUG!

St. James Church is packed; it's August 15, 1997. Waves of applause sweep the congregation as Father Charles M. shares his testimony. It was a sheer miracle that he could be the main celebrant today. Only Our Lady could orchestrate that! I'm not used to clapping in a church at Mass, but on that day, once again, I said to God with a wink, "Thank you, Lord, for having created the Americans!"

I wish I could reproduce here the most delightful New York accent of the 36-year-old priest when he expresses his admiration for the Blessed Mother, or when he plays the songs he composed for her; but if you can't hear the accent, at least take in his words, as they reveal a fantastic gift from Mary:

"I came to Medjugorje for the first time on August 15, 1984; it was the Feast of the Assumption. At that time I was filled with a lot of anxiety, fear, worry, and concern, because I felt in my heart that I was being called to the priesthood, but I wasn't sure whether it was me or whether it was from God! I didn't know what was God's will for me, whether I could live the priesthood, whether I wanted to give up a family, children and a wife. I wanted to get married; I always dreamt of getting married.

"When I was 16, I first began to think of the priesthood. When I first came to Medjugorje I was 24. I now was finishing college, I had studied theology and philosophy, I figured I would become a professor in a university if I didn't get ordained. But at this time of my life I had to apply for the seminary. So I had to make a decision at this point. I was actually very depressed.

"I loved Jesus; I used to pray every day. That's why I used to struggle so much because I wanted to do what was right; I wanted to follow the Lord, but I didn't know what he wanted. It wasn't clear to me.

"On the last day of my pilgrimage, I was walking around the church. I was very inquisitive, so I was kind of checking out everything around the property, and I was very moved by all the priests hearing confessions all day long. It had rained earlier in the day so people were kneeling in the mud going to confession all day, and that was very moving. I was very impressed with the priests bringing people back to Jesus.

"The 2 priests of our group had given the instruction to get on the bus at 6 p.m. and wait for them while they would be admitted to the apparition room. They would pray there, and the second the apparition was over, they would run to the bus which would leave immediately for Split to take a ferry back to Italy. What happened was the whole group went to the bus but me.

"At about 6 o'clock, I happened to see this window on the right side of the church. There were barrels with planks across them and all the people were standing on the barrels looking into this window. I wondered, 'Is this THE window?' I decided to get on top of the barrel as well. When I saw the planks, they were filled. But the second I walked over to the planks, someone jumped off the plank and I jumped on. I was looking in at the window when I realized that that was probably the apparition room, but I was not sure. I figured it could be it, and if it was, I was not about to move. Ha, ha!!

"I stood there and hung onto the bars, for 40 minutes! I figured, I kept thinking, 'This has to be it, this has to be it!' I stood there until they started to bring in the priests. Then I realized that this was it! I saw my friend (one of the 2 priests) coming in, and the expression on his face was: 'How in the world did you find this place, what are you doing here?!? Why aren't you on the bus?,' you know... (here Fr. Charles mimics the silent dialogue and the expression of his face saying, "Yeah, I made it, man!!!").

"At that point he was kneeling there and they brought in the children (the visionaries), and the children were praying. In a split second they all fell on their knees. I kept looking at them and at the ceiling. I remember thinking to myself, 'You know, this is so ordinary...' I was disappointed at first; I struggled, thinking that I would go back home with the very same questions, but I accepted it. Then I heard God say in my heart, '**But I work through the ordinary.**' So I was okay with it—I don't need the angelic sound, the flashes of light—okay, that's fine.

"Then I just kept looking at the children, and all of a sudden I heard Mary speak to my heart. I heard her say, '**Charles, stop all your running and stop being so anxious, and let me prove your vocation to you!**' At that moment what I felt like emotionally was—imagine a big bathtub filled with dirty water, you pull the plug or you open the drain and all of a sudden all that water is gushing down, trying to get through that drain as fast as possible and it's making a sucking... [Here, you're missing the best: the sound of the water being sucked down with a N.Y. accent!]. That's what I felt like emotionally, everything left, I was drained of all the negativity, all the fears, the worries, the questions: 'Can I do it, shall I do it, do I wanna do it?'

"I just felt complete peace. I could feel Our Lady's presence so strongly, I have no words to describe this experience,[1] it was as if she was holding me in her arms, I'll never forget that! I remember being mesmerized that this had happened, I was shocked it happened, I didn't expect this, I did not come to Medjugorje for this, I came to just check it out, to see whether this was real or not, not to hear Mary speak to my heart. Just wondering, you know, "Is this real?" I remember saying out loud at that point, "That's it! This is what I want to do with my life, I want to bring people to Jesus! I definitely want that." I looked to my right and saw the priests hearing confessions...

"It's been an awesome experience; I've just been very humbled by the whole entire experience. This obviously changed my life; it changed my life thoroughly! Bringing people to know Jesus, to love Jesus, to experience Jesus, that's the greatest joy: bringing people to prayer, experiencing God's love and bringing them back to faith and to praying themselves... Back home, I joined the seminary. I was ordained in 1990, and today... HERE I AM, MOTHER!"

---

[1] An English-speaking sister in my community helped me transcribe the recording of this testimony. While she was listening to the tape, I saw her eyes grow moist, and she cried, "But it's incredible!" And in fact, she too had come in the summer of 1984, and had found the same barrels, the same planks, the same window, and had hoisted herself up on the famous window sill to see the moment of the apparition, and had been overwhelmed by the same identical interior experience as Father Charles. That proved beyond a shadow of a doubt that a drain is one of the Gospa's favorite instruments for those who come here, to her beauty parlor, even by chance!

— Message of May 25, 1997 —

"Dear children! Today I invite you to glorify God, and for the name of God to be holy in your hearts and in your lives. Little children, when you are in the holiness of God, he is with you and gives you the peace and joy which come only from God through prayer. That is why, little children, renew prayer in your families, and your hearts will glorify the holy name of God and heaven will reign in your hearts. I am close to you and I intercede for you before God. Thank you for having responded to my call."

STOP SLANDERING!

Hamlet of Unatine, near Bzovik, Slovakia, in a period of scorching summer drought.

Little Patko can't believe his eyes! He's just come back from the pastures where he was watching the sheep with his brother Jozko, and he sees in the distance a huge fire blazing. The village is on fire! The houses are going up like straw, one after the other...and, oh! there goes his own house up in flames! The child is only 6 years old, but he understands what is happening in a flash: as it is, they sometimes go to bed hungry, even though everyone works hard in the fields, but now, with this fire... Oh, Jesus, help us! What will become of us?

Patko's little heart bleeds and prays.

And yet he has not foreseen the worst: the fire was not accidental, but was set by a bunch of kids who were playing with fire near Patko's house. Their father knows what happened; he panics when he sees the extent of the disaster, and he declares loudly that he knows the 'culprit,' and that he is no other than little Patko!

This calumny would never have held water if a serious inquiry had been made, but none was. The little boy's faint protests were drowned out by the loud rantings of the adults, and his weak alibi counted for nothing. All the villagers as one man spread the rumor everywhere without even bothering to ascertain the truth of the matter.

And then began a long agony that was to last 7 years. Little Patko's mother knew her son was innocent. Years later, before she died, she shared with him her memories of what he had said when he and all his family were shunned in the village, pointed at, and made utterly wretched: "Even if people think I did that, and are really angry at me, I know that Jesus isn't angry at me because he knows I didn't do it. Huh, Mom?" This woman, an ardent believer, suffered much more from the unjust persecution her whole family had to endure than from the loss of all her worldly goods.

But one day the village priest was called to a cottage. An elderly father of a family was dying, suffering unspeakable torments due to a bad conscience. He confessed an old sin, an abscess festering for so long in the depths of his heart and which, day after long day, had destroyed his peace. "I confess that we were responsible for that fire, my children set it, and I made up the story about Patko. He's innocent."

The priest hastened to give him absolution and restore to a state of grace this most impoverished of men who, because of his cowardice, had so long been deprived of that essential element of human happiness, peace. But the priest was still unsatisfied: for until the truth was shouted from the rooftops, the evil would continue...

"Jesus has forgiven you everything, but now you must make a public declaration of what you just confessed in secret, for an innocent man remains accused, and his whole family has suffered tremendously. That will be your penance."

The man called together all the villagers and confessed his false testimony and his cowardice. Everyone left in tears, with much to think about, while the poor man breathed his last, garbed in the shining robe of the infinite mercy of God.

This story took place in 1927– and little Patko grew up to be none other than Bishop Paolo Hnilica, who continues today to feed his flock (see

---

[1] Profound love of the truth was born in Patko's heart from this ordeal. He paid dearly for this (Communist work camps). Just recently, in Rome, while we were talking about the sometimes false rumors that had been spread about Medjugorje, he said to me: "If you know the truth, it is your duty to say it and publish it. If you kept silent, it would be a grave sin."

the chapter, *"The Pravda Contained the Truth"*). Nowadays his pastures extend far from his original Slovakia to the entire Eastern Block.[1] And there he seeks out souls to set the world ablaze!

This is only one example among thousands of a situation in which it would have been so easy to stop the evil at its inception, cut it off at the root. Calumny easily arises, but why are people so eager to spread it abroad as soon as they get wind of it?[2]

In my community we have a golden rule, without which the Evil One could have destroyed us long ago, for spreading discord among brothers is child's play to him. This rule holds that we must never give credence to — and even less, spread abroad — something negative that is said about someone, without first asking that person about it. In 90% of cases we perceive that the original situation has been distorted or reported only in part, and we are very glad that we went right to the source to check it out!

The "Father of Lies," who is also the "Accuser" of the brethren, hates this way of bringing everything out into the light, for he needs darkness and shadows to do his filthy work. We can topple his sinister plots like a house of cards by simply seeking out our brother for a calm, heart-to-heart talk, well-prepared in the peace of prayer.[3] Most touching of all, when the person being blamed has indeed been responsible for what he is accused of, he admits it in tears, acknowledges his weakness, and asks for the help of our prayers. So who are we to go rummaging in old garbage cans to fish out what Jesus himself has already purified with his Blood,[4] and even forgotten?

In our chapter *"Tonight They May Touch Me,"* we saw that famous

---

[2] The Holy Curé of Ars used to say: "The slanderer is like the caterpillar who creeps over flowering plants and leaves behind his slime and dirt."

[3] Jesus knows why it is important to go find one's brother and speak to him alone, in privacy (Matt 18:15).

[4] Blessed Miryam of Bethlehem said that this is the same as re-crucifying Jesus. Most of the mystics agree that calumny and slander are a horror in the eyes of God; the instances are numberless where, with the permission of God and for the sake of souls, they have seen the terrible consequences of these sins after death, either a long and excruciating purgatory, or even hell. (See *Martha Robin, The Cross and The Joy*, by Rev. Raymond Peyret, Alba House, NY; Society of St. Paul, 2187 Victory Blvd., Staten Island, NY 10314). I know that some will criticize me for writing this, but I think it is important to warn the reader who might have a grave sin of slander on his conscience and has been putting off confessing it to a priest with all his heart.

episode in which the visionaries took the villagers one by one to touch the Gospa, and her robe was soiled by contact with their sins. Marija adds a very significant detail: "When we (the visionaries) saw that a particular person left a stain on the Blessed Mother's robe, we were furious! In our anger we said to ourselves, 'What! How dare he! I won't forget *that* any time soon!' But right after the apparition, when our role was over, we couldn't remember who had made the stains! That day the Gospa really taught us an important lesson."

The Church has always maintained the sanctity of the secret of the confessional. This affects clergy, but the laity have also been taught to keep silent on the faults of others as well. Keeping alive the memory of an evil done is a subtle sin that the Blessed Mother wants to rid us of, for that is how evil gossip and calumny get started.[5] On April 12, 1984, when the "war of wagging tongues" was putting at risk the outcome of her work in the village of Medjugorje, she gave this message:
> "Dear children, I beseech you to stop slandering and to pray for the unity of the parish, for my Son and I have a special plan for this parish..."

One of my friends in Paris had received the outstanding grace of often visiting with Marthe Robin. One day Marthe begged him to show tirelessly the mercy of God and receive sinners with particular kindness.

Then she told him the episode of the woman taken in adultery (John 8:1) as she had seen it in a state of ecstasy (she was often spiritually present at such scenes from the life of Jesus). This is a summary of what

---

[5] Slandering means to speak evil of a person, to reveal his sins and faults, even when they are **true**. To calumniate is to ruin someone's reputation or honor by accusations that one knows are **false**.

The following quote from an article in *Today's Catholic* (5.5.91, p. 21) is pertinent: "The new Code of Canon Law (1983) specifically states that 'no one is permitted to damage unlawfully the good reputation which another person enjoys.' (#220)

"One way to harm a person's reputation is through calumny. This is when we deliberately tell a lie about him in the hope of injuring his good name. The moral theologian Father Bernard Haring defines calumny as 'a false or exaggerated assertion regarding one's neighbor which is calculated to defame him.'

"Another sin against one's reputation is detraction. Here we harm a person's reputation by saying something about her, even though it may be true. Father Haring defines detraction as any 'unjustified assertion which infringes the good name of another, even though it is not formally untrue.'"

he told me he had heard from her:

In the face of the accusations being leveled at this woman by the scribes and the Pharisees, Jesus kept silent. He seemed to ignore them, and kept his eyes on the ground. He did not look at the woman either, although she was pushed forward for everyone to see her shame. Then he began to write something in the sand with his finger. Irritated at his silence and curious to see what he was writing, a few Pharisees boldly went up to him. What could he be writing?

When the first of the Pharisees reached him, he discovered to his stupefaction that Jesus knew all his most secret sins, for that was what he had been writing on the ground! Deeply embarrassed and scared to death he looked at Jesus, realizing that Jesus could expose him before everyone! But on the contrary, the Savior kindly and majestically erased the sins he had just traced on the ground. The man's sins were wiped away, gone! He read his forgiveness in Jesus' eyes, and silently went away.

Another one went over to Jesus but obviously could not read the sins of the man who had just departed. Jesus then wrote the secret sins of the second man, who read them and also went away, overcome. And so, one after the other all the accusers of the woman departed in deep confusion, but their secrets had been preserved.

Left behind at the scene, with the stones they had intended to kill the adulterous woman with, were the evil slanderings and perverse intents they had brought in their hearts. Yes, the greatest joy of the Lamb of God is to wipe away the sins of the world!

At Cana Jesus changed water into wine; but isn't it an even greater miracle to absorb the vinegar of our bitterness and venom as he did on the Cross, and give back the Blood of his Heart in exchange? And it is just such a miracle that he proposes to perform every day for us, if only we will abandon to him all the poisons that are still festering deep within us and killing our capacity for love.

Who knows if there is not greater rejoicing in heaven for a single slanderer who repents than for 99 prostitutes who have not...? But yes, yes! they do need to repent too! For in order to bring us with him to heaven, Jesus has only opened one door for all, for true sinners and false alike, and that door is the one of his divine, kingly, and unfathomable mercy.

— MESSAGE OF JUNE 25, 1997 —

"Dear children! Today I am with you in a special way and I bring you my motherly blessing of peace. I pray for you and I intercede for you before God, so that you may comprehend that each of you is a carrier of peace. You cannot have peace if your heart is not at peace with God. That is why, little children, pray, pray, pray, because prayer is the foundation of your peace. Open your heart and give time to God so that he will be your friend. When true friendship with God is realized, no storm can destroy it. Thank you for having responded to my call."

A FRANCISCAN IN THE PARKING LOT

It was the end of the year 1993 and the war was raging. The entire Medjugorje region was enjoying a period of relative quiet, but less than 60 miles away Bosnia was being torn apart by the hostilities. Don't expect a run-down of the political situation from me, for there's no one less politically astute than I...

On that particular day I went to the rectory to leave a letter, when I bumped into a Franciscan. He was returning to his car which was parked in the lot, and seemed in a hurry. I called over to him: "Father, what a joy to see you here! So you are still alive, praised be Jesus!"

"Oh, Sestra! You too are alive, thank God!"

This was how we greeted each other here in this country, in 1992-1993. "One will be taken, and another will be left..." says the gospel (Matt 25:40), and this war certainly reminded us that none of us is eternal here below.

"Where are you off to? Don't tell me you're leaving us again; you've just gotten here!"

"I'm already late! I have a long trip ahead of me, and not an easy one..."

("For sure, he'll bring supplies to people in need in a zone that is at high risk," I thought, worried.) "And where does this trip take you?"

A silence heavy with meaning was the only answer to my question. "Okay, if you can't tell me, I will pray for you even though I don't know what it's about—I'm used to it! *Nema problema!*"

He still remained silent, but I saw from his frown that he was hesitating, weighing his options.

"Listen—," he said, lowering his voice. "I know that you pray, so I'm going to tell you where I'm going, but promise me you won't tell a soul. If they ask you where I am, you have no idea. And if you see I don't come back, well...pray for me!"

"You're leaving for Bosnia?"

I will never forget his look, nor the tone of his voice, nor the determination that breathed from his whole being. In a few brief, sober words he outlined the plan that might cost him his life.

"I'm going to—(I keep my promises!) They have been surrounded for almost a month now by the Muslim forces. Hundreds have already been killed; their church is destroyed and they have been surrounded: no one can get in or out, and they have run out of everything. They are facing extermination, and they have no priest. We just can't leave the faithful without the sacraments!"

I put my hand in his, or rather, I took his hand in mine. I swallowed several times to recover my voice, and then I said shakily, "So how are you going to break through the enemy lines?"

He gave a little smile. (Of course, I should have remembered—all the Franciscans around here are bush-whackers in brown habits!)

"You know, this is my homeland, I'm familiar with this region... there is always a way!"

"The Gospa will be with you!"

"All right, time to go! I'll fill up my car and I'm off."

"Bless me before you go, Father."

He placed his hands on my head and pronounced the beautiful Croatian prayer of blessing that includes the Queen of Peace. And then, without another word, he was off!

❈ ❈ ❈ ❈

I saw this brother again many months later, for after his return he came to celebrate evening Mass in Medjugorje. The Lord had protected him, and he took up his ministry in the region as if he had never been away. Even today he sometimes celebrates the mysteries of the Lord for crowds of people from all over the world, speaking many different languages, here at Medjugorje. Amongst all those people, who suspects that this humble disciple of Jesus who looks like so many other priests actually merits the crown of martyrdom? Who can imagine that the hand that gives them the Body of Christ today was almost counted among the missing and dead, and that tomorrow, if the "people" need their priest to help them, peril of death or not, he will not fail the summons? Not one suspects that this priest who proclaims the gospel from behind his microphone, restrained in his gestures and words, had lived the reality of Jesus' words to the death: **"There is no greater love than to give one's life for those one loves."**

This has been the tradition for centuries among my Franciscan brothers in this country. It is fixed in the ancestral memory of the Croatian people. And it is my great joy today to pay homage to it!

— Message of July 25, 1997 —

"Dear children! today I invite you to respond to my call to prayer. I desire, dear children, that during this time you find a corner for personal prayer. I desire to lead you towards prayer with the heart. Only in this way will you comprehend that your life is empty without prayer. You will discover the meaning of your life when you discover God in prayer. That is why, little children, open the door of your heart and you will comprehend that prayer is joy without which you cannot live. Thank you for having responded to my call."

THE SOLUTION WAS LYING IN THE DRAWER

Sherry and Ron? A couple who incarnate magnificently the fruits that Medjugorje can bear even 10 hours away from the village by airplane, for people who have never been there! Last month, when I was in Notre Dame, Indiana, they grabbed me to tell me their story...

Sherry and Ron dreamed of having a child. After 8 years, Sherry found out she was pregnant; she was thrilled. The first ultrasound showed that everything was OK, but after several weeks the baby was not moving the way it should have been at that stage. After the second ultrasound, the doctor diagnosed an incurable heart dysfunction which would shortly bring about the baby's death.

But neither Sherry nor Ron accepted this option. They were heart-broken, and started to pray intensely. Many of their "friends" advised them to have an abortion, but they loved this little life already so much! An operation seemed the only possibility, but the chances of success were minimal: 1%! The doctors attempted a blood transfusion in the umbilical cord, as the little one was very anemic; she was only 23 weeks old and her death could occur at any minute. After this procedure, which was as painful as it was emotionally draining, Sherry and Ron went home, shattered.

Sherry then remembered a wooden rosary that her friend Liz had brought her from Medjugorje, and that she had buried right away at the back of a drawer, among some junk. It occurred to her to put this rosary on her belly while praying, and she pressed it against her as if to make her little girl feel it.

She would never forget what happened next: for the first time, the child began to move, as if to grasp the rosary!

During the next few days, when Sherry and Ron were praying the rosary, the little one made her presence known by all kinds of somersaults and pokes in her mother's womb. A real little John the Baptist!

Sherry demanded a new ultrasound. While Ron prayed near the machine, the physician suddenly seemed all excited and called together all the medical staff present to show them the screen: all the excess fluid that was endangering the baby's life had completely vanished. The doctors couldn't believe their eyes; it was inexplicable! They told the parents to go home and wait quietly for the baby to be born in the normal way. No need for an operation!

Anna Mary was born in September 1994. I saw her last month in the States. She is the picture of health and joy in life, and she's always in perpetual motion! Moreover, she is irresistibly drawn to any statue of the Blessed Mother she comes across.

Mary has transformed the little girl's parents into true apostles for Mary and ardent supporters of her projects; they faithfully invite their friends and family to pray the rosary, because, as they say, "Through praying the rosary, miracles do happen!"[1]

---

[1] But a word of warning here: I don't mean to be saying that the rosary has magical powers, or that such miracles are automatic: no. Sometimes God permits hardships, but, thanks to prayer, he bestows strength and peace. The Cross becomes a way to joy, as the Gospa said in September 1996. Many more healings would be granted if the family involved prayed and fasted for the sick person. In the Rue du Bac in Paris (1830), Mary tells us that she has graces in store for us that she cannot give us yet because nobody asks her for them. So let's ask in all confidence for those graces!

And what about miracles? There are thousands of them just hovering overhead, ready to shower down on us. Fortunately, some people are busy bringing them down into our world. My little friends Allison (6 years old) and Don (5 years old) are real professionals at it, in their own way:

These 2 little ones have a statue in their room of the Blessed Mother appearing in the Rue du Bac. As they were looking at the rays streaming from Mary's hands, we explained to them that Mary dispenses some graces, but holds others back, the ones that are not asked for. The little ones were amazed. They were obviously concocting some plan to do something about this situation!

That very evening, at their bedtime, their mother overheard their conversation. Kneeling on her bed, Allison declared to her little brother, "You take the left hand, I'll take the right one." The little boy agreed to this sharing of responsibility, and then, with their hands clasped and with the deepest concentration, they prayed to Mary with great faith, repeating, "Please, give me those graces, come on, give them to me!"

Indeed, the Kingdom of God belongs to little children, and to those who are like them...

— MESSAGE OF AUGUST 25, 1997 —

"Dear children! God gives me this time as a gift to you, so that I may instruct and lead you on the path of salvation. Dear children, now you do not comprehend this grace, but soon a time will come when you will lament for these messages. That is why, little children, live all of the words which I have given you through this time of grace, and renew prayer, until prayer becomes a joy for you. Especially, I call all those who have consecrated themselves to my Immaculate Heart to become an example to others. I call all priests and religious brothers and sisters to pray the rosary and to teach others to pray. The rosary, little children, is especially dear to me. Through the rosary open your heart to me and I will be able to help you. Thank you for having responded to my call."

SO WHO'S COMPETING
WITH THE HOLY FATHER?

Picture an adorable little Polish grandmother offering you some of her home-made cookies and telling you a sublime story that happened to her personally:

Zofia was born in Wilno in 1930. You can imagine all the privations, humiliations, and losses she suffered, along with all her fellow countrymen who were driven out of Lithuania in 1939...

She married Marek, a great Polish poet, and she lived as a devoted mother and homemaker who had to learn how to deal with the harsh realities of taking care of her brood under an oppressive Communist regime.

As early as 1957 she and her husband were working with Karol Wojtyla, who was just a priest at the time, in a Catholic lay movement. They got very close to him. (Later on Marek continued to work closely with "John Paul II We Love You" in the Vatican, and he still maintains a correspondence with him today. While munching on some of Zofia's goodies I've been able to see some of these letters with my own eyes.)

In Poland in 1982, government censure was once again terrible after the great hope raised by the Solidarity movement. Zofia first heard of Medjugorje on October 1, 1983, and in that atmosphere of sadness, it appeared as a ray of hope that made her say, "God has not abandoned us!"

She felt a new stirring of hope, hope that freedom would once again be theirs... Because the borders were closed and mail was censured, she was unable to stay in contact with her friends in other countries. But lo and behold, on that first day of October, a friend of hers who was a famous pianist, and who could leave Poland for her concert tours, brought her some good news. Zofia, who was fed up with the unbelievable red-tape of the regime, exclaimed: "This just can't go on; you'll see— God will do something to stop the triumph of evil!"

"Maybe he has already begun!" replied her musician friend with an air of mystery.

In Germany, where she had just been, she had heard that the Mother of God had been appearing in Yugoslavia for the past 2 years. Someone even gave her a little book with Mary's words to the visionaries. So Zofia asked if she could borrow the book. The 2 women met at the convent of Sr. Faustina, and Zofia was given the book of messages in front of the tomb of the latter on October 5, the anniversary of the Polish mystic's death.

"I stayed up all night reading that book from cover to cover," Zofia relates. "In the morning I telephoned a friend who knew German better than I and who I thought could quickly translate 20 or 30 pages, the most important, so that here in Poland people would find out that God is intervening in world destiny, and in such an extraordinary way! My friend Maria read all night. She called me in the morning: 'We need to translate the whole book, not just 20 or 30 pages! I'll get cracking!"

"I told her I was afraid that translating the whole thing would take an awfully long time, but she reassured me in no uncertain terms: 'It'll take a month!' And she was as good as her word!

"Her husband Stanislaw was overjoyed to hear that Providence was speaking to the world through the mouth of Mary. He immediately arranged to have 30 or 40 copies of the book reproduced in a place only he knew about, for it was strictly forbidden to publish anything that did not go through the official censuring process, not even a single page. These few copies circulated among our friends.

"We experienced a time of euphoria, of joy, trying to put into practice Mary's recommendations, and dreaming of some day being able to go ourselves to Medjugorje.

"Meanwhile, somehow, my friend Maria managed to lay her hands on another book on the events in Medjugorje; this book was a French copy of Father Svetozar Kraljevic's book *The Apparitions of Medjugorje.* She translated it in no time at all. And we circulated it too, discreetly, just a few copies, and we began to collect the few articles we could get from the foreign press, as well as photographs and videos.

"Maria, Stanislaw and I wanted to go to Medjugorje to pray for all our intentions including the fate of our country; above all, we wanted to thank Mary, and rejoice in her presence. Towards the end of the summer of 1984 Stanislaw got wind of an inexpensive tour to Budva, in the Black Mountains (Yugoslavia). We had to get our passports individually. I got mine the last, with just one hour left to sign up!

"Once we were there, without telling anyone else, we told the tour guide that we were taking 2 days off to go see friends in Mostar. He made no objections. We left on October 4 in a bus crammed to bursting and in stifling heat. After Dubrovnik we changed buses for Mostar. Through hill and dale we finally reached our goal!

"We got to the church 15 minutes before the rosary started. We knelt down before the altar, ignoring how exhausted we were. We knew that in a few minutes the Blessed Mother was going to come, and that was all that mattered!

"My friend Maria clasped to her heart the present she had brought: the 2 books in Polish. You can imagine the state of emotion we were all in: to be able to pray with a crowd of pilgrims in various languages for the first time! To wait for the arrival of the visionaries and their encounter with the Holy Mother! These are the secrets of the heart for everyone, but in another sense these are everybody's secrets too, for all who come here to Medjugorje with faith. I can't describe it—there just are no words.

"And then the bells began to peal, and we heard for the first time the chant: 'Doslismo ti Majko Draga,' that my husband later translated into Polish."

Then and there the extraordinary mission of Zofia was born. The minute she returned to Poland she set about spreading the words of Mary in her country. It took off like wildfire. But let's return to her pilgrimage in

— MESSAGE OF SEPTEMBER 25, 1997 —

"Dear Children! Today I call you to understand that without love you cannot comprehend that God needs to be in the first place in your life. That is why, little Children, I call you all to love, not with a human love, but with God's love. In this way, your life will be more beautiful and without self-interest. You will comprehend that God gives Himself to you in the simplest way out of love. Little children, so that you may comprehend my word which I give you out of love and to forgive all who have done evil to you. Respond with prayer; prayer is the fruit of love towards God the Creator. Thank you for having responded to my call."

LOVE LESSONS

These were days of arctic cold, with a merciless wind blasting over the plains of Medjugorje, freezing everything in its path. January spread its bleak nakedness over the land.

Here we are in the small living room of the Pavlovic home. Marija is looking gravely and intently towards the Gospa, while her friends are praying on their knees all around her. This is the Golden Age of the prayer group, those famous four years during which the Gospa took their education in hand, forming them for a life of love and service to God.

"Tonight the Gospa has given us an exercise to do," says Marija. "She wants each one of us to go outdoors into nature and find something that speaks to him of the Creator. She asks that for tomorrow's apparition, each one brings for her something from nature that they find to be beautiful."

The next day, shortly before five in the afternoon, a strange sight can be seen as one by one the adolescents bring their treasures and lay them down at the feet of the statue of Mary. Each explains the reason for his choice: "Look at the lichen on this piece of bark, can you see its incredible color?!" "And look at this–it looks like an ordinary worthless pebble, but watch what happens when you turn it over. . . Do you see it? It has the shape of two hearts that are touching!" "I looked a long time and couldn't find anything, but then I found this! Look at this bird's nest, the incredible work and skill that went into it, and the little bits of down that the bird has worked into the nest, weaving them in with bits of hay. . ."

While all the children are excitedly showing their booty to the others, suddenly the door bursts open and a gale of laughter greets the new arrival: he has brought in a branch three times as big as he is, and is trying to angle it through the door into the small room which has already been transformed into a museum!

"Don't you think this branch has an extraordinary shape to it?" he explains, hoisting up this trophy with all his might. "You'll see it better when I get it out through the doorway. . ."

That evening the Gospa appeared as if in a new version of the "Burning Bush", and she explained with her unique motherly tenderness: "Dear children, even though it is winter and nature all around you seems bare and bleak, each one of you has found something that speaks to you of the beauty of the Creator. Dear children, do the same thing with each one of your brothers and sisters. When you think that some person is totally unappealing, look harder, and you will find the beauty that the Creator has placed in him, for everyone is lovable. . ."[1]

On another occasion the Gospa gave the young people the following exercise: each one was to write down on a piece of paper the names of the persons he liked best in the prayer group, and also the names of the persons he least liked or tended to avoid. Next she asked them to alter their customary behavior for a whole month: they were to sit down next to the persons they usually avoided and make an effort to talk with them and open up their hearts to them, and in this way put aside their natural inclinations.

At the end of the month, she asked them to write down the name of the persons they liked the best, and then to compare these results with the list they had made a month earlier. All the children were amazed to see how much their feelings about the others had changed: this exercise had opened

---

[1] Marija did not write these words, but related them from memory years later.

wide their hearts in an amazing and totally unexpected way. They realized how closed they had been before, prisoners of prejudices that were totally unfounded, and how much they had lost out on, unable to enjoy the wealth of treasures hidden in the other. . . The commandment to love that we have all received from Jesus[2] was freeing them from the ruts they were in; a new joy filled the group. They had been totally transformed.

This is how the Gospa taught her children about love, not human love, but divine love. She came up with ideas that only the heart of a mother could invent. In countless ingenious ways she helped her wounded children to grow into the fullness of the stature of divine love, just as the sun helps the little rosebud all tightly closed up on itself to open up its petals one by one and to give off its perfume.

When Mary takes us by her motherly hand and tenderly teaches us, she accepts us as we actually are at that point, and not as we perhaps ought to be! She follows our human rhythm, she slows down when we slow down!

As for loving our neighbor, we are all under-achievers! Let us allow God to change our human love into divine love! If we do, we will rise way above our miserable human limits and give our hearts truly divine dimensions. for there has never been a life that has been able to escape this self-evident truth: "Human" love does not last. What is born of the flesh is flesh.[3] And the flesh does not inherit the Kingdom. "Every plant that my heavenly Father has not planted will be uprooted,"[4] said Jesus. All love that does not die to its human and fleshly nature to be reborn in the Spirit is doomed to disappear. Today as never before the bell is tolling earlier and earlier for this disappearance of love in marital and family relationships. . . And this is why the Blessed Virgin, who wants above all else to save true human love, cries out to the world in messages: "Dear children, love not with mere human love, but with the love of God!"

In France, Marthe Robin was sounding the same appeal, and she suffered agony[5] over all the divorces, "free love" living situations, and the rising incidence of the human catastrophes growing out of these practices. But how do we avoid the destruction of our families and our friendships?

---

[2] *"For if you love those who love you, what reward do you have? Do not even the tax collectors do the same?"*(Mt 5:46) And *"Love one another as I have loved you"*(Jn 15:12)

[3] Jn 3:6

[4] Mt 15:13

The answer lies in the practice of mutual respect for all human beings and the courage to ask again and again for forgiveness. A Chinese proverb says that a cup that has been broken and mended is more beautiful than a new cup without a crack! For the reglued cup has a lovely pattern of faint golden lines!

---

[5]"There is no human reality that the secular media and daily life have more deplorably and criminally distorted, soiled, mutilated and corrupted than the divine union between a man and a woman. And yet marriage always has been and always will be the divine symbol of the union of the soul and Christ; because, despite all the distortions it has suffered, the love of two persons who give themselves freely to each other remains one of the most sublime realities of this world. It is not possible to speak of true love without also speaking of unity and eternity. There is no more beautiful flower on earth than the flower of friendship, which is the elevated and lasting element of love: forgetting oneself, mutual trust, the power of the gift of self even to the point of the sacrifice of one's life, and also the sense of presence to each other, even when physically separated for a short or a long time, and the sweetness of mutual support. But alas! Soon it will no longer be love which unites human beings and founds families, but more frequently the desire for pleasure which draws bodies together for selfish and transitory union. How can we calculate the cost of the appalling consequences of this unbraked permissiveness in our modern society which will soon be nothing more than a race for pleasure, a thirst for ephemeral sensuality which is quickly followed by disenchantment and creates so much misery, broken homes, unhappy children, disturbed, sick human beings, innocent victims of criminal passions, today abandoned or orphaned, and tomorrow, in their turn, victims of sin which will kill them.[. . .]" (Marthe's words after having heard Jesus speak of the Sacrament of Marriage to His Apostles, while walking with them to Gethsemany after the Last Supper)

— MESSAGE OF OCTOBER 25, 1997 —

"Dear Children! Also today I am with you and I call all of you to renew yourselves by living my messages. Little children, may prayer be life for you and may you be an example to others. Little children, I desire for you to become carriers of peace and of God's joy to today's world without peace. That is why, little children, pray, pray, pray! I am with you and I bless you with my motherly peace. Thank you for having responded to my call."

THE TRAIN STATION WAS DESERTED

When the Gospa tells us, "I am with you," she is only repeating the famous phrase spoken by God throughout the Bible: I am with you. These words mean: "The victory will be yours for I will be fighting alongside you."

Corinne, however, neither talked the talk nor walked the walk of the prophets of the 1st Covenant. . . Hair the color of gold, beautiful as the dawn, she was going on 24, but lived without any consciousness of God, brainwashed by the unthinking materialism of modern-day Paris, glittering and seductive with its thousands of cheap joys and shoddy trinkets.

But at 25 came the thunderbolt experience followed by a drastic change of life, made as only the young know how to do: without compromise. Medjugorje made it!

Corinne discovers in Medjugorje the love of her Mother, her messages; she encounters Mary's Heart pulsing and burning with maternal tenderness, and from now on she knows she is loved by this Mother. Faith fills her, rushing in like dammed water bursting down into the empty channel below. Mary leads her to Jesus, and the introduction goes without a hitch! Corinne begins to live the messages, taking seriously all the 5 points. Her happiness at having discovered God makes waves of conversion amongst those she knows or with whom she works. There is no room here to tell the full story of her conversion, but one event that happened this fall is well worth telling:

One evening she was returning rather late to Paris, and the train station of Saint-Lazare was almost deserted. . . In surroundings like this, it's not particularly an advantage to be young and beautiful, and Corinne unhappily noticed a man waking in her direction who by his manner left no doubt as to his intentions. So Corinne prayed to the Blessed Mother for him, as she was sad to see this child of God devoured by such passions. With all her heart, but not at all (as she was careful to insist later) with any "magical" intention, she invoked silently upon him Mary's Motherly Blessing just as the man grabbed her by the shoulder.

Suddenly, as if he had received an electric shock, the man jumped back in terror. Backing away he yelled, "What did you do to me?! What did you do to me?!" before fleeing into the night.

Good question! What, indeed, had she done? Nothing but to use Mary's beautiful gift, her blessing, and give it to someone else who needed it, a non-believer. . .

Corinne's case is not rare; it only is a clear example of the power of that blessing[1] when invoked by someone who really lives the Gospel and puts the love of God first in her daily life. Faced with so many young atheists, mired in drugs or other problems, we can be the instruments of Mary who wants so much to bless her children and bring them back to God.

As for the man at the train station, maybe he let go of Corinne, but Corinne did not let go of him! She continues to pray for him, for she knows that the peace of the Motherly Blessing is also for him especially for him!

MESSAGE OF NOVEMBER 25, 1997

"Dear Children! Today I invite you to comprehend your Christian vocation. Little children, I led and am leading you through this time of grace, that you may become conscious of your Christian vocation. Holy martyrs died witnessing: I am a Christian and love God over everything. Little children, today also I invite you to rejoice and be joyful Christians, responsible and conscious that God called you in a special way to be joyfully extended hands toward those who do not believe, and that through the example of your life, they may receive faith and love for God. Therefore, pray, pray, pray that your heart may open and be sensitive for the Word of God. Thank you for having responded to my call."

A ROCK-SOLID MARRIAGE

Does that kind still exist??

That kind will always exist. In the small town of Siroki-Brieg, 20 miles from Medjugorje, parish records show not a single divorce from among 13,000 faithful. Within the memory of the living, not a single family has broken apart. Could it be that Herzegovina enjoys some sort of special privilege from heaven? Do the young couples pronounce some secret formula during the ceremony? Is there some kind of magical trick that protects them from the demon of quarrels and division?

The answer is so much simpler than all that! For centuries the people of this land have suffered cruelly because others have tried to take from them their Christian faith and wipe off the map the precious name of Our Lord Jesus Christ, who died on the Cross and rose again to open up the gates of Eternal Life for us. They know from experience that their salvation lies in the Cross of Christ. Salvation does not come from the UN

Peace Keepers, from disarmament treaties, from humanitarian aid, from peace accords or speeches from the United Nations, even if these efforts can sometimes be channels for bringing a little help to the world. No, the source of salvation is the Cross of Christ!

The humble people of Herzegovina have the intelligence of the poor, that beautiful wisdom that consists of being nobody's fool in matters of life and death. This is why they have linked forever marriage and the Cross of Christ. They have grounded marriage, which is the source of human life, in the Cross, which is the source of divine life.

The Croatians have a particularly beautiful wedding tradition—which delights the pilgrims in Medjugorje—so beautiful, in fact, that people are picking it up in Europe and even in America!

When young people are getting ready to wed, people don't tell them that they found the ideal partner, the person of their dreams. This is what the priest tells them: "You found your cross. And a cross is to be love,d to be carried; a cross not to be thrown away, but to be cherished." If a priest said those words in France, the fiancés would be stuck speechless. But in Herzegovina, the Cross evokes the greatest love, and the crucifix is the treasure of the home.

Father Jozo often tells the pilgrimsabout the tradition that has been upheld in his country. When the fiancés set off for the church to be married, they bring a crucifix with them. This crucifix is blessed by the priest, and during the exchange of vows it holds a central place.[1]

The bride places her right hand on the cross, and the groom puts his hand over hers, so that their two hands are bound together on the cross, grounded in the Cross. Then the priest covers their hands with his stole; the young couple proclaim their vows and promise to be faithful, according to the classic rite of the Church. Once the promises are exchanged, the bride and groom do not kiss each other, but rather they kiss the cross: they know that they are kissing the source of love. Anyone close enough to see their two hands joined on the cross understands clearly that if the husband lets go of his wife, or if the wife lets go of her husband, they let go of the Cross!. And if they abandon the Cross, they have nothing left—they have

---

[1]For several years now I have given a crucifix as a wedding gift to my friends, suggesting they adopt this beautiful tradition for the exchange of their vows. They always welcome the suggestion with enthusiasm. What a blessing for these young couples who hang up the Cross of Christ on the wall of their home and revere it! The day crucifixes reappear in our homes, the numbers of divorces will go down dramatically along with the whole sad list of the secondary ravages of divorce.

lost everything, for they have abandoned Jesus. They have lost Jesus.

After the ceremony the newlyweds bring the crucifix back to their home and give it a place of honor in the house. It becomes the center of family prayer, for the young couple believes deeply that the family is born of the Cross. When a trouble arises, or if they experience some conflict, they will come before this crucifix to seek help. They will not go to a lawyer, or a fortune teller, or have their palms read, they won't rely on a psychologist or a counselor to settle the matter. No, they go to their Jesus, in front of the Cross. They kneel there, they cry there, they pour out their hearts there;and above all they forgive there. They will not go to sleep until they have unburdened their hearts for they will have gone to Jesus for help, He who is the only One who has the power to save.

The first thing the children are given to kill is the Cross. They kiss the Cross every day and don't go to bed at night like the pagans without having thanked Jesus. As far back as the children can remember, Jesus has been the special friend of the family, respected and embraced. They don't go to bed with a "blankey" to hug at night in order to feel secure; rather, they say "nighty-night" to Jesus and kiss the Cross. They go to sleep with Jesus, not with a teddy bear. They know that Jesus will keep them safe within His arms, that there is nothing to be afraid of, and their fears melt away in that kiss to Jesus.

— Message of December 25, 1997 —

"Dear Children! Also today I rejoice with you and I call you to the good. I desire that each of you reflect and carry peace in your heart and say: I want to put God in the first place in my life. In this way, little children, each of you will become holy. Little children, tell everyone, I want the good for you and he will respond with the good and, little children, good will come to dwell in the heart of each man. Little children, tonight I bring to you the good of my Son who gave His life to save you. That is why, little children, rejoice and extend your hands to Jesus who is only good. Thank you for having responded to my call."

HEART TRANSPLANTS

When this message got around, the village of Medjugorje changed. For quite a while people called out joyfully to each other, even in public, making others turn around intrigued. What??!!

"I wish you well!"

"Oh! Uh, that is, well, I wish you well too!"

The essential part is to stick to it, to keep up the level of love even in what St. Theresa of Lisieux used to call "the daily monotony". For years you can just plow on through life, seeing nothing, feeling nothing, and sometimes discouragement begins to peek over the horizon; but then, suddenly. . .

The Gospa burst into Rachel's life. She was a friend of ours, a mother, living in Normandy.

"You know," she said to me, "my relationships with others were a real problem, especially with people I thought were not lovable. I annoyed and hurt others. I was furious at myself, really unhappy, full of scruples and self-doubt, for I know that Jesus was asking me to love them. I tried to repress my negative feelings, but it just didn't work: my natural feelings rushed right back in, time after time.

"Last March, when I was listening to a tape on the messages of Medjugorje as I was sewing, I suddenly heard that Mary wants to give us her heart, yes her own motherly heart and in the case of this "heart transplant", there is no fear of "tissue rejection".

"So I play that tape over and over, that particular passage, and I chew over each word many times. They begin to sink in, and, all of a sudden, as if someone had just switched on the light, I understand that I am supposed to love other people with the heart of a mother! A mother loves her child far beyond the visible aspects, she loves him even when he's being a "pain in the neck". She suffers for him. For through all his scars and even all the ravages of Evil or sin she can see the beauty that God has put in his heart from the moment he was conceived.

"I knew that I had experienced a miracle, and I had found hope again. Right away I wanted to try it out. So I left my pincushion for two minutes and I prayed to Mary that I might be able to live with this new heart of hers starting with my very next encounter with someone. And it worked! And from that day on I no longer suffer from those awful feelings of being blocked when I am with others, on the contrary: I am filled with joy! Everyone has noticed the change in me. this grace has helped me trust more; I know that Mary has more such gifts in store, and that she will always be with me in life's trials. Thanks to her, I can finally live those words of Jesus: **"Love you enemies."** Mary carries out what she teaches in her messages! So I am filled with joy at the thought of her promise: **"In the end, my Immaculate Heart will triumph!"** I no longer just believe it, I *know* it!"

* * * * *

I can't leave out, either, the beautiful testimony of my friend from Romania, Calin.

Calin has been running a jewelry shop for the past seven years. One day in Medjugorje, while he was praying in the church in front of the statue of the Blessed Mother to the right of the choir, Mary herself appeared in front of the statue, and he saw her, real, alive, and incredibly beautiful. She said nothing. full of gratitude and joy she looked at each person who came up to greet her and pray to her. Everyone venerated her according to the customs and traditions of his country. She accepted each prayer with wonder, and her eyes followed each supplicant with a look of tenderness as he or she left. Calin adds: "She looked at me with so much happiness that I was overcome. It was as if I were the most important person in the world to her! I stayed there a long time, gazing at her and praying to her, and when I had finished my Rosary she was still there. I left, telling myself that she would still be there the next day. But when I came back with my wife, Mary was gone."

Since that day, I've never seen her like that again, but a fire of love burns in my heart the moment I meet someone! I see Jesus in the person, it's as if Jesus gives me His love with which to welcome everyone, even strangers who come into my shop. I am not a consecrated person, I don't know how to pray very well, but I love the Gospa with all my heart, I tell her about everything, and God, I love Him even more. . . "

This man just breathes humility and joy, and his life bears witness to the love of God more than any fine words could do. One day he confided in us: "I have everything in life I need: a good wife, healthy children, a house, work. . .; but to tell the truth, if I didn't have God, I wouldn't be able to live. Without God, my life would be impossible! God is everything to me!"

---

[1]Message of Dec. 25, 1988: Dear children, I am calling you to peace. Live peace in you heart and in your surroundings, so that all may recognize the peace, which does not come from you, but from God. Little children, today is a great day. Rejoice with me! Celebrate the birth of Jesus with my peace, the peace with which I came as your Mother, Queen of Peace. Today I am giving you my Special Blessing. Carry it to every creature so that each one may have peace. Thank you for having responded to my call." In regard to this blessing, see chapters "A Satanist on the Hill" and "The Cafes of Lake Como".

— FLASHBACK ON 1997 —

January 2: Mirjana states that from now on, at her monthly apparition, "all those who want to join may do so" as the Gospa said to her.

Early February: Mission of Vicka and Father Slavko in South Africa.

February 6: Il Messagero publishes that after two years of study, a group of Italian theological experts declared that the phenomenon of the tears of blood wept by the Madonna of Civitavecchia (Italy) is "supernatural." This Madonna is a small statue brought from Medjugorje.

February 21: Death of Father Yanko Bubalo, OFM, co-author with Vicka of "1000 encounters with the Blessed Mother".

Early March: Father Jozo preaches a retreat at Medjugorje to a tribe of Native Americans from Canada, the MicMac Nation. The theme of the retreat was "Return to the Eagle's Nest."

March 15: Pilgrimage of President Tudjman of Croatia to Medjugorje. He implores Our Lady to cure him.

April 12-13: Visit of John Paul II to Sarajevo. His appearance draws 50,000 people to the Kosevo Stadium.

June 30–July 4: First international retreat for priests at Medjugorje, bringing together 200 priests.

July 4: Ivan's prayer group celebrates its fifteenth anniversary.

July 19: Birth of Marco, the third son of Marija Pavlovic-Lunetti, in Italy.

September 30: Ivan and Laureen leave Medjugorje for several months. They carry witness to Medjugorje to the United States in particular.

October 22: Sr. Emmanuel is invited by several raking members of the US Congress to travel to Washington, DC. and brief the Congressional Human Rights Caucus on the importance of the messages of peace being given by Mary at Medjugorje. (A video of this briefing is available from Children of Medjugorje, see page 360)

Messages of 1998

January 25, 1998 "Dear Children! Today again I call all of you to prayer. Only with prayer, dear children, will your heart change, become better, and be more sensitive to the Word of God. Little children, do not permit Satan to pull you apart and to do with you what he wants. I call you to be responsible and determined and to consecrate each day to God in prayer. May Holy Mass, little children, not be a habit for you, but life. By living Holy Mass each day, you will feel the need for holiness and you will grow in holiness. I am close to you and intercede before God for each of you, so that He may give you strength to change your heart. Thank you for having responded to my call."

February 25, 1998 "Dear Children! Also today I am with you and I, again, call all of you to come closer to me through your prayers. In a special way, I call you to renunciation in this time of grace. Little children, meditate on and live, through your little sacrifices, the passion and death of Jesus for each of you. Through prayer and your renunciation you will become more open to the gift of faith and love towards the Church and the people who are around you. I love you and bless you. Thank you for having responded to my call."

March 25, 1998 "Dear Children! Also today I call you to fasting and renunciation. Little children, renounce that which hinders you from being closer to Jesus. In a special way I call you: Pray, because only through prayer will you be able to overcome your will and discover the will of God even in the smallest things. By your daily life, little children, you will become an example and witness that you live, for Jesus or against Him and His will. Little children, I desire that you become apostles of love. By loving, little children, it will be recognized that you are mine. Thank you for having responded to my call."

April 25, 1998 "Dear Children! Today I call you, through prayer, to open yourselves to God as a flower opens itself to the rays of the morning sun. Little children, do not be afraid. I am with you and I intercede before God for each of you so that your heart receives the gift of conversion. Only in this way, little children, will you comprehend the importance of grace in these times and God will become nearer to you. Thank you for having responded to my call."

May 25, 1998 "Dear children! Today I call you, through prayer and sacrifice, to prepare yourselves for the coming of the Holy Spirit. Little children, this is a time of grace and so, again, I call you to decide for God the Creator. Allow Him to transform and change you. May your heart be prepared to listen to, and live, everything which the Holy Spirit has in His plan for each of you. Little children, allow the Holy Spirit to lead you on the way of truth and salvation towards eternal life. Thank you for having responded to my call."

June 25, 1998 "Dear children! Today I desire to thank you for living my messages. I bless you all with my motherly blessing and I bring you all before my Son Jesus. Thank you for having responded to my call."

July 25, 1998 "Dear children! Today, little children, I invite you, through prayer, to be with Jesus, so that through a personal experience of prayer you may be able to discover the beauty of God's creatures. You cannot speak or witness about prayer, if you do not pray. That is why, little children, in the silence of the heart, remain with Jesus, so that He may change and transform you with His love. This, little children, is a time of grace for you. Make good use of it for your personal conversion, because when you have

God, you have everything. Thank you for having responded to my call."

August 25, 1998 "Dear children! Today I invite you to come still closer to me through prayer. Little children, I am your mother, I love you and I desire that each of you be saved and thus be with me in Heaven. That is why, little children, pray, pray, pray until your life becomes prayer. Thank you for having responded to my call."

September 25, 1998 "Dear children! Today I call you to be my witnesses by living the faith of your fathers. Little children, you seek signs and messages and do not see that with every morning sunrise, God calls you to convert and to return to the way of truth and salvation. You speak much, little children, but you work little on your conversion. That is why, convert and start to live my messages, not with your words but with your life. In this way, little children, you will have the strength to decide for the true conversion of the heart. Thank you for having responded to my call."

October 25, 1998 "Dear children! Today I call you to come closer to my Immaculate Heart. I call you to renew in your families the fervor of the first days when I called you to fasting, prayer and conversion. Little children, you accepted my messages with open hearts, although you did not know what prayer was. Today, I call you to open yourselves completely to me so that I may transform you and lead you to the heart of my son Jesus, so that He can fill you with His love. Only in this way, little children, will you find true peace - the peace that only God gives you. Thank you for having responded to my call."

November 25, 1998 "Dear children! Today I call you to prepare yourselves for the coming of Jesus. In a special way, prepare your hearts. May holy Confession be the first act of conversion for you and then, dear children, decide for holiness. May your conversion and decision for holiness begin today and not tomorrow. Little children, I call you all to the way of salvation and I desire to show you the way to Heaven. That is why, little children, be mine and decide with me for holiness. Little children, accept prayer with seriousness and pray, pray, pray. Thank you for having responded to my call."

December 25, 1998 "Dear children! In this Christmas joy I desire to bless you with my blessing. In a special way, little children, I give you the blessing of little Jesus. May He fill you with his peace. Today, little children, you do not have peace and yet you yearn for it. That is why, with my Son Jesus, on this day I call you to pray, pray, pray, because without prayer you do not have joy or peace or a future. Yearn for peace and seek it, for God is true peace. Thank you for having responded to my call."

— NOTE —

The use of the expression "Our Lady appeared..." by the author and the publisher does not mean that either has any intention of pre-empting the opinion of the Church authorities as to the authenticity of the apparitions of Mary at Medjugorje. The book contains only the personal opinions of the author, based on the testimony of those who have been witnesses to the events in that village.

The purpose of publishing this book is merely to provide information, and both author and publisher will subject their opinions to the discernment of the Church as soon as any formal pronouncement on these events is made.

Cover photographs:

1) Marija in ecstasy, March 25, 1994, © Tony Cilento
2) Scene in Medjugorje behind the church, © Joseph Mixan

— ABOUT THE AUTHOR —

Sister Emmanuel Maillard was born in France in 1947. She studied theology with Cardinal Daniélou. Further studies were in the History of Fine Arts at the Sorbonne University (Paris) from which she graduated in 1970. She joined the Community of the Beatitudes in 1976, and has been living in Medjugorje since 1989.

> "I wish to thank all the individuals who furnished me with their witness, so that love of Mary will increase in people's hearts. But history marches on, and so I launch here an appeal to all those others who might have their own testimony to contribute, for nothing touches hearts more than such simple and true stories that demonstrate the finger of God in our lives. Once a grace is shared, it multiplies!"
>
> Write to: Sister Emmanuel, "Les Béatitudes,"

If you wish to join the "Children of Medjugorje," a group founded by Sr. Emmanuel and Denis Nolan to help the Blessed Mother's plans for peace, ask for information from: Children of Medjugorje, PO Box 1110, Notre Dame, IN 46556 (USA). Fax: (219) 287-7875.

SEND *"A DOLLAR A DAY FOR THE PROGRAM TO STAY!"*
"MEDJUGORJE: OUR MOTHER'S LAST CALL
with Sr. Emmanuel"

An announcement from Denis Nolan....

While I was praying during Adoration the idea came to me to begin a weekly TV program for America with Sr. Emmanuel sharing the messages being given to us by Our Lady in Medjugorje. The Lord told me two things very clearly from the Blessed Sacrament. First, it was time for me to be quiet and for Sr. Emmanuel to speak. Second, not to worry how the TV programs would be aired - I should just get them done. There were ways for airing I didn't know about.

Sure enough, by the time the first programs in Medjugorje had been filmed and edited, ready for broadcasting - without having initiated anything myself - they were being aired internationally. In the U.S. they were being aired weekly by the Archdiocese of New York, Catholic TV of Denver, SEC TV in Pennsylvania and several other stations. Internationally they were being aired every week in Spanish by "Clara Vision" in Mexico and Latin America; in Lebanese by "Tele Luminere" (the TV station sponsored by the Patriarchs and Bishops of Lebanon to the whole country); in Polish by the Niepokalanow channel in Poland (twice every day!); in Papiemento on the island of Curacao (and its vicinity) in the Caribbean; & the Audio Visual Centre of the Archdiocese of Singapore was spreading videos of the TV programs throughout the Archdiocese!

Hearing about these TV shows, Archbishop Frane Franic wrote: "I am glad that Sr. Emmanuel is chosen to be the main host and the main speaker for these television programs. I think this is providential. She really has a charism of clarity and conviction to explain the messages of the Gospa and what is happening in Medjugorje." Fr. Svet agreed: "I believe that we need Sr. Emmanuel on TV!" Mirjana, the first of the visionaries to receive all 10 secrets, wrote to me: "I have heard a lot about your plans with television and Sr. Emmanuel in America. I like your idea! This is what I said to Sr. Emmanuel, too. 'Go ahead. Don't be afraid. Please do it! The Gospa will always be with you!' Sr. Emmanuel chooses the way which the Gospa likes, simple and with the heart." Mirjana, Vicka and Marija (through whom Our Lady gives her monthly message) are very happy about this program and say they'll pray for and recommend to Our Lady all who become part of it. Fr. Jozo says: "I give my blessing to the project of these

TV Programs. I pray the Gospa will be glorified."

An example of how the Gospa is being glorified: after seeing a program in San Francisco (where it was nominated for an award), a ranking member of the US. Congress (who isn't even a baptized Christian) invited Sr. Emmanuel to come to Washington, DC and brief the Congressional Human Rights Caucus on the messages of peace being given by Our Lady. (His wife, also unbaptized, was so moved she wrote the Preisdent of Bosnia urging him to go to Medjugorje!)

Six months after giving his blessing to Sr. Emmanuel's mission through these TV programs, the Holy Father, lamenting publicly the situation of today's television industry, issued to us a challenge:

> "Public opinion has been shocked at how easily the advanced communication technologies can be exploited by those whose intentions are evil. At the same time, can we not observe a relative slowness on the part of those who wish to do good to use the same opportunities?... It would be a significant achievement if Christians could cooperate more closely with one another in the media as they prepare to celebrate the forthcoming Great Jubilee ," (5/11/97).

Without your help - your cooperation - we won't be able to continue. 60 shows already filmed wait to be edited... Stations around the world are waiting for broadcast quality tapes (which are expensive). Our vision was that these programs offered a way for Americans to help Mary reach her children in less affluent countries - many who couldn't afford the trip to Medjugorje. *But as it's turned out, it has been donations from these poor countries that have been funding the TV programs for Americans!* In the days left before the Year 2000 let's respond to the Holy Father's plea by working more closely together!

SEND *"A DOLLAR A DAY FOR THE PROGRAM TO STAY!"*

I WILL SEND A DOLLAR A DAY FOR THE PROGRAM TO STAY! $30 a month (tax exempt) for the months remaining untiil Year 2000!)

Name   _____

Address   _____

City, State, Zip _____

Send to: Children of Medjugorje • Box 1110 • Notre Dame, IN 46556 (USA)

MEDJUGORJE: OUR MOTHER'S LAST CALL with Sr. Emmanuel
TV PROGRAMS, available on VIDEO

V-1 *"I love each one of you as much as I love my Son Jesus"*
V-2 *"Protect the children" (with Fr. Jozo)*
V-3 *"Give me your worries, and pray for my intentions"*
V-4 *"I am your Mother, welcome me into your life"*
V-5 *"You do not understand the importance of my comings!"*
V-6 *"I have shown you Heaven to let you know it exists"*
V-7 *"I have shown you Purgatory to let you know it exists..."*
V-8 *"After death there is eternity"*
V-9 *"Be reconciled." (Reconciliation • Part I)*
V-10 *"I desire reconciliation among you." (Reconciliation • Part II)*
V-11 *"Your sufferings are also mine"*
V-12 *"I wish your sufferings become joy!"*
V-13 *"Children, Help my Heart to Triumph!"*
V-14 *"I've come to tell you that God exists... "*
V-15 *"Pray for priests, my most beloved sons."*
V-16 *"Pray for unbelievers!" (Part I with Mirjana)*
V-17 *"Take the saints as an example."*
V-18 *"Pray for the sick... "*
V-19 *A Briefing to the Congressional Human Rights Caucus*
V-20 *"For God, divorce does not exist."*
V-21 *"I rejoice to see you here," (in Medjugorje!)*
V-22 *"Pray for the unbelievers!" (Part II with Mirjana)*
V-23 *John Paul II: "My most beloved son."*
V-24 *"I am the Mother who has come from the people."*
V-25 *"If you would abandon yourself to me..."*
V-26 *"Today, rejoice with me and with my angels..."*
V-27 *"I will leave a great sign."*
V-28 *"Pray, for through prayer you will know what to do."*
V-29 *"Go to confession once a month."*
V-30 *Thank you for having created me.*
V-31 *"Unite with me to pray for those who do not believe."*
V-32 *"Fall in love with the Most Holy Sacrament of theAltar."*
V-33 *"I kneel before the freedom that God has given you!" (Part I with Marija)*
V-34 *"I kneel before the freedom that God has given you!" (Part II with Marija)*

Each video is $10.00 - suggested donation.

Order videos for the religion department in your Catholic school, or for your parish library or diocesan resource center; have them aired on your local Catholic TV station or your community public access station. These TV programs are being aired in the US and in many other countries.

TO ENTER MORE DEEPLY INTO
THE EVENTS OF MEDJUGORJE

AUDIO TAPES by Sr. Emmanuel

M-1 The Rosary With Medjugorje
M-2 Touch Your Heavenly Mother
M-3 Prayer With the Heart
M-4 How Wonderfully You Made Me
M-5 True Consecration to Mary
M-6 Holiness Means Happiness
M-7 Prayer Obtains Everything
M-8 Story of a Wounded Womb
M-9 Fasting, door to God's power
W-1 The Most Handsome Saint (*with Fr. Tim Deeter.*)
W-2 In Medjugorje, He Told Me the Secret (*with Fr. Tim Deeter*)
Each audio tape is **US $ 5,** sug. donation **(plus $4.50 s/h per order)**;
minimum order 2 tapes.

For audio tapes send your order to:
        USA: Queenship Publishing • Box 42028 • Santa Barbara, CA
93140-2028 • Fax (805) 957-1631 • Tel:(800) 647-9882
IRELAND "Mir Tapes" • c/o Father Aidan Caroll
87B Stevens Green • Dubin 2 IRELAND
Tel: (353) 147 51 618 • Fax: (44) 1342 89 3515 (for UK)
NEW ZEALAND: Tel/Fax: (64) 9 41 83 428 - NZ $8
ENGLAND: Fax: (44) 1 959 52 3619 - (£2.50)
MALAYSIA: Daniel Tan • 8 Jalan SS 22/20 A
47400 Damansara Jaya • Petaling Jaya • West Malaysia
Tel: 603/ 71 60 762 • Fax: 603/ 71 73 198

Spanish: Write for a catalogue of Sr. Emmanuel's tapes in Spanish:
        Convento di San Francisco
Apartado Postal #208 • CP 74750 Atlixco, Puebla, Mexico
Tel: (52) 244 5 11 45 Fax: (52) 244 5 84 15
Email: csfmecb001@infosel.net.mx

HOW TO GET...

...THE MEDJUGORJE MONTHLY MESSAGE OF THE 25TH:

- On answering machines 24 hours a day: (Partial listing below.)

Arizona		(602) 225-1970
Arkansas		(800) 235-6279
California		(213) 896-2999
		(818) 773-3060
	Spanish	(213) 896-1945
Florida	Spanish/Eng.	(305) 362-7314
Georgia		(800) 245-9846
Kansas		(913) 383-7454
Michigan		(800) 235-6279
Nebraska		(402) 455-6279
New Jersey		(201) 667-6279
New Mexico		(505) 323-9437
New York		(914) 682-8907
	Spanish	(718) 277-6727
Ohio		(419) 385-5841
Pennsylvania		(717) 586-4323
Rhode Island		(401) 944-5683
Tennessee		(615) 329-3332
Texas		(972) 233-6279
	Spanish	(972) 596-6279
Washington State		(425) 481-3676
Wisconsin		(414) 784-4200
Canada (Toronto)		(416) 252-6279

- On the Internet:
    English: http://www.childrenofmedjugorje.com
    Spanish: http://www.fcpeace.com/noti_esp.htm
    Polish: http://www.polbox.com/m/medjug
    French: http://www.beatitudes.org/edm

Information Center MIR (parish): http://www.medjugorje.hz

...THE BI-MONTHLY REPORTS FROM MEDJUGORJE
by Sr. Emmanuel:
- On the Internet: same address as monthly message (p. 362).
- By Fax: dial from hand-set of your fax machine)
(219) 287-5683 (USA) and follow instructions.

This book is available in:

French: Edit. des Béatitudes • Burtin, 41600 Nouan-le-Fuzelier • France Tel: (33) 254 88 21 18 • Fax: (33) 254 88 97 73 • Email: ed.beatitudes@hol.fr

Spanish: #1 - Jesus de la Misericordia • (Fausto Galeano) Av. Eloy Alfaro • 466 Y 9 de Octubre • P.O. Box 6252 CCl Quito, Ecuador • Fax (593) 2 561 445 Tel: (593) 2 564 519 528 519 Email: fjdm@pi.pro.ec
             #2 - Paulinas (Hna Ursula Stoffel) • Association Hijas de San Pablo Nazea 4240 - 1419 Buenos Aires, Argentina • Tel: (54) 1 9517996 / 953 3761 Telefax: (54) 1 571 6226 or 1 952 5924 Email: paulinas@satlink.com
             #3 - Ed bienaventurenzas, Atlixco, Mexico • Fax: (52) 244 58 415 Email: csfmecb001@infosel.net.mx

English: #1 - Queenship Publishing • Box 42028 • Santa Barbara, CA 93140-2028 Fax: (805) 957 - 1631 • Tel: (800) 647 - 9882
             #2 - Archbishop of Kuching • P.O. Box 940 • Kuching 93718 Sarawak, Malaysia • Fax: (60) 82 425 724

Polish: Wydawnictwo Ksiezy Marianow • Ul SW Bonifacego 9 • 02-914 Warsaw, Poland. Fax (48) 22 651 90 55 • Tel: (48) 22 651 99 70 Email: marianie@pol.pl

Flemish: Uitgeverij TABOR, Dampoortstraat 168 • B-8310 St. - Kruis - Brugge Belgium • Fax: (32) 50 37 00 19 • tel: (32) 50 36 06 37

Portuguese:Ed. Loyola (Fr. Gabriel Galache, S.J.) • Sao Paolo, Brazil Fax: (55) 61 63 42 75

Romanian: Ed. Adoremus (Care of Halat Calin) • Str. Nastase Parmfil, 53 • Buil 29, Apt 49 • 72124 Bucarest, Romania • Tel/Fax: (40) 1 22 33 237

Hungarian: Nyolc Boldogsag Katolikus Kozosseg, H-8777 Homokkomarom, Ady E.u.2 Hungary • Tel: (36) 93 356 113 • Fax: (36) 93 35 63 44

German: Parvis Verlag, CH - 1648 Hauteville, Switzerland • Tel: (41) 26 91 59 393 Fax: (41) 26 91 59 399

Italian: Editrice Shalom • 57/bis via San Guiseppe, 60020 Camerata Picena (Ancona), Italy • Fax: (39) 71 74 50 140 • Tel: (39) 71 74 50 440

Lebanese: Publications Daccache • Beirut, Lebanon • Tel/Fax: (961) 33 85 952

Japanese: Pere Alain Quenouelle • Ai To Hikari No Ie • 136 Oaza Sendai-JI • Ibaragi-Shi-Osaka, FU 568 Japan • Email: aitohikari@i.bekkoame.or.jp

Korean: (in preparation) Paul Choi • 21014 Silver Cloud Dr. • Diamond Bar, CA 91765 (USA) • Tel: (909) 861 7105 • Email: lumenglory@aol.com

Chinese: Fr. Francis Ki • c/o Office of the ARchbishop • P.O. Box 940 • Kuching 93718 Sarawak, Malaysia • Fax: (60) 82 425 724 Malaysia

Slovak: Vyd. Serafin • Bratislava • Fax: (421) 754 434 342 • Tel: (421) 754432 159

Thai & Vietnamese transaltions are in progress...

BOOKS on Medjugorje:

The Apparitions of Our Lady at Medjugorje, by Fr. Svetovar Kraljevic, Franciscan Herald Press, Chicago, IL 60615 USA (1984).

Children, Help My Heart to Triumph by Sr. Emmanuel, (for ages 5–13; a coloring book is also included), St. Andrews Productions, 6111 Steubenville Pike, McKees Rocks, PA 15136 USA. Fax: (412) 787-5204.

Is The Virgin Mary Appearing at Medjugorje? by Abbé Laurentin, The Word Among Us Press, Box 3646, Washington, DC 20037 USA (1984).

Medjugorje, the War Day by Day, by Sr. Emmanuel, Florida Center of Peace, PO Box 43106, Miami, FL 33143 USA.

Medjugorje, What Does the Church Say? by Denis Nolan and Sr. Emmanuel, Queenship Publishing Co., PO Box 42028, Santa Barbara, CA 93140-2028 USA. Tel: (800) 647-9882; Fax: (805) 957 - 1631 (USA) 1898

Pilgrimage, by Fr. Svetozar Kraljevic, Paraclete Press, 1991, USA

The Queen of Peace Visits Medjugorje, by Fr. Joseph Pellier, Assumption Publications, 50 Old English Road, Worcester, MA 01609 USA.

Spark From Heaven, by Mary Craig,
Ave Maria Press, Notre Dame, IN 46556 USA.

A Thousand Encounters With the Blessed Virgin, by Fr. Janko Bubalo, Friends of Medjugorje, 4851 S. Drexel Blvd., Chicago, IL 60615. (The Italian edition of this extensive interview with the visionary Vicka was awarded the coveted "Sapienze Award" in 1985 by Cardinal Angelo Rossi, Dean of the College of Cardinals.)

Medjugorje Day By Day, (a daily Meditation book, based on the messages of Medjugorje), by Fr. Richard J. Beyer, Ave Maria Press, Notre Dame, Indiana 46556 USA (1993)

Medjugorje: A Time for Truth and a Time for Action, Denis Nolan, Queenship Publishing Co., PO Box 42028, Santa Barbara, CA 93140-2028 USA. Tel: (800) 647-9882; Fax: (805) 957 - 1631 (1993)

A CLARIFICATION FROM THE VATICAN ON MEDJUGORJE

Finally, a page has turned in the "question of Medjugorje. Faithful Catholics will know from now on the position of the Church on Medjugorje. In effect, the Vatican has just written the clearest letter on the subject since the apparitions began.

Monseigneur Aubry (who gives his testimony in the Preface of this book) wrote in January 1998, to Cardinal Ratzinger to submit to him some fundamental questions concerning the pastoral attitude to adopt toward Medjugorje. One can know that:

– the Ordinary of Mostar has not been in charge of the file (question) since 1986

– the Church refers us to the Declaration of Zadar (1991)

– all faithful may travel to Medjugorje on private pilgrimages

– the Church has not issued a definitive judgement and remains open to more ample studies.[1]

But since these elements are not written in black and white in the highest instance of the Church, certain opponents of Medjugorje pretend to obey the Church by denying the apparitions and ceasing pilgrimages.

Here in its fullness is the response of the Vatican (passed on a little after to all the Bishops of France by official lines):

---

[1] *Two years later a scientific team which had done tests on the visionaries in jApril, 1998, concluded it's work on December 12, 1998. (A booklet was subsequently published with all the meidcal results.) The findings: after 17 years of apparitions, the visionaries do not show any trouble, i.e., trance like states, disassociation or the loss of the sense of reality. They are not experiencing an hypnotic trance.*

These scientific tests showed that the visionaries are not manipulated, that they do not "put on an act" and that this (unexplained) state of ecstacy does not in any way change their "normal" behavior in everyday life. No pathology was found.

Of course, no machine can record what is happening for them in the "invisible" but it is remarkable that none of these studies contradict what they say they experience (as was also the case with Prof. Joyeux's studies in 1985). The document (see www.ChildrenOfMedjugorie.com) was signed by Fr. Andreas Resch and Drs. Girogio Gagliardi, Marco Margnelli, Marianna Bolko and Gariella Raffaelli.

CONGREGATION FOR THE DOCTRINE OF THE FAITH
Pr. No 154/81-06419

May 26, 1998

To His Excellency Mons. Gilbert Aubry,
Bishop of Saint-Denis de la Reunion

Excellency:

In your letter of January 1, 1998, you submitted to this Dicastery several questions about the position of the Holy See and of the Bishop of Mostar in regard to the so called apparitions of Medjugorje, private pilgrimages and the pastoral care of the faithful who go there.

In regard to this matter, I think it is impossible to reply to each of the questions posed by Your Excellency. The main thing I would like to point out is that the Holy See does not ordinarily take a position of its own regarding supposed supernatural phenomena as a court of first instance. As for the credibility of the "apparitions" in question, this Dicastery respects what was decided by the bishops of the former Yugoslavia in the Declaration of Zadar, April 10, 1991: "On the basis of the investigation so far, it can not be affirmed that one is dealing with supernatural apparitions and revelations." Since the division of Yugoslavia into different independent nations it would now pertain to the members of the Episcopal Conference of Bosnia-Hercegovina to eventually reopen the examination of this case, and to make any new pronouncements that might be called for.

What Bishop Peric said in his letter to the Secretary General of "Famille Chretienne", declaring: "My conviction and my position is not only 'non constat de supernaturalitate,' but likewise, ''constat de non supernaturalitate' of the apparitions or revelations in Medjugorje", should be considered the expression of the personal conviction of the Bishop of Mostar which he has the right to express as Ordinary of the place, but which is and remains his personal opinion.

Finally, as regards pilgrimages to Medjugorje, which are conducted privately, this Congregation points out that they are permitted on condition that they are not regarded as an authentication of events still taking place and which still call for an examination by the Church.

I hope that I have replied satisfactorily at least to the principal questions that you have presented to this Dicastery and I beg Your Excellency to accept the expression of my devoted sentiments.

Archbishop Tarcisio Bertone
(Secretary to the "Congregation" presided over by Cardinal Ratzinger)

To summarize:

1 -The declarations of the Bishop of Mostar only reflect his personal opinion. Consequently, they are not an official and definitive judgement requiring assent and obedience.

2 - One is directed to the declaration of Zadar, which leaves the door open to future investigations. In the meanwhile private pilgrimages with pastoral accompaniment for the faithful are permitted.

3 - A new commission could eventually be named.

4 - In the meanwhile, all pilgrims may go to Medjugorje in complete obedience to the Church.

The letter of Archbishop Bertone to the Bishop of Le Reunion sufficiently makes clear what has always been the official position of the hierarchy during recent years concerning Medjugorje: namely, that it knowingly leaves the matter undecided. The supernatural character is not established; such were the words used by the former conference of bishops of Yugoslavia in Zadar in 1991. It really is a matter of wording, which knowingly leaves the matter pending. It has not been said that the supernatural character is substantially established. Furthermore, it has not been denied or discounted that the phenomena may be of a supernatural nature. There is no doubt that the magisterium of the Church does not make a definite declaration while the extraordinary phenomena are going on in the form of apparitions or other means. Indeed it is the mission of the shepherds to promote what is growing, to encourage the fruits which are appearing, to protect them, if need be, form the dangers which are obviously everywhere.

It is also necessary at Lourdes to see to it that the original gift of Lourdes not be stifled by unfortunate developments. Neither is Medjugorje invulnerable. That is why it is and will be so important that bishops be very conscientious about their mission as shepherds for Medjugorje, that they take under their protection the pastoral pronouncement of Medjugorje so that the obvious fruits that are in that place might be protected from any possible unfortunate developments.

I believe that the words of Mary at Cana: "Do whatever He tells you," make up the substance of what she says throughout the centuries. Mary helps us to hear Jesus and she desires with her whole heart and with all her strength that we do what He tells us.

That is what I wish for all the communities of prayer which were formed form Medjugorje; this is what I wish for our diocese and for the Church.

Personally, I have not been to Medjugorje, but in a certain way I have been there many times through the people I have met and the people I know. And in their lives I am seeing good fruit. I would be lying if I said this fruit did not exist. This fruit is concrete and visible and I can see in our diocese and in many other places graces of conversion, graces of a supernatural life of faith, graces of joy, graces of vocations, of healings, of people returning to the Sacraments—to confession. All this is not misleading. Therefore, as far as I am concerned, as a Bishop, I can only see the fruit. If we had to judge the tree by it's fruit, like Jesus, I must say that the tree is fruitful!

Cardinal Christoph Schonborn

Cardinal Schonborn, the Archbishop of Vienna, who gave the Holy Father and his Papal Household their 1998 Lenten Retreat (and who was head of the church's commission responsible for the "Catechism of the Catholic Church"), gave the preceding testimony in Lourdes on July 18k 1998. The Cardinal's words were published in "Medjugorje Gebestakion," #50, and in "Stela Maris," #343, pp. 19, 20.